UNABOMBER:
A Desire to Kill

by Robert Graysmith

REGNERY PUBLISHING, INC.
Washington, DC

Library of Congress Cataloging-in-Publication Data

Graysmith. Robert.
    Unabomber : a desire to kill / by Robert Graysmith. 1942–
    p.   cm.
    Includes bibliographical references and index.
    ISBN 0–89526–397–1
    1. Kaczynski, Theodore John. 2. Serial murderers—
United States—Biography. 3. Serial murderers—United States—
Psychology. I. Title.
    HV6248.K235G73 1997
    364.15' 23' 0973—DC21   97–40485
                                           CIP

Published in the United States by
Regnery Publishing, Inc.
An Eagle Publishing Company
One Massachusetts Avenue, NW
Washington, DC 20001

Distributed to the trade by
National Book Network
4720-A Boston Way
Lanham, MD 20706

Book Design by Marja Walker

Printed on acid-free paper.
Manufactured in the United States of America

10 9 8 7 6 5 4 3 2 1

Books are available in quantity for promotional or premium use. Write to Director of Special Sales, Regnery Publishing, Inc., One Massachusetts Avenue, NW Washington, DC 20001, for information on discounts and terms or call (202) 216-0600.

Robert Graysmith
Author of:

Zodiac

The Sleeping Lady

The Murder of Bob Crane

CONTENTS

PART THREE: The UNABOMBER, Sacramento, California, The Mid-Eighties

PART FOUR: *The New York Times* Bomber, San Francisco, The Nineties

For Aaron

ACKNOWLEDGMENTS

THANKS TO Penny Wallace for sixteen years of constant inspiration, my best and always friend. I am especially indebted to Shane Salerno, Detective Robert Bell, Mark Potter of the San Francisco Bomb Squad, and George and Carol Blowars, the nicest couple in Lincoln. Special thanks for help in the preparation of this book belong to Erica Rogers, David Dortman, Marja Walker, Jennifer Azar, Harry Crocker, Greg Mueller, Patricia Bozell, Christopher Briggs, Jed Donahue, Sandy Callender, and Karen Zach Peck.

Finally, I owe sincere thanks to Richard Vigilante, a fine and sensitive editor, and to Alfred Regnery for asking the most important question a publisher ever put to me—"What is the moral core of this book?"

INTRODUCTION

FOOTSTEPS OF FIRE TRACED THE SNOW along the Great Divide. In pursuit, the FBI padded behind, hounds after the fox. But at each shadowed spot that touched upon the wilderness, around each bend of jagged rock, their quarry vanished as completely as if he had never been. FC was the man everyone saw, few recalled, and no one knew.

A complicated and fractured individual, his goal was simplicity itself. All FC desired was to change the world, to slay technology and "arrogant science," to plunge America back into the wilderness—to usher in his own Age of Wood. His desire was to kill. A certified genius, in these pursuits he was inexhaustible.

Endlessly, the Bureau tracked the most elusive criminal they had ever encountered. It took the longest, most complex and costly (over sixty million dollars and still climbing) manhunt in the nation's history more than seventeen years to play itself out under the Big Sky of Montana at the door of a secluded cabin.

Why couldn't the combined might of three powerful federal agencies and the consolidated intellect and experience of numerous local and state police forces crack this enigma? In the case of monolithic agencies, the timeless human failings of envy, pride, and sloth all played their part. As usual one agency failed to cooperate with another, or so the other said. Important information was not passed on, tribal chieftains protected their kingdoms, men anxious for glory set out to make certain they got credit for bringing down FC, or the Unabomber as he became known. But these human failings impede all big investigations, including successful ones. "Mistakes were made," but in the end the problem with the hunt was the prey.

He was a shadow barely seen and never heard—or many shadows. The FBI file actually contemplated that the prey might be not one man but many complex individuals. He was a chameleon eluding the police because he kept his own counsel and each day became something new. It was hard to fault the authorities—there had never been anything like him before. The Unabomber himself was not one but many bombers. The Junkyard Bomber, fashioning his deadly devices from abandoned household junk—lamp cord and fishing wire, used screws and scrap wood—came first. Then there was the Airline Bomber, who sought to bring down a jetliner filled with screaming passengers through the simple workings of a household barometer.

The University Bomber targeted brilliant professors at UC Berkeley, but left his devices as cunning lures to those curious or gullible enough to disturb them. He was the Good Samaritan Bomber, disguising his bombs to look like road obstacles and drawing those goodhearted individuals to remove them in order to protect others. The first man to do this died horribly. He was *The New York Times* Bomber, selecting his targets specifically from those leaders in computer science and genetics recently profiled in that newspaper. And finally he was UNABOM, the man no one could stop. In the end the FBI was no closer to catching him than in the beginning. Only their final and desperate strategy, to encourage the bomber to explain himself and to finally involve the public in the chase, would prove the Unabomber's undoing.

Though I fought against writing about such a famous case, it drew me into its web. Had there ever been a story this good? As powerful? A brother's anguish at his terrible decision against family loyalty, another man's chilling loneliness, the smashed lives and ruined careers, and amidst it all the howling winds of God's Country, the cloistered life of the university, and the golden sunlight of the Continental Divide. A story biblical in proportions ran with currents as deep as the Blackfoot River as it rushed nearby that lonely shack. The cabin, a little wooden box, had been fashioned after Thoreau's dwelling at Walden Pond. The Hermit quoted Thoreau and set out to live by his tenets, but somehow got it all twisted.

He got a lot of terror out of a cabin that had no electricity or running water. The Unabomber spread fear from coast to coast, striking at airlines, universities, computer stores, geneticists, Nobel recipients, great scholars and psychologists, computer geniuses, and people who'd either crossed his path or crossed him. All were targeted in the bomber's mind, with a logic of overwhelming clarity. But his logic overwhelmed his pursuers, who could find no motive, not even the motive of a madman, and finding no motive, perceiving no mind, they could never, never find the man.

Surely he was mad; but just as surely he was a genius. The bomber was so rare a genius that even his madness never exposed him.

The story of the Unabomber is THE great mystery story, one not only for our time but one for the next century. There has never been anyone like him before, probably never will be again. He was the last person anyone would expect—a Thoreau with bloodstained hands.

Probably I will never erase those images from my mind—a mountain cabin gone walking, the seemingly dull-witted town Hermit, a gold mine that brings pollution to a beautiful river, and, of course, the Professor, ripped from the pages of Joseph Conrad's novel *The Secret Agent*. He strides, legs moving like the opening and closing of scissors, head down and brooding, dreaming of the perfect detonator. But the strongest image is of those beautiful carved wooden boxes. Inside are cunningly-fashioned devices built from society's discards. How could such lovely little wooden boxes hold so much tragedy, fear, and death? How could any man have packed all that suffering inside a tiny box?

THE PROFESSOR, BOMBS FILLING EVERY POCKET, walked like his hero from Joseph Conrad's *The Secret Agent*, "averting his eyes from the odious multitude of mankind. Frail, insignificant, shabby, miserable, he passed on, unsuspected and deadly, like a pest in a street full of men. He had no future. He disdained it. He was a force." Up a short walk, the Professor let himself into a drab room at the back of a house. Outside, brittle branches bent against a single window, outlining a bleak November sky. The solitary man hunched at work over an immaculate table, all the more remarkable in contrast to the clutter elsewhere in the room. Unfinished cartons of milk and sandwiches fermented beneath a foot of trash.

He centered his work in a bright circular light and heated his soldering iron. He methodically arranged tools no one had ever seen before, instruments he'd designed and fashioned himself, on the white desk top. Self-absorbed, self-motivated, and self-contained as an oyster, in this room the Professor became his own universe. He possessed neither military experience nor training in bomb construction. He realized his infernal device would be crude, possibly low-yielding, but perfecting and learning as he went, he labored on.

He'd purchased Hercules Red Dot double base smokeless powder, a relatively weak explosive available in most gun and sporting goods stores. However, when he could, he avoided buying any component he could manufacture himself or salvage from the nearby junkyard, like hinges or switches. He hand-sculpted every nail from rugged wire and made even the tiniest screw himself or reused an old one. He endlessly polished and refined elements that would be destroyed in the blast. Later he occasionally even signed his work on a tiny piece of metal designed to survive the blast, punching his initials into it with an awl.

To enhance the flammability of the smokeless powder the Professor stirred in potassium chlorate, then spooned in liberal amounts of refined sugar. A better trained man would have employed a thick metal pipe. The stronger the pipe, the more gas pressure builds, instigating a more titanic detonation. But instead of a pipe, the Professor used a big, flimsy tin juice can, carefully gluing and taping the open end.

Since he meant to bring down an airliner with his bomb, he required a way to guarantee the device exploded while the jet was in midair. A cheap household barometer he'd salvaged, modified, and repaired would measure the altitude. When the plane's cabin became pressurized at a certain altitude, the barometer's needle would swing like a scythe and close an electrical circuit to four C-size dry cell batteries he'd scraped clean of printing to make them untraceable. The batteries, connected to the initiators, would in turn ignite the powder charge.

What if the barometer failed or someone opened the package while the plane still sat on the ground? He'd need a fail-safe backup. So, the Professor built in a redundancy, a pull-loop switch whose contacts would touch, closing the circuit between batteries and initiators, if anyone lifted the lid of the wooden box he'd carved and hinged at the rear. He was no carpenter, as the uneven and clumsy edges showed, but he sanded, sealed, and polished the box as if the extra effort would somehow disguise the defects. The box lovingly if clumsily handcrafted consisted of four kinds of wood that ranged from cheap crate to fine hardwood, and measured nine and one-half inches by ten and one-half inches by seven and one-quarter inches, held together by a variety of small nails, too many, as usual.

The Professor carved grooves in the hardwood to channel insulated copper wires, cannibalized from an old lamp, down a pipeline to the batteries. He sliced two grooves down each of the two "initiators," wooden dowels each measuring one and one-quarter inches long. He then ran short lengths of wire down each gulley to an improvised pull-loop ignition switch. When the circuit closed, the surge of power from the quartet of batteries would cause the switch to ignite the powder.

Along with the powder, aluminum, magnesium, barium sulfate, potassium chloride, and assorted chemicals commonly associated with fireworks, he'd had to purchase batteries, but every other component was the result of time-consuming labor. He'd filed every brass screw to obliterate any tool mark fingerprints. And he did it all the hard way, apparently taking sensual pleasure in the hours of detailing and polishing. He might have purchased nine-volt batteries and employed the two raised poles on each battery to attach his wires effortlessly. Or, he might have used battery holders with internal metal contacts and ready-to-wire external poles. These items were safely available at any electronics store. Instead he directly soldered the wires leading to his C-batteries, a difficult job because the batteries instantly absorbed the heat of his iron and made it almost impossible to attach his wires. But then, he always over-soldered.

When his box was closed (to open it again would activate the "anti-open" booby trap) the Professor admired it and repolished it to perfection even though, if all went as planned, it would be vaporized. The polishing, of course, served the double task of erasing telltale fingerprints. He carefully wrapped the box in brown paper, sealed every edge and crevice with heavy filament tape, and ran his gloved fingers along the edges.

Naturally, he'd cut his own stencil. He began to stencil an

address in green ink across the brown paper. He falsified the return address, slapped on stamps that had been issued years earlier—including his favorite one-dollar "Eugene O'Neill" stamps—for a total of $8.50 worth, excessive even though the package was to go airmail. He slipped the device under his coat, taking care afterward to button every button. He located a tiny postal station in a little grocery store in Elgin, Illinois, and posted his bomb from there. His bomb existed not only to make a statement (one that he lied to himself about), but also to kill every man, woman, and child on that jet.

The sun behind American Airlines Flight No. 444 burned overhead when Captain Don Tynan interrupted the rhythmical throb of the plane's jets to climb several thousand feet in a matter of seconds, leaving behind three trails of vapor as orderly as a plowed field. It was Wednesday, November 15, 1979. They'd departed Chicago O'Hare at 11:30 AM en route to Washington, DC, National Airport.

Soon after the Boeing 727 gained an altitude of 34,500 feet a great hand seemed to shake the plane. The cockpit crew felt a concussion, a "thump," and heard a "loud sucking noise" come from the area of the forward cargo hold. Captain Tynan suspected a can of shaving cream in a passenger's suitcase might have exploded, as they often do, and said so. But the sleek, silver outer skin of the fuselage began to peel and blister, just outside where the bags of mail were stored in aluminum pods.

Twenty minutes later, a sickly sweet smell, like the burning of a sugar field, filled the cabin where seventy-two passengers lounged. Many passengers had their seats in reclining positions. A few, drowsy after eating, actually slept. Others read while Captain Tynan, still concerned, explained the odor away by telling the passengers, "There's a problem with a sticking valve. Happens all the time." But then the first acrid, dense clouds of black smoke billowed into the passenger cabin. Disorientation and panic took over. Oxygen masks automatically dropped down from in front of choking passengers, and flight attendants sprang forward to move passengers away from the smoke. Passengers wept and prayed as the jetliner shuddered. The captain advised passengers to place their heads between their knees.

Neither Tynan nor his first officer was immune to the choking fumes seeping under the locked door of the cockpit and partially blinding them. The captain took one long look back into the passenger section before reclosing the door and donning an oxygen mask and goggles himself. "Stygian," he later called the scene. But now he had only a few minutes to prepare for a heartstoppingly rapid descent. He strapped himself into his seat, threw switches, jettisoned fuel, and brought the bucking plane under control.

Meanwhile, Tynan's co-pilot could not raise the flight tower at Dulles International, twenty miles west of Washington, to request an emergency landing. They had no way of knowing how near the fire was to the fuel tank. The plane had to go down now.

Flight No. 444 descended from thirty thousand feet at over six hundred miles per hour, twice the normal velocity of an approach, and the co-pilot still could not reach the Dulles tower for clearance. Finally he made contact, and now the field below became as busy as the cockpit.

Tynan saw below the busy red lights of what he fervently hoped were firetrucks and ambulances scrambling across the field. The men on the ground looked like ants. But then, as Tynan lowered his wheels, he saw the small plane on the runway ahead. It was too late to take the plane back up. Miraculously, the light plane cleared the jet's path seconds before Tynan touched down. Doors flew open the minute the plane rolled to a stop, smoke roiled out, and an emergency slide was rolled down from the door nearest the wing. Medics packed twelve passengers, each suffering from various degrees of burns and smoke inhalation, into ambulances and rushed them to the hospital. None were dead. None of the injuries were serious.

Firefighters eventually extinguished the blaze, then cut an eighteen-inch-wide hole into the hold to pinpoint the origin. The regular mail shipment, not screened by metal detectors, had produced the worst of the toxic smoke and done more damage than the nearly intact bomb beneath. Since the blaze had not been accidental, they called the FBI as required by federal law.

BACK IN NOVEMBER OF 1955, the first air homicide by bomb in the United States took place. Jack Gilbert Graham took out a $37, 500 life insurance policy on his mother, Daisie Walker King, then placed a homemade bomb in her luggage and saw her off on a United Airlines DC-6B bound from Denver to Portland. Flight No. 629 carried forty-four passengers (five crew, thirty-eight adults, and one baby). Graham's time bomb consisted of twenty-five sticks of dynamite, a timer, a six-volt battery, and two electric primer caps. The device exploded and destroyed the plane ten minutes into the flight, the fragments raining down onto a beet farm near Longmont, Colorado.

Jack Graham stood to inherit $150,000 from her estate, over and beyond the air insurance policy on his mother. "Of course I'll make a statement," he said when questioned. "Why shouldn't I? And I'll do a lot more—I'll take a lie detector test if you wish. What's more, you have my permission to search my house, my car, or anything else. I haven't done anything wrong."

In his garage, agents quickly found incriminating copper wire like that used in the bomb. Eventually the son confessed to the murder. In January 1956, he literally bounded to the gas chamber, screaming gleefully, "I'll be with mother tonight!"

AS A RESULT OF THE GRAHAM CASE Congress enacted the Federal Aviation Act of 1958, making the threat of destruction of an aircraft in interstate commerce a federal crime. Thus that day at Dulles Civil Aeronautics Board agents and Federal Aviation Authority (FAA) officials were quickly joined by teams from the Bureau of Alcohol, Tobacco and Firearms (ATF) and the FBI. Chris Ronay, a bomb expert, was one of the FBI agents.

While Ronay waited the Virginia State police bomb squad dragged the charred aluminum mail pod from the still-smoking hold and placed it on the runway. Ronay observed immediately that the device, though designed to explode, had instead burst into flames. He first assumed the cunning contraption had been intended not specifically for Flight No. 444 but for the addressee, whose address still partly showed on the wrapping. A Chicago postmark showed in the upper right-hand corner along with far more postage than necessary to mail the package. Some over-anxious individual, a typical mail-bomber, seemed to want to make doubly certain his deadly delivery reached its destination.

But when Ronay rooted out the remains of a barometer in the debris of the box, he realized the bomb had been intended for the jet after all. In the meantime, in Chicago, where Flight No. 444 originated, the *Chicago Tribune* and two radio stations received phone calls claiming responsibility for the pipe bomb. One caller claimed that the act was the work of the Iranian Student Association (ISA). "There will be more bombs, larger bombs, unless the deportation of Iranian students is stopped," the caller said. Only eleven days earlier Iranian militants had seized the US Embassy in Tehran and taken sixty-five American hostages. The nation was on edge, and all of a sudden the threat of domestic terrorism seemed real.

An FBI spokesmen said they took the anonymous call seriously, but noted the twelve-hour delay between detonation and claim of responsibility was uncommon. "Usually such calls come immediately before or immediately after," he said. In Washington, which was the destination of the ill-fated American Airlines flight, an official spokesman for the Iranian Student Association said they had no part in the bombing. "There is no way the ISA or any other Iranian student group would have done it. It's a lie," he maintained. Still, the ISA had many extremist factions, said the FBI.

Since the incendiary bomb had been mailed and exploded in a US mail pouch, postal inspectors were also involved. FAA authorities responsible for airport security enforcement met with them in the afternoon to discuss means of improving mail pouch security.

Almost immediately the three major nonstop carriers between Chicago and Washington—Trans World, American, and United Airlines—started refusing to carry mail, fearing a second bomb. By day's end, all were carrying letters again, but still refusing packages. Jamison Cain of the Postal Service announced the temporary embargo on all airmail packages, but promised this move would have no effect on letters.

Protecting aircraft from a mail bomber was all but impossible since, as a rule, mail pouches were never screened. "It would be impossible to target a specific flight with a package bomb," an official explained, "because all mail is dispatched on a first-plane-out basis."

But the detonations were just beginning. The fuse had been lit, creeping and crawling with flame, a full ten years earlier, at the most radical university in America.

PART ONE

THE JUNKYARD BOMBER
Chicago / The Late Seventies

CHAPTER 1
The Vanishing Professor

T*he industrial revolution and its consequences have been a disaster for the human race. They have greatly increased the life-expectancy of those of us who live in 'advanced' countries, but they have destabilized society, have made life unfulfilling, have subjected human beings to indignities, have led to widespread psychological suffering (in the Third World to physical suffering as well) and have inflicted severe damage on the natural world.*

—UNABOMBER MANIFESTO

TWILIGHT ABIDES IN THE CITY of late afternoon, a golden twilight that commences just under the arch of the Golden Gate Bridge and stretches across the flat plains of Berkeley to tint students at coffee house tables and professors on their redwood terraces with equal quantities of gold. The bleak flatness of the land sends long, distorted shadows across this city of one hundred thousand, dark lines that reach across the neighborhoods of West Berkeley, the Flatlands, and Downtown, all the way to the base of the Berkeley Hills, towering some two thousand feet above.

Berkeley, the world center of radical politics, of campus unrest, of social and cultural upheaval, the birthplace of modern feminism, black power, and the environmental and antiwar movements, remains one of the most tranquil, cloistered, and lovely places on earth. Its gently lit paths welcome evening. Its stately trees swaying in the long golden afternoon are more golden here, where only the sea separates the city from the sun. From just the right spot, a little toward Richmond perhaps, one can best see the region's most immense wonder, Mount Tamalpais, a vast granite mountain shaped like a sleeping lady. At the northern end of the Golden Gate Bridge, this stone maiden rests on a soft bed of fog, a thick blanket that gradually covers her over until she vanishes. This same blanket of fog can reach Berkeley in as little as forty minutes, swallowing up the long afternoon until people can't see their hands before their faces.

The day the Professor's resignation became final, June 30, 1969, ten years of simmering campus unrest came to a boil. A sad, slim figure, five feet ten inches tall, with a sensitive face, the Professor thrust his pronounced, pugnacious jaw defiantly at the world. His tie and neat coat made him as unfashionable at Berkeley as he'd been at Harvard and Ann Arbor. Twenty-seven years old, the scholar wore his sandy hair just as unfashionably— short, and parted neatly on the left, like his father's politics. Turk, his dad, an introspective, pipe-smoking sausage maker, was an avowed liberal. His discussions around the dinner table were about many of the same social inequities that campus firebrands now rallied against. But the soft-spoken, quiet instructor of mathematics kept aloof, working out his unfathomable but no longer fashionable calculus problems and showing no interest in politics of any stripe.

His "quietly arrogant" personality, which some students gauged as adding up to "absolutely zero," his conservative coat and tie, and his introspection served to segregate him. Was it such change after a solitary childhood as a "boy genius"?

His brisk walk quickly took him from Campbell Hall, south along Conte, and then west at Sather Tower. The twelve bell campanile, designed by John Galen Howard, who had also framed Sather Gate, was meant to resemble the campanile of St. Mark's

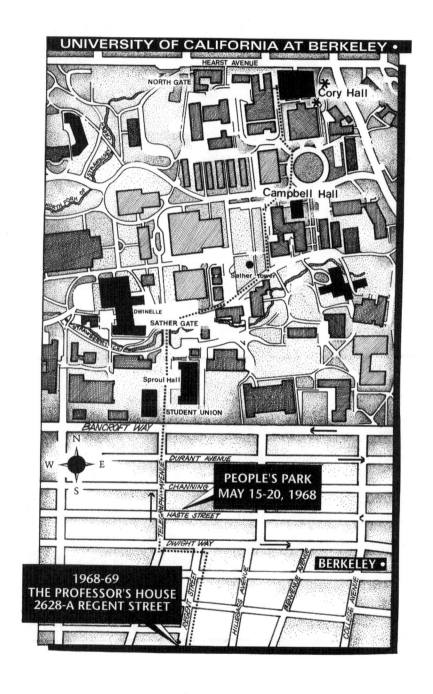

Map of 1969 Berkeley, CA.

Plaza in Venice. On the final day of classes, the carillonneur played an Irish folk song about the bandit Danny Deever who would be hanged in the morning.

The Professor passed Moses Hall, then Wheeler Auditorium. Ahead he saw Dwinelle Hall and recalled the bomb that was discovered there. Police had unearthed a timing device connected to two quarts of gasoline under a table, several weeks after a fire had gutted Wheeler and caused $300,000 in damage. The bomber had never been caught. The Third World Liberation Front, prime suspect in the case, denied responsibility for both incidents.

Unchallenged, the Professor stalked through the graceful arch of Sather Gate, flanked by two lights glowing like torches of genius. It led to the heart of the 1,232-acre campus. Only months earlier, militant black students at San Francisco State had struck over the issue of instituting a black studies program on that campus. The strike had crossed the bay to Berkeley. To enter Sather Gate during the strike one had to cross a picket line manned by the militants, be inspected—or barred—as the spirit moved them, or risk being gassed and clubbed by police. In the end it came down to power, and, disillusioned with politics, the Professor looked neither right nor left.

This evening the gate stood unguarded. The Professor passed quickly between the two lights and, head down, trod a wide, inclined path south toward the Student Union across open Sproul Plaza. He walked the domain of Mario Savio, Jerry Rubin, Tom Hayden. Here flowered the Peace and Freedom Party, the Free Speech Movement (FSM), Students for a Democratic Society (SDS), teach-ins, and the Panthers: Huey Newton, Bobby Seale, Eldridge Cleaver. In October of the previous year, activists had occupied Moses Hall and done considerable damage as they protested the conservative regents' refusal to allow Cleaver to teach an accredited course.

When Simone de Beauvior had visited the Berkeley campus in 1953, she complained that "the universities only confirm these young people in their apathy and conformity."

What a difference a decade made—in 1964 a scowling, sandy-haired Mario Savio, the son of a machinist, spoke for many students at a pre-sit-in noon rally:

> There is a time when the operation of the machine becomes so odious, makes you so sick at heart, that you can't take part; you can't even passively take part, and you've got to put your bodies upon the gears and upon the wheels, upon the levers, upon all the apparatus and you've got to make it stop.

HE PASSED LEAFLETEERS AT THEIR tables clustered around the main administration building and kiosks festooned with political tracts. He waited with Hare Krishnas at the three-way light to cross Bancroft Way and proceed down Telegraph Avenue at the southern edge of the university. The Professor walked on, his head locked down, legs moving briskly.

In his pursuit of mathematical enigmas, the Professor wandered a landscape barren of human contact. Standoffish, bright, and clever from the beginning, he'd skipped a grade in elementary school, then leaped past his junior year, and by age sixteen had been packed off to Harvard as a scholarship math prodigy.

By June of 1962, the Professor had finished with Harvard, and, at twenty, set off to the University of Michigan to earn his masters. There the scholar perched in the front row of Professor Peter Duren's math class, hanging on every word. Duren noticed him because of his conservative dress and introspective manner. "This was a time when the hippies were coming in, and I never remember him looking disheveled," recalled Duren. "He was always wearing the tie and jacket, which was very unusual."

When Duren saw the youth set out to solve a complex math

problem proposed by George Piranian, another professor, the teacher realized how good he was. "He was off doing the problem on the side without anyone knowing about it. He was really extraordinary," said Duren. "By the time he got his degree, we all had tremendous respect for this guy."

As a graduate student the Professor cracked a tough problem on "Boundary Behavior of Function Theory," upstaging two of his instructors. One of them, Piranian, recalled, "His papers were highly detailed, nothing was omitted. He was a brilliant young mathematician." Duren agreed, saying he might have presented too much proof. "He liked to construct ideas on his own without things being just handed to him."

The Professor who built so many boundaries against the world wrote his thesis on "Boundary Functions" and won the annual Sumner Meyers Prize for best doctoral thesis in 1967. He had already published three meticulous, highly detailed articles in respected scholarly journals.

Nevertheless his college advisor had attempted to lead the young man into a more active field of research such as an area of advanced calculus. His "Boundary Functions" specialty was a backwater already out of favor, leading nowhere, unfashionable quite soon after he'd won his prize. His work had no apparent practical application.

In the summer of 1967, after five years, the Professor left Ann Arbor, leaving behind barely a trace that he had ever been there: no photographs or yearbook entries. People barely remembered him and if they did, recalled only his oddness. He seemed to be vanishing piece by piece, like some cheerless Cheshire Cat, leaving behind only a frown.

Eyes averted, the Professor moved along Telegraph, passing outdoor cafes, filled with laughing, long-haired students in army surplus clothes or ponchos. He passed secondhand bookstores, head shops, health food stores, and vegetarian restaurants, and the Studio and Guild theaters where Pauline Kael wrote monthly reviews.

In 1967 the shy scholar arrived at the Berkeley Math Department as one of the faculty's twenty-eight assistant professors with a two-year contract to teach. He found Campbell Hall, where the department was located, huge. It was a six-story building near Cory Hall, home to the Computer Sciences and Electrical Engineering Department up the hill to the north, on the eastern edge of the campus near the Faculty Glade. Under its chairman, Professor John Addison, the department had fifty full professors and three hundred graduate students, including people like Professor Robert Vaught, Assistant Professor Hung Hsi Wu, and math student Hugh Scrutton. Of the ten young math scholars Addison hired that year, three would get tenure.

No doubt, the Professor ran on the fast track to tenure in the world's premier math department. But he was not a popular teacher and probably not a good one. He taught three graduate courses but received bad marks from his own students, especially on his presentation of the "curvilinear convergence of a continuous function as defined in the interior of a cube."

Six undergrad students, polled in an unofficial course evaluation, dubbed his lectures "useless and right from the book." Others remarked that "he showed no concern for the students." Still others complained the Professor "absolutely refused to answer questions by completely ignoring the students." But he published two more papers, again on boundaries.

The Professor entered Cody's bookstore, gigantic and well-lit at 2460 Telegraph. He fingered some books on calculus, and climbed to the fiction department on the second floor. He saw Conrad's *The*

Secret Agent, one of his favorites which he'd read many times. Conrad's original name was Konrad Korzeniowski, a name not too distant from the Professor's true name. Like Conrad, he was of Polish extraction and had on occasion reportedly used "Konrad" as an alias. *Secret Agent* tells of "The Professor" who stalks the boulevards with his finger around an india rubber ball that will blow him and all around him to smithereens in the event of his capture. The tale suggested itself to Conrad by, as he put it, "the absurd cruelty of the Greenwich Park Explosion of 1894," a true event.

Conrad's Professor, a nihilist fueled by rages, labored from dawn to dusk in his room constructing the perfect detonator. "Madness and despair" are his allies, which he says will provide him with a "lever with which to move the world."

The real-life Professor continued down Telegraph and passed Channing Way. The gray mantle of fog, speeding on its way, met a blue-tinged and fading golden light. There were many on the street but the Professor had mastered the ability always to be alone, even in crowds. And what crowds they were to the unhappy man. Grim, wide-eyed skeletons. Walking skulls, their features etched away by the street lights leaving only staring eyes. The streets were gray now. Lights glowed in each Telegraph Avenue window.

Visible from most of the campus, the Rad Lab was the oldest national lab in the United States. There, researchers had discovered fourteen different elements and were probing subatomic particles. The "Father of the Bomb," J. Robert Oppenheimer, then a UC professor, also toiled there, now horrified by his own creation: "I am become Death, the destroyer of worlds."

The Professor chose the summer of 1968, his second year at Berkeley, to resign. On a hiking trail he'd come upon a colleague, Maxwell Rosenlicht, and the two instructors had paused to chat.

"I'm going to quit my job," the Professor said abruptly.

"Why?" said Rosenlicht. "That's a silly thing to do. You've got a good position, and it'll be hard to find another job that good if you just up and leave."

The Professor shrugged. "I just have to go," he said.

A lot of people were dropping out in those days, and for once the Professor seemed not so far out of place. Ultimately, however, he stayed until the summer of 1969. By then the country had lost Martin Luther King, Jr., and Bobby Kennedy, Vietnam had boiled over, and the "Chicago Seven" were standing trial.

The Professor now came to the corner of Haste and Telegraph, where he saw signs of the recent riots over People's Park. It had been a terrible event, occurring as it did on his birthday only a month earlier, and may even have changed his life.

The university had bulldozed some old houses to get rid of agitators living there and left behind a muddy field. A rally that noon attracted several thousand angry radicals and hippies to Sproul Hall, chanting, "Take the park! We want the park!" They marched down Telegraph, but they never reached their destination. The San Francisco Tactical Squad arrived and fired tear gas and birdshot into the crowd. When they ran out of tear gas, troopers threw stones back at the demonstrators. The mob unscrewed a fire hydrant and, under a jet of water, smashed windows in the Bank of America at Durant and Telegraph. Bullets ricocheted into classrooms as the battle raged all afternoon.

Just a block from the Professor's house, protesters torched a city car. One youth was wounded by the police, and a demonstrator fleeing down a side street was shot in the back from a distance of thirty feet. By early evening, rioters took control of the two-story rooftops lining Telegraph, showering the police with concrete and metal debris. The police replaced their birdshot with buckshot. Far more lethal, one buckshot blast killed an innocent rooftop bystander, James Rector. One hundred twenty-eight demonstrators were shot, but no police were injured.

Governor Ronald Reagan called out the National Guard to restore order that night, Thursday. Tuesday, the Professor's birthday, the riot still raged. The National Guard formed a line across Bancroft in the early afternoon, blocked access to and from the campus, sealed Sather Gate, cleared and locked the Student Union, and trapped thousands of students and professors in a virtual box.

When a National Guard helicopter appeared overhead the university personnel and eight hundred students had no place to flee. The copter swooped down in pass after pass, dousing the confined crowd with the most potent tear gas manufactured. The Professor and students, along with the crowd, panicked and tried to flee, but gas was everywhere, covering more than a mile of the campus. Eventually it drifted up the hill to Cowell Hospital, where it choked and tortured polio victims locked into iron lungs.

The day after a police helicopter sprayed tear gas on the People's Park protesters, I sat drawing a political cartoon of the event in the city room of the *San Francisco Chronicle*. I'd been their editorial cartoonist for almost a year now.

But I found nothing remotely humorous about what was going on in Berkeley, the city which, after San Francisco, I loved most. And so I leaned more toward the serious, hard-hitting cartoons of the last century. Soon I would buy a house there, not on the flatlands, but among the Queen Anne homes overlooking the north side of the campus. I remember a wonderfully fine Maybeck house stood across LeRoy Avenue from mine, all sloping redwood shingles and superannuated bricks. A golden city.

On May 22, mass arrests began. A *San Francisco Chronicle* reporter, Tim Findley, was arrested, and Berkeley residents grew as outraged as the students over the situation. The strife appar-

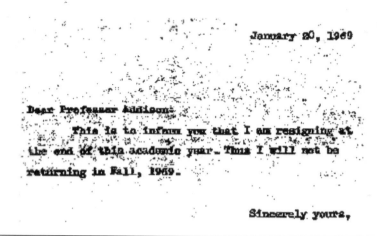

January 20, 1969

Dear Professor Addison:

This is to inform you that I am resigning at the end of this academic year. Thus I will not be returning in Fall, 1969.

Sincerely yours,

The Professor's letter of resignation from University of California at Berkeley.

ently also made up the Professor's mind for him. He would resign because, as he later said, "Math wasn't relevant for the times."

John Addison, the Professor's boss, had attempted to dissuade him from resigning once before, January 20, 1969, in fact, the day Nixon was sworn in as President, but now he saw that the scholar was determined.

"He was very calm and relaxed about it on the outside," Addison wrote, "but he seemed pathologically shy and as far as I know made no close friends in the department. Efforts to bring him more into the swing of things had failed. I think there was a lot of inner tension there. My guess was it probably had something to do with the atmosphere on campus and around the country."

The chairman recalled how the Professor had remarked with disgust over the widespread drug use and liberal politics on campus. Additionally, there was tremendous pressure among science and math scholars—not only in Berkeley, but all over the country—not to "undertake work or research that might contribute to the Vietnam War effort." He told Addison, "I'm tired of teaching engineers math that is going to be used for destroying the environment." Alan Shields, the Professor's former advisor at Ann Arbor, had led a group of fifty mathematicians in signing a petition not to help the war effort.

"What will you do?" Addison finally asked.

"I'm going to give up mathematics. I'm not sure what I'm going to do now. I want to do something of more immediate social value. I wonder if I'm not wasting my time."

That was the last time Addison saw the Professor. After a short while he was unable even to recall the young man's appearance.

Soon no one would remember him at the single-story stucco house he'd rented for two years, number 2628 Regent Street. Students at Ann Arbor and Harvard, when later pressed to recollect him, couldn't, though they could summon forth, with great concentration, the fleeting image of a vanishing, solitary man walking briskly.

Now the Professor's shadow stretched before him like the exaggerated shadows cast by the Golden Gate Bridge across the Bay. He walked on and as he walked he seemed to become more and more insubstantial until it was as if he'd never been at all.

As fog the closed in over Berkeley none of us knew the trouble that awaited us.

BERKELEY: DEPARTMENT OF MATHEMATICS

Sunday, March 2, 1969

Dean Walter D. Knight
College of Letters and Science
207 Moses
Campus

Dear Walter:

I submit herewith the sudden and unexpected resignation of Assistant Professor Theodore Kaczynski. Dr. Kaczynski has decided to leave the field of mathematics.

Vice Chairman Calvin Moore and I have tried to persuade him to reconsider his decision but have not been successful.

Sincerely,

J. W. Addison
Chairman

JWA:at

Chairman of Math Department's (UC Berkeley) reaction.

UNIVERSITY OF CALIFORNIA, BERKELEY

BERKELEY · DAVIS · IRVINE · LOS ANGELES · RIVERSIDE · SAN DIEGO · SAN FRANCISCO   SANTA BARBARA · SANTA CRUZ

DEPARTMENT OF MATHEMATICS   BERKELEY, CALIFORNIA 94720

Sunday, March 22, 1970

CONFIDENTIAL

Professor Allen Shields
Department of Mathematics
The University of Michigan
Ann Arbor, Michigan 48104

Dear Allen:

Thank you for your inquiry about T. J. Kaczynski. I apologize for my delay in providing you with the information you requested.

Kaczynski did indeed resign effective June 30, 1969. He submitted his resignation last year quite out of the blue. At my request he came in and let Cal Moore (our Vice Chairman for Junior Faculty) and me talk to him about his decision. He said he was going to give up mathematics and wasn't sure what he was going to do. He was very calm and relaxed about it on the outside. We tried to persuade him to reconsider, but our presentation had no apparent effect.

Kaczynski seemed almost pathologically shy and as far as I know he made no close friends in the Department. Efforts to bring him more into the swing of things had failed.

He left the following forwarding address:

Sincerely,

John

J. W. Addison
Chairman

JWA:at

A letter from J.W. Addison responding to Allen Shields's request for information about the mysterious Professor.

CHAPTER 2

The Missing Years

By *'freedom' we mean the opportunity to go through the power process, with real goals... and without interference, manipulation or supervision from anyone, especially from any large organization.*

—UNABOMBER MANIFESTO

THE LONG LEAN FIGURE topped the misty crest of a ridge and stopped to take in the expanse of forest spread out before him. He peered down on ancient forests, the packed stands of trees, and the thick canopy of leaves that shadowed the forest floor. His jaw thrust squarely from the clean-shaven face, his reddish hair, sun-streaked, fanned in the breeze. Cinching up his pack, he went down into a glade by a stream to set up camp.

The forest everywhere was soundless, except for the rush of streams and the hushing noise of the waving tops of trees. The mosses here were brilliant green, the ice-blue water frigid, and rain dripped from branches among toppled trees and scattered trunks.

"In wildness is the preservation of the world," Henry David Thoreau had written. "Would it not be a luxury to stand up to one's chin in some retired swamp for a whole summer's day?" The

Professor sat brooding in front of a fire he'd made of several different kinds of wood. The aroma of the smoke curled round him,
stained his clothes, got in his hair and in his mind. He drank it
deep into his lungs, and it kindled the rage slowly building there.
He had time to think in the woods, and ultimately that may have
been the worst thing of all.

The imagined and real slights of the past festered and began to
smolder. He heard the howl of what may have been a wolf in the
distance, but it may not have been. Even wolves had become an
endangered species. The Santa Barbara oil spill, a blowout at
"Platform A," had occurred while he'd been at Berkeley. Now
Boeing Aircraft was in the news, having secured in May 1970 a
government contract to develop a prototype of a supersonic, commercial aircraft over the next seven years. The growing environmental movement was outraged, and many an ordinary citizen
opposed. An ad in the *San Francisco Chronicle* and *The New
York Times* concluded in huge letters—"AND WILL HASTEN
THE END OF THE AMERICAN WILDERNESS." Reportedly
the SST, as it broke the sound barrier, trailed a fifty-mile-wide
sonic boom behind it and damaged the ozone layer, affecting the
balance of heat in the upper atmosphere and theoretically bringing about global warming.

"Boeing," he must have thought. "Boeing, someone should do
something about that." His eyes roved the still-rich timberland.
Still-rich near him for now. But after World War II clearcutting
had become so prevalent that now, in 1970, it accounted for some
60 percent of all logging operations in the national forests. How
could they? Magic throbbed in the trees all around, in the gnarled
trunks, in the roots of the world.

Magically, he himself had disappeared. The Harvard Directory
had placed him at Number 788 Banchat Pesh, Khadar Kheb, in
Afghanistan during these lost years, 1969–1971. But the

Professor's passport showed no record of such an excursion. During 1970 he paid no taxes, had no photos of himself taken, had lost himself entirely. Even his practical jokes were about changes of identity and sleight of hand. Just after he'd resigned from UC Berkeley he'd forged a letter to one professor supposedly from another and brought it off in a highly convincing manner.

HE HAD NO ACTUAL FRIENDS of his own. Seemingly so cut off, he could be terribly observant, even a good gossip. Math instructor Nolan R. Wallach had taught with the Professor at Berkeley and recalled that "[h]e told me all about everyone in the department who had been divorced, who was sleeping with whom, and so forth. When he told me those things, I thought he was telling me nonsense, but they all turned out to be true."

No, the lost years were not spent in some exotic foreign land, but in wandering, moving from one woodland shadow to another, then to the cloak of a mountain ledge. After his resignation, the Professor had driven to Wyoming and met his brother, and they traveled to British Columbia to see if they could buy some land. Near Prince George, the Professor found a site that fit the bill and filed homesteading applications for the property. Some days he fell silent, ignoring all questions, but the next day he would be normal. In the summer of 1969, he returned to the family home in Illinois while waiting to hear about his land application. He haunted the library, hiked the woods, and worked as a gardener at the mall.

In the winter of 1970 the Professor received a brief letter from Canada denying his request. For days he secluded himself in his room reading and writing letters to magazine editors about liberty and, specifically, technology. On February 28, 1970, he wrote to the editor of the *Saturday Review*:

C.W. GRIFFIN, JR., exaggerates the extent to which Americans romanticized the freedom, independence and adventure of the frontier. In any case such romanticism should be regarded as a symptom rather than a disease. A happily married man does not daydream about romantic love. Similarly, a man does not romanticize frontier freedoms unless he is suffering from a lack of personal autonomy. Mr. Griffin apparently would like to change people to make them fit the restrictive structure of society. Perhaps the better solution would be to change the structure of society so that it becomes possible to allow some of the freedom and independence they seem to crave.

A society, after all, is supposed to be designed for the benefit of the people that live in it, not the other way around. Griffin would put the blame for our environmental problems on excessive *individual*[sic] freedoms. Actually, most of the problems are direct or indirect results of the activities of large organizations—corporations and governments. It is these organizations, after all, that control the structure and development of society. Perhaps the most unfortunate thing that has ever happened to individual liberty was its being used as an excuse for the misdeeds of huge corporations. Now the evils perpetrated by these highly collectivist organizations are blamed on "individual liberty."

THE PROFESSOR'S MOTHER, a constant early riser, went downstairs one morning and caught him leaving.

"There's a note for you on the table," he said.

"Aren't you going to say goodbye?" she said.

"It's easier this way."

Around August the Professor went to his brother's apartment in Great Falls, Montana, and spoke of a conflict he'd had with their parents. "I have to get away," he lamented. A month earlier, his brother had received a note from their parents who quoted a letter the Professor had written them. In it he said they were the "best parents anyone could have" and he was sorry if he'd disappointed them. "Please don't worry about me. I just want to go my own way," he'd scrawled.

Now, the Professor asked his brother if he wanted to go fifty-fifty on a land purchase, and his brother agreed. The Professor's wandering years had been spent on two extended camping trips—through Canada, and in Montana. The glaciered peaks of the Western Montana mountain range; the sharp rimrocks and bitten, saw-toothed terraces; the varied grasslands and geysers; and the towering waterfalls, hot springs, and high plateaus claimed his heart. The flat, wide gravel beds of the prairies charmed him, and he knew he'd found a home. The forest would be his family.

CHAPTER 3

The Scapegoat Wilderness

The industrial–technological system may survive or it may break down. If it survives, it MAY eventually achieve a low level of physical and psychological suffering, but only after passing through a long and very painful period of adjustment and only at the cost of permanently reducing human beings and many other living organisms to engineered products and mere cogs in the social machine.

—UNABOMBER MANIFESTO

"I LIVED ALONE, IN THE WOODS, a mile from any neighbor, in a house I had built myself... and earned my living by the labor of my hands only."

The moment I saw the Hermit's high-peaked shack with its green roof and got the lay of the land, saw the placement of the root cellar and gardens, I knew I'd seen it before—it was Thoreau's cabin at Walden. There were some similarities in the Hermit's own writings and the philosopher's. But the design of the two Recluses' properties was identical. Then I realized that both shacks were identical because both had come from the same plan, blueprints called the "pioneer plan."

In describing his land, and thus the Hermit's, Thoreau said: "My house was on the side of a hill, immediately on the edge of the larger wood, in the midst of a young forest of pitch pines and hickories, and half a dozen rods from the pond, to which a narrow footpath led down the hill. I have thus a tight shingled and plastered house, ten-feet wide by fifteen long, and eight-feet posts, two trap doors, one door at the end, and a brick fireplace opposite.

"I dug my cellar in the side of a hill sloping to the south, where a woodchuck had formerly dug his burrow, down through sumac and blackberry roots, and the lowest stain of vegetation, six feet square by seven deep, to a fine sand where potatoes would not freeze in any winter.... My furniture, part of which I made myself—and the rest cost me nothing of which I have not rendered an account—consisted of a bed, a table, a desk, three chairs... a kettle, a skillet... two knives and forks, three plates, one cup, one spoon and a jug for oil."

Thoreau had felled tall pines with a borrowed ax for the cabin's timbers, rafters, and studs, and brought it all in for a total cost of $28.12. The Walden writer allowed himself a weekly outlay of 27¢ for necessities. His home, he said, reminded him of mountain houses, high-placed, airy, fragrant, and he liked that moles lived in his cellar and that a hare visited once a week. Space, air, a few tools, his journal, a copy of Homer—what more could a man wish for?

In the beginning the Hermit lived in a tent on Baldy Mountain property, then on June 19, 1971, he purchased almost one-and-a-half acres in the rough footlands on the pitted trail to Stemple Pass. It was all in section five, "more or less," along the jagged edge of the Continental Divide. A local rancher, Clifford David Gehring, sold it to the shy man for $1 down and $2,100 total and had the Hermit's younger brother cosign for the property. The Professor obtained money for his half from some invested certificates of deposit. Gehring died August 1, 1974, was buried on his ranch property, and was succeeded by his son Butch, who eventually took on the running of the saw mill. As for the Recluse, he

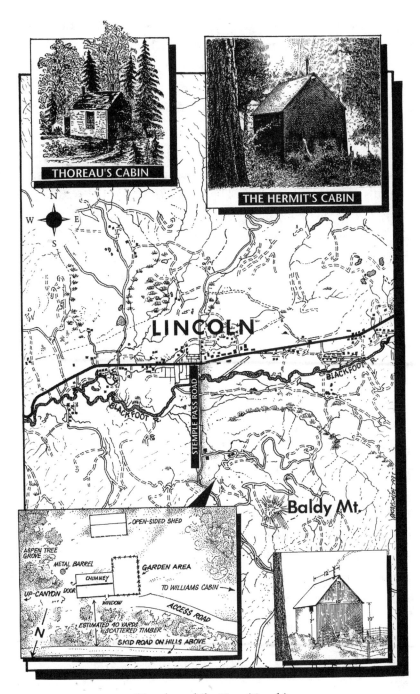

Lincoln and the Hermit's cabin.

figured he could scrape by on $200 a year, a relative amount to what Thoreau had allowed himself annually.

The Hermit's mountain plot under the Big Sky stood down a glorified dirt path, Humbug Contour Road, near Poorman's Creek and one-quarter mile up Canyon Creek from Gehring's lumber company. To the north, about five miles away, lay a summer resort, mining, and lumber town, Lincoln, Montana, situated midpoint between Missoula and Great Falls in the western foothills of the Divide along Highway 200. At a half-mile north of Highway 200 lay the richest farmland in Lincoln Valley. The big Blackfoot River, of "A River Runs Through It" fame, cuts through the town alongside the highway.

About five hundred people live in Lincoln, but the town doubls its population every summer when tourists flowed in from Helena, fifty-five miles away. Lincoln boasts a

full-time doctor,
medical center,
pharmacy,
part-time dentist,
part-time vet,
part-time eye doctor,
part-time chiropractor,
master electrician,
volunteer fire department,
sheriff's office and jail,
and its own newspaper and printer,
plus a beef jerky plant.

In addition, the town supports
five motels,
five cafes,

204 340

WARRANTY DEED IN JOINT TENANTS WITH RIGHT OF SURVIVORSHIP.

This Indenture, Made the __nineteenth__ day of __June__

A. D. one thousand nine hundred and __seventy-one__ _____BETWEEN

Clifford D. Gehring, Sr., a single man,

of __Lincoln, Montana__ PART Y of the FIRST PART

and

of __Lombard, Illinois__ and Great Falls, Montana the PART ies of the SECOND PART;

WITNESSETH, that the said PART Y of the FIRST PART, for and in consideration of the sum of __one__ Dollars ($__1.00__) lawful money of the United States of America to __him__ in hand paid by said PART ies of the SEC-OND PART, the receipt whereof is hereby acknowledged, do es by these presents grant, bargain, sell, convey, warrant and confirm unto the said PART ies of the SECOND PART, AS JOINT TENANTS AND TO THE SURVIVOR OF SAID NAMED JOINT TENANTS, (and not as tenants in common) and to the heirs and assigns of such survivor forever, the hereinafter described real estate situated in the city or town of _____ County of __Lewis and Clark__, and State of Montana, to-wit:

beginning at the N ¼ Cor. Sect. 6, T. 13 N., R. 8 W., M.P.M.;
thence N 82°03' E a distance of 333.2 feet; thence N 57°53' E a
distance of 2014.3 feet; thence S 44°55' E a distance of 787.0 feet;
thence N 67°59' E a distance of 373.4 feet; thence S 67°26' E a
distance of 220.0 feet; thence S 86°47' E a distance of 198.0 feet;
thence N 77°36' E a distance of 265.0 feet; to the true point of
beginning; thence S 12°37' W a distance of 300.0 feet; thence
N 82°52' E a distance of 217.2 feet; thence N 12°37' E a distance
of 300.0 feet; thence S 82°52' W a distance of 217.2 feet to the
true point of beginning, containing 1.5 acres, more or less, all in
Section 5, T. 13 N., R. 8 W., M.P.M., Lewis and Clark County,
Montana; together with the right of ingress and egress to the
above-described property from Stemple Pass Road over existing
road.

TOGETHER, with all and singular the hereinbefore described premises, all tenements, hereditaments, and appurtenances thereto belonging or in anywise appertaining, and the reversion and reversions, remainder and remainders, rents, issues, and profits thereof; and also all the estate, right, title, interest, right of dower and right of homestead, possession, claim, and demand whatsoever, as well in law as in equity, of the said PART Y of the FIRST PART, of, in or to the said premises, and every part and parcel thereof, with the appurtenances thereto belonging. TO HAVE AND TO HOLD, all and singular the above mentioned and described premises unto the said PART ies of the SECOND PART, as joint tenants with right of survivorship (and not as tenants in common) and to the heirs and assigns of the survivor of said named joint tenants forever.

And the said PART Y of the FIRST PART, and __his__ heirs, do es hereby covenant that __he__ will forever WARRANT and DEFEND all right, title and interest in and to the said premises and the quiet and peaceable possession thereof, unto the said PART ies of the SECOND PART, as joint tenants with right of survivorship (and not as tenants in common) and to the heirs and assigns of the survivor of said named joint tenants, against all acts and deeds of the said PART Y of the FIRST PART, and all and every person and persons whomsoever lawfully claiming or to claim the same.

IN WITNESS WHEREOF, the said PART Y of the FIRST PART ha s hereunto set __his__ hand and seal the day and year first hereinbefore written.

Signed, Sealed and Delivered in
the presence of

_____ Clifford D. Gehring (SEAL)
_____ (SEAL)
_____ (SEAL)
_____ (SEAL)

Deed to Hermit's cabin, June 19, 1971.

two grocery stores,

three gas stations,

two laundromats,

one supper club,

one general store,

one convenience store,

one video store,

and four churches.

THE HERMIT SALVAGED LUMBER from an abandoned log cabin and used it to build his own ten-by-twelve-foot shack, topped by a dun-colored, sharp-peaked roof with a tin chimney. It had thin, plywood walls, leaned a bit, and was covered on top with green tar paper. But the roof let in rain.

Like Thoreau's cabin, the Hermit's shack had two, single-pane, twelve inch by twelve inch windows on either side, providing the only sunlight. At night he read his volumes by the illumination of homemade candles. One window he'd installed above eye level, but the other allowed him to look out and scan for interlopers.

Inside, the cabin had no wires or plumbing of any kind. A makeshift padlock locked the cabin when he went into the woods, and inside it was secured by two deadbolt locks. Over the years only two visitors were ever known to have been inside.

Once a volunteer fire department lieutenant working as a census taker knocked on his door. Most locals knew better than that. Even when they carried provisions to his house for him, he would wheel and close the door behind him. But this day he let Joe Youderian, who also worked at the beef jerky factory, inside. Youderian took the only chair in the cabin and surveyed what he later called "a real bachelor pad." Piles of clothing were strewn on the floor and books lined the walls, about sixty volumes in all. Joe saw names he scarcely knew—Thackeray, Thoreau,

Shakespeare, and Victor Hugo. The Hermit crouched on the thin mattress that covered the hard wooden cot. Simple tools, boxes, and a slop bucket were in one corner. Papers, homemade candles, and more books crowded a small table.

Over the years the Hermit's cabin would acquire a remarkably un-Thoreau like number of items packed inside such a compact area. For tools he had a hand-bowed wood saw, two spades, a welder's mask (but no torch or acetylene tank), a drill, a compass on a string, and a wood-handled hammer. Rough, woodsman's implements, simple and plain.

However, his garments were more varied, even colored like the woods, than the people of Lincoln who glimpsed him riding his patchwork bike suspected. He had a blue zippered sweatshirt, a blue jacket, a green hooded jacket, a rain poncho, a brown raincoat, a hat, a camouflage jacket with green and brown pants, and a canvas jacket. He also had a woodland green coat, mittens, a blue scarf, a turquoise and verdant scarf, and even a red hat that went with two pairs of plastic glasses. For shoes he chose from among eight pairs of Northwest Territory hiking shoes and also a pair of boots.

His cooking implements consisted of two steak knives, a metal pan and stick, cans with matches, four measuring spoons, a metal pot, two white Mix 'n Drink plastic cups, a metal frying pan without a handle, and a wood-handled knife inside a sheath constructed of newspaper. He'd organized his small bits and knickknacks in discarded cans and boxes: A Tater Tots box held books and maps, Hershey's Cocoa cans held nuts and bolts.

He kept his degrees in a Samsonite briefcase, and thirty-nine yearbooks in a green plastic bag. He had student guides and publications from the University of Montana and Carroll College, a number of rolled up maps, and a shopping bag that held his Montana driver's license and less than fifty dollars in cash. He owned a radio, though he had no electricity, and a map of Lincoln.

The Hermit's library eventually consisted of 233 volumes, two walls of books that would have astounded his neighbors by their complexity and variety. Their brightly colored jackets contrasted with the dark wood of the shack, an army of old friends. One brown-covered paperback was by Paul Goodman, a psychotherapist and social commentator who wrote of how society attempts to suppress the humanity of its citizens. Goodman applauded students who dropped out rather than yield to the constraints of organized life. In his book of social criticism, *Growing Up Absurd,* Goodman found his greatest audience, and through the sixties it was influential on college campuses throughout the nation.

He had *Asimov's Guide to the Old Testament* and, somewhere, *Asimov's Guide to the New Testament,* as well as the *Holy Bible-Dictionary Concordance* and a Bible. Among the books on chemistry and electrical circuitry were *Comes the Comrade, Eastern Mysticism,* and, two volumes of Victor Hugo's novel *Les Misérables.*

As for art, the most perfect piece would have been Van Gogh's claustrophobic painting of his solitary room—two chairs with no one in them, a window with no view, a mirror reflecting nothing, and a lonely bed. In this airless, solitary cell, the artist writes his brother saying that here he feels "tranquility and restfulness." Yet the little room vibrates with frustration, anxiety, and mental stress. In reality, a picture he painted of one of his rare friends—a postman—hung on the wall.

Joe and the Hermit, who actually looked somewhat alike in dress, spoke face-to-face for some time, long enough for Joe to realize that the Recluse was far more intelligent than he'd imagined. They discussed Vietnam, and then the topic turned to gardening. "What kind of plants and vegetables grow best around here?" the mountain man asked, perhaps thinking of Thoreau's experiments with roots. "Why?" "I'm interested in growing my own food."

The only other known visitor was Glenn Williams, who owned a hunting cabin near town. He recalled how the Hermit had helped him out for quite a few years. The two shared meals, went hunting together in the mountains surrounding the cabin, and the Recluse sometimes did chores for Williams. "He did so many things for me," said Williams. "He was always a straight shooter. At least he was to me."

Outside the narrow entrance to the shack, the Hermit had piled glass and plastic bottles. Four plastic one-gallon jugs hung from a piece of wood between two aspen trees. More aspens surrounded the cabin; groves of ponderosa pine and lodgepoles weaved in the wind. One large tree on the site had a ladder made from two-by-fours going up its side to a tree stand, perhaps as a lookout for the animals he hunted or an outpost to spy for unwanted outsiders. A large plastic bucket, probably a food cache, hung from a limb. But other buckets hung from limbs with no apparent use.

The Hermit got his water from Poorman's Creek, just a short walk away. The stream was probably just short of two feet wide at that juncture. He kept his garden watered with a spring-fed hand pump, a cunning arrangement of black tubing that to this day lies among the tall grass. On the far side of his shack flowed Canyon Creek, where the mountain man had constructed a tumbledown root cellar. The cold (20 degrees on the average in January) and the short growing season made a garden difficult. But in the root cellar he kept his potatoes, parsnips, carrots, and other vegetables that he grew. He hunted rabbits with a .22-caliber rifle, the same caliber as the gun with which his terminally ill father had committed suicide.

On the occasions he showered, he washed under a five-gallon

bucket of water suspended from a tree limb. The constant wind in the trees made the grove sound like the rush of a river, but the actual Blackfoot River flowed fast close by, steeply dropping, charged with power.

Big River, as the locals call the Blackfoot, roars loudest in the canyon just above the Old Clearwater Bridge, a fishing access site on Sunset Hill Road that intersects Highway 200 just east of Greenough Hill. "The river is a straight rapids until it strikes big rocks or big trees with big roots," writes Maclean. "This is the turn that is not exactly at right angles. Then it swirls and deepens among big rocks and circles back through them where the big fish live under the foam."

Two of the Hermit's gardens measured larger than the cabin. The smaller stood only scant feet from the shack, but the other, nine hundred square feet, lay fifty feet away and was surrounded by a ten-foot-high barbed wire fence, to keep foraging bears and deer away. The solitary man kept a ladder to get over the towering wire fence and down into his garden. He also maintained an open-air drying shed near the garden and hung game in it. But he could use this shed only in the winter when bugs wouldn't get at the meat. The Hermit was careful to keep his local deer-hunting license up to date. It wouldn't do to break the law.

Throughout 147,000 square miles of Big Sky country, May and June are the wettest months, when feather, cheat, and needle grasses drink their deepest. Summers heat up to 117 degrees. Blustery, ripping winds plunge the temperature to forty degrees below zero on winter nights. Snows come early to the Continental Divide, and the Hermit industriously cut and hauled his own firewood. But that shack must have gotten cold beyond description.

Thoreau knew the same cold and loneliness in the heart of winter. "At this season I seldom had a visitor," he wrote. "When the snow lay deepest no wanderer ventured near my house for a week or fortnight at a time, but there I lived as snug as a meadow mouse, or as cattle and poultry which are said to have survived for a long time buried in drifts, even without food."

The Hermit's house, in the rugged northwest Montana terrain near Big River, lay in the open, yet among the remote trees it didn't have to be hidden to be private.

Since the mountain man had no electricity, reaching him proved more than difficult. If his family needed to reach him in an emergency, they had to write and mark the envelope with a red line just below the stamp. Any letter without this code might remain unopened for weeks or be destroyed.

The rasp in Thoreau's social relations may have been a defect of personality, rather than a truth of his character. The silence, shyness, and alienation of the Hermit may have been his only personality. He had no friends because he possessed such an exalted standard of friendship that no friend could meet his requirements. Yet many times he'd helped neighbors cut lumber and labored with such energy and speed they were astonished.

Whenever his root garden delivered more vegetables than he could use, he brought the extra to a couple who lived close by. From time to time he reportedly played pinochle with another couple, Irene Preston and Kenneth Lee, who lived in Lincoln. One evening he came upon two black bears rooting through barrels behind a neighbor's hunting cabin, and waving his long arms shooed them back into the forest.

The bearded Hermit kept his hair long and a bit unkempt, but didn't clothe his gaunt frame in the army fatigues and all-black outfits people later claimed he habitually wore. When he traveled into town he donned jeans and a shirt, neat and clean, but tattered. He wore sunglasses on these trips, but when he took them off people found his gaze as penetrating as an X ray.

The Hermit conducted life as he chose, just as Thoreau had done. The village had looked askance at the pugnacious ascetic writer. The Hermit was silent because he'd been taught that he'd been given two ears and one mouth in order to listen more and speak less. He had no time for small talk, and a complete sentence seemed to tax his attention.

They say wild birds perched on Thoreau's shoulder; that he and a woodchuck once conversed for half an hour, looking into each other's eyes until they felt mesmeric influences at work over them both; and fish nibbled from his fingers. But the Hermit feared animals. When he heard the rustling of leaves or a woodpecker tapping, he sometimes feared an ill-fed village dog had turned wild and was afraid.

"Simplicity, simplicity, simplicity!" proclaimed Thoreau. The country had strayed far off the path of simplicity. Americans had sacrificed their independence, laid up corruptible treasures on earth, and made the mistake of seeing the means—manufacturing, the trades, professions—as the ends of life itself. "It is a fool's life, as they will find when they get to the end of it, if not before," Thoreau said. "Our inventions are wont to be pretty toys, which distract our attention from serious things. They are but improved means to an unimproved end.... As with our colleges, so with a hundred 'modern improvements'; there is an illusion about them; there is not always a positive advance." The Hermit thought, "Exactly so!"

In the journal he kept he wanted to compose something durable, sinewy, significant—a thesis that did not reek of the scholar's study, nor the poet's cabin, but would be saturated with the fragrance of the mountains, fields, and woods, with the exhilarating tonic of wildness.

Once or twice a month he "commuted" to Lincoln, making the trip on a bike of his own invention. But the Hermit was not mechanically inclined. His closest neighbor, Leland Mason, thought he was not a smart worker and short on common sense. He'd driven an old pickup all one summer until it quit on him. "He just let it sit there," recalled Mason, "until somebody bought it from him. It only cost the new owner $25 for the part."

Once he tried a chainsaw to cut firewood, but quickly abandoned it for a handsaw. Butch Gehring thought this showed the man's disdain for technology. He briefly had worked at Butch's small sawmill down the hill from his shack, but quit the same day. Peeling logs was not for him.

His customized, one-speed, high-handlebar confabulation was one of his rare successes. The twenty-six-inch wide-tire bike could not be called old, since every mismatched part came from a different vintage. It had no gears, but in rain or snow, summer or winter, the Hermit jounced along a four-mile gravel road to Lincoln. The only concession he ever made to the elements was to strap on chains as traction when the snow was deep.

He made no concession to style, only function. He tied his pants legs close to his ankles, then tucked the cuffs into his socks to keep them from snarling. He had no chain guard. As he bounced along the way, his backpack flew out behind him.

When the weather was too severe even for the stoic Hermit, he sometimes hitched a ride into town with the mailman who delivered mail between points in the Scapegoat Wilderness and Helena, almost sixty miles away. Dick Lundberg never knew when he'd see the Recluse standing silently at the three mailboxes at the bottom of the rutty road leading half a mile up to his cabin.

"It was four or five times a year," Lundberg recalled later. "Usually he had a small backpack but it didn't amount to nothing, like a kid would wear, like it would hold his lunch."

The Recluse turned his bike onto the potholed Stemple Pass Road, toward Lincoln, passing over the river. As he swung around the curve to Lincoln, all the village dogs pricked up their ears, switching and scratching to beat the band. They sniffed the breeze, got the scent of his jeans, steeped in the smoke of his wood fires, and followed the trail. The Hermit was coming! They chased alongside the vintage bike, growling and barking, ears laid back like a pack of wolves. The Recluse was genuinely frightened of dogs. His arms flew straight up in fear, then he peddled for all he was worth onto Highway 200, as the dogs, sensing his fear, bayed on. The phantom slid across the gorgeous landscape, lean, denim-clad legs pumping, pumping, pumping. But so often he saw not beauty but smoldering ruins, flashing lights, and pale faces. Averse to technology as he was, furious at the manipulators and mind controllers, he nevertheless kept up with his prescription.

The Hermit was troubled. The gradual loss of the wilderness was driving him to make terrible choices. He might love the forest, but not everyone else in Northwest Montana did. At first he'd imagined that the handful of folks in Lincoln would be foursquare behind the environment (the Blackfoot River was in real danger), but the town's history had shown him the opposite.

Lincoln perched precariously on the spine of the Western Hemisphere. Beyond the community lay endless wilds. Big River, undammed, snaked to the south of the village and generally followed Highway 200, but doubled back and slipped under it at various points. The river wound thirty miles through the Swan and Blackfoot valleys.

The town's big ore strike in 1865 occurred when President Lincoln was assassinated, so his name christened both gold-laced Lincoln Gulch and the valley's major town. Indians, cowboys, ranchers, miners, and financiers had ruled Big Sky country, but in the 1920s Anaconda Copper seized control of the state and most of its resources. The Company, as it was known, also ran logging camps on the Blackfoot River.

"The lumberjacks were registering their customary complaints about the Company—it owned them body and soul; it owned the state of Montana, the press, the preachers, etc.," wrote Norman Maclean. "The grub was lousy and likewise the wages."

When Lincoln general store owner and pioneer environmentalist Cecil Garland took on The Company, Montana was not yet environmentally conscious. Too many big interests—the railroads, mines and timber companies—dominated the state. And Lincoln, and for that matter most of northwestern Montana, was desperate. World War I, the drought, an inferior banking structure, the collapse of the homestead boom and the stock market, and the decline of agriculture drove many farmers away. Little Lincoln was nearly busted and the Company's plans to reopen Mike Horse Mine might mean salvation. But Mike Horse had been abandoned in a contaminated state, leaving behind silted streams, bare mountainsides and eroded hillsides, mining pits, whole areas stripped of trees, and piles of waste. The principal product of Mike Horse Mine was silver and zinc, but its by-products—toxic waste metals like arsenic, lead, mercury, and cadmium—were left behind as poisonous mountains. Rains and wind swept these toxins into the streams of the Scapegoat Wilderness and finally into Big River.

For a hundred years Montana's lenient mining laws had allowed any mining company to pay a modest annual fee, tunnel, drill, build roads, clear-cut, and cart off any mineral it wanted. No provision in the law said anything about cleaning up behind. To reopen Mike Horse, the Company would dam part of clear, freshwater Alice's Creek, a tributary of Big River, to form a pond to hold toxic mining waste and sludge.

Montana Governor Forrest Anderson generally supported The Company, but Cecil Garland, a Lincoln storekeeper, convinced the Montana Wilderness Association to petition Congress to make the land around the mine a federal reserve. Thus, in March 1969, for the first time, a Montana mining lease was denied and Blackfoot River was temporarily saved.

The desperate townsfolk, however, retaliated with a boycott of Garland's store that eventually forced him out of business. "By 1973, Garland had won his environmental battle, but lost his home in the process," wrote Marc Mowrey and Tim Redmond in their book, *Not In Our Backyard*. "The people of Lincoln had spoken, loudly: they'd rather have Anaconda Mining, and its jobs, than Cecil Garland, and his cause. Garland parked his car, bid his family good-bye, and left Montana forever."

In 1972, a year after the Hermit came to Humbug Contour Road, the state revised its constitution to provide increased environmental protection, setting a precedent for the country. However, throughout the 1980s two giant timber companies began to cut heavily for maximum profit in huge clear-cuts, a strategy conservationists in Swan Valley and Blackfoot Valley called "cut and run" policies. Champion International was one company, Plum Creek the other. In 1968 Burlington Northern bought the small Montana timber company, Plum Creek, and harvested old-growth timber on its land-grant territory, making mile-square clear-cuts.

Plum Creek sold the timber as "raw" unmilled logs to Japan and then sank its profits into operations in Idaho and Montana, driving out the smaller mills around Lincoln. Huge clear-cuts in the Swan Valley north of Lincoln threatened wildlife habitats and watersheds.

Today the Hermit had come to town to buy groceries, mostly organic and generally healthy fare, do some laundry, pick up some used clothes, visit the post office to pick up mail he probably would never read, and visit the two-room Lincoln Community Library, a long building with a corrugated metal roof and painted wood siding, redwood logs for posts, and oak tables inside.

The mountain man read books in German and Spanish borrowed from bigger libraries, issues of *Omni* and *Scientific
American* like his mother used to read him, and the only newspapers available, Montana papers. "It was hard-to-read stuff,"
recalled Linda Bordeleau, a library worker. "A lot of books he
wanted had to be ordered because they were extremely intellectual works. He would bring back his books, and I would ask him,
'You can read and understand this stuff?' I couldn't. I'm more the
Danielle Steele type." Chief librarian Sherri Wood was his closest
friend. Many of the reference books were years out of date,
including directories he sometimes consulted, but the Hermit
loved that library.

From Anna Haire, owner of Aunt Bonnie's Books in Helena,
the Hermit bought used texts and obscure books, always careful
to inquire about the cheapest prices. "What he took out was very
obscure stuff, stuff that people often don't bother with, stuff we
would often toss," she said.

After he'd made a phone call at the library, the Hermit would
buy his groceries at the Blackfoot Market. Karen Potter, the store's
co-owner, always noticed him. He walked with his head down and
rarely smiled, but that might be because of his poor teeth, and he
kept his sentences short. Potter thought he looked fit. "He was not
what you'd call well-groomed," she said, "but he was not dirty. It
amused him that I was concerned with his health."

If someone asked the Hermit's name, he reply with a shy smile,
"Why?" and run one hand through his matted hair. Where some
would say, "OK" or "all right," he'd say "quite correct." Potter
liked him. "He was sweet and quiet," she said. "I would have
trusted him with my life." He avoided questions like "Where have
you been lately?" When Potter remarked she hadn't seen him for
a while, the Hermit seemed startled. "Thank you for your concern," he said. But many Montanans avoid questions. This was

the land of rugged individualists and people who'd come to get away from questions.

His backpack was big enough to fit a ten-pound bag of Montana Flower and Grains Company whole wheat flour inside, $4.25 a bag and the only kind he would buy. He loaded canned tuna, Beach Cliff fish steaks in Louisiana hot sauce, Spam, ingredients for baking his own bread, and bananas into the pack. He wouldn't buy anything with pesticides in it.

Next he went to the Grizzly True Value Home Center for hardware. "We have a lot of Hermits here," recalled Anna Wood, the cashier. "It's a quiet little town." She thought of him as typical of the kind of person who lived here in what she said was "the most boring place in the world." Anna was Sherri Wood's cousin.

Every few months he bought packets of vegetable seeds. "I understand he grew a fabulous garden," said Wood. "I know a lady he shared vegetables with." Over the years he'd purchased a bow saw, some gloves, bolt nuts, and batteries.

Probably few Lincolnites, with the exception of Sherri Wood and the rest of Lincoln's book people, knew how smart the Hermit was. But Butch Gehring had realized it when the Hermit pitched in to help Butch repair his house in exchange for some wood to build his cellar. As they were hammering, the Hermit instantly calculated fractions in his head, complaining his annual cost of living had risen from $200 to $300.

The Hermit's intelligence also revealed itself to Roger Holm, a cattle rancher who lived down the road from the Hermit's shack. The Hermit had entered a local newspaper competition in which readers were asked to find grammatical problems in a story. He'd circled 147 errors quite quickly, marking up the page with so many lines it was almost blackened. "Up until then, I had no clue he was educated at all," said Holm.

Another Lincoln resident, Ann Pryor, said, "He rarely spoke,

The Hermit and his bike.

but when he did he was friendly and courteous. Everybody knows him. Everybody knows everybody in Lincoln. We see him downtown at the library, the grocery store. We don't see him at any community functions. He's not community involved."

The Hermit once told Vicky Morris's ex-boyfriend that he got through the year on one hundred dollars. Morris worked at Lambkin's Restaurant, and Bette Love, a construction company secretary who moonlighted at Lambkin's, the local gathering place, knew a little something of the puzzle herself. "I never paid much attention to him, but he fit right in around here," she said. "The main thing we saw him doing was riding his bike to and from the post office.

"You would never think he had an education. He looked like a cross between a hippie and a bum. Everybody knows him as 'the Hermit.'" He seemed "a man without a life, without a home, without any motivation."

"He used to leave his bike at our office," recalled Carol Blowars, a GRI broker with Dallas Land Company, "which used to be down by the post office where the video shop is. He would come and he was always very polite. Knocked on the door, said he was going to park the bike, but first he'd come in and ask. He visited for a little bit, and said he'd like to be able to leave it there. Every time he came to the office, he'd always knock and park it out back. We didn't have a good spot for it so he just parked it by the back door." But she never once saw him pick the bike up. "We'd go around to the back of the office, and it'd just be gone.

"He'd leave vegetables for us either on our deck or at our office. He brought them in, gave them to me, and we put them in the sink and washed them. He was extremely polite." She always assumed the vegetables were his thank you for letting him leave his bike on the property. She wondered at his gardening skill. "He grew a great garden down there, parsnips, beets, carrots, potatoes, and leaf lettuce, I'm telling you—I can't believe it yet, because this is a beautiful but *cold* area to grow a garden in."

When the bike was left, which could be for days, "what it means is that he's left town."

Though "he was never dressed to the nines," says Carol, "I never saw him dirty, and we saw him a lot—between leaving his bicycle there and passing him on the road. My husband George would actually put his bike in occasionally and give him a ride home."

George, a roof builder and realty sales associate, and Carol, a realtor on Highway 200, which cut through the center of Lincoln, were fond of the Hermit on the Hill. They lived just down the road from his shack—a downhill ride on his wide-tire bike.

"He would never flag you down," for a ride, Carol told me much later. "He never went out of his way to be pesky or anything to get you to take him." She used to kid him "because the hill coming into here is pretty steep off of Stemple Hill and we ride bikes too. George can ride to the top of the hill, and I can't. Of course, he had to push his bike up and I stopped a couple of different times, rolled the window down, and said, 'Come on, get on in. George can ride to the top. What's the matter with you?' He laughed, 'I've got a one-speeder, and he's got a fifteen-speeder'."

Some years later the solitary man came into Carol's office.

"Do you have time to visit?" he said.

"Sure." The Recluse sat down across the desk from her and said, "I'm short of funds. Could you give me any idea of what my property is worth?"

Carol got out her yellow pad and a pen.

"How big is your lot?" she asked.

"1.4 acres."

"How big is your little cabin?"

"Ten by twelve feet."

Carol wrote that down and took notes as she questioned him. "Oh, you got a potty?"

"No."

"You got an outhouse?"

"No." Carol sat there, poised to write. Then the shy man said, "That's what I fertilize my garden with."

Carol blanched. She was thinking about all the carrots he'd brought her over the years. "You know home-grown carrots are all squiggly—they're not the nice straight store carrots," she said later, "and you can't ever get all the dirt out of them. When I looked up at him he had a kind of smile. He knew exactly what I was thinking, knew what was going through my mind. A sly grin crossed his face."

Carol asked, "Are you the sole owner?"

"When I bought it my brother's name was on it, but he quit-claim deeded it over to me." Afterward Carol was surprised to find his brother's name was still on the property. "He must have needed money badly to lie."

She told him his one acre with the cabin on it was worth twenty to twenty-five thousand dollars. She recalled later, "The area around his cabin is a great area for hunting, really secluded, so it's the kind of piece of property everybody's looking for." Carol asked him if he wanted a written appraisal, thinking he might want a bank loan, but he said no. Perhaps the bank had already turned him down, she thought.

"Do you know about employment in the area?" the solitary man then asked.

"Of course, the jerky plant is always hiring—Hi-Country Beef Jerky."

"I have no interest in working there." Making beef jerky is a terrible job, working with frozen meat at relatively low pay. The

Hermit's friend, Joe Youderian, worked there.

"Gee," said Carol, "you're at the library all the time. Can't they use you down there?"

"I don't think so."

Much later Carol learned that he'd applied down at the Blackfoot Market for a job. This was about the time he was getting serious about the environment. "If I don't get a loan on my property," he lamented, "I'll have to find some sort of employment." He obviously needed money badly, she thought, but for what?

Carol and George often walked up to the shack by Poorman's Creek early in the mornings. "He'd have a little campfire going outside a lot of mornings to cook his coffee over." When he was away she missed the smell of his pine, fir, and larch woodsmoke. "He had really good-smelling woodsmoke."

He was consistently pleasant, she remembers, and "would always wave as he biked past." But he was afraid of their dogs. "The border collie is real hyperactive, and whenever he'd see our friend, he'd shoot down the hill." Then the Hermit's arms would shoot straight up over his head and he would stand frozen until Carol took the dog away.

"Later people claimed he smelled bad, but I never smelled him," she notes with some annoyance. "He was in my office several times, and I sat across from him the width of my desk when I came in for the appraisal," and he was clean though "he never dressed fancy. His clothes were jeans and a shirt."

"When George and I moved here we'd always been told he'd come from money back East, that he was just an eccentric bachelor. There's a lot of people like that in the mountains. People think they can get away from society, and so they come here. There's a lot more people who would frighten me more than him. I was never afraid of him and would never have hesitated giving him a ride anywhere. He seemed quite gentle. You know, he was soft-spoken, and he had never done harm to us up here. He was just an excellent neighbor." One January morning George and Carol were walking and right before the turn to go up to his property, she spoke to George.

"'You know, George, we sure haven't seen our friend around this winter,' I said, 'I wonder if he left?' 'Well, no,' he said, 'I thought I'd seen him.' And right there were his bicycle tracks in the snow—right at the end of the logs there—in or out on this road, but he just never bothered anyone. You'd just pass him on the road or whatever.'"

CHAPTER 4
Birth of the Junkyard Bomber

I f the system breaks down, the consequences will still be very painful. But the bigger the system grows the more disastrous the results of its breakdown will be, so if it is to break down it had best break down sooner rather than later.

—UNABOMBER MANIFESTO

ON OCCASION THE HERMIT RODE the entire route from Lincoln to Helena with Dick Lundberg, who carried the mail six days a week. As they jounced along, Lundberg listened to the Recluse rattle on about the weather, his garden, and the difficulties of pumping enough water from Poorman's Creek to keep his garden flourishing. He'd made a list of things he said he intended to do in Montana's capital city. "I'll be paying my taxes," he'd remark, "might get some books, or run some errands." As far as Lundberg could tell the Hermit usually stayed for some days, though he could not imagine why, or where, in Helena he went. All the mailman knew was that at some point in the future he'd glimpse the Hermit standing patiently outside Buttrey Food and Drug in the downtown area waiting for a lift home.

The FBI later said that the Recluse had stayed at the Park Hotel of Helena on at least twenty-two occasions since 1980. Actually the neatly printed registration cards suggest at least thirty visits. When the Hermit climbed the wide stairs to the eighteen-room hotel above a karate studio and an office furniture store, he arrived without a reservation, as he always did. At the top of the stairs to his right was the registration desk of the 1917 hotel. A sign read: "432 Park Hotel" and "No dogs allowed." Barbara McCabe, the wife of owner J.R. McCabe, let him fill out one of the three-inch by five-inch registration cards. In the early eighties the cheapest room, which is what he always took, was nine dollars for one day, but by the midnineties the cost had gone up to fourteen dollars. He placed three dollars down as a key deposit and strolled to Room 104, 105, 118, 119, or 120. He stayed in Room 119 the most often, the room directly to the left at the top of the stairs. Like the Lincoln Lodge back home, the hotel offered a public shower for these five rooms. Of course, there was no phone in the room. The Recluse carefully put his backpack away. A pink coverlet shrouded the bed, and a dark wooden writing desk, a light, and a flowered chair hugged one wall. A white-painted chest of drawers stood at the foot of the bed, with a wash basin to its right.

He shut the door behind him, used the public phone in the lobby, then walked downstairs and cut diagonally across the street to Aunt Bonnie's Books. There, he traded for inexpensive books, mostly technical volumes. Back at the hotel, J.R. considered the shaggy man who'd been coming to his hotel since the late seventies. "He looked like a drifter, but he never drank," he said later. "He never took drugs. He didn't smoke. He'd leave an empty bottle of fruit juice or spring water behind, that's about all. Actually, he was an ideal guest. He came with a backpack that didn't look like it had much in it, and when he left it didn't have much in it."

The Rimrock Trailways bus station was only four blocks away, so the Hermit could leave at any time for anywhere. In fact, he rarely stayed at the Park Hotel for more than two days, usually checking out around 11:00 AM. He would leave his pack in the lobby and retrieve it only in late afternoon. Then he would be gone for a few days a week, a month, or longer. He would not be seen in Lincoln. Then at some unknown future time, always unexpectedly, Lundberg would see the Hermit outside the Food and Drug and drive him back to where the lonely mailboxes stood on Stemple Pass Road. On the way home, walking the gravel road, he'd pass George and Carol Blowars's fine home, a gambrel (a barn house), which is a sort of wood chalet with a low, pitched pyramidal roof. An old buckboard sat in the yard, and a rocking iron grid—a cattle guard—filled the gap between their driveway and the road, spaced just right so a car could drive over it, but deer, with their tiny hooves, could not walk over it.

Evening would be falling as he hiked along the road to his shack, a golden light coming from his right as he began to climb. He looked warily about for George and Carol's dogs. At a slight ridge he started down by a white rail fence. The countryside changed as his own shadow stretched out before him, long and impossible. The road beckoned, high ridges of pines stretching upward, larch, fir, spruce, and lodgepole. He was in shadow now, but just a yard before his cabin and the steep incline that led down to it, the full glow of golden light framed the aspen to his right.

Home. The Hermit's house, in the rugged northwest Montana terrain, lay in the open, yet ringed by trees. Once he'd wandered in a mathematical landscape—unsentimental, pure, and abstract—but smoke now curled on that bleak plain. What fueled the curling column and invisible thunderstorm—revolution? revenge? Framed against the Big Sky, he hustled down the rocky hill and vanished into the glade.

IN LATE 1972 THE PROFESSOR TRAVELED to Salt Lake City and labored for the next six months as an unskilled carpenter's helper for a private contractor. On one occasion his brother David stayed at the Professor's apartment overnight. Around June 1973, the Professor quit his job and left Salt Lake City, writing in the winter of 1974 that his family shouldn't worry about him because he'd "be away camping for awhile."

Briefly, the Hermit toiled at a six-pump gas station and truck stop as an attendant and unsuccessful tire salesman. In all likelihood, he was too truthful, too guileless to be a salesman of any sort. While the Hermit worked at the stop, he developed one of his infrequent crushes on a woman who worked there as a cashier. In a series of letters, each one growing more icy and formal, he complained to the woman, Sandra Hill, a nineteen-year-old North Dakota native. The first letter, she later remarked, was "basically an invitation or a request for me to move to northern Canada and be his squaw. The second letter was more like a résumé." In the third and final note the Recluse complained that she was ignoring him, so he assumed she had no interest in a relationship.

But he had one more letter to write, this time to Joe Visocan, the owner of the truck stop.

Visocan considered the note "so weird" that he slipped it into a desk drawer until events twenty-two years later prompted him to take it out again.

In 1978, just two years before he began staying at the Park Hotel, he needed money. He traveled to Lombard, Illinois, where his mother Wanda, his father Turk, and brother David lived. Possibly he could get employment where his father and brother worked—Foam Cutting Engineers, Inc., a foam-rubber plant in Addison. On June 26 the Professor began the tedious job of sawing foam, laboring under the watchful eye of his younger brother who acted as one of the supervisors there. It must have been humiliating working for his younger brother under the giant rounded white letters "FC."

Stemple Pass Road
Lincoln, Montana 596:
Oct. 1, 1974.

Dear, sweet Joe:

You fat con-man. You probably think I treated you badly by quitting without notice, but it's your own fault. You gave me this big cock-and-bull story about how much money I could make selling tires and all that crap. "The sky's the limit" and so forth. If you had been honest with me I would not have taken the job in the first place; but if I _had_ taken it, I wouldn't have quit without giving you a couple of weeks' notice. Anyhow, I have a check coming. I am enclosing a stamped, self-addressed envelope in which you can send it. I had better get that check, because I know what authorities to complain to if I don't get it. If I have to complain about the check, then, while I'm at it, I might as well complain about the fact that you don't have a proper cage for putting air in split-rim tires, which, if I am not mistaken, is illegal.

Love and Kisses,

Letter from the Hermit to Joe Visocan, owner of the Kibbey-Corner, a Raynesford, Montana, truck stop.

The job gave him time to think and brood on his roots in Evergreen Park, of his troubled days in high school and at Harvard. In childhood, his legs were short and spindly, but he already had the familiar head-down, straight-ahead walk. Dr. LeRoy Weinberg lived across the alley from the Professor's childhood home and found the boy to be "an old man before his time. He always walked by, not even answering my greeting, just staring at the ground. He was a brilliant boy, but most unsociable. I would see him coming in the alley. He'd always walk by without saying hello, just nothing. No other youngster in all my years has ever done that."

Dr. Weinberg, a veterinarian, recalled the Professor's parents as being "hypereducated." They didn't mingle with the people on our street very much," he said. "Their kids didn't, as far as I know, play with anybody." He said the little boy just came home and descended into the basement and "did his thing."

The boy's mother ran the local grade-school PTA in conservative blue-collar Evergreen Park, Illinois, a Chicago suburb. She'd left her teaching job to raise her child, and opened a neighborhood preschool for toddlers. "The parents lived for the kids," said Weinberg. "Wanda helped the kids at home studying."

Dorothy O'Connell lived next door to them and recalled the day when the boy, just ten, bounded into her house carrying a book titled *Romping Through Mathematics from Addition to Calculus* under his tiny arm. The bookish little gentleman often perched on his mother's lap as she read to him from *Scientific American* on the front porch of their two-story, three-bedroom frame-and-brick colonial. At that time he'd been in first grade. Once the boy had defeated his mother Dorothy and two other women at *Scrabble*. "We were all pretty flabbergasted," said Dorothy.

His mother and some experts on infant trauma believe the root of the Professor's troubles, that aloof and troubling shyness, that aversion to being touched, could be traced to infancy.

He had appeared a perfectly normal infant after his birth in Evergreen Park on May 22, 1942. "He'd be bouncing around and he'd nuzzle, talking and gurgling—pull my hair," said his mother. "He was a bundle of joy." However, nine months after leaving the maternity wing of Chicago Hospital's Lying-In Hospital, the baby suffered a dangerous case of hives. Seeing his tiny body so blotched, Wanda rushed to the hospital.

Once there a nurse pushed her out the door while the doctor examined her baby. "Hospital policy," she said stonily. "No visitors with sick children." Wanda turned to see her child, crying, shaking, standing in the crib, and holding out both arms to her. "And I had to go out the door," she recalled. He would be in the hospital for more than a month. Hospital visits to sick children were limited to one a week. During that horrible time, not only was her son not held or comforted, but (as a hospital photo showed later) he was pinned down with splints, spread-eagle and naked, to a hospital bed. The restraints kept the child from touching his ointments or disarranging the compresses. The hospital photo showed him as helpless, little hands clinched, and so terrified his eyes crossed. In the third-person diary Wanda kept of her firstborn she wrote:

"Feb. 27, 1943. Mother went to visit baby.... Mother felt very sad about baby. She says he is quite subdued, has lost his verve and aggressiveness and has developed an institutionalized look."

Whenever she returned, he refused to look at her. "It wasn't that happy, bouncing, joyous baby, but a little ragdoll that didn't look at me," she said, "that was slumped over—completely limp."

Once her baby was home she noted a perceptible personality change.

"March 12, 1943. Baby home from hospital and is healthy but

quite unresponsive after his experience. Hope his sudden removal to hospital and consequent unhappiness will not harm him."

She characterized him as "flat," listless, cold, considerably less trusting than before, and "like a bundle of clothes." Though she cajoled, rocked, sang, and cooed, he lay unresponsive to her caresses. Wanda marked that experience as setting in stone her son's lifelong pattern of withdrawal—"Always apart, aloof, alone," she said.

In nursery school at age three, the teacher drew Wanda aside and said of her boy: "He has very strong ideas as to what he wants to do and how he wants to do it. He will not play with other children. He will play beside them, but does not want them interfering in anything he is doing."

When he was four, the child saw the picture of himself spread-eagled and helpless. After a quick glace, he couldn't look at it again. His mother recalled, "He refused... and I thought, 'Oh my God, he's having the same feelings that he had when he was held down that way.'"

The boy was always going upstairs, closing his door, and being alone. Whenever he heard a car drive up, he'd say, "Oh, there's so and so—don't call me down. I don't want to see them." Worse, when they thought about it, no one could recall the child ever smiling.

Wanda took her boy to the Museum of Science and Industry, showed him Adler Planetarium. She read aloud articles in *Scientific American* and explained them to him as they perused the museum. So intent on her only child's academic excellence was Wanda that the boy's aunt cautioned: "Wanda, the boy is too young. He isn't learning anything." But Wanda wasn't concerned about pushing her child too hard academically. "I never felt I went beyond the attention span of the child because I felt you couldn't coerce children into learning," she said. "You can intrigue them, you can fascinate them, but you should not coerce them." When the boy did well in class, Wanda told the aunt, "You see? He *was* listening."

His brother David's birth in 1950 seemed to make him even more withdrawn. Later Wanda agonized that she'd tried too hard to make her eldest son more sociable. "I was getting a lot of pop psychology from people all around. 'Well now, he is too bookish, he should be out playing more with children, he should be socializing more.'" She used cookies and lemonade as bait to attract neighborhood kids, praying her lonely boy would finally snare a friend. "I would try to draw him out. 'What's bothering you?' I would ask him," remembered Wanda. "I don't know whether he knew himself what was bothering him. All he knew, I think, is that he felt rotten."

The eldest child would close down, avoiding eye contact and refusing to speak, then make for his attic room. One time his dad cajoled him into going to a scout meeting, but once there the boy only locked his eyes to the floor. "Don't push him," said the scout leader. "So he came home," recalled Wanda, "and it was a great disappointment. Maybe by trying so hard we were just making him more stubborn."

At Sherman Elementary School on West 52nd, the boy studied more and more, but still he had no friends, and his growth seemed stunted—at least compared to his brother David. He sped quickly through high school, finishing a year ahead of everyone else, with his shyness, glasses, and pocket protector, his sly smile and sweet face. Skipping a grade in elementary school had made him younger than his classmates and even more cut off socially.

He invested his time in woodcarving, studying, and haunting hardware stores looking for everyday products he could transform into explosives.

With the bright child's fascination with chemistry and its potential for surprise, he tinkered in the school lab with Russell Mosny, a pal almost as bright as himself. The boys experimented with nitrogen triiodide in liquid form and watched it become explosive as it dried. But the young Professor was not alone in this.

"We all played around with that stuff," said Roger Podewell, another classmate. The Professor, though, simply loved blowing things up. He and Dale Eickelman made explosions that shook the rafters of the house and forced his mother to apologize to the neighbors for the noise. One metal trash barrel was blown to bits. But more often than not, the blasts were duds. But Eickelman said his friend had "the know-how of putting things together, like batteries, wire leads, potassium nitrate and whatever, and creating explosions. We would go to the hardware store, use household products, and make these things you might call bombs."

The young high school boy's crush on pretty Jo Ann Vincent De Young expressed itself in odd ways. He put in her locker a catskin he'd borrowed from the biology department, then watched to see her discover it. Once he handed her a rolled piece of paper, filled with chemicals, that exploded with a pop like a small firecracker when she opened the knot. The incident made the local news, and he was briefly suspended.

Joyce Collis, a childhood friend of the Professor's, later remembered, "He was quiet. Once in a while, when I'd see him coming out of the house—my brother and I shared a car that we had to get to school—we asked him, 'Do you want a ride to school?' He would either just nod, or just say a simple 'yes.' And there might not be any conversation in the car. We'd try and include him in on whatever the conversation was that day. You could tell by his look from the backseat he didn't necessarily want to be included in on what you were talking about. He really had nothing to add."

He played trombone during his freshman and sophomore

years, but mechanically and without inspiration. A friend, Jerome
De Runtz, said that "technically he was very good. But there was
a missing quality to his music. He didn't have the feeling." After
school he lost himself in German, coin, and math clubs. In the
moments between, he whittled intricate, quite lovely wooden
boxes, once sending a beautifully carved sewing box to a teenage
family friend.

A brilliant student, he sailed through school in three years,
skipping his junior year. Not quite the nerdiest pupil there, he carried a perpetual sly grin "as if he'd pulled a fast one." He got the
blame in his senior year when an explosion rocked the chemistry
class. He hadn't actually set the explosion, but when another student asked him how to put the chemicals together, he told him
without explaining how dangerous it might be. As Morris remembers, "His personality was not robust, and he often got left holding the bag." The explosion blew out a window in the class and
damaged a girl's hearing.

A year later he would write a clever and ironic article,
intended for *Harper's* magazine, titled "*How I Blew Up Harold
Snilly,*" in which the Professor described the dangerous results
of such experiments:

> When I was in high school I took a course in chemistry. There
> was only one aspect of the subject which interested me, as any
> chemist could have seen from a brief inspection of my rather spe-
> cialized home collection of reagents [sic]; powdered aluminum,
> powdered magnesium, powdered zinc, sulfur, potassium, nitrate,
> potassium permanganate... in suitable combinations these things
> are capable of exploding.
>
> One day in the laboratory, having finished my assigned experi-
> ment early, I thought I might as well spend the extra time pursuing
> my favorite line of research. On theoretical grounds, a mixture of
> red phosphorus and potassium chlorate seemed promising. (I did

not know at the time that it is the red phosphorus in the scratching surface of a match-book, together with the potassium chlorate in the match-head, that makes a match light so readily. I later found that the mixture is extremely sensitive to friction and practically impossible to work with. The reader is advised not to play with it.

But generally, as one student put it, he "aced everything," and, a National Merit finalist, he was accepted at Harvard at age sixteen with a scholarship.

"Much of his time," the Professor's mother wrote for inclusion in his Harvard file on July 16, 1958, "is spent at home reading and contriving numerous gadgets made up of wood, string, wire, tape, lenses, gears, wheels, etc., that test out various principals in physics. His table and desk are always a mess of test tubes, chemicals, batteries, ground coal, etc. He will miss greatly, I think, this browsing and puttering in his messy makeshift lab."

THE PROFESSOR—WITH FAST, LONG STRIDES like the opening and closing of scissors—marched to Eliot House. Even at Harvard Eliot House he stood out as "different," and even in Eliot House, the two suites down the long corridor on the fourth floor stood out as more different yet. The Professor headed straight down that long corridor to suite N43. As he passed each of the rooms branching off the hallway, he ignored heads that popped out to say, "hello." At any noise, any recognition, or glance that suggested someone might like to speak to him, he sped up. Faster and faster he went to his cramped and dismal chamber.

In a few seconds, the dorm would echo with the bang of his slamming door. It was a thunderclap so predictable you could set your watch by it. The slam, suitemates said, was his trademark. "There he goes," they'd remark, "regular as can be."

At Eliot House—a four-story brick Georgian brick house spiring along the shore of the Charles River—two to four or seven guys shared a suite—a living room, bedrooms, and bathroom. The rooms the Professor shared with Keith Martin, Blaine Persons, Michael Rohr, and Patrick McIntosh were the odd suite, nestled in the low-rent wing, the place they put students who didn't find a roommate or *want* one.

"Eliot was quite an odd assortment." McIntosh explained to me. "At the end of freshman year you kinda nominate which house you would like to live in. You always get at least your third choice. Eliot House was my eighth choice." For McIntosh, already intimidated by Harvard, banishment to this house of oddities was one more depressing reminder of how badly, he thought, he fit in.

In the year the Professor had been at Eliot, he'd never had anyone come to his room. "I saw him on campus always walking," recalled McIntosh, "and always by himself." McIntosh had never seen him with a date either. "Was he still a virgin?" he recalled. "Well... I think it's likely."

The Professor—thin, sensitive, even good-looking, hair leaping crazily in all directions—was considered strange even among a group just barely not as strange. McIntosh judged him the most unusual man of his acquaintance. "He was the hardest person to get to know I ever met," he recalled. Though few had ever seen the inside of the Professor's room, McIntosh was the exception. "I was the one who collected money for the phone that we shared," he said later, "and for other necessities that we shared in the bathroom, so I had to talk to him at least once a month. "But these were not social calls. "It was, 'Hey! Where's the money?'"

"Most of the time the door wasn't open very far to get much of a look anyway," McIntosh later told me, "but there were a few occasions... where the door was wide open... and it was such a mess in there... there was an odor after a while.... Of course I got nominated to be the one to go stir up the trouble and talk to the headmaster. He came up personally to persuade him that things had to be improved. If there was ever an occasion where he could have vented anger on any of us, that would have been then."

THE FOOTSTEPS OF JOHN FINLEY, the "Master of Eliot House," echoed along the long hallway. Finley walked purposefully. He'd heard again from the Professor's suitemates and the other students on the fourth floor about untidiness and other sins. Not that the other members of what was known as the "lone wolves' section" weren't almost as eccentric, but the shy Professor had crossed the line. At the door of the withdrawn boy's room, Finley gave a sharp rap.

Finley entered and glimpsed his quarry, endlessly rocking in his chair and banging against the wall (McIntosh's room was on the other side), completely absorbed in his math text. Finley had to wade through snow drifts of paper to reach him. The debris was two feet deep in places. And there was a sour odor. "Now see here," he said, "this won't do at all." How rare a visitor to the withdrawn seventeen-year-old Finley was probably even he didn't know. Ordered to clean up his room, the Professor retaliated in the only way he knew—indirectly.

"He'd done a soap drawing, probably with shaving cream, on the bathroom mirror that I found after everyone had left for class," McIntosh recollected. "I don't know for a fact that it was him, but I'm pretty sure he was the last one in there. It was a face of a pig, rather well done, and I couldn't read the words because they weren't in English. I get the feeling that maybe he really thought he was superior to all of us and therefore couldn't talk on our level or we couldn't talk on his.

"And after the first year of trying to get to know him we kind of turned our backs on him," the suitemate remembered. "We had too much to do to compete with the other students at Harvard. So we didn't have the compassion to try and go problem solving."

He had a "genius for the abstract." The long, mournful sound of his trombone flowed from behind his closed door and down the long hall.

WHILE THE PROFESSOR WORKED as a press operator, his brother's future wife, Linda, was about to receive her doctorate at Northwestern University. It seemed everyone was passing the isolated man by as he labored in the Addison plant. The name put him in mind of his former boss, John Addison, head of Berkeley's math department.

Northwestern math professor Donald Saari told ABC News some years afterward that he recalled a young man who brought in a manuscript on modern technology and asked his help in getting it published. Faculty members at Northwestern and at the University of Chicago declined to back the publication, which made the unknown young man furious. "I'll get even," he'd allegedly snarled. But later there was doubt even about the year of this encounter.

The Professor started at Foam Cutting Engineers on June 26. Later his brother David would recall that the Professor had begun work within a few days to at most "30 days" after arriving in Lombard. With both his father and brother at the plant and his brother a supervisor, and the Professor having come to Lombard specifically to work, it would make sense that the delay between his arrival and going to work would be brief. That would place him in the Chicago area no earlier than late May.

On May 26, 1978, a full month before the Professor started at Foam Cutting Engineers, an unusual incident had occurred at the University of Chicago.

THE GOOD SAMARITAN RETURNING home caught sight of a parcel lying unattended in a parking lot used by the engineering department. It was a shoe-box-sized parcel, wrapped in brown paper. The sun curled the edges of ten one-dollar Eugene O'Neill stamps stuck to the wrapping. She bent down and felt through the paper.

She could feel the edges of a rugged surface, possibly that of a carved wooden box. She lifted the package. It was addressed to Professor E.J. Smith, who was on the engineering faculty of the Rensselaer Polytechnic Institute (RPI) in Troy, New York. The return address was local, one Buckley Crist, a professor of materials science and engineering at Northwestern University's Technological Institute in nearby Evanston. That was only sixteen miles away, so she decided to call.

"Mr. Crist, I found your package," the Good Samaritan said when she'd gotten through.

"What package?"

"The one you mailed to Professor Smith."

"Who?"

"E.J. Smith."

"I don't know any Professor Smith, and I didn't mail any package to Renssalaer."

Suspicions aroused, Crist arranged to have a messenger pick up the parcel and deliver it to Northwestern, then called the university police, Department of Public Safety, to check out the package. Crist's secretary noticed that the handwriting was not his when the parcel arrived at 4:00 PM at the institute's ground floor mailroom. She, Crist, and several onlookers were crowded into that twenty-foot square room when campus police officer Terry Marker arrived. After some joking that the package might be a bomb, something no one there seriously believed, Marker unwrapped the brown paper.

The explosion was fairly minor, and injured only the officer, searing Marker on the left hand, between the index finger and thumb. He was rushed to Evanston Hospital.

After Crist made several vain attempts to locate the apparent target of the device, a Professor Smith, he contacted the Bureau of Alcohol, Tobacco and Firearms (ATF). They later spoke with Smith, who knew nothing of the parcel. The agent judged the bomb to be the work of a beginner, made out a report, and snapped a few photographs of the remnants. Crist had never heard of a match head bomb before, and, though the ATF man could not tell him how to make a bomb, they discussed it generally. "It has match head igniters. You see, a good ignition material can be gotten from the heads of safety matches. The composition must be scraped away with a knife or crushed with pliers to get a sufficient supply. It's tedious work to get enough to fill a pipe with a quantity of igniter material."

"But it just sounds childish."

"No, simple safety match heads in a pipe, capped at both ends, make a devastating bomb. This number had wooded initiators."

"Initiators?"

"For any explosion to take place, an initiator, some flammable material, must be available. It's a device whose function is to set the material ablaze or to cause the explosion. The only odd feature of this case is the carved wooden box it was packed in. I've never seen that before."

Later, ATF analysts examined the litter of pieces of what had been a nine-inch-long, one-inch-diameter pipe in a wooden box held together with nails, rubber bands, screws, epoxy, three-quarter-inch black plastic tape, and half-inch filament tape. The explosive charge was two kinds of smokeless powder contained within the pipe. The improvised mechanical firing mechanism was almost like a child's toy: a nail held under tension by multiple rubber bands. Lifting the cover of the handmade wooden box released tension on the firing pin and caused the nail to strike the match heads, touching off the powder. Oddly, the pipe had been sealed on one end with a *wooden* plug. The bomb was largely made from discarded items—handmade nails and recovered screws, stuff people might throw away. The Junkyard Bomber had been born.

CHAPTER 5
A Failed Romance

W e therefore advocate a revolution against the industrial
system. This revolution may or may not make use of
violence; it may be sudden or it may be a relatively gradual
process spanning a few decades. We can't predict any of that.
But we do outline in a very general way the measures that
those who hate the industrial system should take in order to
prepare the way for a revolution against that form of society.
This is not to be a POLITICAL REVOLUTION.

—UNABOMBER MANIFESTO

ELLEN TARMICHAEL, ONE OF THE MANAGERS at Foam Cutting
Engineers, caught the Professor's eye, and he asked her to dinner
at a suburban restaurant. The evening went well enough, and two
weeks later he invited her to go with him to pick apples.
Afterward, they returned to his family's home in Lombard and
baked an apple pie together.

On this second date, however, she ended the relationship. He
seemed to take it calmly, and Tarmichael assumed that was it. But
the Professor thought differently. Her words, "I do not wish to see
you on a social basis," must have rung in his ears because the
rejected suitor responded by making crude remarks in her presence. Ellen didn't understand the vehemence of his reaction—"It
had never been a romantic relationship," she explained, describing
him only as "intelligent, quiet." Later, she characterized the bizarre
theory that she'd pushed him over the edge as "grossly unfair."

Soon the Professor composed an insulting limerick about her, duplicated it, and pasted the copies on walls throughout the packing material factory.

"He didn't sign the limerick, but another supervisor sees it and figures out that it was something he would do," recalled a coworker. "That supervisor, his brother [David], tells him to cut it out, basically. But instead of cutting it out he goes and puts another limerick on the wall in front of where that supervisor sits."

"He wrote a limerick that was offensive," his brother David said later, "and he pasted it in various places around the factory where we worked about this woman who'd rejected him. I approached him and I told him in an angry way, 'You have to stop that, and if you don't I'll fire you.' He came up to the machine where I was working and pasted one of these limericks right in front of me and said to me, 'So what are you going to do about this?' I said, 'Go home.'"

He lasted just four weeks on the job. The firing had been hard on David. He admired his elder brother with that fervor common to younger brothers and, for most of his life, emulated him. Now a chasm began to grow between the two.

At home the former professor of mathematics locked himself in his room for days. His father went to the room and said, "How could you humiliate me that way?" But when the tortured son, his face filled with "pain and despair," looked back, the father ceased his complaint. He could not add to his son's pain.

Finally, the elder son came down and said, "Well, don't worry about me. I'll be leaving."

"Please, please, don't leave now," said his mother. "Not now. We'll all live through this, but this is not the time to leave." He had brought three pages of written explanation down with him. He wrote of how cruel the woman had been (something David knew not to be true in any respect), then ended the "apology" in a disturbing manner—he repeated the insulting limerick. "Like he wasn't going to take it back," said David, "no matter what. It was the first time that I felt, hey, he's not functional."

After his foam-cutting job the Professor found work in August or September 1978 at a plant, Prince Castle, that manufactured restaurant machinery. He remained in Chicago until May 9, 1979, when the Junkyard Bomber struck once more.

JUST UNDER A YEAR after Terry Marker was injured by the bomber, another suspicious container was found at Northwestern University, this time on the second floor of the Technological Institute, Room 2424. For several days grad students had noticed a "Phillies" brand cigar box, its lid taped shut, sitting between two cubicles on a drawing table. Though it was a cardboard container, finger-sized pieces of unfinished wood had been glued to it, making it in effect a wooden box.

John Harris, a thirty-five-year-old grad student in civil engineering, considered the container in midafternoon and decided it would make a fine box for his pencils. He reached over and began prying the tape off the lid.

Either of two independent circuits could have detonated the device. Each circuit entailed two C-cell batteries wired to improvised wooden dowel initiators, bearing a pair of wires joined at their end by a thin bridge wire inside the main charge of match heads and smokeless powder.

Opening the lid completed the electrical circuit, and the bridge wire began to glow, detonating the mix of powder and match heads.

The resulting detonation startled students in the other study cubicles, sent thousands of match heads and shrapnel-like twigs everywhere, and caused a rain of black coal dust to shower over

Harris and much of the room. He felt for his eyeglasses, which had been blown off. The powerful smell of sulphur assailed the student, and he staggered to the hallway where he was seen by an administrative assistant, Joel Meyer. Meyer ran for an extinguisher.

Just before Meyer extinguished the fire, he glimpsed rags in the box, or paper, and flashlight batteries with the metal skin removed. Many wires were protruding from the batteries, lamp cord initiators, wooden dowels, loop switches, and filaments.

Harris was treated for his minor cuts and burns. No connection was made between the May 25, 1978, and the May 9, 1979, devices. Both were considered amateurish, though the second was an advancement in technique and power.

Investigators listed everything they recovered from the scene of the explosion. It was indeed junk—a cigar box, match heads, four Ray-O-Vac C-cell batteries, wood fragments, maple wood sticks, tape ends, and monofilament fishing line. The rubble also included an anti-open switch (wire-loop switch); a paper pouch that once contained match heads and powder; white insulated duplex stranded wire; solder; wooden dowels; epoxy; white glue; and three-quarter-inch filament, plastic, and friction tape. One-half-inch filament tape and tape tabs had been used to seal the brown paper wrapping.

After the Professor resigned from the Prince Castle Restaurant Equipment Division, he stayed at his parents' home for a few weeks, then took David's car and traveled into Canada for seven to eight weeks more, searching for land in Saskatchewan. After returning his brother's car he set off for his wilderness home. Wanda walked with her son to the local commuter train in Lombard.

Wanda spoke of her son sometimes to neighbors, and when she did, a hint of pride came through as she enumerated the Professor's great academic accomplishments. "He worked hard and saved his money," she said, "and that's why he was able to retire and buy his own place." But to others it seemed that below the surface the parents were "deeply disappointed" in their eldest's inability to make a go of a promising career. Wanda often spoke of what the world would see when her son's "book" was finally published. She extolled the lifestyle he'd chosen and his ability to survive without recourse to modern technology.

The Professor's feelings for his family vacillated from gratitude to hatred. In May 1970 he wrote that he considered them the best parents anyone would hope for and asked that they forgive him for disappointing them. Uncharacteristically, he closed with the word "love." His feelings for David were as ambivalent—he expressed disgust and contempt for him and said he often found him "repulsive," while in a second letter he explained that seeing him "enjoy life" brought him comfort.

Later the Professor wrote that he was satisfied now that his parents had conceded their failure as parents. "The resentment I have toward you," he wrote them, "will always remain, but your last letter does soften my attitude a little. Enough anyway, so that I will take back what I said about hoping you drop dead on Christmas—'cause it's true that you were always good to me on Christmas."

By the mid-seventies, the Professor had convinced himself that his parents were insensitive, if not cruel, to him during his formative years. He found the basis for his antisocial tendencies to be rooted here, and not in his mother's belief that his extended hospital stay during infancy had created all the anger and pain he felt now.

"OK, now let's take your contention that because I was a 'gloomy' etc. kid, the parents had reason to believe I really was 'sick'.... Let's go even further and assume I was a real nuthouse case—let's suppose I went around insisting that I was Napoleon

Bonaparte," he wrote in an April 1986 letter to his brother. "Far from justifying our parents' behavior, that makes it even worse. They certainly knew enough to realize that if someone really is mentally ill, one of the worst things you can do to them is to shout at them in a hostile and accusing manner, 'You're sick! You're sick! You have the mind of a two-year-old!'

"Neither you nor they seem to be able to get this obvious point through your thick skulls. They (and now you) keep citing supposedly 'sick' symptoms of mine in order to justify their behavior toward me. The only way to explain this is by assuming that they (and you) are more anxious to justify themselves than they are to get to the heart of the matter. I flatly refuse to accept any contradictions on this point. No doubt this is unreasonable. But you're just going to have to humor me if you want to get along with me."

CHAPTER 6

Something a Kid Might Make

IT WAS AN ODD BEGINNING, an inauspicious inauguration for the most cunning opponent in the annals of the FBI. That first little wooden box appeared so simple in comparison to the elaborate devices that lay ahead that it would be a lie to say that anyone gave it a second thought, with the possible exception of Terry Marker, favoring his scorched finger and thumb. And the custodians who had to clean up the tiny room scattered with match heads.

The Bureau of Alcohol, Tobacco and Firearms, a part of the Treasury Department, had looked at the device at the end of May 1978 and had seen nothing of importance in what seemed obviously the work of a prankish student or disgruntled former employee. They didn't even ask themselves if Crist had any serious enemies. But the carved box was different enough to cause them to file the photographs of the device. This would be valuable later, because soon afterward the fragments of the bomb would be thrown out.

The ATF did conclude that "this device was capable of causing serious injury or death to persons in close proximity of the explosion." When interviewed by ATF agents, Professor E.J. Smith had no knowledge of the package.

"Do you have any idea who might have wanted to send you such a parcel."

Smith thought for a moment. He was well-liked and hadn't an enemy in the world. "I just don't," he said finally. The ATF agents left and went back to see what they had. The first item they examined was a one-inch-diameter galvanized pipe approximately nine inches long. But there was something unusual about the explosive device.

In the case of most pipe bombs the ends are sealed by screwing caps on the end of a pipe. But this bomber had done something neither of the two ATF men had seen before. "Come over here and take a look at this," one said gesturing to the work station. The other pushed back his chair, came around, and peered at one surviving wooden disk on the brightly lit formica table.

"What the hell?" The bomber had sealed the ends of his pipe with wooden plugs, not the usual metal. "Now what's the idea behind that?" he asked.

The oddness of that and the carved wooden box caused them to study the other fragments in search of more unusual qualities their man might have used.

"Well, right off," the chief technician said later in the afternoon, "our man has used not one but two types of smokeless powder. It has an improvised firing mechanism consisting of a nail held under tension by several rubber bands."

"It's like something a kid might make, isn't it?"

"Opening the cover of the wooden box releases tension on the nail, the firing pin as it were, and strikes the match heads. That ignites the smokeless powder."

It was an odd bomb at that and probably worthy of more of their time. But they quickly completed their survey of the scattered parts, screws, nails, bits of three-quarter-inch black plastic tape and half-inch filament tape, all spread out next to charred brown wrapping paper.

Near the red, white, and blue mailing label was an odd stamp—a commemorative issue of the great American playwright, Eugene O'Neill, author of *The Iceman Cometh*.

The first bomb had gotten only moderate media attention, a few write-ups in the local papers but nothing outside of Chicago and Evanston. Then the second bomb came only two weeks shy of the anniversary of the bomb directed at Smith. Investigators noted that the second bomb also used match heads.

But when set off it had not sounded at all like the first "embarrassing ineffectual" device. It was more sophisticated, and certainly more powerful. The rubber-band-and-nail trigger was gone. In its place were two independent electrical circuit fuses, either of which could have detonated the device if the other failed. He was a careful SOB. On the other hand, here again were the wooden dowel initiators and "two kinds of smokeless powder." But this time, the bomber had enclosed his match heads and powders inside a paper pouch.

Weighing all in the balance, the investigators made a mistake typical of what was to become a nearly two-decade-long case— they did nothing to publicize the odd wooden bomb and they felt the device was inconsequential enough that they didn't even notify their federal brothers at the FBI.

With the next bombing, the attempted downing of a jetliner, the FBI would become involved and treat its own federal brethren a bit better. Through cooperation with the ATF and the postal inspectors they would even garner an early lead. But this spirit of cooperation would not continue for long.

CHAPTER 7
The Airline Bomber

A lmost everyone will agree that we live in a deeply troubled society. One of the most widespread manifestations of the craziness of our world is leftism, so a discussion of the psychology of leftism can serve as an introduction to the discussion of the problems of modern society in general.

—UNABOMBER MANIFESTO

"**ON NOVEMBER 15, 1979,** I was directed to go out to the Dulles International Airport where a bomb had exploded on an airplane coming from Chicago," recalled FBI Agent Chris Ronay. After the explosion on Flight No. 444, it was Ronay who realized that the FBI was dealing with a serial bomber.

"I took the evidence into the laboratory and we started to examine it, and as soon as we had some information we communicated it to Chicago (because that's where the flight originated) where they were waiting to start covering leads such as, 'What's the return address?' 'Who was it mailed to, if you can tell?' and 'What sort of device was it?'

"In a few days Chicago came back to us and said, 'We've shown the photograph around and we've located another bomb [the cigar box device], and there are some real similarities here. We want to send it to you.' And they did." As soon as the cigar

box remnants came in, Ronay made the call: It had been made by
the same person who made the airline bomb. Ronay, the FBI's
leading bomb expert, along with the ATF and postal authorities,
had linked the two devices through the bomber's meticulous construction of his elaborate machines, his signature showing up in
the cunning way he used metal and especially wood, in the use of
smokeless powder, in the absolutely distinctive manner in which
he tied certain elements of his bombs together, and especially in
his use of improvised loop switches and initiators.

Agents dubbed him the "Junkyard Bomber," though Ronay at
first tried to call him the "Recycle Bomber," because his devices
were crafted from common, hard-to-trace materials. The list
grew: mostly low-tech household items—lamp cord, epoxy, white
glue, fishing line, flashlight batteries with their casings removed
so the brand couldn't be identified, string, match heads (twice so
far), handmade nails, sink traps, handmade switches, towels,
wrapping paper, newspaper, a barometer, plumbing parts, and
smokeless powder. The bombs, intricately fashioned by hand of
components that could have been easily, even safely, purchased at
any local hardware shop, were impossible to trace. By manufacturing the most elemental parts, the bomber had completely covered his tracks. As one agent commented, "It was clearly the
intention of the bomb-maker to conceal any lead value from the
investigators from the onset."

THE BOMBER WORKED, hunched over a partially completed device.
Methodically, he hand tooled precise components designed to fit
neatly into a hollowed-out book. But before he finished he paused
to write a short letter.

He tried several variations but they all said virtually the same
thing: "You will soon receive a book that you will find of great
social significance.... You will soon be receiving a book in the

Big River.

mail that all executives should read.... I will be sending you a manuscript to read...." He signed the name "Enoch Fischer" to the message and gave a Ravenswood address from the Chicago metro area, a vacant lot. There was no such person as Enoch Fischer. He went out and posted the letter.

Over the years men who had only briefly crossed the Professor's path would become the bomber's victims, and men he never met might qualify on something so simple as a name. United Airlines President Percy A. Wood met both criteria. Wood, as FBI profiler John Douglas later pointed out, had served on the Bay Area Air Pollution Control Board while the Professor taught at UC Berkeley... and he had an irresistible name. Also, the bomber may still have been angry at the airlines.

A mail carrier delivered Enoch Fischer's letter to Wood's Lake Forest, Illinois, home, but inexplicably the envelope carried no postmark and the stamps had not been canceled. While the

Junkyard Bomber had so far not explained his motives, he had at least begun to send advance messages to some of his targets. There was a reason for this, as a bomb expert explained much later in the manhunt.

"If I tell you a book's coming," he told me, "then OK, I'll look at the book. You know there's some reason for it. If the book comes from nowhere the recipient may send it back never even opened. But if I set you up ahead of time, you're going to open the book, and trigger the device."

A few weeks later, on June 10, 1980, a sweltering summer day Wood had just celebrated his sixtieth birthday. In a buoyant mood, he strolled the short distance down his sidewalk to his roadside mailbox, a box not unlike the Hermit's in remote Lincoln, Montana. Inside sat a parcel wrapped in brown paper and tied with white twine. Another present, he thought, then noticed it was addressed to "Percy Addison Wood." Addison was a middle name he almost never used. John Addison had been the Professor's boss at Berkeley.

Wood carried the parcel by the twine back into the colonial two-story red-and-white house and into the kitchen; he estimated that it weighed about three pounds. He plunked the five-by-eight-inch package onto the table. It carried far too many stamps and of a wild variety—the one-dollar "Eugene O'Neill" stamps (in roll version, first issued in January 1978), a twenty-five-cent "Frederick Douglass" stamp (first sold in February 1967), a fifteen-cent "Will Rogers" stamp from the Performing Arts and Artists Series (first issued in November 1979), and a "Rush Lamp and Candleholder" stamp (first sold in July 1979).

At 3:40 PM the airline executive began to peel back the brown paper. He first observed cardboard from a "Bugles Cereal" box, probably used in packing. Then he saw an Arbor House logo on a book spine, a tree leaf trademark. Inside someone had posted him a copy of Sloan Wilson's novel *Ice Brothers*. O'Neill, whose stamps were on the package, had been the only American playwright to win a Nobel prize and was famous for *The Iceman Cometh*. Wilson had penned the penultimate denunciation of the Madison Avenue conformist, *The Man in the Gray Flannel Suit*. *Ice Brothers* told, in 517 pages, a World War II tale of a Greenland Coast Guard Station and two brothers, one a Yale grad who distinguishes himself, and their adventures on the patrol ice trawler *Valkyrie*. The story follows the Allied Underground's attempts to disrupt German U-boat travel among the ice floes. "What social significance could this hold for me?" wondered Wood as he pried back the red and blue cover, only to discover that many pages had been glued together.

Every explosion begins with a thermal event, an extreme burst of heat. Inside a pipe within the book, activated by a pressure-sensitive trip device, a firing system investigators would never quite figure out, ignited three kinds of smokeless powder, which as it burned changed from a solid to a gas. The gas built up, distending the metal pipe sealed on each end by a combination of epoxy and nails. The pipe began to bulge until, like a steam boiler, it could no longer contain the enormous pressure, and burst out in all directions.

A powerful shock wave followed, and razor-sharp fragments flashed outward at supersonic speeds. Wood fragments glued to the book acted as more shrapnel, piercing Wood's face, hands, and thighs. One section of the three-quarter–inch galvanized pipe ripped into the executive's thigh while another shot into the air and punched a gaping hole in the kitchen ceiling. Wood could feel nothing in his hands, yet his hands were also burning.

The process of recovery at the Wood crime scene was as difficult as most bombings are, and all are very difficult. Every fragment had to be located, marked with numbers, photographed, and reassembled into a device that had been specifically designed to be blown to bits. But the Junkyard Bomber had designed one section of his bomb to survive fragmentation, one that the detectives would find in all but the first three bombs.

Investigators laid out the surviving components of the package wrapping and of the bomb—first the pipe container, a fragmented copy of *Ice Brothers,* tape tabs, a mailing label, and the stamps. They catalogued newspaper, the cereal box cardboard, and the blue-lined white paper. They swept up the wood fragments and sifted through screens, noted the use of white glue *and* epoxy, the different kinds of smokeless powder, the oversoldering, the plastic, friction, cellophane, and filament tapes, all three-quarter inches wide. The remnants of the galvanized pipe, its threaded pipe cap ends, the common nails used as shrapnel, white and black insulated stranded wire, and D-cell batteries were gathered up—some fragments with tweezers—and one small round metal disk with the letters FC punched into it with a nail. It had been designed to survive the explosion.

"It wasn't until the fourth device that was to the president of United Airlines, that initials were affixed to the device," said FBI agent Jim Freeman, "and they were affixed to the device in such a way that they would survive the explosion."

Obviously, the flat end plates on the pipe were especially unusual to the investigators. Pipe bombs, the most common type of criminal explosives, most frequently are sealed by screwing caps onto threaded ends of a pipe. The Junkyard Bomber sealed his with flat end plates, drilled and screwed into place with two bolts. It was on such a metal end plate that forensic chemist James Upton at the FBI lab discovered those initials, FC. But what did the letters mean? Could they possibly be the name of a group?

Did the answer lie in a Joseph Conrad novel, *The Secret Agent?* Years in the future, detectives would note the parallels between the story of a professor who blows up *universities*, to the Unabomber, or UNABOM, the designation the terrorist earned from the FBI by targeting Universities and Airlines. One paragraph from *The Secret Agent* in particular was telling:

> Mr. Vladimir let fall disdainfully a grey sheet of printed matter. "What are all these leaflets headed F.P., with a hammer, pen, and torch crossed? What does it mean, this F.P.?" Mr. Verloc approached the imposing writing-table.
>
> "The Future of the Proletariat. It's a society," he explained, standing ponderously by the side of the armchair, "not anarchist in principle, but open to all shades of revolutionary opinion."

And later Vladimir says:

> "The demonstration must be against learning—science. But not every science will do. The attack must have all the shocking senselessness of gratuitous blasphemy. Since bombs are your means of expression, it would be really telling if one could throw a bomb into pure mathematics. But that is impossible."

The Professor had read and loved all of Conrad's works since childhood, so much so that he apparently used the alias "Konrad" once or twice. His brother David had noted that he'd read "Conrad novels for about the dozenth time." Conrad's alienated, brilliant but mad Professor often walked abroad in rags and thought with severe exultation of "the refuge of his room with its padlocked cupboard, lost in a wilderness of poor houses, the Hermitage of the perfect anarchist."

BECAUSE OF THE UNCANCELED POSTAGE and lack of postmark, Postal Inspector Ruberti had both the victim, Wood, and the postman hypnotized to see if they recalled anything pertinent, but they didn't. The Postal Service offered a $5,000 reward for the capture of the Junkyard Bomber. Meanwhile, the detectives got computer tapes of names connected to both Northwestern University and United Airlines. They cross-referenced them to see if the same name appeared on the lists, suspecting that some bitter graduate or fired employee, possibly a machinist, might have had an ax to grind against Wood.

Meanwhile, members of the FBI Academy in Quantico, Virginia, devised an early psychological profile of the Junkyard Bomber—a typical loner with "an obsessive-compulsive personality." Murray S. Miron of Syracuse Research Institute, who'd profiled San Francisco's Zodiac and New York's Son of Sam, pegged the bomber as a white male in his early twenties to mid-thirties, probably raised in the Midwest, and college educated. At the time the Professor was thirty-nine years old.

The Hermit had stayed at the Park Hotel in Helena from May 3 to May 4. Percy Wood's bomb was mailed on June 3, 1980, according to the FBI. From June 27 until June 29 the Hermit was at the Park Hotel. Then he retreated to his Hermitage. That fall he hunted deer with Glenn Williams. "One time, I was hunting by myself," Williams said later, "and he'd just killed a deer, and we got to visiting, and I asked him if he ever killed an elk."

"Naw," said the Recluse. "I can't afford the tag [elk-hunting permit]."

"I got an idea," said Williams. "I'll take you to Lincoln. I'll pay for the tag, and if you get an elk, you go to the nearest phone, call me collect, and I'll be up there with a four-wheel drive the next morning."

When the Hermit killed an elk, he did as promised. "I went up there," said Williams. "We got it out, and we split it, fifty-fifty. It was way back, about seven miles back in there. We had to go way back in there on a snowmobile and bring it out."

Williams volunteered to take the hide from any deer that the Hermit killed into Great Falls to Weissman's hide and scrap-iron business and give the Recluse the money from the hides when he came up to his own log cabin. The Hermit's shack had an access road to Williams's place to the west, which came off a skid road used for logging. But the Recluse's was the last cabin up Canyon Creek.

Williams passed the money on to the Hermit each time, but once Pacific Hide & Fur offered a pair of deerskin gloves as trade for one of his raw hides in lieu of the regular payment of three dollars. "He didn't know what to do! Boy, he had a heck of a time deciding!" recalled Williams. In the end he chose the gloves.

Leland Mason, another neighbor, visited the Hermit's cabin at Christmas. He knocked at the door, and it opened a hair-thin crack. Mason, former owner of the beef-jerky plant, held out a plate of cookies and sweets his wife had made. The Hermit didn't ask him in, only thanked him. "We exchanged Christmas greetings, that was it," said Mason. "I was surprised that he could withstand the winters, whenever they got bitter cold.

"He'd be gone for a week, maybe two, but not real regularly." All Mason knew was that at times the Hermit was simply gone and no one knew where.

CHAPTER 8

The Utah Bombing

B ut what is leftism? During the first half of the 20th
century leftism could have been practically identified with
socialism. Today the movement is fragmented and it is not
clear who can properly be called a leftist. When we speak of
leftists in this article we have in mind mainly socialists,
collectivists, 'Politically correct' types, feminists, gay and
disability activists, animal-rights activists and the like....

—UNABOMBER MANIFESTO

ON OCTOBER 8, 1981, at the end of a sixteen-month period during
which the Junkyard Bomber had apparently retired, the terrorist
placed yet another of his infernal devices. He carefully chose a site
that guaranteed maximum damage. At the end of a tiled third-
floor hallway between two classes in the University of Utah's
Milton Bennion Hall, Business Building, he laid his trap, prop-
ping a large paper-wrapped parcel beneath a window. When his
package detonated it would transform the hallway into a tunnel
of flame, trapping students in their classrooms in the computer-
sciences building.

But as the day dragged on, no one took the bait. Finally, a
maintenance man finished cleaning a business classroom and
paused to inspect the abandoned parcel. He bent down and carefully studied the brown paper covering. No address showed—
only minute ballpoint squigglings, arrows, and tiny letters. He

reached and, with a single motion, lifted the shoebox-sized package from the floor.

As he did so, a wooden lever dropped down four inches with a soft click. But nothing more happened. Administrators summoned Staff Sergeant John Wooten from a nearby army base. Immediately, the expert recognized the booby trap. A six-inch rod, an improvised slide switch, had been set to drop down and make contact, exploding the device. This was attached to a one-gallon gas can. If the bomb had functioned properly, many would have died. The ordnance-disposal man gingerly carted the parcel to the ladies room, where the tile might cushion any blast. Inside, he defused the device by rendering it harmless with a small explosive charge.

Once safe, Wooten X rayed the bomb and observed an elaborately carved box with dovetail joints and tapered corners, and fabricated from a variety of woods. He saw a General Electric household on/off switch, and an improvised initiator arranged in series. The attached can, filled with gas, had its spout sealed with both wax and a wooden plug. The bomb itself was a galvanized eight-inch-long, one-inch-diameter pipe sealed on both ends with wooden plugs and packed with three kinds of smokeless powder.

The bomb had failed because the detonator had burned out. He'd used three-strand wire in the detonator and Wooten felt that a single-strand copper wire would have carried the current from two D-cell batteries effectively and with much loss of life. In his last three bombs, the Junkyard Bomber had used his unique loop switch, but this time he had not.

Much later, as the detectives disassembled the device, they saw that he'd also put together, then taken apart, his bomb numerous times. The three-quarter–inch metal tag bearing the punched initials FC, as usual, had been designed to survive any detonation.

In his coded journal the Professor recorded his thoughts on the business classrooms. "Last fall," he wrote later, "I attempted a bombing and spent nearly three hundred bucks just for travel expenses, motel, clothing for disguise, etc. Aside from the cost of materials for the bomb. And then the thing failed to explode. Damn."

The Hermit was restless once more, and tossed through the night of November 9 at the Park Hotel, a month after the gasoline bomb had been placed at the University of Utah. He checked out the following morning looking little rested.

On April 23, 1982, the Junkyard Bomber mailed from the BYU campus post office in Provo, Utah, a package to Professor Patrick Carl Fischer, a computer scientist who had gained a national reputation in the sixties. The forty-seven-year-old scientist and educator, St. Louis–born, had studied at the University of Michigan in 1957, where he'd received his MBA the following year. He'd been an assistant professor at MIT, Harvard, and Cornell, and an associate professor at the University of British Columbia. He'd been head of the computer department at Pennsylvania State University from 1974 until 1978 and had become a member of the computer science department at Vanderbilt in 1980.

The bomber addressed Fischer incorrectly at Penn State. He frequently got the addresses wrong, suggesting he might have been using out-of-date reference books. The three Eugene O'Neill one-dollar stamps on the parcel had been canceled *before* he mailed the package. The bomber had used invalid postage, suggesting he may have wanted it to be rejected by the post office and sent back to the name on the return address. His intended target *may* actually have been Professor LeRoy *Wood* Bearnson at Brigham Young University's electrical engineering department. But, Bearnson was on sabbatical and, for whatever reason, the package sailed through the mail system, despite invalid postage, and inexorably trailed Dr. Fischer to Nashville.

The Junkyard Bomber, true to his name, had manufactured his latest device from a one-and-one-half-inch-diameter household U-shaped sink trap, packed it with five different kinds of smokeless powder, and sealed both ends with wood and metal plugs.

He'd packed the bomb into one of his wooden carved boxes, incorporating twin pivoting levers held in tension by several rubber bands. When the brown wrapping paper was removed, pressure would be released on the levers and the loop switches would close, detonating the bomb.

Fischer was on sabbatical and lecturing in Puerto Rico, and thus was absent when his secretary, Janet Smith, received the box on May 2. "My secretary sat down," Fischer said later. "She was just doing her job and opened the package. She was seriously injured. There was shrapnel inside, and she received severe lacerations and, bleeding, was taken to Vanderbilt Hospital. I don't think this bomber knows his victims personally. I think the victims are symbols, not individuals this person personally knows and dislikes. I will be careful the rest of my life."

Fischer was genuinely perplexed as to why he had been targeted. "For a while I thought he opened up *Who's Who* and threw a dart until he got a computer scientist. That's probably wrong. There has to be a link."

In Fischer's past was a brief visit to the Michigan math department at the same time the Professor—who was easily angered for long periods—had studied there.

During the period when he was operating from Utah, the Junkyard Bomber changed his style of bomb, making it more sophisticated, and changed himself as well. The University Bomber of Berkeley, California, was about to be born.

CHAPTER 9

Silence

YEARS LATER THE AGENT TURNED TO HIS COLLEAGUE and asked: "Why can't we catch him?"

The second agent only placed his finger across his lips to signify silence. And he was right. In silence lay the secret of the Unabomber's extraordinary success at eluding his pursuers.

The line of the Hermit's lips. Tight, thin, and with a downward slash like the gentle curve of a hill. Negligible they seemed, as if any flow of words might wash them away. But he hoarded his words, and his silence built a boundary that rendered him unknowable and inaccessible.

The silent man kept only his own counsel and thus could never betray himself. When this stony silence, all the more protected by the solitary, sub-zero Montana winters, finally found expression in a flow of words bottled up for a decade and a half, springing finally from those reddened, chilled fingers typing at his little work table, those words would lead him to disaster. Only as long as the solitary man kept his silence would he remain free.

The lone wolf factor shows up in most psychological profiles of sociopaths. But few serial killers that the federal agents had pursued before had mastered silence and solitude so well, had felt so little need for the company of men. It was the silence that drove Chris Ronay, former chief of the FBI's explosives unit, to tell *Newsweek* magazine as late as the summer of 1995 that he didn't "hold out any hope we'd ever catch [the Unabomber]."

A killer who didn't communicate, didn't explain his goals, or give a motive for his lethal actions, whose very existence was almost unknown outside his family and a small town in Montana, could not be captured. Naturally, there would be no co-conspirator to leak to the police pertinent information or to forge a deal with a DA. As Murray S. Miron, one of the nation's top psycholinguistics experts and on staff at the Syracuse Research Institute, had written in his analysis of the Zodiac case, a similar type of serial killer also of high intelligence, who similarly remained at large for more than twenty-six years: "He lives the secret life of seclusion... Miron said of this type, He will be 'secretive and guarded in his dealings with the world... will repeat his crimes, is highly intelligent... feels no remorse... is incapable of forming normal adult relationships... and takes great pains to avoid capture.'"

Also confusing to the investigators was that the man did not fit the mold of the serial killer in many ways (though he was ultimately classified as that). Most importantly, he killed at a distance, whereas most serial killers did their work at close, even intimate range, relishing the kill itself. Though he may have observed the maiming of Gary Wright and death of Hugh

THE INVESTIGATION

Campbell Scrutton from under cover, he rarely gave himself the chance to relish the kill up close. Did he, like a posioner, imagine his victim's death agonies from afar?

The bomber deviated from the stereotypical profile in several other ways—he was not a police groupie, and his "sociopathic personality" did not, as was the norm, "naturally burn out as he ages." He also thought of his victims not as objects to exercise power over, the motive of sadistic serial murderers, but as a means to a possible political end. And finally, as was later learned, he did not torture small animals as a child, but in fact was an animal lover and protector.

And then for seven years, from 1987 to 1993, the silence was complete, unbroken even by the occasional blast of a bomb. Ronay had pursued this phantom for over a decade and in twenty-two years with the Bureau had never faced a more puzzling or challenging adversary. And the Great Silence since he had been glimpsed planting his Salt Lake City bomb in 1987 made their prey even more difficult to figure. And what to make of the odd gaps between explosions?

"Perhaps UNABOM [the FBI casefile designation] had been out of touch or in prison during the lull periods," conjectured Ronay.

"Or," remarked another agent, "maybe he was just happy."

Even the most quiet of animals will leave a track, but the bomber cunningly covered his. His first name, given to him by investigators, had been the Junkyard Bomber, because the bombs were built of common materials such as lamp cord, flashlight batteries, scrap wood, match heads, and smokeless powder. Though intricately constructed, almost all components were manufactured by hand though they could have safely been purchased at nearly any hardware store. Of course, by handcrafting the most elemental parts the bomber made it impossible to trace where UNABOM had acquired his materials. There was no paper trail for the detectives to follow.

The Unabomber, to this point, had left no identifiable fingerprints or clothing and hair fibers. As far as the FBI lab could tell, UNABOM had not licked either the gummed labels, envelope flaps, or stamps—so there was no DNA for them to analyze. He used postage stamps, not a postage meter, and mailed or placed the bombs himself. Therefore, no postal clerk could be counted on to ever come forward and identify him.

The bombs themselves, of course, told investigators that they were seeking one man. Or seemed to. FBI bomb expert Ronay, among others, had determined in 1986 from the remains of the bomber's handiwork that the same hand lay behind all twelve blasts. But even this link was not easy or obvious, because the devices showed great variety over time. "He is creative because almost every one of his bombs has been crafted in a unique way," said Ronay, "so much so that to the untrained eye, they may not be related. And two of the bombs may yet prove Ronay and the other investigators wrong about their authorship.

He was a chameleon, constantly altering his tactics and geographical location, his choice of bombs, as he upgraded and improved his devices. His modus operandi was too varied to reveal a discernible pattern to his life. Lacking a pattern, too few leads became too many leads, because it was too difficult to distinguish and shed the irrelevant. "More leads than you can believe," said one cop. "You start to look at everyone and think he might be a suspect."

He was a man of immense contradictions. He had to be insane,

THE INVESTIGATION

but in many ways he behaved more like a terrorist than a mad-man. Yet a terrorist usually communicates his motives with great clarity. The Unabomber's motives were clear only to him. And, though mad, he was enough in touch with reality to cover his tracks for almost two decades. He was a killer who, as was later learned, wanted to live in harmony with nature. None of the official profiles steered investigators to the wild. He was a self-taught bomb-maker and machinist who abhorred technology. So all the searches for machine shops and airline mechanics led to nothing.

He lacked one of the most useful of all paper trails: an arrest record. Many bombers turn out to be recidivists, or to have other criminal records suggesting their infernal potential.

If the Unabomber was the least typical of cases, here is the way a more typical case follows, the case of Walter Leroy Moody, which the Bureau likes to point to with pride.

In mid-December 1989, a package was delivered to federal appeals court Judge Robert S. Vance outside his home on the outskirts of Birmingham, Alabama. When Vance sliced through the white cord securing the parcel, he noticed idly that the red mailing label on the brown paper package bore no return address. Then he noted that excessive postage had been applied. Carefully, the judge peeled back the tan plastic tape binding the wrapping and revealed a corrugated paper box with a hinged lid.

As Judge Vance lifted this lid, he triggered an electrical booby trap and exploded double base smokeless powder inside a pipe packed with nails. The razor-sharp shrapnel killed the jurist.

Two days after the Vance slaying, a similar device was delivered. The detonation snuffed out the life of a Savannah civil rights lawyer and official of the NAACP, Robert E. Robinson. Soon after, authorities unearthed two unexploded bombs of the same type at the Jacksonville NAACP offices and at an Atlanta federal court building.

Fragments of a message in the two undetonated bombs placed responsibility on the doorstep of a right-wing hate group. An exact amount of excessive postage, type of stamps, wrapping, and identical construction linked all four devices to each other. Agents labeled this case VANPAC, and scanned a list of thousands of known bombers.

Moody's name made the very first suspect list of dozens of previously convicted bombers in that region. But his motive usually involved revenge, and occasionally financial gain. That seemed to argue against his complicity in what was apparently a race crime. But race was a ruse.

Moody had once been charged with three counts of attempted murder, having taken out life insurance policies on three of his employees and allegedly abandoning them in water two miles off Grassy Key, Florida. That resulted in a hung jury. But Judge Vance had sat on the three-judge panel that denied his appeal on a counter suit.

At an FBI luncheon at Ryan's Steak House in Atlanta, Lloyd Erwin, a forensic chemist with the ATF, saw photos of the recent bombs. He recognized Moody's work and pointed out, sketching the design on a napkin, that Moody had used bolts to strengthen his 1972 bomb. The four civil rights bombs had contained this feature.

Surveillance of Moody began, and finally, using an ATF list of firearms salesmen in the region, the FBI ferreted out a dealer in Georgia who recalled that Moody had purchased four pounds of Hercules Red Dot powder from him, the type of powder employed in all four explosive devices. As Robert Ressler wrote,

THE INVESTIGATION

"Moody had been on a list with thousands of known bombers. Without the critical link between his techniques and the most recent devices, the case would likely never have been made." Erwin, the chemist, saw the point—and the reason the Unabomber might elude capture altogether—while Moody hardly stood a chance of getting away with it. "They [criminals who use explosives] start with something and stick with it. If he had changed, he would still be running around today."

In 1991 Louis J. Freeh (pronounced Free), the man most often considered as Sessions's replacement, conducted the case against Moody. As prosecutor, Freeh constructed a strong examination and delivered the closing arguments himself. Co-prosecutor Howard Shapiro called Freeh's remarks "the single most powerful piece of courtroom advocacy that I have ever witnessed."

Bizarrely, Moody used some of the same techniques as the Unabomber, including that unusual use of bolts to help secure his end caps (whereas most pipe bombs employ screw-on caps). Yet Moody came after the Unabomber was established. Of course UNABOM eventually improved the end cap bolt. In his typically vicious fashion, he began to design them to fail at the crucial moment so that the bomb would send out two additional walls of force perpendicular to the main blast.

Bob Bell of the Sacramento Sheriff's office had only been on the job a few months when he was handed one of the toughest serial cases in history. On a sweltering day in Sacramento, after I had just visited the former site of the first Unabomber fatality, I had an opportunity to see how he met the challenge. I asked him "What did you feel like when you got this case and realized how big it was?" I asked.

"Actually, confusion. There was nobody that could provide us with a motive, and without a motive, you're sort of treading water when it comes down to trying to solve a homicide investigation. You really need some direction to go in and we could not figure the motive out. Even the prior victims, once they told us that they had a series—electrical engineering and all that kind of stuff—there was nothing that seemed to connect other than maybe he was angry at technology. That from the get go was sort of suspected because he was angry at computers, and the impact of technology on society.

"But that really wasn't clear. Why would he go bomb all those people [professors] except again there is technology, but it's good technology—trying to help people."

PART TWO

THE UNIVERSITY BOMBER
Berkeley, California / The Early Eighties

CHAPTER 10
Angelakos

T*he two psychological tendencies that underlie modern
leftism we call feelings of inferiority and
oversocialization. Feelings of inferiority are characteristic of
modern leftism as a whole, while oversocialization is
characteristic only of a certain segment of modern leftism; but
this segment is highly influential....*

—UNABOMBER MANIFESTO

ON JULY 2, 1982, Diogenes James Angelakos, an electrical engineering educator at UC Berkeley, spent the day before his sixty-third birthday on a busman's holiday. Over the weekend he sauntered over to Cory Hall. He walked around the Mining Circle, Evans Hall to the west, and Campbell Hall to the south directly behind him, then strode past Donner Hall and reached the five-story concrete home of the computer science and electrical engineering departments. A few mathematics professors also toiled there.

Angelakos, professor of applied physics and engineering and department vice-chairman, had a long and illustrious career. He'd attended Notre Dame and also Harvard, where he got his Ph.D. in 1950. He then served as an engineer for Westinghouse Electric and had been with the computer science department at the University of California at Berkeley from 1951 to the present, and a professor there since 1960. Angelakos was named director of the research lab in 1964–65, and vice-chairman in that same year. The kindly professor was a celebrated expert in the areas of electromagnetic fields and waves, wireless communication, and microwaves.

The Chicago-born Angelakos married Helen Hatzilambrou on December 29, 1946, and the couple had two children, Erica and Demetri. Demetri developed sickle-cell anemia and died in 1979. Angelakos then established a fund in his son's memory, recognizing an outstanding graduate student each year for both scholastic and altruistic achievements in the departments of computer science and electrical engineering. When his wife became ill with cancer, the blow, closely following the first, was almost unbearable. He realized life's true fragility.

Endlessly, he tended his frail and bedridden mate, washing and cleaning, changing the linen, and cooking. Surely, if he'd not been there to serve as her arms and legs, she'd have perished. Angelakos was a true ministering angel and was beloved on the campus. When he left their home on Euclid Avenue in Berkeley to visit the campus, he was greeted by students who adored the balding, portly fountain of wit and good fun. Angelakos always had a "joke du jour" and a disarming smile for students he happened upon as he wandered the hallways. He was famous for his "high spirits and boundless energy." He heard greetings of "Hi, Diog" at every step.

Angelakos trudged up to the fourth floor of Cory Hall where some math professors had offices. He entered Room 411, the coffee-break room across the hall from the then Electronics Research Lab, presently the Microfabrication Facility, at 7:45 AM. Two minutes later he glimpsed what he described as "a can of something." He guessed, "Maybe paint thinner." It sat like some odd space age contraption on the floor. "I guessed a contractor left it," he said. "Workmen had been busy on this floor." It piqued his curiosity....

The homemade green cylindrical box perched atop a can on the floor was studded with "dials and gauges," or so the instructor said later. Angelakos saw wires—loop switches attached to the sides running up each upright shaft of a wooden handle. This in turn was attached to the wooden box that rested on top of the gallon can. Angelakos reached out for it tentatively, and this slight movement was enough to stretch the wires. The bomber had incorporated into his device an ancillary component built to look like a piece of test or measurement equipment. In reality it was a piece of faux technology serving no function except that of exciting curiosity.

The tension he unwittingly applied when he lifted the handle detonated an eight-and-a-half-inch-long, half-inch-wide galvanized pipe sealed on either end with threaded caps. The bomber had suspended the pipe, packed with four varieties of smokeless powder and detonated by four D-cell batteries arranged in two independent circuits and an improvised wooden dowel initiator, within the can of gasoline.

The pipe shattered into shrapnel along incised lines the bomber had made in its surface for just that deadly purpose. But at the base of the box, the can of gas failed to ignite into a fireball. Other debris from the blast, however, did terrible damage. Metal tore the flesh off three of the scholar's fingers and ripped the tendons of his right hand to shreds. Hot metal burned his face, smoke curled from his cheeks, and Angelakos flew backward.

A single thought raced through his mind, as he said later— "What will Helen do without me? How will *she* live?" But within a moment he knew he would survive. The small scrap of paper that had been affixed to an ancillary device on the cylinder of the bomb fluttered to the floor.

The words on it read: "Wu—It works! I told you it would. RV"
What could it mean? And why hadn't the gasoline exploded and
burned the bomber's victim alive?

"The idiot filled the tank to the top," explained Angelakos
later, "and did not leave enough air for the gasoline to explode. I
was really lucky."

Police evacuated Cory Hall and cordoned off the northeast corner of the campus. Within, police sifted and combed through the
wreckage for clues.

The remains of a half-inch pipe with threaded end caps, a one-
gallon gas can, blue-lined paper, brown paper, and white insulated duplex-stranded wire littered the coffee room floor. Wooden
dowels, part of the initiator assemblies, and a wooden handle lay
among three-quarter-inch black plastic, filament, and masking
tape. The bomber had used insulated duplex-stranded wire,
epoxy, black rubber, green paint, and white putty. He'd employed
brass screws, U-nails, staples, an improvised wooden knob and
nail spindle, and solder in the construction of the device. He'd
also used four types of smokeless powder, a wire-loop switch,
Leviton toggle switches, GE flashlight bulbs, red and black insulated stranded wire, a flattened nail pointer, and alligator clips.

For Angelakos, the aftermath of the bombing brought more pain
than the attack itself. Surgeons at Herrick Hospital attempted to
repair Angelakos's ruptured tendons, but his right hand remained
crippled. Far worse, the formerly sunny man was plagued by dark
thoughts. Fear of another attempt on his life played upon him. He
no longer greeted every cry of "Hi, Diog" with a cheery grin or a
joke. Jokes became suspicions, and the suspicions were terrible.

He feared the turn of a key in the car ignition, an unbidden letter, or a birthday present left on his desk. He dreaded crank phone
calls. Yet his own terror was nothing compared to the greatest
tragedy of his life.

With his right hand crippled, Angelakos could no longer care for his ailing wife. Even worse, one suspects, was that in his darkness he could no longer cheer her. Within a month she was dead.

As investigators puzzled over the arcane scrap of paper that was the note from "RV," and mentioned Wu, Ricky Timms, Cory Hall custodian, came forward with some information. He'd seen a man, a stranger, loitering in the corridor. "I think he might have placed the bomb," he said. Timms worked with the police, who produced a composite drawing of a fair-skinned man with a narrow mustache, possibly the first portrait of UNABOM. However, the sketch received little circulation. The building had been unlocked until 10:00 PM the previous night, and anyone might have entered to place the infernal device.

After hundreds of hours trying to interpret the message on the scrap of paper, Lieutenant Foley of the campus bomb squad said, "We have run that 'Wu' thing every which way to Sunday. We have interviewed people with that name. We tried to figure out if it was left by the bomber, or if it was left by someone else. We ran all this down and really came up with nothing."

Six-story Cory Hall, home to the computer science and electrical engineering departments, stood just uphill from Campbell Hall on the eastern edge of the campus, where the Professor's second Berkeley office had been located starting in 1968. Two of his math department colleagues in those days were Professor Robert Vaught (RV) and Assistant Professor Hung Hsi Wu.

Like Conrad's Professor, this Professor sought the perfect detonator, the perfect bomb, and to this end kept a journal partially in numerical code of what he considered "experiments" and their outcomes. He had hidden away a "key" that would decode them. In the journals, which he'd kept since 1969, he discussed his trip to Cory Hall.

"I went to U of California Berkeley and placed in Computer

Science Building a bomb consisting of a pipe bomb in a gallon can of gasoline," he wrote. "Traveling expenses for raids such as the foregoing are very hard on my slender financial resources."

The Professor kept a second, complex, multilayered scientific log book of his bomb tests, carefully cataloging all the construction techniques and materials employed in his devices.

The Professor studied his deadly and growing chemistry set— potassium nitrate, sodium nitrate, and ammonium nitrate, a yellow-gray salt. Potassium chlorate gleamed white and his sulphur a dun color. The colors of the Professor's dispassionate, abstract universe were subtle indeed.

Don Shannon, Lincoln Baptist Church's minister, came upon the Hermit at the little post office one morning. The quiet man was pawing through the flyers and junk mail that people had thrown away. Carefully, he sorted the piles and placed them in his backpack and peddled away. In mid-December, 1982, he seemed to vanish again, but on December 13 J.R. McCabe checked him into Room 119, where he stayed until December 17.

CHAPTER 11
The Welder

"**O**h," say the technophiles, "Science is going to fix all that! We will conquer famine, eliminate psychological suffering, make everybody healthy and happy!" Yeah, sure. That's what they said 200 years ago. The industrial revolution was supposed to eliminate poverty, make everybody happy, etc. The actual result has been quite different....

—UNABOMBER MANIFESTO

THE HERMIT HAD NO MUDGUARD on his wide-tire, homemade bike, so when he rode in the mud, he'd have a mud streak up his back all the way to the top of his head and over. Mud balls clung to his beard and hung from his hair, but he never complained about them, and in fact seemed not to notice them.

Each time he rode his one-speed bicycle past the home of Chris Waits, a black-bearded, 220-pound, 6' 2" Lincoln music teacher and welder, he paused to talk. This was not at all average behavior for the Recluse. His relationship with Waits, says Waits, became one of the longest friendships the Hermit ever had, lasting twenty-five years.

"I got in with him early on when he first came. He was obviously a different person then. The change was kind of a progressive thing," Waits later told me.

"He came in '71, and I met him sometime shortly after that—

within the first year." Waits several times offered the walking man rides but was refused. "Finally, one day he took a ride with me and that's kinda how everything started. I live quite close to him, just over the hump across the road. If you just go on past his place."

When Waits first laid eyes on him, in the early seventies, he thought he looked like a man who needed some help. The music teacher found out the Hermit was fascinated with history, especially about the old-time Lincoln prospectors and how they lived a hundred years ago. Waits had a vast library of history and mining books. "I've been putting together an area history compilation for years on this property I own." he told me later. Waits's property was completely surrounded by national forest and included a four-mile-long gulch that was utterly isolated. "That's why he loved it up here so much. He had permission to be here, and it was so private." The Professor would come and go to the gulch and never see a person. "It was kind of a neat situation for him," Waits explained.

Except for Waits's love of technology and especially electronics, the two had much in common. Waits had a big library, "thousands of books" on everything—chemistry, math. I like the book nobody else likes.... I like to read something that's true.

"I have such a wide vocational range that sometimes people accuse you of being arrogant. If you start to tell them things that you're capable of doing, then the first thing they do is say, 'Oh boy, that guy really boasts.'"

In time, he says, the Hermit grew less tense with him. In fact he says the two spoke a great deal, and the Hermit frequently visited him. The Hermit liked to talk to Waits about gardening, and spoke proudly of his ability to live on twenty dollars a month. Then the rough-hewn pianist and the grizzled mountain man played music together. Waits had played piano since he was three or four years old and was a certified piano tuner and classical pianist.

But Waits quickly learned that anything personal was not to be discussed with his friend. He did not think this so odd in itself since many men do not express their feelings easily among each other. However, it did strike the music teacher as odd that the Recluse never, not once, made reference to any female. And when Waits got married he noticed there was "definitely" some slight friction between the Recluse and himself.

"My wife has been here her whole life," Waits explained. "He obviously knew who she was, but he never would wave to her and never took a ride from me when she was with me. He was polite, but it got to where I just stopped asking if he wanted a ride. He'd just say no if she was with me. I consistently asked her, 'Did he *ever* wave to you?' 'Never.' Even when she came into the store. We've been married for eighteen years, but he absolutely never took a ride when she was with me. And I never saw him with a woman."

Waits may have held one other attraction for the Hermit. "I had a rather large junk pile out back of my repair shop, and there was every type of metal thing—aluminum and magnesium. Everybody's got a scrap pile. I had a large one because I ran my business downtown." Waits had seen his friend purchase cheap silverware at garage sales around Lincoln on two occasions, one around May of 1993. "It seemed odd to me at the time because he had enough silverware," recalled Waits years later.

Also, of course, Waits was a welder and kept welding equipment. The Hermit had none of his own.

Once in June 1985—about the time the Boeing aircraft in Auburn, Washington, received a mailbomb postmarked to Oakland—he glimpsed his shy friend nervously hitchhiking home, and dressed very differently than he usually did. "He was dressed up—dressed for travel. He didn't seem agitated in any way, but it seemed like he was anxious to get home," said Waits.

"I thought he could be a very sane, intelligent person—a person you tried to help, confiding as a friend to come and visit with you."

After the long winter, when the thaw set in, the Hermit would hike miles into the hills. "There it's very remote, very quiet," said Waits, "but you can do naturally anything that you wanted to do and be undetected." Later, he elaborated on this.

"And I spent time talking to him up there," he said. "I own a lot of acreage, and he spent a lot of that time right here—more time than probably anywhere outside his own home. Even probably more than his own home. And you'd have to understand the logistics here to be able to appreciate what I'm saying." I didn't quite appreciate what he was saying so I asked him to elaborate.

"I can't even begin," concluded the welder, "to tell you... how deeply I was involved even unknowingly in a lot of areas.... I choose my words carefully. You just have to—there's too many ramifications for disaster in the future if you're not careful about your choice of vocabulary and the way you come across."

Danny Wood, a thirteen-year-old, sat dejectedly on the bridge spanning Big River on the way from Lincoln (right at the stoplight) along Stemple Pass Road. He swung his feet over the water, watching the torpid gray waters and thinking of a school bully who'd mocked him for making good grades. In the distance he saw the Hermit kicking up a cloud of dust on his old bike. He saw Danny, the son of his close friend Sherri Wood. Sherri was the town librarian and the Hermit often spent long hours in the one-story library down and across from Carol Blowars's realty office. The ragged man pulled to a stop and asked what was wrong. Danny affectionately called him "Uncle," though the rest of the town mostly called him the Hermit on the Hill. Wood told the Recluse his story.

In his past, the Hermit had been the target of jeers and taunts for his intelligence. He recalled with a grimace and a twitch of his beard his own days in high school. Some boys had crammed him into his own locker for a "giggle and a grin" one day. Thus for once the Hermit could relate and, not only that, could give advice.

"Don't worry about the other boy," he counseled. "You have a loving dad, a good mom, and a good home life. Remember, you're a really smart boy, and right now the kids will be jealous of you. So hang in there, because you are really smart and you don't want to waste that."

CHAPTER 12
Abel

*Political correctness has its stronghold among university
professors, who have secure employment with comfortable
salaries, and the majority of whom are heterosexual white
males from middle to upper middle-class families.*

—UNABOMBER MANIFESTO

THE PROFESSOR'S BROTHER DAVID had also attended an Ivy League
school—Columbia University—and had received his degree in
English in 1970. The two, seven years apart, were alike in many
ways. David, introspective and highly intelligent like the Professor,
intended not to use his prestigious degree as a way to make
money, but to become a serious writer. After graduation he took
various jobs, one as a copper smelter in Great Falls, after which
he headed back to Lombard, Illinois, to teach school.

In 1974 David joined the staff of Lisbon High in Iowa. Though
not much of an athlete, he played passable basketball in a league
on Thursday night with fellow teacher Jim West. To West he
seemed to adore "being one of the guys, hanging out." The fact
that he loved to listen to and was interested in the students was
not lost on his pupils. And that he was not in the least interested
in material possessions did not escape his colleagues. He served

his guests soft drinks in glass jelly jars whenever they dropped by his little apartment.

Recalled another teacher, Bob Bunting, "Dave was a very sharp guy, and he said he was the dummy in the family and his brother was a genius. I thought David was knowledgeable in everything, good at everything he did."

He left Lisbon High and between 1975 and 1976 and wrote a novel about baseball, but it remained unpublished. He was "aghast" when he submitted it to a publishing house and the editor wrote back that they wanted to cut it and make certain revisions.

He served as a supervisor at Foam Cutting Engineers, Inc., in 1978, then drove a Commuter Bus Systems bus in Lombard for six months to build up a nest egg that would enable him to take time off for his serious writing. Then in 1985, still unpublished, he appeared destined to follow in his brother's footsteps to the margin of society and beyond. He packed up his old camper van, which had flying fish hand-painted on the side, and headed from Chicago to the Christmas Mountains of western Texas.

Near Big Bend National Park, he purchased a moderately priced parcel of land, five acres, about sixty miles south of Alpine, in Brewster, the largest county in Texas. Spanish conquistadors had dubbed this area *despoblado,* "unpopulated." Before he got around to building a modest cabin in Nine Point Draw, he lived in a hole dug in the ground. To keep rain out he covered the opening with a tarpaulin and sheets of corrugated roofing material. To hold the metal sheets down against the howling wind of the Chihuahuan Desert, he heaped heavy stones on top. Mexico lay forty miles to the north. He rode a dilapidated bike into a town some thirty-five miles away in the valley. There, he'd buy a few weeks' groceries at a time. Sometimes he hiked the Chalk Mountains.

Eventually, the gentle, bearded author acquired a thirty-acre spread at Terlingua Ranch Estates and, with the help of Mexican friends, built a Thoreau-like cabin. David had two rooms measuring eight by twenty-four feet, which were lit by hurricane lamps. He was so Thoreau-like that the locals dubbed him "Henry David."

"David wanted to be next to nature," his neighbor Mary Ann Dunn remembered. "He gave me a photograph of his brother's cabin. I'm sure he was pretty fond of his brother. During bad weather he'd come and stay at our bunk house."

The young, bearded idealist was a strict vegetarian—berries and fried cactus pads cooked in a skillet over an open fire. Eventually, he got a propane stove for his meals of meatless chili or rice. Being a gentle man, he never killed a rabbit, or scarred a tree, or fouled a water hole.

"I never ran into anyone who didn't like David. He was a person who enjoyed his solitude," said San Benito Episcopal priest Father Mel LaFollette, "but also enjoyed being around people. When in a group, he loved to talk.

"He found a flint knife or scraper while hiking in the Dead Horse Mountains and he took it to Enrique Madrid of Ojinaga across the river in Mexico, who is an expert on such things. Enrique laid such a guilt trip on him for removing the artifact that he turned right around and hiked forty miles back to the spot where he found the object and put it back on the ground.... He had a sense of honor."

Father LaFollette spent starry nights around a camp fire in the Big Bend wilderness with David discussing poetry; the ideas of Thoreau, Gandhi, and others; and philosophy.

David spoke glowingly of his brother who was more self-reliant, saying he was "doing a lot better than me," LaFollette told *Time* magazine. "Then we had this discussion about what a Hermit was. He envied his brother for the purity of it. He was looking up to his brother, the man who went off and divorced himself from the world in a very Thoreauvian way. I think in Dave's eyes his brother was up there figuring out some new math or something.

"David, like his brother, fretted about computers and other technology and what it would do to humanity. The destruction of mankind from too much emphasis on technology concerned us." LaFollette was so taken with the lively arguments and the character of David's brother that he penned a novel, *Phobia,* about a Berkeley professor at odds with the modern world.

In 1987 Wanda and Turk, the Professor's parents, came to visit David from Chicago and were appalled at the sight of their bearded, longhaired son living in a cabin. Turk, now seventy-five, checked into a motel. The Professor had intended to visit his brother's Alpine cabin in 1985, but as he said in a February 10, 1986, letter, "Well, I can't come to see you after all. I am extremely sorry to inconvenience you with all these changes of plans. All I can say is that these changes of mind are not frivolous and arbitrary—they are due to changes of circumstances. There is more to this than you realize." That was the winter the Unabomber had struck again, for the first time fatally. On March 8, 1986, the Professor said he'd gone to "a warm weather state" to seek work, but by September or October David was able to visit his brother, but only under strict rules. The Professor had written a letter September 2 that read: "Dave—you can come between Sept. 27 and Oct. 4 inclusive, but not outside those dates." There was no known Unabomber or bombing attempt in that fall of 1986.

Two years later came a turning point in David's life. He'd gone into town to buy supplies at a store but was turned away because of his disorderly appearance (and this in a town often frequented by Hermits). Then citizens paved a nearby road, and David felt civilization moving in on him. "It's getting too crowded," he moaned. Coincidentally, his brother had written, "...my life in the woods has been ruined by progress." Whenever a train whistle penetrated Thoreau's woods, "it seemed to his ears the piercing scream of a hawk... a harbinger of outside encroachment on his preserve."

David had been in love with Linda Patrik since his school days, for almost a quarter century. Finally, he decided to change his life so that he could be with her. Juan, a Mexican worker who did maintenance work on the nearby estates, repaid David, who had secured him a green card, a thousandfold. "I taught him how to write a love letter," Juan said happily. "He translated it into English."

Mrs. Dunn, the neighbor David had known the longest, pitched in, too. She gave him dancing lessons on the desert sand and trimmed away not only the long hair, but his beard.

The amorous conspiracy succeeded. In 1989 David wrote his brother of his marriage plans. The Professor responded with fury, telling David not to communicate with him again. He ordered that his brother write to him "only if he had something really important to say," and to do so by marking the envelope with a red line under the stamp so he would know it was important news. "I intend to destroy any envelopes that do not have" this code, he said.

David sent his brother a letter asking him to be best man at the wedding. The Professor did not respond. In one letter the Professor had warned his brother of Linda, painting her as evil.

David and Linda held a beautiful wedding in their backyard in July of 1990—a hundred friends and relatives, as well as both sets of parents, moved among huge colorful tents. One of the guests was Susan Swanson, a childhood friend of Linda's. It was a Christian and Buddhist ceremony, and the couple—Linda in beige gown with trim and lace, David in white shirt and slacks—knelt on pillows sprinkled with raw rice before Buddhist images. They chanted, chimed finger cymbals, and exchanged vows before a Christian minister.

"David was not one to compromise or hurry or lose hope," Joel Schwartz, the best man and a former roommate of the groom's at Columbia, told *Time* later. "He made a commitment to her way back when he was a young man. But not many people wait twenty-five years to be with the person they love.... Had it not worked out and they not got back together again, I think he would have accepted that, too."

Newly clean-cut David did not abandon his cabin, now a tan structure with a metal roof that gleamed for miles. Instead he brought his wife home. He soon installed enough electric power for her to use her computer, then poured fresh cement in which he drew a heart and their initials with the same whimsical flourish with which he'd colorfully decorated his van and cabin door.

Soon after, however, David and Linda relocated to live most of the year in Schenectady, New York, she toiling as a philosophy professor in the morning at Union College, and teaching existential literature and ancient art theory in the afternoon. As for David, his caring side expressed itself in his selfless work at Residential Opportunities, Inc., an adult care facility where he worked with the developmentally disabled. He played his guitar for them, took them to church on Sunday, and showed his thoughtfulness in uncountable ways. It was as if unable to reach his brother, he yearned to touch as many lives as possible.

In 1993 he took a job at Equinox, an Albany halfway house ministering to troubled teens and young runaways. One of his main jobs was to find them housing. Their neighbor, Mary Ann Welch, thought the reason he did so well working with young boys was that he was a good listener. "Dave cares about people," she said.

David joined the local softball team, and successfully published his short stories in literary magazines. But a sad event, and the most life-changing, came in September of 1990 only a few months after the wedding, and widened the rift between the two brothers. Turk had become seriously ill with lung cancer. David wrote his brother of his father's probable mortal illness, using the envelope code to signal the importance of the communication. The Professor stonily responded that "this was an appropriate use" of the signal.

When Turk died a month later, David wrote to ask his brother to attend the memorial service in Chicago, but this time the Professor did not even respond. Then, in January 1991, the Professor wrote, demanding a share of the father's $60,000 estate. He didn't receive this money, but Wanda sent $7,000 to him under separate circumstances. By summer, the Professor was writing that he didn't want anything further to do with the family. But first, of his mother, he wrote that he wanted "the bankbook in my own hands so that I could withdraw money myself. Apparently she likes power and wants to keep it in her own hands."

"Dave, because he has a little ego problem vis-a-vis big brother," wrote the Professor in another letter, "resorted to further rationalizations in order to avoid having to make any concession to my reasoning.... Now I want to make it clear that my decision to break off communications with Dave is neither frivolous nor petty—it's a very serious matter for me."

And again: "It is a matter of life and death, and this is not an exaggeration..." the Professor wrote to his brother in the summer of 1991. "I seriously believe I will die if you can't accomplish this for me [get him his share of the estate]... I won't be able to eat or sleep or stop my heart from pounding until this whole thing is settled.

"I have got to know, I have *GOT TO, GOT TO, GOT TO* know that every last tie joining me to this stinking family has been cut FOREVER and that I will never NEVER have to communicate with any of you again…. I've got to do it NOW. I can't tell you how desperate I am…. It is killing me."

CHAPTER 13
Cain

*M*any leftists have an intense identification with the
problems of groups that have an image of being weak
(women), defeated (American Indians), repellent (homosexuals)
or otherwise inferior. The leftists themselves feel that these
groups are inferior.

—UNABOMBER MANIFESTO

FROM 1988 UNTIL 1995 THE HERMIT HAD A PEN PAL, who became in truth a close friend. Juan Sanchez Arreola, of Ojinaga in the Mexican state of Chihuahua, corresponded with the Hermit. Juan kept the letters, eight a year, some fifty in all, in a leather satchel and often read the precise, formal, fluent letters that were written in Spanish. They spoke of their friendship with joy. Over the years, though, all but four were lost. Most of all he prized the miraculous carved gift the Recluse had sent him in 1991. He hung it proudly on his wall.

In 1991 the Hermit had carved the gift—a cylinder out of redwood, hollowed out and with a cap. Meticulously, he incised the hardwood with images of twisting vines, red-stained berries, a frisky white rabbit like those in the brush by Poorman's Creek, and painted carved lettering that read "Montani Semper Liberi" ("Mountain Men Are Always Free"). The hard-muscled, steel-haired, stolid farm worker guessed, "I think it's for carrying pens."

Each of the Hermit's letters came in a plain white envelope with a red, white, and blue "Old Glory" stamp and was written on three-ring binder paper. Each sang the praises of friendship. The Hermit had been introduced to Sanchez through his brother and found the poverty-stricken, loving family man to be generous in all respects. Though he had little material possessions, the ranch-hand offered his poorer friend everything that he had.

But it pained the Mexican that the Hermit's parents were so estranged from their son and that the son was so angry with them. Sanchez knew the Hermit's parents had reprimanded him for leaving a promising career for the wilds and said that his American friend was "on bad terms with [his] mama and papa— he doesn't want anything to do with them." When the Recluse's father died, he didn't even mention it to Sanchez. "He called his mother a dog," he'd heard. "It's very sad when someone doesn't love his parents.

"He lived a very poor life. Once he wrote that to travel, he would have to give up eating for a year."

The two men never met. They learned of each other through the Professor's brother, David, then living in Texas in his shack, who had befriended Sanchez and helped him to get a green card. Sanchez did errands for David, and on one occasion David cared for Sanchez when he was involved in an accident that broke his leg. Both men apparently were short of funds, and for some reason, which is not clear, Sanchez ended up appealing to the Professor, by letter, for help. That was the beginning of their friendship, which the Hermit affirmed in the first letter to Sanchez we have. "I am very pleased that you call yourself my friend," wrote the Hermit, November 14, 1988, "And I, in turn, call myself your friend."

"Mountain Men Are Always Free."

ON FEBRUARY 17, 1994, the Hermit wrote to Sanchez in Mexico:

> My very dear and esteemed friend:
> For now, just a short letter because I am in a hurry. It is not possible for me to spend two months with you. If it were a question only of going to El Paso to visit the immigration office with you, and then returning here right away, and if this were to make the difference between bringing your family with you to the United States or not, fine. I would go. But spending two months there is impossible. Aside from other reasons, I have much need of money, and here there is little work in the winter. The best season for work is summer, so the best time to look for work is spring, and so I must be here to look for work. If I did not find work for the summer, I would die of hunger when winter came.
> I have just mailed two letters, looking for information that, with luck, could prove beneficial for you.
> I don't have time to write more at the moment.
> Fondly, one who values your friendship.

Though he had only two years of formal education, Sanchez was wise in common sense and in the ways of the heart. He would peer through his dusty, scratched reading glasses, as old and battered as himself, and, holding the Recluse's letter in thick, calloused fingers, devour it. Sanchez would scrunch up his wonderful face, honest and plain as a loaf of salt-rising bread. Jose Sanchez, Juan's son, said, "We always sent greetings to him in my father's letters.... He seemed very nice and always was very nice with my father. He wrote about his economic problems. He wanted to know how my father lived in the United States [when he worked on a Texas ranch] and about Mexican history. I think it was a hobby for him." But—to have a friend at last! How delicious, yet calming. It was almost enough to silence the roar of the blackening river and splitting sky, to tame the demon inside for years at a time.

The Hermit was especially interested in the revolutionary Pancho Villa, who'd roamed the remote border area where Sanchez lived, but some sixty years earlier. "I was born four years after Pancho Villa was killed," said Juan, "but I proposed that he come down for a history tour with me." The Hermit refused in his usual manner, by sending back a neutral, dispassionate reply.

On May 17, the Hermit, concerned, wrote:

> My dear and esteemed friend:
>   It angers me and shames me that those merciless and lying officials want to take away your pension. They should live up to their promises. But it is not surprising that government officials do not live up to their promises, because they are either stupid and incompetent, or they are liars who twist the law to be able to commit any injustice. Well, keep me abreast of what happens with these matters of immigration and your pension, so that I can know how things are going.
>   Although what the officials are doing is a great injustice, consider that your fortune is not all bad, because you have a wife and three children and all are healthy. Even though you have to endure these difficulties, you will probably overcome them in the end, and your children will thrive

and some day they will have children of their own. I wish I had a wife and children! Nevertheless, I know these things are very painful for you. Even though I can do nothing for you now, I never forget you; instead, I think of you and your problems often, and perhaps someday I can help you in one way or another.

But I do not have a lot of hope that I can visit you at Christmastime. Things are very bad for me. I still do not have work, and without work there is no money and without money there is no bus ticket.

But, with time, things will improve for us. In the meantime, I leave you with affection and esteem and good will, as always.

Your friend,

Over the long years, Sanchez became more a father figure than a friend to both the Hermit and his brother, and at David's request began to give the Recluse advice. The Hermit wrote back, "If you want to be my friend, don't give me advice."

Toward the end, Sanchez offered the Hermit $200 for bus fare from his shack to Mexico. He said he had a rich family life, with his wife Rosario and three fine children, and "a bunch" of money. The Hermit, said Sanchez, "had written his brother twice in 1995 to ask for money, but not saying why." Four years earlier, the Recluse wrote that he'd slipped and cut his foot on a can. "He cured it himself, without seeing a doctor." The Hermit distrusted doctors, though reportedly he had developed a heart condition. However, it was possible that the symptoms were the side-effect of a powerful prescription antidepressant that he took.

On February 15, 1995, the Recluse wrote:

My very dear and esteemed friend:
I am so sorry that you have had some problems, according to

what you told me in your last letter. I hope they were not serious and are now in the past. In your letter, you expressed the hope that your family would get their papers. Does that mean there is a possibility that your wife and children will get the documents that would permit them to come and live with you in the United States? I hope they get them, because they have a right to live in this country, since the immigration officials promised it to you previously. But, even though they may be able to live in the United States, it is an injustice that the officials did not live up to their promise, and that they caused you so many difficulties and worries, and forced your family to return to Mexico. Do me a favor and write to me when you know whether your family is going to get their documents to enable them to live in this country, because I am very anxious to know.

In this region where I live, there has been little snow this winter. It seems as though there is less snow every year. When I first came here, it snowed about four feet, or almost 1.25 meters, near my little house. But nowadays it is rare to have more than a foot, or 30 centimeters, near my house, and this winter I don't think there has been more than four or six inches or 10 or 15 centimeters of snow on the ground near my little house. The bad thing is that the snow there melts when it is not very cold, and it freezes when it grows cold again, so that many parts of the ground are covered with a layer of ice. This is very dangerous, especially on the hills, because one can slip very easily if you don't step on the ice carefully, and you can fall very suddenly, so that you can break a bone. But up until now I have not broken any bones, and I hope to continue to avoid that by being very careful.

Well, give my regards to your wife and children. Good health and good luck to you and your wife, and I hope you get the papers you need. (And do not hesitate to write to me when you find out whether you will receive them.) With affectionate greetings, I am your friend who esteems you.

The Hermit corresponded on "Noviembre 28 de 1995" with this message:

My esteemed and valued friend:

It is time to send you a Christmas greeting. It is almost December, and here there is a good snow cover on the ground, and at this moment more snow is falling, a sign that Christmastime is approaching.

I am fine here. I am poorer than ever, but I am in very good health, and this is more important than anything. As to my poverty, I have $53.01 exactly, barely enough to stave off hunger this winter without hunting rabbits for their meat. But with the rabbit meat and a little flour and other things that I have put away, also a few dried vegetables from my little garden, I will get through the winter very well. And when the spring comes, perhaps I will have better luck with work and money, so that I can go visit you. We will see.

About these rabbits, which are called "liebres de raquetas" ("snowshoe hares" in English), they are very beautiful and interesting, and also very useful, because often they have provided me with meat when, without them, I would not have been able to eat any. I can hunt them freely, without buying a license, and I do so with a .22-calibre rifle in the following way: during the night, I go out into the woods and I walk until I find some fresh tracks made by rabbits, then I follow the tracks until I find the rabbits. In general, this is easy if it has snowed within one or two hours before dawn, and then stopped. But when snow has fallen during the first part of the night and not during the rest of the night, then it is hard to track rabbits, because they rest during the day and they move around at night, and they change directions constantly, so that they cross their own trails repeatedly and the trails of other rabbits, and so in the course of a single night they leave trails that are very tangled and hard to follow.

Anyway, when it is known from the freshness of the tracks that the rabbits are near, you must look closely, because these rabbits are white in the winter, and they are not so easy to see in the whiteness of the snow. In general, what you spot first are the black eye and the black tips of their ears, which stand out against the snow. Then you

must find a good position from which to shoot, and you
must take care not to frighten the rabbit, because if it
becomes frightened and runs, sometimes you have to chase
it two hours before you get another chance to shoot....

The Hermit added that he'd mail this last letter, then, "[a]fter-
wards I probably will spend the rest of the winter without going
to the village of Lincoln and therefore will not visit my post office
box [524] until spring." He concluded with, "May God bless you
and all your family."

When the Hermit's father had visited him, he was "appalled"
that his eldest son lived with no water or electricity "in a hut."
But the Recluse went on happily baking bread, hunting deer, and
shooting squirrels, coyotes, and even porcupines, slowly roasting
them over a fire in his yard by the miraculous sprawling garden,
which grew larger by the day.

CHAPTER 14
The Campus Astronaut

F eminists are desperately anxious to prove that women are
as strong and as capable as a man. Clearly they are
nagged by a fear that women may NOT be as strong and as
capable as men.

—UNABOMBER MANIFESTO

FOR SEVERAL DAYS a small beige plastic box with a three-ring black binder on top and held in place with a rubber band had lain in front of a terminal in the computer lab of Cory Hall at UC Berkeley, the same building in which Dr. Angelakos had been bombed. Students using Room 264 A soon found this to be a hindrance, and over days its position was subtly altered, nudged this way and that. Initially, the binder's spine had faced away from the researchers and toward the computer screen it was obscuring. Finally, one student moved it so that it now lay like a closed book, its spine facing left.

Electrical engineering grad student and astronaut candidate USAF Captain John Hauser entered the lab for the first time on Wednesday afternoon, May 15, 1985. The seemingly perpetually smiling young man was clad in a blue-striped T-shirt and tan pants, and sat down to work on his master's project. After a few minutes he noticed the box with the binder on top. He thought the rubber band holding the two together was unusual, and when he casually ruffled the notebook pages, he saw that those inside appeared to be blank. Hauser's curiosity was aroused.

The Unabomber counted on the curious and numbered them among most of his victims. Hauser peered over at the right side of the box and saw its latch was open. He thought, "I wonder who this belongs to?" Perhaps one of the other graduate students who worked regularly in the research laboratory was missing his property. Seeing that it was open, he thought to check and see what it was. Hauser picked up the latch. It was just 1:41 PM.

UNABOM had booby-trapped the card file with two, or perhaps three, detonating devices, including a microswitch, and had concocted his most powerful bomb yet—a titanic mix of aluminum powder and ammonium nitrate inside a pipe. If someone had not turned the device sideways, if Hauser had opened it facing him as one might open a briefcase, the full force of the bomb would have blasted into his chest, killing him instantly.

Instead, Hauser had opened it from right to left, as if opening a book. The main thrust of the detonation, which he characterized as making a loud "ZZZZZAT," funneled into his fingers and right arm and knocked it to the side. It tore the Air Force Academy ring off his hand and shot it into a plaster wall with such force that the letters of the word "Academy" were imprinted in the surface a full six feet away. A spinning piece of pipe embedded itself in the same wall, narrowly missing Hauser.

The first thing that went through his mind was, "Why would they do that? Why?" Whatever was happening to him was incredible—his whole arm felt on fire as if he'd hit his funny bone, the medial epicondyle, a thousand times harder than he ever had before. The blast had severed his medial nerve, one of the most important nerves in the human body.

"I grabbed my arm," Hauser said later. "It was now pretty weak because I'd lost many of the muscles, and so I stood there kind of looking around. I noticed that blood was pooling in the wound in my arm, coming up to the level, and then starting to spurt out. At this point I realized there was some serious business here and so I backed up a little bit, still holding onto an edge of the binder, and screamed for help.... I was twenty-six years old at the time, in the prime of being able to do things, and suddenly I nearly crossed over that line between a healthy, active life and none at all.

"I could see a large divot was taken out of the inside of my forearm," he told *Time* magazine afterward. "It was just destroyed. There was a tremendous amount of blood spluttering out and pooling around me. Both major arteries, including the one that gives you a pulse on your wrist, were ripped open. All of my fingers were missing two sections; the index finger a little more, the pinkie a little less."

Professor Mike Lieberman, running down to Hauser's aid, barely paused to absorb the scene before trying to control the bleeding through direct pressure, while elevating the forearm higher than the heart. Minutes, or possibly only seconds later, Professor Diogenes Angelakos, the only UNABOM victim to be involved in *two* blasts, hurried into the room to help. Angelakos's tie was the necessary two inches in width called for in a tourniquet. He quickly placed it over the artery, slightly above the gaping wound, wrapped it around twice, and tied it in a half knot. Then he placed a stick or some part of the wreckage on the tie–tourniquet, finished the last of the knot, and turned the stick until the bleeding stopped. He looked at his watch to be sure of the time he'd applied the tourniquet. The medics would need to know.

When the medics arrived they searched for the finger parts severed from Hauser's hand to save those they could. Then they carried Hauser, already suffering from heavy blood loss, by stretcher from the second floor, his right arm hanging uselessly at his side, his left thrown over his face as if shielding himself from a blast that was just occurring. He couldn't understand why he couldn't see out of one eye and in the midst of this tragedy, the one great fear that raced through Hauser's mind was for his flying career.

"I can remember lying on the gurney in the emergency room, my arm swollen by my side," recalled Hauser. "I guess I didn't realize how bad the damages were." He kept asking, "I can't see out of my left eye. Am I going to be able to fly again?"

He never would. The severing of the medial nerve meant he could no longer "see" with his right hand, say to reach into a pocket and pull out change or find the right key among several. "This ability to see with your hand is very important in everyday life, but especially in flying a jet fighter."

"I had hoped the Unabomber had blown his brains out trying to make a bomb some place," said Angelakos bitterly.

A week after the crippling attack on Hauser, the captain received a cordial letter inviting him to join the astronaut training program. Instead of heading to astronaut training, he learned to write left-handed, and endured terrible pain and a year of occupational therapy after two extensive microsurgeries. Hauser received a fellowship from Berkeley, then taught at the University of Southern California after being medically discharged from the Air Force.

The conclusions of the experts studying the latest bomb were chilling. While his first seven explosives were composed of smokeless powder and match heads, the latest showed a startling change. The primary charge was now composed of a mixture of aluminum powder and ammonium nitrate—a far more explosive combination.

The device that so tragically maimed Hauser had been a three-quarter-inch-diameter pipe sealed on either end by metal bar stock plugs and held in place with metal securing pins some five-sixteenth-inch by one-half-inch. Nail fragments, lead, and double-pointed three-eighths-inch tacks had been used as shrapnel. The letters FC, as usual, were stamped into the end of one plug. This time, though, the bomber had used six D-cell batteries, with their identifying casings removed, arranged in a series to include a metal/wooden initiator inside the pipe and an improvised loop switch outside. The plastic file box had been reinforced with a wooden framework. The bomber was beginning to take greater pains with his machines.

Once more the investigators totaled the vicious shopping list of untraceable parts. In the end they had not gained a single step on their cunning quarry. They had as much chance of catching the bomber as the Hermit of snaring bare-handed the swift white hares that nibbled his lettuce.

The Hermit checked into the Park Hotel on April 29, stayed a single night in Room 119, then using the halfway house as a springboard for other parts, vanished. But on May 22, he was back to the same room for one night. In between, on May 15, the tragic maiming of Hauser had occurred.

CHAPTER 15

Notes of an Unidentified Detective

IN THE COURSE OF ANY INVESTIGATION, certainly one as long, involved, and costly as this (some fifty million dollars, not including payment of the reward), it's not unusual to become discouraged. The case started for me in the early nineties. I believe you came along about the same time—trying to write a book about a case nobody really knew anything about; our trail was still cold.

I had gone to the Timber Association scene in Sacramento. The drive had taken me about an hour, and by the time I got there almost everyone had gone. Inside the floors were shiny with liquid, and the smell of chemicals was overwhelming. A picture blown off the reception desk or one of the walls lay smashed in a corner. Some of the debris still smoldered. I moved from office to office and saw the damage had penetrated walls. I looked at Gil Murray's desk and saw a picture of his wife and almost grown sons there. It too was smashed.

THE INVESTIGATION

I went to where the front lobby had been and craned my neck to observe damage to the skylight as high as seventeen feet up. Shards of metal were riveted right up all four sides like machine gun fire and, where the door had been, I was able to look out on a city office building across the street. People there paused, then continued on their way in the evening. The day had been hot but the April night would be cool.

Whoever this bomber was he had a soul of ice because Gil Murray was liked by everyone we spoke to.

As you recall, some time earlier we had scoured dingy Emeryville and ransacked every metal works and scrapyard between there and Sacramento. This was back in '93. That summer day we headed for Oakland for lunch. We were sweating by the time we reached Lake Merrit by way of Grand Avenue, then headed Bayward to check out a hole-in-the-wall yard that did do some work with aluminum. We mostly suspected an aircraft machinist, though.

A sense of hopelessness about the Unabomber case had gripped me for some time, and I was having a tough time shaking it off that afternoon. I put on a big smile, though, and began to ask the subtle list of unrevealing questions we'd been told to ask. Meanwhile, I racked my brain to ask, "Where did we go wrong?"

Just past the shells of rusting cars, I glimpsed a portly young man in a flack jacket. I knew they had a machine shop there, but my first priority, or rather that of my partner and I, was to determine the availability of aluminum and other metals our bomber had employed in the odd wood-metal construction of his bombs. As I said, our questioning was delicate. It had to be because at that time we were still under orders to keep the whole case secret. The bosses were still operating on the theory that if we tipped our

THE INVESTIGATION

hand that a serial bomber was at large, we risked a panic and the worst case scenario of alerting the master bomber that we were on to him or at least aware of his methods. This would have been before the Task Force in Frisco made some news and Freeman started to call those big press conferences.

The chemical chase. That's where I held great hope for the solution to the UNABOM question. Some of the chemicals he was using were not common. But today, I was stuck tracing the metals he used as shrapnel in his devices. These shavings implied a tooling machine of some sort, which to me suggested sophisticated or at least professional machinery. My partner felt even more strongly that our man had a home welding shop.

"It would have to be private though," he said. "Hidden somewhere inside a separate home, most likely a basement complex or room that he forbids anyone to enter. Now the existence of such a room tells me that we have a guy who has a job, has money to travel the country and purchase expensive, high-tech tools to work metal, to turn a pipe like an expert, to construct those end caps...."

"He'd need an acetylene tank and torch, a welder's mask. Those are things we should look for. But today we do shavings," said my partner. "We'll have to take some samples."

"He'd have an assortment of drill bits and electric drills, and probably a tool or simple awl to punch those initials into the end caps. Those metal disks capping the pipes are professionally done."

"Oh, yeah, he's educated, middle class, and probably high up enough in a company to have the time and money to expend on his enterprise."

"He has to be management because he has time to be traveling from one end of the country to the other," I told him.

My partner decided to take the questioning. He must have sensed I wasn't up to par. As you know my wife was still recovering and I was pretty near retirement anyway.

When my partner finished speaking with the scrapyard boss and had gotten the names of a few employees who'd left under cloudy circumstances, we went inside to check the machine shop. My partner bent down and collected a few of the scrapings from the lathe. I passed him a glassine envelope and he packed them in to send to the lab in DC.

"FRED CHURCH," THE NAME I'VE USED on my correspondence to you regarding this more interesting member of our club of constantly changing priority suspects, lived as I said, in Palo Alto, a college community not unlike UC Berkeley, but with just a shade fewer Nobel prize recipients. Church ran the small department of a large Silicon Valley computer company. Like many in the Valley he worked underground. I gather the reason for that is not so much for security reasons as to keep industrial spies from picking their potentially lucrative patents clean.

I remember on the occasion I showed him off to you, that you remarked on his tidy blandness. Just the way I'd imagined UNABOM. I've seen that Eastwood film [*In the Line of Fire*] about the presidential assassin who handcrafts every component of his plastic gun, or was it wood? He had that same look. The white sleeves rolled up, the receding hairline, the hint of a paunch, the business suits with red-striped ties. He had the glasses too, though they weren't of the tinted aviator style. He looked like the kind of man who could manufacture death after a hard day's work as a slave to a computer and not blink an eye.

THE INVESTIGATION

After breathing that pristine environment all day, did he roll up those sleeves and hunker down to his real work? Was his shop that highly illuminated or did he work in dankness with only a tensor light focused on his work? I saw the latter in my mind—but good tools, gloves, lots of power, and a key no one was allowed to touch. It was too bad the case was being kept under wraps. Surely, someone would recognize a man who kept one key to himself. Who had a room so private that his wife and children would be banned. At the time I wanted to see that basement workshop more than my pension.

I drove my wife crazy with conjecture about that little man. About two months after you and I visited his place—long, low, tan, and in a grove of trees, I began to do my own background check. He'd been well-educated, and that fit. He'd lived here at the time of the Angelakos and Hauser maimings at Berkeley. He made trips into Oakland, but he had two or three clients in that city. He had been passed over for promotion. I was working on the idea that Church had some grudge against his company, but had transferred that to computers and the industry itself.

Of course, now that I stand back from the facts, it does seem odd that a man who hates technology should go into computers in the first place. Anyway, cracks began to appear in my case against Church.

Still, he was tempting. Late, late in the game, the year after we were finished combing scrap yards, we began to get the letters. I saw the hand of an intelligent man. As *Newsweek* put it, FC's letters were "alternately preachy, chatty, ironic, and even subtly self-mocking. They are surely the most remarkable letters any serial killer ever wrote." In the meantime, our man continued to haunt the Stanford bookstores. I recollect at the time *Newsweek* had a

a

great quote and I've included it in my file to you. Keep the clipping, shred the file. "[UNABOM] has arguably raised murder by mail to the level of performance art," it read in July 1995. "His mainspring—the apparent reason for it all—is vanity and narcissism. Consider the power trip inherent in watching the FBI chase its tail, or watching authorities at LAX (and other California airports) get the shakes."

My point in taking this literary turn at this time was that our guy had a habit of quoting Eric Hoffer, the longshoreman and political philosopher, around the office watercooler. Now admit it, that seems out of place. Especially since our bomber down the lane had enough Hoffer in his writings to make me curious. Hoffer wrote something called *The True Believer* back in the sixties, real popular then, and the time period the Unabomber seems most comfortable in. Hoffer's book spoke, if I'm not mixing it up with the other influential books in the case, of "the dark, satanic mills," and was pretty much a dissection of mass movements.

So the last time we met, I drove to his office parking lot and we got another look at him when he went to lunch. Everyone else left in groups, but he ate alone. He ate alone and read a book. What struck me was the absolute lack of emotion his face held.

I recall how you read sadness there, but I just didn't see it. He was a blank sheet of paper. And so we abandoned him while his whereabouts during every bombing was checked.

Well, you know the rest. He did not have the opportunity to commit the bombing in Salt Lake at CAAMs Computer Store. Our stand was that one man did them all. And so he slipped from the short list. Then he slipped lower and lower on the long list. Then one day he was gone into the limbo of unrealized expectations.

THE INVESTIGATION

But I sure liked him back in those days. However, I see now there was no way he could be the bomber.

And now of course it looks as if we know most of the answers.

[end of report]

My friend was of old school police work and knew little of the space-age technology that now existed to track bombers. He was as much of a Luddite as myself and the long-sought bomber. The Bureau had a number of high-tech items on their side—DNA analysis, microscopic analysis of letters on a typed page, and infrared spectrophotometers.

Reflected light from bomb debris can pinpoint the device's chemical composition. Splinters of wood, metal, and plastic give clues to the bomb's shape prior to detonation.

And detection now occurred at a molecular level—a portion of a strand of hair, a old damaged droplet of blood, or a single molecule of tissue. Fibers from bomb fragments may later be found in the suspect's home and one cloth fiber can yield the dye lot of an article of clothing. Whether its tip is "bi-lobed" or "tri-lobed" is meaningful to the experts. Until they made their big arrest, the Feds vowed to use technology to bring down the man who hated technology. But most of the technology only helps after you have a good suspect.

After the arrest, long after my friend retired, the FBI inventoried every item inside. They found a "welding-type mask" but no welding equipment—no tank or torch. There was no electricity in the dwelling.

The suspect had "seven large drill bits, one drilling base, and a hand drill with a blue and red handle" but nothing that would drill through double-thicknesses of metal to secure end caps to pipe bombs. Where is the machine shop?

CHAPTER 16
Student Bombers

L*eftists tend to hate anything that has an image of being strong, good and successful. They hate America, they hate Western civilization, they hate white males, they hate rationality....*

—UNABOMBER MANIFESTO

THE BOMBER TOOK ONE LAST SWIPE at the airline industry on May 8, 1985, when he posted a brown-wrapped package from Oakland, California, to Boeing's fabrication division in Auburn, Washington. Lost in internal mail or the postal service, the package turned up in Building 17-04, the company mail room, on June 13. The return address read Weiburg Tool & Supply in Oakland, a fictitious name and address.

Because one of the thirty clerks on duty there considered the parcel suspicious (it had been sent to no specific person) he only partially opened it, then called King County bomb squad. X rays confirmed it was a bomb.

For the next six hours technicians dismantled, then blew up one of UNABOM's most powerful devices. Inside had been another wooden box, but with cutouts that resembled shipping containers for prosthetic devices. The bomb had been big, a thirteen-and-three-quarter-inch-long, one-and-one-fourth-inch-diameter pipe sealed on both ends with aluminum plugs and secured by steel bars and epoxy glue. Each metal plug had FC stamped onto it. The Unabomber had used aluminum powder and potassium sulfate this time. The bomb would have been triggered by the recipient removing the wrapping paper on the box.

Carefully, as they'd done in each case, forensic experts listed the remnants recovered from the blast scene:

- 1¼" steel pipe
- End plugs (aluminum/magnesium alloy, letters FC stamped into ends of both plugs)
- Rectangular securing pins
- Metal shim material
- Metal bands, ³⁄₈" width
- D-cell batteries
- Brown paper
- Three types of tape
- Picture cord style cable
- Beige insulated duplex wire
- Green insulated stranded wire
- Epoxy
- Elmer's glue
- Screws
- Nails
- Wooden box
- Wooden chocks
- Wooden switches
- Wooden wafer (part of initiator assembly)
- 2 transparent type ³⁄₄" black plastic-tape
- ³⁄₄" black friction tape
- ½" filament tape
- Wooden stick
- Wooden pegs
- Coil springs
- Metal strips
- Solder
- "Of the People By the People For the People" $.22 US postage stamps
- "America's Light Fueled by Truth and Reason" $1 US postage stamps
- Red, white, and blue mailing label

So much evidence, yet Chris Ronay, the FBI bomb expert, and all the rest of the tireless investigators seemed unable to get anywhere. In between explosions it was as if the earth had swallowed up UNABOM.

A labyrinth of minutiae as elaborate as the bomber's overdesigned infernal devices crowded the Professor's landscape. When he gave his brother permission to send him a book for his birth-day in May, he said he would accept it only if its width did not exceed seven inches. Anything larger required that he make a journey to the post office since his mailbox accepted only narrow packages. A second requirement was that David understand that he would be allowed to trade it for another book if he wished. "You get the sense of how deeply he thinks about details and has to anticipate every contingency in advance," David later said. "It's as if he can't take things as they come."

Previously, he'd sent his aunt the dimensions of his narrow mailbox with the complaint, "I had to walk a mile in the snow and wait two hours for the mailman [because of your package]."

And when the father of the girl he'd carved a sewing box for wrote in 1986 to say, "Thank you. Maybe we could all get together sometime," the Professor reacted testily. "Who invited you?" he fired back.

When a rift occurred between the two brothers, the Professor wrote: "Since I'm still mad, don't write to me for a while. Permission to send me a book for my birthday is rescinded."

The brother concluded his letter with a warning that he had no intention of communicating with David, other than exchanging Christmas greetings. "You're a fool. Go to hell," he signed off. "(But I say that affectionately.)"

The Professor, in arranging a visit to his brother's place in Texas, set January 25, 1986, as his date of arrival, then January 27. On February 10, he canceled the visit. In March the Professor claimed he'd gone to a "warm weather state" to look for work. David visited his brother September 27 through October 4, 1986. It would be their last face-to-face meeting to date. "The social world was not a safe world for him, like it was loud music he could not shut out," David reported later. Then in March, the Professor was still doubting the sincerity of missives from his parents apologizing to him. "Isn't there a hint there of something like, 'we are truly sorry you turned out so rotten'?" he wrote. "It was cold and curt and afterward she seemed to just shove it under the carpet and forget about it."

CHAPTER 17
On Bombs

AT THE LITTLE SAN FRANCISCO CAFE where I always wrote, I looked across the table at the head of the city's six-man bomb squad. I was hungry to know every aspect of the UNABOM story: how, for example, the cunning bombs were painstakingly constructed. Yet I had no desire to print how to build such a machine. I was ravenous to glean all the secrets these brave men had about defusing bombs, but knew that to reveal too much was to provide terrorists with clues to circumvent police bomb-disarming techniques.

Recently in a German publication, for instance, an article explained how German bomb squads used cryogenics to freeze bombs and disconnect them. In answer the terrorists fashioned a mail bomb with a thermostat next to the detonator that would explode the bomb at freezing temperatures. The terrorists would have succeeded had the device not sat overnight in a mailbox. When the temperature dipped toward zero, the bomb blew up the box and made the bomb squad aware of a new danger.

Bomb squad head Mark Potter's world was a frightening one of high-tech, sheer guts, constant danger, and heroism, a world of eighty-pound, $60,000 Kevlar, Nomex bomb suits that protected almost every part of their bodies, save one: In order to perform the delicate work of defusing, their hands were completely exposed. Israeli bomb experts defined the bulky, space suit-like costumes as "body bags," preferring instead lighter more flexible protective suits.

In Potter's world, cunning Mark 6 robots rolled on treads across bombed out landscapes, peering out through twin electronic eyes, panning, tilting, and slightly off-spaced to provide the men at the monitor with a sense of depth perception. They could pick up or find bombs, but not disarm them. That was still left up to Potter and his men, vulnerable hands gently probing the wires. "It's always the red wire. Cut the red wire," goes the old bomb squad joke.

From the space-age costumes to $140,000 robots, Potter resembled a NASA employee more than a policeman. And his clear, intense eyes, his confident, easy manner suggested an astronaut more than a cop. He looked remarkably fit—he had to be. As a member of the EOD (Explosives Ordinance Disposal) unit, he had to muster the strength to drag the heavy eighty-pound bomb suit around for at least a half-hour at a time. He had to be in top shape to avoid dehydration inside the claustrophobic costume.

The air is drawn in from the outside through a tube providing little protection from the so-called ACDD bearing sarin gas used to kill in the Tokyo subway, but earmarked for the US by the cult leaders behind the plot. Potter and his team had recently come up against CDDs (Chemical Dispersion Devices) and BDDs

THE INVESTIGATION

(Biological Dispersal Devices) from chemical agent bombs. Potter's bomb suit did give him a certain amount of "frag-protection" and overblast shielding. The Kevlar material had steel plates in it.

He told me about a typical bomb call as, outside, the light-rail "J" car passed, dogs barked in the little Sunset neighborhood, and the Unabomber, somewhere, still walked free.

"When we get there the police department has already been notified that they have a suspected device or suspicious package. The police would come, interview these people who received it as to why the device seems suspicious." If it seems indicated they will move everybody out, close the place, and put in a call to EOD. "We always come out in pairs and one of the techs" again questions the recipients and the cops. If the device seems "very intricate, we'd call in the whole unit, and have somebody call the FBI and ATF. At Harrah's at Tahoe [which was mined], they had the local bomb squad, the military command, the FBI, and the ATF."

Potter had been summoned to Oklahoma City a week after a bomb weighing many thousands of pounds bit the Alfred P. Murrah Federal Building in half. The horror was still fresh in Potter's mind. The team had discovered debris "at six blocks" which meant the investigative "perimeter was *nine* blocks, because it's half again the distance."

Potter has seen the aftereffect of many bombings but still calls the scene in Oklahoma City "unreal." It looked more like a contract demolition crew was just tearing down the building rather than the result of a terrorist bomb. One reason Potter was there was to learn how to cope with a strike of similar proportions in San Francisco.

"At that time San Francisco was going through UN Fifty. We wanted to see how their response was to a large incident like that so if we had one in San Francisco, we'd have a foot in the door of how to react to something that major—how their command post functioned, how their evidence gathering worked.

Potter told me about negative blast pressure and positive blast pressure. "Oklahoma City," he explained, was a textbook example of the large blast. The Murrah Building was destroyed by the initial or positive blast pressure, the pressure blowing *out* from the explosion itself. "That building was cut up by that blast pressure—there was nothing left."

An ATM video camera had picked up a partial image of a yellow Ryder rental truck parked in front of the building. Later, an FBI agent found a charred, misshapen portion of a truck axle two blocks away from the thirty-foot-wide, eight-foot-deep bomb crater.

"One axle was one block one way, the other axle was one block the other way. That was the positive blast which cut through the building so powerfully there was very little damage when the blast came back."

"Came back?"

The blast "comes back" with the negative pressure. The negative blast pressure is the vacuum created when the initial blast pushes everything, even the air, out, leaving a dangerous emptiness behind. "A block out there was a one-story building—the blast came in, but the front side of this raised the roof up. Right then the negative blast pressure took over, the vacuum so to speak, and instead of blowing this wall in, it sucked the wall out, sucked everything in the building out onto the ground toward the blast. That's negative blast pressure."

"Blasts don't work the same way as a bullet's trajectory. If I can find a piece of evidence directly across the street from the blast I might think it got blown directly from the blast point." But that's not necessarily so. "That thing could have gone all the way around the block and come back," because of negative and positive blast pressure. The *Journal Record*'s Building directly across the street was so big, he explained, that it actually funnelled the blast so that some evidence was flown out and half way around the block by the positive blast and then sucked back by the negative blast, so it completed a circuit of the block.

I asked Potter about the connection between Oklahoma City and the Unabomber.

"Yeah," said Potter, "within a week UNABOM hit in Sacramento so they theorize that everyone's attention went to that and he became jealous."

"He hit after the World Trade Center attack as well," I said.

"I think what happens is that deep down inside he wants the attention and so if anything takes the attention away from him, he has to do something to draw the limelight back to himself."

Potter feels that Americans are too cavalier about taking precautions: "In European countries they do far more searches and checkpoints. You leave a bag for over a half a second and somebody's onto it. European countries have gone through these terrorist-type situations for years. The US has been slow—we're very reactive as opposed to proactive.

"The New York Trade Center bombing put us on alert for the first time: We've never had a bombing that was of the same caliber. Up to that point the truck was the transporter of the bomb, the New York Trade Center changed it so the vehicle *was* the bomb."

I asked about UNABOM's construction of his bombs. "Anything unusual spring to your mind?"

"His end caps were built differently. Most people would go to a warehouse or Ace Hardware and get a pipe nipple and a couple of tap-ins. UNABOM would start with a piece of pipe and then he would build the caps. His caps were handmade, drilled, and pinned."

I wanted to know what kind of emotions EOD guys felt in a bomb situation.

"A lot of it is based on how much training you have or how confident you are with your training," he told me. "There's always apprehension. Your safety is on your mind. You *try* to keep that on your mind, though most of our calls turn out to be a package somebody lost. We still go through every step as if it were a real device."

Much of their squad's training is done by the FBI and the military. And so one comfort is that if a bomb squad gets "into a situation that was over your head, it's easy to call for help. You can call military—87th EOD.

"When I was a patrolman I originally signed up for" the bomb squad "and then saw the movie *Juggernaut* [about bombs on an ocean liner]. It scared the hell out of me and I took my name off the list. I finally got over that. When I got close to becoming a sergeant in charge of EOD I purposely watched *Juggernaut* again."

"It's a scary movie."

It is to a bomb technician.

Potter particularly admires Israeli bomb units. But points out that even they have been stymied lately, not by technology but by suicide bombers. "They don't know what to do with these guys."

THE INVESTIGATION

In the United States he tells me "85 percent of the devices we run into are pipe bombs. The gangs are starting to get into pipe bombs, so they're using them as grenades basically."

"What about the nested three-pipe bomb that UNABOM mailed to Sacramento?"

"It increases the frag. The more you confine the blast the more power or energy you're going to eventually develop. The blast itself goes out 360 degrees, so if one part of the pipe is weaker then that's the area that will go.... Usually pipe ends are the weakest area because they're not one solid core."

"Bombing," he explains, is "the safest way to do somebody in—to a certain point. Devices don't disappear. There's a lot of evidence left over. But the Unabomber was very, very careful. He made his own devices from scratch, but there's a lot of clues in there—the fact that he might have licked the stamps, the DNA testing."

"Why do you think he camouflaged his bombs to look like something else?" I asked.

"UNABOM was meticulous. If you build a bomb into something that looks like it belongs where it's at, there's less chance it'll be discovered until the person you want to discover it will be there," especially if it has the victim's name on it.

"Do you think there could be bombs UNABOM planted that no one ever connected him with?"

"Only in the beginning, before he became who he was." In the beginning "it could be anybody's guess. He's experimenting. He's building things. His devices went from very, very simple to more complex as he refined the whole system. He may have tried a lot of different techniques" early on.

As I watched Potter leave to return to his patrol car, I recalled the bomb expert down south who'd gotten sloppy. He came upon an assortment of eight pipe bombs laid out in the grass and began to pick them up one by one. One through seven were safe and he began to rush, his niece's birthday party in the back of his mind. But the last pipe bomb blew up in his face and killed him. Its trigger had been set to explode when the device was moved.

Outside the street was quiet. Another light-rail car sped by; evening and its gunmetal gray fog arrived. Somewhere out there the Unabomber was thinking, perhaps constructing his most powerful bomb yet.

CHAPTER 18
Ishmael in the Wild of Parma

T*he moral code of our society is so demanding that no one can think, feel and act in a completely moral way. For example, we are not supposed to hate anyone, yet almost everyone hates somebody at some time or other, whether he admits it to himself or not.*

—UNABOMBER MANIFESTO

THE HERMIT HIKED UP THE SLOPES of Mount Baldy. Below, the world lay simple, uncomplicated as his philosophy. He turned his gaze to the sky, and a frown wrinkled his brow. Above, he could feel the atmosphere coming apart, great rents in the delicate, eggshell-thin ozone layer that kept the forests alive. Some twelve to thirty miles up, a hole over Antarctica the size of the United States let invisible high-energy solar radiation, ultraviolet light, stream through, causing skin cancer and cataracts. More importantly, he thought, it played havoc with the genetic structure of the plants and trees all around him.

Though some doubted it existed, the Recluse feared the global warming of the earth. The 1980s had so far included six of the hottest years on record, and the staggering possibility that the temperature could climb nine degrees in the next fifty years shook him.

Man-made heat was the culprit, he thought. The burning of fossil fuels, petroleum, wood, coal, natural gas, the fierce inferno of the burning Amazon tropical rain forest—all, as they burned, emitted the carbon dioxide, which was floating up into the ozone layer. There, along with the methane, sulfur dioxide, nitrogen dioxide, lead, and toxic chemicals that flew upward in a never-ending stream, it blocked the escape of heat back into space and overheated the globe enough to melt the polar icecaps.

At least, he thought, the use of aerosol propellants, chlorofluorocarbons (CFCs), had been banned through the Clean Air Act of 1970 and 1978. But that was only in this country. As for the Recluse, he did his part, for he genuinely believed in protecting his wilderness; he used no electricity, drove no car, and used only a wood fire or a wood stove when he baked bread.

In 1982, November 17, the Hermit wrote in a letter of the "...partial destruction of the ozone layer in the atmosphere, which is caused by releases of fluorocarbons..." and five years later, "They predict that in the coming years there will be increasing more drought... because of the greenhouse effect."

When twenty million Americans had turned out on the first Earth Day, April 22, 1970, the Hermit took note. There were "wilderness fundamentalists" and "purist environmentalists" who answered this call to save Mother Earth and, in turn, mankind. Radical environmental groups such as Earth First! believed that in defense of mother earth no compromise must be made.

"Too often," wrote Dave Forman, a founder of Earth First!, "philosophies are rendered impotent by their inability to act without analyzing everything to an absurd detail. To act, to trust your instincts, to go with the flow of natural forces, is an underlying philosophy. Talk is cheap. Action is dear."

Mike Roselle, another Earth First! leader, said, "When television brought Vietnam into America's living rooms, it made the horror of war more real to the people at home; if those same people could see what the oil drillers, loggers, miners, and road builders were doing to America's wilderness, maybe it would create the same sort of outrage."

George Alexander became the first seriously injured victim of tree spiking, a dangerous practice used by some extremists. Tree spiking involved intentionally driving long nails into trees so that when lumberjacks cut into them it ruined their chain saws. As Alexander toiled on the ground floor of the Cloverdale lumber mill, working one of his nine- to twelve-hour shifts, his station lay not three feet away from the machinery that dragged enormous logs into the saws. The saws, fifty-two-foot-long strips of tempered steel with footwide teeth, spun nine thousand revolutions a minute around a pair of huge metal cylinders.

The redwood that roared down the metal, chain-driven conveyor roller that morning had been spiked at its core after it was felled. At 7:30 AM, the blade came to an eleven-inch nail sunk into the butt end of the log and met it head-on. The saw exploded off the cylinders in a cloud of smoke and wood chips, and a twenty-foot piece of razor-sharp metal blade twisted in the air like a snake. That blade coiled around Alexander like a metal cocoon, smashing out all his upper teeth and severing his jugular vein. In a frenzy, welders worked to snip the steel carcass from his badly injured and bleeding body.

Reportedly, fringe elements in the environmental movement were deliberately spiking trees in the hope of causing just such accidents, to drive the lumber companies out of the old-wood forests. Later, the FBI would claim that they suspected the Unabomber was following a "hit list" that Earth First! had developed of enemies of the environment. Then they would say that one November the Unabomber had attended a meeting, under his

real name, of ranking members of the group in Montana. No
proof of this has yet surfaced. Judi Bari, a leader of Earth First!,
called the claim "outrageous B.S. We've all checked with each
other and other groups and no one ever heard of this guy. He's
not our style."

Unlike his brother David, the Hermit's environmentalism did
not move him to forswear meat or violence against animals. The
Hermit had become a skillful hunter, bagging porcupines and
snowshoe hares with his .22-caliber rifle during the night. It provided the only meat he would have during the winter. He'd
changed so much from childhood. Back then he'd never have
harmed a little animal. The sight of them hurt or caged broke his
heart and drove him to care for them. Once, when he was about
ten, his dad trapped a shrew and called for the children to come
and see it. When the Hermit saw the confined animal, he cried,
"Let it go! Let it go!" His startled father handed the shrew to his
son and told him to let it run free.

Another time he'd found an injured rabbit and, in spite of his
aversion to hospitals and doctors of any kind, he implored his

The Lincoln Library.

father to take it to an animal hospital. When his dad saw his son's "violent reaction" to a rabbit he'd killed during a hunting excursion, he gave up hunting altogether. His brother often recalled him as a "young boy crying over a rabbit." David knew that his older brother had a conscience and was capable of human sympathy, "but," he said, "you had a sense that these capabilities were not integrated into a whole personality." The family saw the isolated man as unhappy and moody, a figure of "strange contradictions."

The Hermit had discussed Thoreau and his essay on civil disobedience, a deliberate act of public lawbreaking. He spoke of Immanuel Kant in college in all-night "bull sessions," and owned a two-volume set of *Les Misérables*. Possibly, he pictured himself as Jean Valjean, Hugo's heroic former convict who struggles to escape his past and reaffirm his humanity. But of course he'd read Dostoyevsky's *Notes from the Underground* and should have recognized himself in it most fully.

Dostoyevsky's antihero lived in a dismal basement room, his underground, and was, as A.D.P. Briggs described him, a man "incapable of living anything like a normal life because of [his] inability to establish conventional relationships with anyone, male or female... [in him] love has turned into malevolence... gentleness into violence, sociability into reclusiveness."

Notes attacked rationalism and the premise that science and reason held the keys to prosperity and human happiness. These ideas, Dostoyevsky implied, "would lead inevitably to a totalitarian society in which rules for human behavior were worked out according to scientific formulae and imposed upon the society for its own good."

"I just crouch here in this den of mine," said the underground man, "and worry myself with the irritating, the useless, reflections that, after all, a man of parts cannot become anything; for only a fool does that.... Of course I hated to despise my colleagues. Yet somehow, also, I was afraid of them, and at times felt them to be my superiors."

Before the cabin by Poorman's Creek, the Hermit had another "underground" as a child—the attic-like room at his home. "It's his escape hatch, you know," his mom said. "He has everything he wants up there—his books... and whatever else he wants." When company called, he hid there. Noise bothered him, too, and his father gave up watching the nightly television news when his son visited from college because the sound irritated him. "When you live with someone who's unusual," his brother said, "there are certain things you can't do without creating further upset."

When the Hermit as a young man closed himself off, it was a process physically discernible—he'd stare silently at the ground and, as his brother frequently noted, "a kind of veil would come down across his face." As far as the family could tell the spells of withdrawal came upon the man for no particular reason and at no particular time, but they came with greater regularity and increasing power.

The first time the Hermit's parents came to visit his new cabin, they saw the Recluse at the bend in the road before the cabin. He held up his hand as if to say "Hi." But he then looked away, his eyes lost on the distant horizon. The now-familiar, almost palpable veil had dropped down over his face. He'd known they were coming, but, all the same, instead of speaking to them or bringing them up to the cabin, headed off in the direction of the sawmill and soon vanished in a cloud of dust.

Bewildered, his parents returned to their younger son's apartment, who at the time was living relatively nearby. There, they found the Hermit seated on a couch. He still wore the veil, and appeared unable to speak. His mother sat down next to him and began to stroke his hair. "What's wrong?" she said soothingly.

"Talk to us. Let us know what's going on." He said nothing, and unmoving, remained on that sofa until night fell. Next morning, though, he was more sociable than they'd seen him in some time. "He was cheerful and convivial," recalled the brother. As if nothing had happened the Recluse spun delightful tales of Lincoln, Montana, history, and myths of his Baldy Mountain for them.

"I ponder endlessly over it," recalled his mother. "What could I have done to keep him out of the wilderness? What could I have done to give him a happier life? And yet there were so many happy, wonderful times with the family. I just don't, I just don't know." She remembered the family's musical evenings when the two boys and their father would play Vivaldi and Gabrielli on trumpet and piano for her, and her eldest son would write music compositions and study music theory. From without, it appeared as a happy family and in reality might have been. But to the isolated man, a gloom prevailed as dark as the rushing, blackening river.

CHAPTER 19
On the Move Again

D rugs that affect the mind are only one example of the new methods of controlling human behavior that modern society is developing.

—UNABOMBER MANIFESTO

PROFESSOR JAMES VERNON MCCONNELL, author of a widely used college text, *Understanding Human Behavior,* one of the top five best-selling books in its field, and a specialist in theories of human controllability and modification, had taught at the University of Michigan while the Professor studied there to earn his doctorate, and was now professor of behavioral psychology at Michigan. He routinely provided his students with free copies of his popular text and insisted they call him Jim. McConnell, had recently been featured in a *New York Times* article detailing his significant advances in learning and memory transfer in invertebrates. On the six-year anniversary of the bombing of Flight No. 444, November 15, 1985, he received a request to review a scholarly manuscript contained in a package from one Ralph C. Kloppenburg.

"Dear Dr. McConnell: I am a doctoral candidate in history at the University of Utah," the letter attached to the parcel began.

"My field of interest is the History of Science, and I am writing my dissertation on the development of the Behavioral Sciences during the 20th century.

"I am attempting to analyse the factors in society at large that tend to promote vigorous development in a given area of science, and especially I am attempting to shed light on the way in which progress in a particular field of research influences public attitudes toward that field in such a manner as to further accelerate its development, as through research grants."

There was no return address, though the postmark read "Salt Lake City." The one page note said, "I'd like you to read this book. Everyone in your position should read this book." Thus, when the book-sized package arrived at McConnell's home, 2900 East Delhi Road in Ann Arbor, his assistant, Nick Suino, opened it for him.

Ammonium nitrate (fertilizer), which explodes at up to 1,400 feet per second, is 60 percent nitro. When mixed with aluminum it makes a devastating bomb. The Professor had made certain that the aluminum flakes he used were free from oxide, keeping the copper content low. As for aluminum tubing, it burns almost as fiercely as finely ground magnesium, which can ignite as low as 900 degrees and cannot be extinguished with water.

Knowing the power of his materials the Professor had worn goggles and gloves as a precaution as he toiled.

A ten-and-one-quarter-inch length of one-inch galvanized steel pipe, sealed on either end with two plugs fabricated from steel bar stock and secured by two steel pins with epoxy and shim material, was concealed inside a hollowed-out ream of paper. Once more the bomber was making his infernal devices appear to be something else.

As if never satisfied (he continually oversoldered), the bomber reinforced each end with short metal sleeves made from a separate piece of pipe with an outer diameter of one-and-five-six-teenth inches. His fusing system was powered by four D-cell and six AAA-cell batteries arranged in a pair of independent circuits, each wired to a spring-loaded triggering switch mechanism linked to a single initiator within the pipe.

When Nick Suino undid one end of the package, tension was relieved on the switch. The package initially seemed to bulge and expand in his hands, then an explosion propelled shrapnel into his arms and upper body, and powder burns seared his legs and the left side of his body. A piece of the pipe punched a six-inch hole in the kitchen cabinet. As for McConnell, a full eight feet away, his hearing was permanently affected, a tragedy for such a great music aficionado. "Who could hate me this much to send me a bomb?" he said to the end. His assistant, Suino, eventually recovered.

The following components were recovered from the blast scene by the FBI and ATF. FBI Special Agent Terry Turchie, who would be the heart and spirit of the investigation, again dutifully listed the remnants as if the recitation might hold the magical qualities of a chant that would lead them to the truth.

- Remnants of 1" galvanized steel pipe
- $^3/_4$" diameter metal end plugs (Letters "FC" stamped into end of one plug)
- $^5/_{16}$" and $^5/_{32}$" diameter securing pins, tick marks present on securing pins
- $^{15}/_{16}$" diameter metal sleeve
- Metal bands
- Four D-cell batteries
- Six AAA-cell batteries
- Solder
- Remnants of Douglas fir wood
- Brown insulated duplex stranded wire
- Red insulated stranded wire
- Single strand steel wire
- $^1/_2$" filament tape
- $^3/_4$" black friction tape
- $^3/_4$" black plastic tape
- $^3/_4$" masking tape
- Epoxy
- 0.060" sheet steel
- Brass and wood screws
- Nail
- Wire staples
- Red paint

- Lead split shot
- Black plastic binder
- Brown paper
- "Of the People By the People For the People" $.22 US postage stamps
- "America's Light Fueled by Truth and Reason" $1 US postage stamps
- Red, white, and blue mailing label

McConnell's mention in *The New York Times* and his fame as an author might not have been the only things to attract the attention of the Professor to him. He'd appeared on the "Steve Allen" television show with some flatworms he'd experimented with. First, McConnell had trained some worms (using alternating light and shock to produce a conditioned reflex) to work through a maze. Then he had ground them and fed them to a second set of worms who'd never been in the maze. Once they'd consumed the worms, the new flatworms were able to navigate the labyrinth successfully. He did the same with worms cut in half. The tail-end grew a head, and the head-end grew a tail. The new worms both remembered what the original worm had been taught. McConnell had once suggested that people might be able to learn calculus by taking a pill or master any other skill in the same way. McConnell's name had also been prominent in *People* magazine in a feature that had spoken of his royalties; his Mercedes; his greenhouse, wine cellar, and record collection; and his opulent home.

The Professor was probably drawn to McConnell because of his own definite ideas on the dangers of the behaviorist's research. "As this behavioral engineering grows more and more extensive and effective," he wrote, "people would become, to all intents and purposes, mere robots, designed and built to serve specific purposes, like automobiles or adding machines....

"Each baby when it is born will have its mind adjusted by scientists anxious to be useful to the community... it's disagreeable to admit the extent to which we've been influenced by all that brainwashing—attitudes to which we are constantly exposed in school, in books, in the mass communication media, etc."

Elsewhere the Professor wrote: "A growing number of educators want to take over from the parents the task of molding the personality of the child and superintending his emotional development.... Sex 'education' properly should be called sex indoctrination, because sex 'education' courses usually seek not merely to provide students with bald facts, but also to influence the students' attitudes toward sex.... The issue is whether parents have a right to try to guide their own children's sexual attitudes or whether these attitudes are going to be engineered on a mass basis by educational psychologists."

OF COURSE DRUGS TO ALTER THE MIND were hardly a brand new invention. The Hermit took some himself, daily usually with meals. He occasionally increased the dose, giving himself an extra 50 milligrams once every three days. Sometimes he went even further, but the maximum he could take was 400 milligrams in daily doses. A bottle of this medication was later found in his cabin. It did serve temporarily to combat his depression and anxiety. But there were side effects. Vivid images and dreams haunted and shook him, enough to cause him to describe one to his brother.

In the grip of a nightmare, after taking his medication, the Professor tossed in his bed. In his dream he saw himself home again one winter. Three members of a cult, who had come to "tighten their control" over his brother, invaded the family house. The Professor fought valiantly for David and quickly dispatched the first two. As they lay dead, he "tore to pieces" the last cultist with his bare hands. But the tension did not let up even then. All the family dreaded the imminent appearance of the sect's leader.

Soon the door swung open and, as the Professor later described him, a "short, portly, middle-aged man with a pleasant demeanor" entered. He discerned something "sinister" about the stranger, who soon introduced himself as "Lord Daddy Lombrosis." He bore a remarkable resemblance to the Professor's father.

Then, before the Professor's eyes, the stranger altered and his shape changed until he'd become a tall, handsome figure with "a paternal, dignified" appearance. "I felt awed by him and thought, 'This is God!'" the Professor later wrote in a 1985 ten-page letter to David. "Yet in my heart I defied him."

Through "some sort of deception" the leader tried to gain psychological control over them. "Gradually, the room became dark," recalled the Professor, "and his face turned into a television screen; the pupils of his eyes became two black dots that flew around on the television screen in symmetrical patterns.

"But still I defied him and stood between him and you. The room became light again, the television vanished, and the man reappeared. As he walked out of the house becoming invisible and leaving only footprints in the snow," a pall fell over the family.

A terrible fear, an overwhelming panic, raced through the scholar's heart. "I knew that ALL IN THAT HOUSE WERE TO BE LEFT WITHOUT HOPE," he said. The Professor raced through the snow after the handsome figure, "begging him not to leave like this, not to leave my little brother without hope."

The Professor awoke in a sweat, eyes wide and gripped by a sense of foreboding. It was then he realized that "Lord Daddy Lombrosis stood for the Technological Society itself."

A tricyclic antidepressant, trazodone inhibits the re-uptake of serotonin to the brain. Doctors had been warned against prescribing trazodone (aka Desyrel or *triazolopyridine*) to anyone suffering from epilepsy, psychosis, or suicidal tendencies. Trazodone interacted badly with alcohol and other CNS depressants. It has been known to cause heart problems such as the Hermit later came to suffer or claimed to suffer, problems that prevented trips to see his friend, Sanchez. In addition, a trazodone-induced mania has been documented. Trazodone HCl causes provocative behavior and a considerable loss of impulse control—all actions that the Recluse's family was well aware he demonstrated.

The Hermit's anger, threats, and hostility, his palpable dreams and vivid nightmares, nightmares so real that he actually felt he was experiencing real life, could be explained by a reaction to this drug. Hallucinations, the flight of ideas, and psychosis walked hand in hand with trazodone, which exacerbates any tendencies already present and perpetuates any mania. One odd side effect was priapism, a permanent or prolonged and sometimes painful erection, that must have been disconcerting to the shy woodsman.

CHAPTER 20

Profiles

THESE DAYS THE FBI AND HOLLYWOOD set enormous stock in the delicate art of psychological profiling of serial killers. This wasn't always the case: Not until the profilers proved themselves with some dramatic successes did the technique become popular. The examples of George Metesky and Dr. James Brussel was one of these early successes and shows the way profiling is meant to work.

In the fifties, from 1950 until 1957, a reign of fear gripped New York. "The Mad Bomber" terrorized the city, secreting homemade bombs in much-frequented locations such as Penn Station and Radio City Music Hall. He rocked the Empire State Building and Macy's, convulsed the Fifth Avenue Public Library, and impacted Grand Central Station. His earliest bombing was of the Consolidated Edison Power Company. This proved to be the key to the mystery.

On December 2, 1956, he bombed the Brooklyn Paramount

Theatre; the blast injured seven people. In all, the Mad Bomber left fifty-four infernal devices in public places. Thirty-seven actually exploded and although twenty-two people had been maimed, remarkably no one had yet been killed. But it was only a matter of time before the city's worst fears were realized. Authorities had no idea, in those more innocent days before serial killers, what could possibly be motivating this madman.

As the devices became increasingly more sophisticated, assaulting the city with ever more powerful detonations and in such public locations, the climate of fear became paralyzing. Surely, the bomber was mad, so senseless, so random was the blitz. Did a rationale exist behind the letters and carnage, one that the investigators had just not as yet divined? Dr. Brussel, who more accurately might be described as an early day psycholinguistic analysist, later wrote about the investigation in *Casebook of a Crime Psychiatrist*. He believed there was a motive.

At his Greenwich Village office he wondered, like most of New York, "Who was FP?" This was the bomber's signature in his letters railing against Con Ed. Brussel had reached some conclusions on the matter which he shared with the investigators. Brussels contended that the long-sought bomber was paranoid, narcissistic, and most likely an Eastern immigrant in his forties who lived with his mother. Furthermore, the doctor conjectured, the "Mad Bomber" would be unmarried and probably never have had sex. "When you find him," Brussel predicted, "chances are he'll be wearing a double-breasted suit. Buttoned."

Because the bomber's communications singled out the Consolidated Edison Power Company as instrumental in his contracting tuberculosis, detectives suspected the maniac had planted his first device, a crude pipe bomb that had been a dud, there in

THE INVESTIGATION

1940. The terrorist block-printed a letter to the NYC police head-quarters which read in part:

> Later I will bring the Con Edison to justice—they will pay
> for their dastardly deeds.
>   F.P.

In another letter to the *New York Herald Tribune* the bomber said:

> "I merely seek justice."

A GRUELING SEARCH THROUGH CON ED'S FILES for disability claims eventually unearthed George Metesky, a fifty-three-year-old Waterbury, Connecticut, toolmaker and bachelor who resided with his mother. Metesky had been a generator wiper at Hell Gate Plant, a precursor of Con Ed, when he was injured in 1931. Detectives discovered letters Metesky had written the power company containing the same phrases the "Mad Bomber" used in his communications with the press. After they'd arrested him on January 22, 1957, four detectives led the suspect past the press. A broad, crooked grin crossed Metesky's face; his pale-blue eyes danced behind rimless glasses. Obviously, he enjoyed his fame. As predicted by Dr. Brussel, Metesky wore a light-colored hat, dark top coat, and double-breasted suit—buttoned.

The "Mad Bomber" had signed himself "FP" for Fair Play. The bomber the FBI wanted so desperately to capture signed himself "FC." Could this modern mad bomber be a student of past bombers? If so, just how much had he imitated? What could "FC" possibly mean to UNABOM? A religious fanatic saying "For Christ," "For Commonsense," "Fair Control?"

And like Metesky, UNABOM linked himself to each of his terrible machines with a fingerprint of personality—his intricate, almost loving construction of the infernal devices.

Law enforcement still likes to point with pride to the classic profiling done on Metesky. Dr. Brussel, a private psychiatrist, had been accurate down to the last detail, but it was his prediction that the suspect's double-breasted suit would be buttoned that is impressive.

The profilers have had some recent successes as well. Back in the early 1980s I saw the exceptional work done by Dr. Murray S. Miron of the Syracuse Research Institute on the San Francisco Zodiac case, a very early example of profiling. I studied some of the work he'd done on Son of Sam. I thought both hit the mark. In the case of David Berkowitz, New York's .44-caliber Killer (aka Son of Sam) his findings accurately predicted patterns that were useful in tracking a mad killer who sent letters to newspaper columnist Jimmy Breslin that were peppered with street names and neighbors from his daily life.

In recent years, however, just as profiling has become more prominent and popular, the profiles have had a tendency toward sameness—time and again one reads of a thirty-five-year-old white male, a white-collar worker, who is an unmarried loner. As profiling has become routine, no longer the work of creative geniuses, but a standard investigative tool, it has often seemed as if the profilers are studying other profilers as much or more intently than they analyze their prey. Within many investigative units, it almost seems as if deviations from stereotypes are met with scorn.

In all, there were five major UNABOM psychological profiles done. In the beginning the FBI's behavioral experts were in the midst of compiling the first criminal profile of a man they only

THE INVESTIGATION

suspected of being a serial bomber when the bombing of Flight No. 444 elevated the investigation to a "major case." "Now it's called UNABOM," they were informed by the intruder. "That's UN for University and A for Airlines."

From the beginning, the Unabomber was pigeonholed in the "quiet loner file." True but that was such an across-the-board cliche that it was hard to go wrong. "Quiet loner" to the profiler is a relative term. Married or at least divorced may have denigrated quiet loners. Nothing in the profile suggested the subject might be the quietest loner the FBI had ever pursued, a Hermit living on a mountain. The 1991 psychological profile compiled by the FBI envisioned him as a meticulous dresser and in all likelihood a compulsive maker of lists. The FBI pictured him as the kind who'd drive an older car, but would keep it not only well-maintained, but in perfect running order. In the end this was about as far off as one could go.

This profile was updated in 1993 at the time of the revitalization of the UTF in San Francisco when just about every aspect of the case was being updated. Taking into account the passage of years and any noted changes in the bomber's pattern, the new report suggested that the Unabomber probably worked at menial jobs and spent his formative years in the Chicago area since that was the site of the first four bombings.

Agents continued to scrutinize the names of more than eighty thousand former residents of Chicago. But they were also convinced he'd resided in Utah where two bombs were set and had moved to California. So far the serial bomber, cutting a swath of fire across America, had been behind detonations at universities in Illinois, Michigan, Tennessee, Utah, and California. Failed college students, along with disgruntled airline employees and odd ducks reported by co-workers and neighbors and family, were questioned by agents to no avail. Girlfriends turned in their boyfriends and wives their husbands.

Investigators thought they knew why UNABOM spent hours buffing and polishing his bomb material even in the realization that it would be vaporized in the fulmination. They conjectured that the elaborate refining, assembling, and re-assembling of his devices' wooden and metal components gave him some sort of bizarre sexual satisfaction. Director Sessions had lamented that his men "have been unable to establish any motive for the crimes," but a few experts in the private sector were working on a possible motive.

Bruce Hoffman, a terrorism specialist with Rand Corp., believed the attacks might not be acts of political terrorism, but instead the product of a deranged mind or individuals acting independently. "I just never knew what to make of these things [the UNABOM series of explosions] because no group ever took responsibility. It's just not clear what this is."

What this was, some worried, was a form of anti-Semitism. The speculation that the Unabomber might have anti-Semitic tendencies was based on the fact that some of his latest targets were Jewish, and some return addresses and some signatures used on letters had had Jewish-sounding names. Was this the long-sought motive?

In 1995 the physical profiling represented all that the agents knew of the Unabomber's appearance, which wasn't much. He was "a white male, about five-feet, ten-inches tall, 160 pounds, in his thirties or forties, with a ruddy complexion. He may have resided in the Midwest in the late 1970s and moved to Northern California in the early or mid-1980s."

THE INVESTIGATION

Added to the psychological profile was that "he is well educated [A previous FBI strategy had been to suggest that the bomber was uneducated in hopes that his vanity would be pricked and he would write to contradict them], familiar with universities and university faculties. He most likely has a background in metalwork or carpentry... possibly never married." The suggestion of a background in metal work or carpentry was not only wrong, but should have been obviously wrong. As intricate and ingenious as the bombs were, the crude craftsmanship, however painstaking, suggested no technical training in wood or metal work whatsoever.

At one point dozens of amateur profilers sketched out their own estimations of the Unabomber—a numerologist informed the FBI that the bomber had a secret code buried in his writings that revealed his true identity and another was certain that "he lives in Boston and drives a Volkswagen."

It has been said that Chris Ronay, longtime head of the FBI's elite explosives unit, knew more about the Unabomber than anyone else. He likened his experience to a "roller-coaster ride. Every once in a while, you get that thrill, then you go down that hill again." He was the first to have pieced together that they should be looking for a serial bomber. However, the aspects of the Unabomber psychological profiles I kept seeing remained all too familiar. The one constant that jumped out at me was the "quiet loner" image. Safe. As was the determination that the Unabomber was in his thirties or forties. Early psychological studies showed the years between eighteen and thirty-five to be the years of violent activity for most violent offenders. The profilers were studying profiles, not the bomber.

Late in the investigation, Special Agent Bill Tafoya out of the

San Francisco office floated a heretical profile, unburdened by the profiles.

The first point that Tafoya made was that the "bomber had an advanced degree in a 'hard science' such as engineering," directly contradicting the third FBI profile, which had stated that "any advanced training the Unabomber had was probably in one of the social sciences." As the brilliant profiler John Douglas wrote in his own book on the Unabomber in 1996, "Tafoya kept trying to get across his point that the UNABOM had to be someone not only from academia but with a hard science background. It seemed clear to him that the concepts the Unabomber was employing to develop his bombs came right out of the hard sciences."

Douglas himself made the shrewd, and as it would turn out, accurate suggestion that the bomber would be an obsessive diary keeper. When discovered, the bomber's diary would exceed twenty thousand pages, some in an elaborate numerical code. Even more important Tafoya also questioned whether the subject actually lived in the Bay Area. He suggested in fact that he might live somewhere considerably more remote.

Finally, Tafoya insisted the bomber was not in his thirties, the prime age for serial killers, but his fifties.

Most FBI officials reacted as organization men tend to react to heretics. They were "baffled and angered."

Tafoya was not believed.

PART THREE

THE UNABOMBER
Sacramento, California / The Mid-Eighties

CHAPTER 21
The Trips

F or primitive societies the natural world (which usually changes only slowly) provided a stable framework and therefore a sense of security.... Modern society changes very rapidly owing to technological change. Thus there is no stable framework.

—UNABOMBER MANIFESTO

GEORGE BLOWARS FOLLOWED HIS DOGS, Blue, Shotzi, and Joe, a quarter-mile up Canyon Creek from Gehring's Lumber Company, then glanced back toward his own home. There he saw a herd of nine elk cropping at the hay he'd laid out on the snow-covered ground. George couldn't help but recall the identical scene last spring with what appeared to be the same elk, but they'd nibbled among deep grass and clover then. What a magnificent country! he thought, and continued on.

He soon reached the faded, reddish-colored shack. He stopped, his breath frosty in the air, and studied his friend's home. It had no eaves. A single door, tightly shut, peered up-canyon. A single window looked out on the trailside of the cabin and reached to where the roof and north wall joined. A single chimney at the eastern peak of the roof overlooked a garden area.

Nearby was the root cellar where parsnips grew. It had been

constructed by the Hermit sometime in the mid eighties, about the time he was beginning to cultivate a beard. Visible from the front door, the cellar was located just across a small running creek about one-hundred-plus feet from the shack, cut neatly into the hillside, and covered over with sod. Two doors, like garage doors, barred the opening. Other underground construction had gone on—so the rumors went—and George guessed there was a cellar under the cabin. No one really knew. To the east stood the cabin of the Hermit's hunting buddy, Williams. There, a white trail of smoke curled upward. The lack of any smoke from the Hermit's crude pipe chimney told him that his friend was not home. The odd times the Recluse went wandering had not escaped George. Possibly, the man had hiked up into the desolate hills or left Lincoln entirely. All he knew was that the Hermit hadn't left his bike at their office this time. Nor had George seen him on the road. All-in-all, it was a winter like all the others that blanketed Lincoln in flurry after flurry and covered over your tracks.

AS EARLY AS 9:00 AM, a Rimrock Continental Stages bus chugged out of the Trailways depot in Helena and plunged south toward Butte. Though memories can be tricky, much later ticket agents and bus drivers vaguely recalled the Hermit, an admittedly unusual character, riding this route over the years. One driver for Rimrock Continental recollected an unusual, lanky man riding with him to Butte several times. At Butte there is a Greyhound station, a transfer point. A Butte Greyhound agent specifically remembers an unkempt mountain man, much like the Recluse, buying tickets on over a dozen different occasions between 1990 and 1995. Another bus line employee said that same man "hops on a bus and goes and visits a lot more than anyone thought." One Greyhound bus driver's fiancée thought she'd seen a "very geeky-looking man," a kind of "transient" who should "have been riding a freight, not a Greyhound," as many as fifteen times over a five-year period. Other ticket sellers along the way to Missoula or to Idaho Falls dimly remembered such a striking individual... but then memories *can* be tricky.

Since the Hermit disappeared for long stretches at a time, it is possible that he was the man huddled on the Rimrock bus as it hurtled south from Helena on Interstate 25 past Unionville, Clancy, Alhambra, Corbin, and Deerlodge. He whizzed past Basin and into Butte, a switch point, then dropped down further into Idaho, still clinging to the interstate. Through Dillon, past the Clark County Reservoir, down along Garfield Mountain and through Monida Pass, then Roberts further on and into Idaho Falls.

At Idaho Falls, to continue further, he transferred to a Greyhound bus for the trek to Salt Lake City. He'd gone 276 miles from Helena in a little over five hours, but many hours lay ahead. For more than a day this lonely man, a man who kept his own company and counsel, steeped in woodsmoke and isolation, would be packed in with a hoard of strangers and assailed by gas fumes, pitted roads, crying babies, and talking travelers. How he must have squirmed in the midst of unwanted company as towns and desert crawled by and the bus slowed at stop after stop.

Outside the light lowered, the sky darkened, and lights inside the bus leaped on as people read or played cards. Billboards and other vehicles, blaring trucks and trailers, roared by. And at each stop, he remained rooted in his seat, shoulders tense, with his backpack balanced on his knees. The trip from Helena to Great Falls to Salt Lake and ultimately San Francisco or Sacramento would take twenty-five-and-a-half hours.

Once, the Hermit actually made a friend on the bus. The man was drunk and telling his tale of sadness in a loud voice. As the Hermit told the story later, he said to the stranger, "Let's go in the back seat where nobody's around. We won't disturb anybody, and you can tell me your story." In the back, the drunken man sobbed that he had no one in the world but a daughter who'd left some money for him in the post office in Missoula.

As the bus rolled on, the Hermit, naturally touched by a story so similar to his own, spoke of his own lonely life. Then he dug deep into his own meager reserves and pressed a "few dollars" into the drunk's hand.

ALONG A TRAIL OF FIRE, the FBI moved its agents silently as falling snow. They were under great pressure to solve the unsolvable, but suspected the stress must be equally telling on the bomber. "I would say the pressure is certainly building up," said veteran investigator Lou Bertram when the case had dragged on seventeen years. "What he's got on his soul is more than the average person could live with."

UNABOM *might* be coming apart psychologically, but the FBI knew enough from experience to realize that their man would be inspired to greater boldness. If he followed the familiar pattern of serial killers (which they were coming to view him as, although he had yet to claim a life), then the future was predictable. More and more outrageous acts on his part would be required to gain attention. With each new boldness, his complacency and confidence would increase. Emotionally detached, the bomber would begin to exhibit more and more obsessive-compulsive behavior patterns. He loved power more than his criminal acts, and this might prove to be his undoing. But, obviously, he possessed a great knowledge of law enforcement and science and, as more than one FBI agent commented, "had examined and studied every bomb in history." He would not stop of his own accord—he enjoyed the game. He relished outwitting the government. And he relished reigning vengeance and disaster upon his enemies.

Expert FBI profiler John Douglas became convinced that the

Unabomber would be on the scene for some of his explosions. "He would have to be standing there," said Douglas, "and he would have tried to inject himself into the investigations." For his most fiendish device to date, UNABOM did just that. Moving gingerly among the Christmas shoppers in Sacramento, he checked into a small hotel, then went out to reconnoiter the area. He paused at an open parking lot. A stiff wind cut across the pavement and moved among the empty Dumpsters, making their lids rattle like snakes.

CHAPTER 22
Hugh Campbell Scrutton

W*e are going to argue that industrial-technological society cannot be reformed in such a way as to prevent it from progressively narrowing the sphere of human freedom.*

—UNABOMBER MANIFESTO

FOR A TIME HUGH CAMPBELL SCRUTTON had lived in Plains, Montana. If you traveled through Lincoln on Highway 200 west to Missoula, then sightly north, but still holding west, you would come to Plains at an elevation of over two thousand feet in the midst of the National Forest. Scrutton had been there helping his close friend, John Lawyer, start his nursery.

Scrutton had lived in Berkeley attending the University of California as a visiting summer student for several summers around the time of the Professor's tenure there. Scrutton had taken math classes. After graduating from UC Davis, Scrutton had opened RenTech Computer Rental at 1537 Howe Avenue in Sacramento. His family was deeply involved in the business.

On December 11, 1985, only two weeks before Christmas, Scrutton got up from his desk and made ready for a lunchtime appointment. Most often, though, he took lunch at no particular time. He opened the rear door of his store and looked out upon a windswept parking lot in the strip mall and pulled up his collar. Near a Dumpster he saw a block of wood about four inches high and a foot long. There were sharp nails protruding from the block, a road hazard or, even worse, a real danger to the trash men or the transient who occasionally came by to pick through the Dumpsters. He bent over to move it. It was heavy. Lead weights had been inserted in the lower two inches of the block.

The device the bomber had constructed this time was his most powerful to date, correcting several of his mistakes that had caused such disappointment in the past. This time, he'd used potassium chloride, potassium sulfate, ammonium nitrate, and aluminum powder and packed it into three pipes of equal length, ten inches, but of slightly differing circumferences, nesting, one inside the other. Of course, he employed the familiar lamp cord and used batteries, with their jackets removed, four D-cells this time instead of C-batteries, and a 9-volt battery, and placed them all inside a carved wooden box.

The biggest change from his earlier devices was in the plugs capping the ends of the outermost pipe. Instead of wood, they were made of steel dowel. Handmade pins, five-sixteenths of an inch in diameter, were driven through the pipe, and steel dowels held the caps in place. The letters "FC" had been punched into or drilled through the one-inch-diameter cap in such a way as to survive detonation.

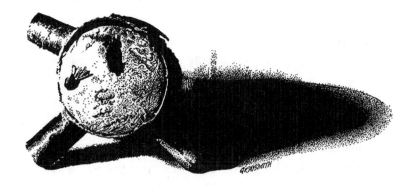

Scrutton bomb part.

This device was especially cruel—a back-up fail-safe system of wires and batteries, two independent systems, and a spring-loaded lever triggering system made sure any movement would explode the package. He'd also filled the device with nails, razor-sharp pieces of metal, and splinters. This bomb was meant to be lethal.

The roar of the explosion filled Scrutton's ears. The blast cut off most of his right hand and shot holes in his right lung and liver. The blast then snapped his right ankle in half. The same fragments penetrated his heart, exposing it completely. His employees saw Scrutton, still standing at the back door and facing them, stagger, then rock back on his feet, a dazed look spreading across his face. He seemed to be saying, "What happened?" and attempting to raise his arms in supplication. He gave a shout of "Oh, my God, help me!" then crumpled into a heap and collapsed on the pavement.

Employees from other businesses, hearing the explosion, raced out. A clerk at a nearby software store came on the run, as did his customer. Printed reports later said the customer was a former medic in Vietnam who began to administer CPR. This was untrue. Everyone knew it was too late; Scrutton was dead. Only a half hour after he'd touched the device, Scrutton was formally pronounced dead at the emergency room of the University of California at Davis Medical Center.

The Unabomber had so far struck nineteen people in eleven attacks over six states, and now he had taken one life.

Lieutenant Ray Biondi, a dark, intense man with a strong moral code, and Detective Bob Bell, youthful and eager in his first months in homicide, came from the homicide unit of the Sacramento sheriff's office. Biondi was his supervisor. They had reached the scene within "half an hour of the bomb going off," tearing down bright capitol streets decorated for Christmas.

"Looks like we may have a fatality," a dispatcher had told them on the phone. "He's been transported from the scene with a serious, serious injury." Bell commented on the high winds scattering the evidence, in this case a fine black powder. What the wind had not strewn, the blast had dispersed. Bell knew driving up that this was a "new kind of murder scene." He told me later, "We didn't know a serial bomber existed until that cold day in December."

He shivered against the chill, driving wind. "It was extremely exasperating," he said of the scattered evidence. The crime scene grew worse. "We found body parts of Hugh Scrutton on the roof," he told me later. "Tissue. Stuff like that. Obviously, this particular device was wrapped in some sort of paper sack because we had a little bit of paper underneath we found near the blast site. With this wind and everything kind of going away on us and not much we could do to stop it. That was just one of the considerations that we had."

The fire department and ambulance crews had rigid rules as to when they have to transport versus whenever they can leave someone on site. "A person has to be decapitated, has to be in rigor—certain factors which totally wipe out any possibility of that person surviving," Bell told me later. "When you have a device, when he's still warm, where this just happened within minutes—in spite of the fact that he has a gaping hole in his chest—they still have rigid rules by which they have to transport."

They secured the scene as best they could, then began to wonder if Scrutton could have been a specific target. "The bomb was placed at a spot where he regularly traveled, but Scrutton had no set routine and since that area was heavily visited, and the Dumpsters were routinely gone through by the occasional transient, virtually anyone could have detonated the booby-trapped block of wood at any time.

Scrutton bomb parts.

The twenty-mile-per-hour winds showed no sign of abating as Biondi, Bell, and reinforcements bagged every scrap of clothing, labeling each bag with the initials of the man who had recovered it. They retrieved every twisted, unworldly piece of metal and shattered wood component. On each bag they printed neatly: EVIDENCE AREA C, Grid No. 7, 14A-SF-106204. Then they began to collect and study the "abundant black foreign matter."

As always, the bomb and the box were filled with contradictions. The bomber was meticulous, highly inventive, even ingenious at times. He put enormous work and care into his devices, often taking them apart and reassembling them repeatedly (as the light feathery penciled numbers indicated). But for all that, he was a *careful* craftsman, not a *skilled* craftsman. The bombs were often overcomplicated and too much of their "genius" was of the "we can hold this together with wire and chewing gum" variety. The boxes were lovingly and obsessively finished, sanded, polished, and re-polished. Sometimes the results, as far as could be told from the remnants, may have appeared beautiful. Certainly the hollowed tube box he gave as a gift to Sanchez was beautiful. But in many ways he was not even a good carpenter—too many nails, imperfect right angles. Even in his favorite work, he was out of place.

The two men checked lists of every RenTech customer, transfer student at close-by California State University, airline reservations, and absentee ballots. Their searches would eventually take them to Salt Lake City and Texas, then to Colorado as they followed the slimmest of leads. Eventually, they would amass seventeen black looseleaf binders which they kept on the top bookshelf in the homicide unit in plain sight. It reminded them of the case they intended to solve—no matter what.

CHAPTER 23
The Secret Strategy

MURDER CHANGES EVERYTHING. Logically, perhaps, there should not be much difference between the way the FBI or a local police department treats a near miss, an attempted murder, and the way they treat a murderer who succeeds. A serial attempted murderer represents just as much of a threat to public safety as one who has succeeded. Several of the Unabomber's previous devices could easily have ended in the deaths of his victims—if the bomber had used multi-stranded wire instead of an old lamp cord in the trigger of his American Airlines Flight No. 444 device and if he had used a stronger containment vessel, one without a faulty end seal, then his victims would already number more than 100. A Boeing 727 carries as many as 189 passengers and crew.

But most police forces, perhaps fortunately, are motivated by passion and politics, the press and public opinion as much as by logic. And especially in law-abiding suburbs with low murder rates, such as Sacramento County, the cops are also driven by the primal imperative that all murders *will* be cleared and that an uncleared murder file is never closed.

And so for the FBI and the rest of the Unabomber Task Force, one thing that the death of Hugh Scrutton changed was that for the first time the Feds were forced to collaborate or at least appear to collaborate indefinitely with a local police force. Neither the FBI nor the other federal agencies involved hold direct jurisdiction for most murders, and until Scrutton's death was established to be more than a local phenomenon, the Unabomber team would be working, at least technically, at the sufferance of local authorities. And no matter what jurisdiction the Feds eventually acquired, Sacramento County's right to pursue the murder of one of its citizens would endure, at least technically.

As Detective Bell told me, "It was the first fatality" in the Unabomber case, "so in essence we held the only murder." The Feds "realized that it was going to be necessary to deal with us because we held the[ir] murder." Bell and his colleagues would stay on the case for more than ten years.

As with most local police forces, the Sacramento detectives would come to view the FBI's cooperation as grudging at best. Their resources, especially through the then still revered crime lab, gave the Feds leverage. They could require the locals to pass on all evidence and leads, but information was usually slow to come back the other way. One problem was the frequent turnover in the command of the Task Force. "Every time they had a new commander in charge of the UNABOM Task Force," recalls Bell, "he'd have a meeting of concerned federal agencies and invite the cops." At one point they were actually called down to San

THE INVESTIGATION

Francisco where the Task Force was headquartered, so the commander could proclaim "'Janet Reno has dictated that we work directly with you. She wants local agencies involvement.' And it sounded great.... You know, I thought, 'Well boy, that's terrific.' And that lasted until I got back and realized that they had several other meetings right after that and nobody bothered to tell us."

That first day at the crime scene, the agents seemed to be trying to avoid even informing the Sacramento cops that they were facing a serial bomber. "We didn't know a serial bomber existed," Bell told me, which was why at first the crime scene was so baffling. The best place to start any homicide investigation is with motive, but that seemed unreadable. Bell and Biondi quickly dismissed the idea that Scrutton was a deliberate target. Placed as it was out in the parking lot in full view of any observant passerby, "anyone could have picked up this device—disturbed it and caused it to go off." Scrutton did not have a well-established routine of, for instance, always coming out that back door at 12:05 to go to lunch. And even if he had, no one had seen the bomber, so the cops did not know how long the bomb "had been placed in this location before it was disturbed and detonated." Not only could any other employee have been the first to see the device but any of the homeless who come by and go through the Dumpsters "trying to look for garbage or anything like that could have pulled the device up and had it detonate on 'em."

It seemed a bit more plausible that the business, rather than Scrutton, was the target. Otherwise why "would you pick this particular business when you had six others that you could have gone to—all of them identical in the configuration of their back doors and the garbage cans? So what difference does it make?"

So their first approach was to "look at the business records to see what about their business" might have angered someone. Was the business being sued? Were they suing someone?

"None of that cropped up, of course. It was like a day and a half later the FBI finally told us." Offering little explanation, about noon of the second day the agents "asked if we had any initials on our device and we told 'em, 'Yeah, we do.'" The agents reviewed the crime scene debris gathered by the cops and then "the following evening we had a meeting... on the fourth floor where we met with the FBI, ATF, and postal inspectors and they sat down and told us it was a series.

"The agents explained that UNABOM series had been going on for a long time and that the bomber had tried to bring down an airliner." Beyond that the Feds had little to tell them. "We'd ask, 'Who are the targets?' 'What's the motive?'" and all the agents would say was 'We don't know.'"

In truth the agents had relatively little useful information even ten years into the bombings. The bomber's obsession with making or obtaining untraceable parts for his devices was paying off: So far the physical evidence left behind had been all but useless in narrowing either the profile or the search for a home base. And the bomber's bizarre choice of targets, which seemed both so personal and so random at the same time, was equally confusing. Seven years, ten bombs (apparently), and, as Bell remarked, still without a clue.

BUT THERE WAS ANOTHER, larger factor in the FBI's reticence: A strategic decision that controlled and, in the opinion of local cops like Bell and even some of the agents themselves, undermined the investigation until the mid nineties. The federal strategy was to keep the Unabomber a secret, or at least to severely control the information available about him. The reason Bell and Biondi did not know, at first, that there was a serial bomber working was that, practically speaking, no one knew, though the bomber had been at work at that point for almost a decade. There had been no really informative national alert to police forces and certainly not to the public.

This was not because of a fear of public panic. The federal position was that they should keep the Unabomber from knowing how much the investigators knew about him, or even that they knew the bomber existed. In this way, says Bell, the Feds argued that Unabomber would not be alerted to how readable his bombs were as the product of the same bomber. As long as the bomber did not know what the investigators knew, he would take no additional steps to conceal his "signature." The evidence would accumulate and, with the FBI's vast capacity for amassing data and sifting through thousands of potential suspects, eventually the overconfident bomber would be caught.

Bell says that when he and Biondi first grasped the FBI strategy he and his partner were extremely shocked. Our "foreheads hit the table," he told me. The FBI was seriously arguing "that if we release this information—if we even release that the series is going on—'He will then know that we know.'" Bell found this incomprehensible, since obviously the bomber already "knew that we knew." After all, the first question the agents had asked Bell was whether there were any initials on the bomb fragments. This guy wasn't simply leaving a "signature" inadvertently in the technology of his bombs: He was signing them for real and in indestructible metal. "It's like they didn't want the Unabomber to know we'd connected these cases and were working them as a series in spite of the fact that the Unabomber is doing everything in his power to tell investigators, and the world, 'I'm here.'"

In Bell's view, however the decision to maintain silence took away what the cops considered their most powerful weapon against any serial killer: public awareness. The Sacramento detectives had had experience with several serial killers over the years and they had learned that turning over a growing mound of evidence in a vacuum was not the best way to catch a serial murderer. A tip from a citizen linking a neighbor's eccentric behavior, a family member noting a brother or father's erratic actions with reports on the evening news was one of the more effective ways to close these cases.

One of the cops' first recommendations at their early strategy meetings with the Task Force was "a media blitz—release everything we can about this—'cause in our history of solving serial murders we had determined that the best thing to do was to work with the media." In fact Bell had become convinced that he should even give the press information investigators did not want made public. "Give 'em everything you got, tell 'em what you want to hold out. We've found most reporters to be honorable people who want to do the right thing. If you tell 'em you're going to screw up the investigation if you release certain information— this is why we want to keep it secret—they'll bend over backwards to help you out."

When the press believes the police are being straight with them, argues Bell, they can be very cooperative because they don't want "to burn that bridge. If we get to the point where we can't trust you and you can't trust us, then all we're going to be doing is lying to each other—then we're going nowhere. We've solved a lot of cases just working with the media."

THE INVESTIGATION

Bell's team had almost immediately "prepared a media release that we thought should go out," even suggesting that FC be released. The Task Force strongly objected, not only for fear of letting the bomber "know that they knew," but because of the danger of copycats. Bell and Biondi conceded that was a reasonable concern. But at least one FBI agent, bomb expert Chris Ronay, thought the Sacramento sheriff's investigators were right, even to the extent of releasing "FC," says Bell. "He's saying, 'I can tell this guy's bomb. Don't worry about copycats—I can handle it.' So all the more reason to put out this media blitz and try to get this going.

"The idea was to try and get this guy to explain why he was doing this. Just get a dialogue started. I thought that somehow, someone might put this together."

The Feds could not have been more opposed. At times secrecy seemed to be their greatest concern. Bell argued, for instance, that the bomber's typed letter to Professor James McConnell, the recipient of a bomb just prior to Scrutton, should be released, not only for content but to impress upon the public the terrorist's use of the old manual typewriter. They hoped this particular eccentricity might ring a bell with a witness. "The FBI was afraid if they talked about that, he'd get rid of that typewriter. I understand that, but the fact of the matter is—he don't care. He's continuing to use that typewriter and telling us he is. Let's tell the world he's not using a word processor here. He's not handwriting it."

At times the results of the federal obsession with secrecy were comic. At one point the Task Force leadership called "a hush-hush secret meeting" where agents and detectives "would meet and discuss how to attack the investigation." Unfortunately for the advocates of secrecy, they chose as a meeting place a hotel in

Seaside, California, right on the shore near Monterey, a big area for tourists. And when the investigators drove up to the Day's Inn, right off 101, they saw spelled out on the marquee in huge block letters: "WELCOME UNABOM TASK FORCE." Somebody had forgotten to tell the hotel the meeting was secret.

Because the Task Force knew the cops opposed the secrecy strategy, the Feds became even more reluctant than usual to share their information with the cops. Inevitably as the media worked the bombing story "there were leaks... little things that went out that were attributed to us because they knew that Ray and I were anxious to work with the media." Every time there was a leak "they went crazy with thinking we were the ones doing it." Viewed as "a conduit to the media" Bell says, the cops "were no longer invited to the meetings. As for getting updates it was very difficult... we were stonewalled—there was no information coming from the FBI to us about *our* murder."

Soon Bell began to echo a complaint common to homicide detectives around the nation. However brilliant the FBI may be in its own fields of expertise such as organized crime, white collar crime, counter-intelligence, or even kidnapping, the agency does not do many homicide investigations. Most FBI agents' practical instincts about how murders happen are inferior to those of the homicide units of a good municipal police force.

"I had never had any experience dealing with the federal authorities at this level at this time," recalls Bell. "The FBI does not get involved" much in homicide. But "locally we had worked with several serial murder investigations here. So we had already developed a certain expertise having to do with serial murders. We had a feeling how we should solve these and then we start meeting with the FBI and began to get frustrated because we real-

THE INVESTIGATION

ized they weren't going to approach this in the same manner we would."

Bell admires the FBI and the state-of-the-art resources they bring to bear on investigations. He thinks the recent criticism of the famous crime lab may be exaggerated and certainly thinks the lab was functioning well on this case at the time. "I honestly believe they were still doing a good job... doing an excellent job because I had so much respect for Chris Ronay and some of the other criminalists who were looking at the [Unabomber] case. I met and talked with them and discussed the evidence. I have no doubt they were absolutely objective and did everything right." The agents he worked with were always willing to go back to the evidence and entertain new approaches. "I give the FBI a large credit for a lot of the work they did. They did a wonderful job."

But in the final analysis, he says, "I just don't agree with the strategy they took" on secrecy. That one strategic error may have outweighed a great deal of hi-tech expertise. "They just don't have a lot of experience at actually working murders," he argues and so they went with the impractical and ultimately arrogant approach of cutting out the public.

With so little traceable evidence and no motive clear enough to help build the bomber's profile, "I didn't have a clue how we were going to solve this, other than going to the media. Let the public know. That was the only thing we could hang our hat on. Then they took the hat away, picked up the pole, and walked out with it."

Bell grew irritated when he heard the case referred to as unsolvable because the evidence was so thin. That's true only if the approach one takes is to simply resift that non-evidence in a secret vacuum. "But it's not unsolvable—it is solvable," he argued, "if we reach out."

For the time, it was not to be. The local cops needed the resources of the FBI too badly to defy their approach, and only the Feds could do an effective national PR campaign anyway.

Eventually, however, a reach-out strategy would be put in place. By the bomber.

CHAPTER 24
UNABOM Described

B ecause of the constant pressure that the system exerts to
modify human behavior, there is a gradual increase in the
number of people who cannot or will not adjust to society's
requirements: welfare leeches, youth-gang members, cultists,
anti-government rebels, radical environmentalist saboteurs,
dropouts and resisters of various kinds.

—UNABOMBER MANIFESTO

IT WAS FEBRUARY 20, 1987, a bright Salt Lake City morning at
CAAMS, Inc., a sales and service company owned by Gary
Wright. The company secretary, working with the store owner's
mother, had parked in the lot behind the building at 270 East 900
South. Three windows were in front of the secretary's desk, which
faced the lot. A shadow—a silhouette of a man—crawled over the
blinds of the first window, then disappeared. Next, it crept over
the second window, and the secretary looked toward the third,
where the silhouette should have appeared next. When the shape
of the passing man did not, she walked slowly to the third small
window and cautiously peered out.

Some fifteen feet away she glimpsed a man with a white canvas
bag slung carelessly over one shoulder. He was bent over the left
front section of her car, placing some sort of object (a package? she
first thought) beneath the wheel, slightly between two parked cars.

She turned to Gary Wright's mother and yelled, "Take a look!" She might even have knocked on the window. Her sudden movement, her shout to the owner's mom, the disruption of the blinds, or her tap against the glass—one of them must have alerted the stranger.

He turned suddenly and looked directly at the secretary through dark, aviator-style glasses. The eyes were invisible beneath the reflection of the lenses. She later described the person she saw as a twenty-eight-year-old white male, about five feet, ten inches tall and weighing roughly 165 pounds. She could just see the prominent jaw that jutted like a boulder from beneath the smoke-colored lenses and above a gray-hooded sweatshirt. She caught a glimpse of a light, strawberry-blond, thin mustache on the ruddy face. If that was the man's real hair showing just above the glasses, it was curly and blondish and quite unlike the straight hair above his lip.

She saw his face as expressionless (an effect enhanced by the cold glasses), unscarred or marked in any way, thin, with a reddish flush or a rough-looking complexion. Overall she judged him healthy, even fit, but it was his hands that held her attention for a moment—long, thin fingers, hairless and clean, uncalloused, with close cut nails. He wore no jewelry, perhaps not even a watch, and the witness saw the cuff on the white sweatshirt bunched at the wrist.

He finished his work, rose, and calmly strolled away. The secretary watched him a moment, shared a joke on his appearance with her coworker, and was interrupted by a ringing phone. She temporarily forgot the unusual event of the stranger near her car and answered the phone.

A few minutes later, at 10:30 AM, Gary Wright, the store owner, returned from a service call and parked his truck in his usual spot in the lot. As he rushed toward the office, he saw the abandoned object, two wooden two-by-fours with nails sticking a good two inches out of them. A Good Samaritan like Wright naturally couldn't allow this road hazard to remain in the parking lot where someone might run over it.

"When I pulled into the parking lot I noticed there was a piece of wood that was lying in the parking lot," recalled Gary Wright later. "It had nails sticking out of it. I didn't want anyone to run over it, so I got out of the car and I walked over toward the wood. I knelt down and lifted it up. As I knelt down I released the...."

The device, concealed within a block of wood, was fashioned from a three-layer concentric assembly of one-inch and one-and-one-quarter-inch steel pipes separated by a layer of steel shim, and sealed on the ends by plugs made from one-inch bar stock. Three metal pins and shim material held each of the plugs securely in place. The bombs were growing steadily more powerful.

The Unabomber had connected his fusing system to a spring-loaded lever switch that was designed to detonate the bomb if anyone moved it, which Wright did.

The blast shook the lot. People came on the run, and smoke billowed up. Debris was scattered everywhere, and pebbles rained down. An unearthly wind whipped the lot. Wright's mother actually watched the explosion rip into her son's throat, face, arms, legs, and smash his left hand where it inflicted permanent damage through fragmentation wounds.

"At first I thought I'd been shot. It was just this huge impact that hit me. The force of the impact knocked me back a good twelve to fifteen feet, and I started to go into shock. I started to bounce around quite a bit, and I could see my pants were missing from about my knee down on my left leg. My shoes had been burned. There were quite a few holes in my body, and a lot of the 'bullets' in the top of the device came up and struck me under the neck. I couldn't move much. It was like a porcupine—a lot under-neath there."

The bomber had made one fragment of his device invulnerable to detonation, as had been his practice. Printed on the one-inch diameter end-cap and punched into the metal with a nail, were the familiar letters, "FC." Still, the FBI kept the bomber's signature a secret. Shouldn't the public have been told?

Hardly anyone doubted that the Unabomber had been watching. A hotline was established, the Bureau received almost four hundred messages daily, and agents poured in from San Francisco and other jurisdictions to work the scene. Almost immediately after the brief sighting, police combed bus stations and flophouses asking for I.D. and looking for anyone who resembled the description. An unknown FBI sketch artist drew what the secretary had witnessed. This composite was released on February 23, but was little used.

Instead, at Biondi's urging, the ATF and the postal inspector arranged for Bob Exter, a Powell River, Canada, freelance artist, to do another composite, which he did in watercolor. He would be called in again in 1994 to do another one.

"I completed my job on March 18, 1987. I was there for about a week doing this thing, and I did one. Then the witness thought that the hair was a little different, and she was right because that second one on the eighteenth came out with the hair the right way. They later flew me back to Salt Lake to change the too-curly hair. 'There wasn't supposed to be bangs,' the witness said. 'It wasn't bangs. It was in front, and it was sticking out from the hood.' In my composite the hair looks right, but it's a little too high. The hair was right on the first, but I just got it high on the one I later did in '94.

"The only thing the witness was really worried about was the chin. She was trying to talk about the protruding chin so I made

$50,000 REWARD

---------- WANTED BY THE ----------

POSTAL INSPECTION SERVICE FOR

MAILING OR PLACING AN EXPLOSIVE DEVICE

THE U.S. POSTAL SERVICE MAY PAY A REWARD OF UP TO $50,000 FOR INFORMATION AND SERVICES LEADING TO THE ARREST AND CONVICTION OF ANY PERSON(S) FOR PLACING OR MAILING AN EXPLOSIVE DEVICE IN A POSTAL DEPOSITORY.

ON FEBRUARY 20TH, 1987 A PACKAGE EXPLODED AT A COMPUTER BUSINESS AT 270 E. 900 S. SALT LAKE CITY, UTAH 84111. BOMBS HAVE BEEN EITHER RECEIVED IN THE MAILS AND OR PLACED IN THE FOLLOWING STATES: UTAH, PENNSYLVANIA, ILLINOIS, CALIFORNIA, MICHIGAN AND WASHINGTON. THIS INCIDENT HAS BEEN LINKED TO 11 OTHER INCIDENTS WHICH HAVE OCCURED ACROSS THE UNITED STATES SINCE 1978 INJURING 21 PEOPLE AND KILLING ONE.

2/21/87

White Male
25 - 30 Years Old
5'10" - 6' tall
165 pounds
Slender Build
Blond hair (reddish tint)
(hair sticking out, not bangs)
Light Mustache
Ruddy Complexion
Wearing Blue Denim Jeans, Gray Hooded Sweatshirt
Tear drop Sunglasses (smoked lenses)

IF YOU HAVE ANY INFORMATION ABOUT THIS INCIDENT PLEASE CONTACT THE UNABOM LAW ENFORCEMENT TASK ---- FORCE BY TELEPHONE COLLECT (801) 359-1917 (24 Hr.) ----

The first Unabomber sketch by an FBI artist, February 21, 1987.

a strong chin on mine, but that was probably the weakest point of the first sketch."

At the time one of the ATF inspectors wanted Exter to let the bomber's eyes show through his sunglasses. But he resisted because the witness had not seen the eyes. Later in 1994 he changed his mind and tried to put the eyes in.

"I'd worked on the Green River Killer case and done other skull reconstruction where you take comparisons of other people and see how the eyes vary and you can get a basic idea of what the eyes would look like. So he examined pictures of men with similar skull structures to the bomber's. "They all had similar eyes, and I said, 'How can I go wrong?' And that's how I came up with those eyes."

As he points out, a composite is not meant to be evidence. "Evidence is the witness being able to convince the jury that this is the person they saw." The point of a composite is to help identify suspects. Then investigators look for real evidence. When Exter redid his composite in 1994 he no longer had access to the witness. "The FBI, ATF, and postal inspectors are always hiding evidence on each other. They can be obstinate. That's why Jeanne Boylan [who did the final and very famous composite seven years later] got into it. They wanted to do the composite over because they figured it wasn't working. But actually when investigator Tony Mujat appeared on "Larry King Live" one night, he said they believed that first composite actually made the Unabomber hide."

The FBI continued to process the elements in the CAAMs booby-trap device. Exhibits 1 through 50 were received in Washington, DC, on February 22, two days after Gary Wright's injury. Three days later exhibits 51 through 62 were received, and the single final exhibit arrived at the FBI lab on March 9. In part the report read: "A clear epoxy adhesive was sandwiched between

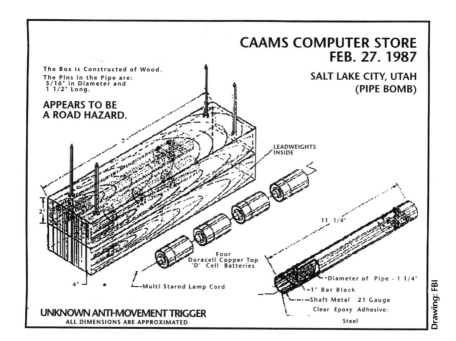

The Box is Constructed of Wood.
The Pins in the Pipe are:
5/16" in Diameter and
1 1/2" Long.

CAAMS COMPUTER STORE
FEB. 27. 1987
SALT LAKE CITY, UTAH
(PIPE BOMB)

APPEARS TO BE
A ROAD HAZARD.

LEADWEIGHTS
INSIDE

2"

11 1/4"

Four
Duracell Copper Top
'D' Cell Batteries

4"

Multi Starnd Lamp Cord

Diameter of Pipe - 1 1/4"
1" Bar Block
Shaft Metal 21 Gauge
Clear Epoxy Adhesive:

UNKNOWN ANTI-MOVEMENT TRIGGER
ALL DIMENSIONS ARE APPROXIMATED

Steel

Drawing: FBI

FBI drawing of the 1987 Salt Lake City road hazard bomb.

the layers of [concentric] pipe and tubing." Some of the pipes
were galvanized, some were twenty-one-gauge sheet metal. An
FBI diagram of the device was drafted on February 27, 1987, and
portrayed the arrangement of the four batteries and an equal
number of protruding nails, two at each end.

Two months later, however, the extra agents who had been
assigned to the case returned home, and interest waned. Whether
the composite had any effect or not, the bomber ceased all activity. He would remain silent for seven years. The case fell into
limbo.

CHAPTER 25
Big Yellow, 1992

D *ue to improved techniques the elite will have greater*
control over the masses; and because human work will
no longer be necessary the masses will be superfluous, a useless
burden on the system. If the elite is ruthless they may simply
decide to exterminate the mass of humanity.

—UNABOMBER MANIFESTO

TO HIS BROTHER, THE PROFESSOR CONFIDED in a long letter in the summer of 1991 that "my social self-confidence... my good social skills" were pretty much "destroyed" by the age of twenty. "I had very little social self-confidence [because] I experienced so much rejection both at home and in school.... I became an outsider," he said. This awkwardness and stress continued to cause him great pain. It was never far from his mind because of the long hours of loneliness.

In a letter written to his mother during the same summer, the Professor explained carefully over many pages how he was perpetually "under stress" in the presence of others because he couldn't believe they'd accept him. "This fear of rejection—based on bitter experience both at home and at school—has ruined my life," he wrote, "except for a few years that I spent alone in the woods, largely out of contact with people."

The wayward son maintained that he paid for the constant rejection he endured in school and at home (as he perceived the situation) physically as well as emotionally. He believed that this explained why he was a full three inches shorter than his brother, David. He ended his long letter to his mother by accusing her of failing to nurture his social skills, thus barring him from relating normally to people. He stated icily that he would hate her forever "because the harm you did me can never be undone."

Later he wrote, "One might possibly see a connection between the physical abuse you suffered as a kid and the psychological abuse you inflicted on me during my teens.... The psychologists claim that people who abuse their kids are usually people who were abused themselves as kids."

Convinced his formative years had been shaped by traumatic social experiences, the Professor said they left him wary of other individuals. He attempted to explain this more fully to his mother in that summertime letter:

> Suppose that for a period of years whenever you touched—let us say—a banana, you got a severe electric shock. After that you would always be nervous around bananas, even if you knew they weren't wired to shock you. Well, in the same way, the many rejections, humiliations and other painful influences that I underwent during adolescence at home, in high school, and at Harvard have conditioned me to be afraid of people.

The Professor felt that he'd not made a single close friendship during his entire adult life and now consistently enjoyed his solitude, finding it "congenial." His greatest sense of loss came not from being deprived of male friendships (which he found nonessential), but "female companionship is another matter," he lamented.

"Women are gentle, nice, pleasant to be with, they represent warmth, joy, family life, love and, of course, sex. Naturally, women have their faults too and moreover not all women have the good qualities I've just mentioned. But for 37 years I've desired women. I've wanted desperately to find a girlfriend or a wife but never have been able to make any progress toward doing so because I lack the necessary social self-confidence and social skills.

"I am tormented by bitter regret at never having had the opportunity to experience the love of a woman." At forty-nine, he saw himself as soon being an old man—with no friends, children, or wife to console him. His only future lay in old age and death.

David deemed his brother's memories of their parents distorted, but still they constantly plagued him—"amplifications or exaggerations of what happened that seem quite unreasonable, though they seem quite real to him," David later said. "It was as if he had created a system of interpretation so that there was nothing you could do to get him to look at something differently. Nothing could alter his way of looking at the world."

The Professor took his family's analysis of him with increasing irritation. "You can write to me whenever you like," he said, "but please DON'T try to psychoanalyze me, and TRY not to get me upset." With the scholar's growing hypersensitivity, every word and action seemed to scald.

David stated later, "Progressively, more and more subjects were off-limits because they upset him so much to talk about. I came to sense over time that he literally could not stop thinking or obsessing about some things. It would interfere with his sleep or heartbeat. Many of these subjects could plunge him into deep distress." He also got the distinct impression, as the Professor grew ever more defensive at hints that he might have mental problems, that his brother was projecting his own mental difficulties onto others by diagnosing one of David's friends as a potential schizophrenic.

"I agree there is no clearcut line dividing insanity from sanity, and that 'mental illness' often is a mere label pinned on those who don't act as society demands. Further," said the Professor, "I would question whether 'mental illness' and 'insanity' are even useful concepts.... On the other hand, when someone is tormented by strange visions and disagreeable feelings that pass through his head owing to a hereditary peculiarity of brain chemistry it seems absurd to refrain from calling his condition a disease."

At another time, the Professor reacted with irritation to his brother's attempt to have a his mental stability gauged by a professional: "In at least some of these interviews the psychologists seemed to be trying to get chummy with me, presumably in an attempt to get me to loosen up and reveal more of myself. Because I resented having been talked or manipulated into participating, I refused to loosen up or get chummy with them."

Becky and Theresa Garland, daughters of pioneer environmentalist Cecil Garland who had attempted to clean up Big River, owned and ran Garland's Town and Country Store in little Lincoln. At one point the Hermit would give Becky a letter that told of his childhood, lost youth, and lost love. It was his cold, but practical way of telling about himself. Like everything else, he did it indirectly. "He wrote about things that hurt him in his heart really bad, so that I would understand his feelings, that he was human," she said afterward. He left something for Theresa, too— in 1992, she received a handmade packet of carrot seeds and a handwritten note from him that explained how to grow them:

WILD CARROT BIG YELLOW 1992
Plant these just as you would regular carrots. Some will
probably put up seed stalks the first year. Pull these out,
since the roots get tough as soon as they put up seed stalks.
The white roots have only so-so flavor. The tasty roots

are the pale-yellow ones. If you like them and want to grow
the seeds, dig around the plants in the fall to see which ones
have large, pale-yellow roots. Leave these in the ground
over the winter, with soil mounded up over them to prevent
mice from getting at them, and the second year they will
put up seed stalks.

CHAPTER 26

Fleeting Images

WHEN I RAN INTO JEANNE BOYLAN on a television show in New York she had just been approached about doing the most important composite sketch in her career. A lot of composite drawings lead nowhere, but Boylan's had had a remarkable success rate in the past. This time hers would fail on one level, but succeed wildly on another, contributing in an unexpected way to the Unabomber's eventual apprehension.

Back in the beginning of June 1994 I found myself in New York in the green room of the "Rolanda" television program. I had flown there to comment on the unheard phenomenon of a second copycat of San Francisco's Zodiac killer, a physically powerful costumed genius who sent taunting letters to the police along with diagrams of bombs. I mention this because at a later point he would also be suspected of being UNABOM. The original Zodiac's bombs were meant for schoolchildren. He intended to place them in Bay Area mountainsides set to the height of school buses and programmed to count the windows as they rolled by to identify the target. Then they would be triggered. He had never been officially caught (though police considered the case cleared). Exactly four years earlier I'd been summoned to New York to study the case of a Zodiac copycat, and now there could be two copycats of the original West Coast Zodiac. My ten-year case study was undeniably being followed. As disturbing, at the time of this writing [June 1997], a *third* copycat surfaced in Japan where my book had been translated. The murderer of students in Kobe left the Zodiac's crossed-circle symbol on the bodies, crimes of the most horrifying character. He was captured soon after.

Some cases were so compelling that copycats fell under their spell. I could only hope that the Unabomber did not engender the same kind of imitation. Jeanne Boylan was on the same show. Young, blonde, attractive enough to be a model, she had brains, intuition, and an almost uncanny way of reading a witness's mind. No one worked like her.

Boylan, a Portland artist, was a veteran of over seven thousand cases and instrumental in bringing to justice the killer of Polly Klass, a kidnapping victim in Petaluma, north of San Francisco, where I lived. I especially admired her drawing of Richard Allen Davis, who was speedily arrested and ultimately convicted for the murder of the little girl because of the accuracy of her portrait. Boylan and I exchanged drawings and small talk. The following month she would produce the most famous composite sketch in history, an icon widely reproduced all over the world.

Boylan knew the witness to CAAM's Computer Store bombing in Salt Lake City had sighted UNABOM in 1987 for brief seconds. Over the years she'd moved three times, but the FBI had continued to monitor her phone calls, and some FBI agents had even lived nearby for a time. In the back of the secretary's mind, she knew the first drawing hadn't quite captured what she'd seen. It had been close though and since the FBI was dissatisfied, she was willing to undergo another ordeal to improve it.

Agent Max Noll had met Jeanne Boylan at the San Francisco International Airport and flown with her to Salt Lake City, showing her his stack of three-ring binders filled with the Unabomber case background on the way.

Boylan had known it was a long shot when police called her in July and requested she reinterview the witness. Bob Exter, the original artist, had gone back recently at the FBI's invitation and done a new version.

Boylan settled down to face what she considered a challenge. "You're going back an awfully long time in memory and this woman was aware through all those years of the significance of the information that she had." Boylan itemized the obstacles—a "slightly contaminated" witness, an aged description. In the interim the witness had been shown a great number of photographs, and when the hooded sweatshirt and dark aviator glasses were added, it made the task all but impossible.

A Salt Lake City FBI sketch artist had done the first portrait one day after the crippling attack, February 23, 1987. Then Exter had painted a color composite of the young man seen kneeling by the witness's car, finishing in mid-March.

Because of the "silent strategy" however, neither portrait was much used, except locally. Not until the end of 1994 was any portrait used to create national awareness. In a 1994 drawing, Exter had removed the glasses, drawing eyes he'd only visualized in his mind, but backed up by experiences in forensic reconstruction during the Green River case. Boylan felt this visualization might be a problem. After all, the eyes were never discernible at any time during the brief sighting.

Boylan also believed that the techniques most police used to produce composites were archaic. "They're out of the forties," she said. "They bring a victim down and have them go through catalogues of facial features and have them pick out features. That tends to contaminate, destroy, and bury the memory. In addition, when somebody's been through trauma, the mind is very powerful in wanting to protect you and wants to transplant new information that's more emotionally palatable. So that new image takes the place of the original image."

Boylan considered the amount of time the witness had actually seen the suspect. The bomber had been fifteen feet away and she'd only noticed him because he'd been alongside her car. Originally, he'd been less than an image, only a fleeting shadow. First his shadows crawled over the two windows. When the shadow failed to reach the last window, her curiosity sent her to the last window to peer out. Her shout at seeing a man by her car caused him to turn and look back at her for a second. And this was seven years ago.

Boylan spent six hours trying to rebuild that moment. She believed that for information to be embedded in the memory, trauma has to exist alongside. Her working methods were unique in composite work. "I might ask, 'Would you elongate something or would you lengthen it?' 'Would you broaden it?' 'Would you make texture?' 'Would you create a smooth surface?' So that when I say, 'Would you,' I'm not saying, 'Was it?' because 'Was it?' is going to take her back emotionally into that memory."

She talked about textures and shapes, working below the cognitive level and on the emotional level. She kept everything in the present tense and found the constant interruptions of the witness's son to be beneficial.

Boylan sketched as she talked, but it was almost inadvertent. "The sketch is in my lap," she said. "She's not seeing it all because if she were to see it she would be dwelling on the task at hand— what I try to do is a diversionary system of variance so she's almost unaware of it.

"We're having a conversation about anything I can find that will elicit a positive emotional response from her. We're going to talk about her kids, her job, travel. Anything that she loves. Periodically, I reach in and interject a question and the answer will be there because she's not trying. When you try, it's like the tip-of-the-tongue syndrome where you try to know someone's name or something and you're trying really hard to think of it. You can't do it.

"So I keep them occupied over here with anything that's going to be positive, relaxing, keep them in a sense of being in control and then sort of reach around and pluck these answers out. And they're there.

"Fortunately, the only thing we had left in that face in spite of the disguise was that prominent jaw line, the chin, and the underbite."

In her first version, reproduced here for the first time, Boylan drew the wanted man without his moustache. The second version showed the sketch as we know it now. What Jeanne Boylan produced in those six hours became an American icon—the white male in a hooded sweatshirt, black aviator glasses covering a third of his face and imparting almost an insect look to him, a wispy mustache on his upper lip, and curly, reddish-blond hair just showing under his hood. Boylan had used strong shadows to bring out the most salient characteristics of the wanted man—the strong, powerful chin, full of defiance, calm in the midst of inner rage. Drafted in half-tone crayon, the image when printed as a line cut took on tremendous power as the shadowed area blended and simplified.

But was what she drew a likeness of the Unabomber?

I would have to say no—with the exception of the strong chin. Her considerable contribution came from the power and spirit of her drawing. The image so transfixed the country that new interest and more attention was focused on the case. When Boylan's portrait was finally widely publicized in late 1994, it galvanized us.

Bob Exter, the original UNABOM sketch artist, perhaps predictably, criticized Boylan's work. He told me after the release of the new composite, "You're dealing with a witness that's spent seven years straining on this thing and to do as good as they can from a five-second contact. Boylan got that chin a little bit better, but it was the other direction. It was stronger. If they had consulted with me, they would have avoided such problems as the hair [which was still too curly]. Boylan didn't realize what went into that Salt Lake City composite that I did and if a witness gets a better idea you'd best consult with the first artist because the first artist remembers things that maybe she told him. I would remember things that would be important to an investigation.

"When I saw Jeanne Boylan's drawing I said, 'They're crazy— that looks more like me.' My mother thought so too....

"I brought out how the composite had changed. If you look at that one I did with no glasses, that's the closest they came to doing it through investigative means. But they [the FBI] were abusive to me because they didn't give me the credit for knowing things that were important."

But Exter and Boylan were part of a team, the army of men and

THE INVESTIGATION

EXCLUSIVE: The Unabomber in his first Boylan sketch.

women dedicated to capturing the most elusive criminal in US history, and both had done their part as well as could be expected based on a sighting in 1987, lasting mere seconds, of a man concealed in a hooded sweatshirt and dark aviator-style glasses.

What is remarkable is not that the composites were not more accurate but that they were so gripping and in that way useful. A perfect example of how the composite portraits proved valuable happened late in the case. If this sighting was true, it would have predated any earlier sighting of the suspect agents eventually arrested as the Unabomber.

The federal worker at the Bay Area passport office had a reputation for veracity, and so many months later when she told this story to the *Chronicle,* many believed it. I have not been able to personally verify their story. One day in mid-September 1995, she was working when a strange man came to her office only one hour before closing time. It was 3:30 PM as he showed her outdated identification to support his passport application.

"Such outdated information can't be accepted," she explained, gesturing to his expired 1978 California driver's license and university identification. "This material is twenty-three years old. It won't do."

"But he's still me," he said.

She looked carefully at him. He was wearing a fatigue jacket and glasses. "The glasses had a plastic frame," she recalled. "The bridge was wire, and when I was looking at him he had all this green mold like bread mold on the bridge of his eyeglasses. So I thought, 'God, why would anyone wear mold on their glasses?'"

She studied his hands as he ransacked a packed wallet looking for any identification she might find suitable. The woman began to read his application. "From there I went to his occupation on the application and saw it was carpenter."

CHAPTER 27
Turk

*I*n any technologically advanced society the individual's fate
MUST depend on decisions that he personally cannot
influence to any great extent. A technological society cannot be
broken down into small, autonomous communities, because
production depends on the cooperation of very large numbers
of people and machines. Such a society MUST be highly
organized and decisions HAVE TO be made that affect very
large numbers of people. When a decision affects, say, a million
people, then each of the affected individuals has, on the
average, only a one-millionth share in making the decision.

—UNABOMBER MANIFESTO

PITTSBURGH, PENNSYLVANIA-BORN, the Professor's father was married at the age of twenty-six by a Cook County judge. For a while he and Wanda lived at 4755 South Wolcott Avenue in Chicago, then Turk began running a Polish sausage storefront factory on South Ashland Avenue. Laboring alongside his first cousin Felix, he made some of the best kielbasa in the city.

But Turk's greatest disappointment came when he failed to get two sausage-making patents, one based on his idea for new casings for the meat. Finally, the store closed in 1969 and the hardworking sausage maker began casting about for a new line of work. The couple and their first child lived in the 1940s at 5234 South Carpenter Street, a two-family dwelling with front and back yards. Then in 1952 they moved to Evergreen Park on South Lawndale, this time into a larger place—a three-bedroom colonial.

In the mid sixties Turk accepted a job as a supervisor at

Cushion-Pak, Inc., near Lisbon, Iowa, just outside of Cedar Rapids. The family quickly got involved in local politics and were labeled "intellectually elite" by the less than two hundred town residents.

Chicago Tribune columnist Mike Conklin grew up in Lisbon and fondly recalled dinners with his neighbors, the Radls (Dick Radl was a Democratic State Representative) and the Professor's family. Over wonderful meals, political and philosophical discussions spun like gossamer over the thoughtful participants. Wanda herself was "enamored with words," and avidly read Shakespeare and Austen. Conklin remembered Turk as "one of those old-school ethnic liberals, very left-leaning, very compassionate, and he raised a supportive family, where ideas were more important than anything else." Wanda unfailingly nudged the boys—David had been born by now—into speaking out on political issues.

Paul Carlsten, professor of political science at Cornell College in Mount Vernon, sat in on the discussions, too, and noted that Turk believed "the best minds were being recruited into military research for the development of instruments of violence." Both boys listened carefully to their father's words. As the saying goes, "Little pitchers have big ears."

Turk exercised enormous influence on his two children—especially his espousal of pacifist views. He believed technology kept the war in Vietnam boiling, and told his son, when he was a professor teaching math at Berkeley, that he should step down and not aid students in learning to design weapons of war and nuclear bombs. "Shut down the war machine," he said. And he meant it.

Turk later told friends that the reason his son had resigned from Berkeley was because he didn't want to help students learn how to make nuclear weapons. "Or harm the environment," he added.

The father's powerful antitechnology leanings—beliefs rooted in Emerson and Thoreau, the love of learning he shared with his wife—were passed on to his two boys. He was outspoken in his admiration of the Amish in Lisbon. The Amish, a conservative Protestant sect, were members of the Old Order Amish Mennonite Church. They spurned technology, lived simply, and were self-sufficient, believing that technology could subjugate the world. Their lifestyle obviously offered healthy benefits. On the whole, they suffered depression at less than one-fifth the rate of nearby big cities.

The family resettled in Lombard, Illinois, in 1968, and Turk took another factory job. Turk and Wanda, active supporters of left-leaning Democratic presidential candidate Eugene McCarthy, revered the Kennedys and Martin Luthur King, Jr., and soon became strong doves in the Vietnam War. Both joined the Lombard Democratic Club.

Neighbors in church-filled Evergreen Park discovered the little family was not religious, but the parents were devoted to the two boys, in love with learning, and a couple who got things done. Wanda, a very visible presence at each PTA and school board get-together, was a Northwest booster along with her husband, and through neighborhood organizations got the streets paved and kindergarten classes set up.

Several doors down from Wanda and Turk, neighbor Dorothy saw how concerned about people they were. "They taught their boys that." When Dorothy's daughter contracted polio, the two boys came daily to the front step of the quarantined house, put dishes of food there, and then slipped away without waiting for thanks. She saw the boys as also very different from each other, perceiving David as "bright and precocious with a wonderful vocabulary." She said, "He was outgoing, pleasant, and sweet, and happy-go-lucky." But Dorothy and another neighbor, Evelyn

Vanderlaan, noted that the elder child was "in a different world." For instance, when Turk once remarked that his older son "has the brain of a two-year-old" or when both parents thoughtlessly remarked, "You're nuts" or "You're crazy," the boy recalled it for literally decades.

Turk, always political, wrote to the editor of the *Chicago Tribune* on October 17, 1988, saying:

> Isn't it puzzling that lately the "L" word is used so pejoratively? That the word "liberal" is used to evoke something bad? Here are some things that the liberals have given us: Social Security, later the Social Security COLAS, federal deposit insurance, unemployment insurance, the right to join or not to join a union, the G.I. Bill (giving educational opportunities to veterans), Medicare and student loans for education. By what twist of the imagination can anyone call the above bad? Let us treat the word "liberal" with the respect it deserves.

When he was at Berkeley teaching mathematics, the Professor had purchased a rifle and had begun to hunt deer in the woods. He recalled how his father had loved the outdoors, and taken pride in teaching his two boys fishing and hunting, and most especially the skills involved in surviving in the wilderness. Their camping trips, usually joyful, would last for a week at a time.

Once David and Turk discovered a wild rabbit with a hurt leg, and the father took the animal home, mended it, and gently nursed it back to health, then released it back into the woods.

The family joke was that the Professor would go off on his own into the woods someday, "and they were all afraid for him because, being a pretty urban kid, he couldn't even boil water." But the eldest was withdrawing. Once the boy passed up a fishing expedition with his dad to stay home and peruse a new calculus book. It set the pace for the future.

And finally, the gentle father passed on to his sons a passionate love of gardening. At twilight he tossed horseshoes with the neighbors among the cabbages. Then, tragedy. A longtime pipe smoker, Turk was diagnosed with terminal lung cancer in 1990. As the disease crippled his body, he convened a family meeting to arrange his personal affairs and to allot his possessions to his loved ones. Everyone was there, grieving and sharing the sadness, everyone except the Professor. It was right in character; after all, he'd not even attended his brother's recent wedding. After the conference, Turk appeared moody and began to sink within himself. Finally, on October 2, 1990, he gravely took down his .22-caliber rifle, the same one he'd taken his boys hunting with, and committed suicide.

The Professor had warned his mother and brother to use a code whenever there was an "urgent and important" message they had to send to him. In emergencies they were told to draw a wavy red line directly under the stamp on their envelope. Otherwise, estranged as he was, the Professor would put off reading any letters from them until later, and possibly never open them. The reaction of the Professor to the terrible news of his father's death was frigid. He allegedly wrote back that such news was "an appropriate use" of the "red line" treatment.

In Lincoln the snows began to fall.

CHAPTER 28
Thinking, Writing

The conservatives are fools: They whine about the decay of traditional values, yet they enthusiastically support technological progress and economic growth. Apparently it never occurs to them that you can't make rapid, drastic changes in the technology and the economy of a society without causing rapid changes in all other aspects of the society as well, and that such rapid changes inevitably break down traditional values....

—UNABOMBER MANIFESTO

FOR THE REMAINDER OF THE EIGHTIES, the Hermit continued his odd pattern of wandering and sporadically visiting the Park Hotel, a sort of halfway house for him. In 1986 he stayed from April 7 to April 9 in Room 118, and then he was back again on May 28, this time occupying Room 119, for two more days at a cost of twenty-two dollars. When 1988 rolled around, the Hermit checked into Room 119 and stopped over for two more days, May 9 through May 11. His sojourn included a day's stay on May 25 (although his registration card showed he had departed on May 27). From May 31 until June 1 he resided in Room 112 and stayed there on June 14 for another day's stay, again in Room 119. He might have still been there on June 20 as other records showed. On September 6, 1989, he checked into Room 105 and departed on September 8.

When the nineties came, he continued the pattern—sleeping

one night at the Park on June 5, 1990, and paying the new, increased rate of $12 a night. Because 119 was taken, he slept in Room 104 as a temporary abode. Back again on July 16, 1991, he lodged a single night. In 1993, May 6, he resided in Room 120 until the following day, then went his way.

As the years went by, the Hermit continued to pour forth an endless stream of thoughts into the mail system. He wrote letters to his mother, to a Dr. Goren (expressing his feelings of anger), and to his brother. In an undated letter he told David:

> **As you know, I have no respect for law or morality. Why have I never committed any crime? (of course, I'm not talking about something like shooting a grouse out of season now and then. I mean felony type stuff—burglary, arson, murder, etc.) Lack of motive? Hardly. As you know, I have a good deal of anger in me and there are lots of people I'd like to hurt. Risk? In some cases, yes. But there are other cases in which I can figure out ways of doing naughty things so that the risk would be insignificant. I am forced to the humiliating confession that the reason I've never committed any crime is that I have been successfully brainwashed by society. On an intellectual level I have only contempt for authority, but on an animal level I have all too much respect for it. My training has been quite successful in this regard and the strength of my conditioned inhibitions is such that I don't believe I could ever commit a serious crime. Knowing my attitude toward psychological manipulation of the individual by society, you can imagine how humiliating it is for me to admit to myself that I have been successfully manipulated.**

The Hermit's concerns about the environment intensified as Big River grew more polluted and new roads intruded on the privacy he enjoyed in his cabin. In July 1991, tank cars plunged from a railroad bridge into the Sacramento River and sent shivers through the soul of every nature lover. Twelve hundred gallons of herbicide contaminated the forty-two-mile stretch between the derailment and Shasta Lake, riding the current swiftly and decimating all fish within that area. He thought of the International Nickel smelting plant in Sudbury, Ontario, and that one factory's pollution accounting for 5 percent of the world air emissions of sulfur dioxide. And finally the Hermit, with all his reading in the little library with eight chairs, may have considered Foundry Cove on the Hudson near Cold Springs, New York, next to a plant where military munitions and batteries had been manufactured for a century. The cove represented the "highest concentration of toxic cadmium and nickel pollutants in the world." It set his mind to burning. Vice President Gore had sparked national awareness of the invisible rent in the fragile ozone layer which seemed to be widening.

Gore had written a widely read book, *Earth in the Balance,* which the Hermit may have read although it wasn't among his personal library of 233 books (the FBI individually catalogued everything recovered from the Hermit's cabin except the books). "In the speech in which I declared my candidacy, I focused on *global warming, ozone depletion and the ailing global environment and declared that these issues—along with nuclear arms control*—would be the principal focus of my campaign [emphasis added]."

It is probable the Unabomber or, as he called himself, "FC," heard that speech or read Gore's book because he later wrote, "No one knows what will happen as a result of *ozone depletion, the greenhouse effect, and other environmental problems that cannot yet be foreseen. And, as nuclear proliferation* has shown, new technology cannot be kept out of the hands of dictators and irresponsible Third World leaders [emphasis added]."

As Tony Snow noted in his *Detroit News* column much later, "Gore, like the Unabomber, distrusts unbridled technology. He frets over the fate of the planet and thinks people must embrace revolutionary cures.... Gore sells books; FC detonates bombs. But the two men still take an amazingly similar view of modernity."

Agitated in the manner of all highly intelligent eccentrics, the Hermit went about his property, tending his garden, doing various good deeds for his neighbors, and searching out the furtive rabbits in the brush. Anyone seeing him might have been put in mind of John Randolph's line—"The chameleon on the aspen, always trembling, always changing."

CHAPTER 29

FBI Labs

IT WAS 1989 WHEN FREDERIC WHITEHURST first blew the whistle on the FBI lab and launched a series of inquiries that would result in a scathing Justice Department report some seven years later. Inspector General Michael Bromwich would write more than five hundred pages about the FBI forensic operation being "sloppy and biased." This was the same lab that had been analyzing the UNABOM devices from the very beginning. What would this mean if the bomber were ever caught and brought to justice? Would all that had been gathered so far be thrown out of court, and would a conviction ever be possible?

The study reported on twenty-four cases, and examined three of the Bureau's thirty-five special units. Ten lab technicians were accused of "shoddy analysis" and significant failures, affecting a number of high profile cases.

THE INVESTIGATION

These included flawed testimony in the World Trade Center bombing; inaccurate testimony in a Florida case in which a man was convicted of homicide by adding poison to a bottled cola; and about Jeffrey MacDonald, the Green Beret doctor chronicled in *Fatal Vision* as the murderer of his two daughters and wife. The result of the report affected thousands of trial motions and resulted in many retrials.

Principal findings were "improper preparation of laboratory reports" by three bomb unit technicians who allegedly altered, omitted, or improperly supplemented some of Whitehurst's internal reports.

The report pointed to "insufficient documentation of test results" by the examiner who worked on hundreds of cases (including UNABOM) and by the central toxicology chief. "Scientifically flawed reports" were cited in the mail bomb murder of Judge Vance and in the Oklahoma City bombing, "and in a few instances by an explosives unit examiner who altered Whitehurst's report." The Justice Department concluded with charges of "inadequate record management and retention system," pointed to "failures by management" to resolve allegations in many cases, and finally spoke of "a flawed staffing structure of the explosives unit."

Seventeen pages of the report, and eighteen months' labor, focused on the Unabomber investigation and six of the bomber's devices in particular. It was critical of explosives examiner Terry Rudolph's work on the UNABOM case from November 1979 to December 1985. The Bromwich report concluded that his "performance... lacks competence," or was "unacceptable and unprofessional," recommending that the government not rely on any of Rudolph's work in the prosecution of a Unabomber suspect.

THE INVESTIGATION

THE BOMBINGS WORKED ON BY RUDOLPH included Scrutton and the November 15, 1979, attempt to bring down a jetliner. In the investigation of Flight No. 444, the report cast doubt upon Rudolph's assertion that the bomber had used smokeless powder, that his work "lacks competence.... The case files do not contain sufficient information to identify the analyses performed, if any, or to understand the basis for the stated conclusions."

In the October 1981 business classroom bombing in Salt Lake City, Rudolph concluded that a matchlike substance was employed in the attack, but failed to support his conclusions. "Again," read the report, "Rudolph's answers strongly suggest a lack of competence. His work is of little value if the files do not document the basis for the stated conclusions, and Rudolph must rely on his uncertain memory of what he 'probably' did in the particular case."

In the bomb attack on Angelakos the report stated that the examiner did not use accepted standards in examining evidence from the blast, and called his work unprofessional. In the subsequent attempt on Hauser, Bromwich said he should have run more tests on the device.

Finally, regarding the June 13, 1985, bomb dismantled at the fabrication division of Boeing in Washington, the inspector general stated that Rudolph could not have concluded from the tests he ran that the device contained black powder, and questioned how the examiner could have identified aluminum in the bomb: "Nothing to back up that conclusion existed within the file."

"As we have observed earlier," read the report, "an examiner's subjective impressionistic 'experience' is no substitute for scientifically valid procedures."

THE INVESTIGATION

As for Whitehurst the man, FBI agent Rick Smith had some strong opinions, which I'd seen him express one morning on KTVU when revelations about the fifty-five cases became known.

"In my twenty-five years in the FBI," he said, "it's the worst thing I've seen. No one ever thought that was possible in the FBI. I think they did consider that there was some exaggeration, but they did conclude they had some validity."

I spoke with Smith later and he made some criticisms of Whitehurst. But bottom line, he was convinced that at least some of Whitehurst's criticisms were true. "I'd be amazed, he told me, if the allegations against the lab actually affected the Unabomber case adversely. But the fact is, there were some lax standards."

IN THE BLISTERING MIDST OF A HEAT WAVE, my photographer and associate, Penny Wallace and I exited the elevator on the third floor of the Sacramento County sheriff's department and made our way to the homicide Bureau to see Detective Robert Bell. The air conditioner hummed. It seemed as cold inside his office in summer as it had been outside that December day in 1985 when the Unabomber claimed his first kill. Then, by streets hung with scarlet bells, silver stars, and holly garlands, Bell had watched Christmas shoppers, arms filled with wrapped packages, peer into the windswept, bloodstained lot at the back of Hugh Scrutton's computer rental store.

At the time we spoke, long after it was over, the FBI labs were in the news and I was anxious to learn how the evidence in the first UNABOM fatality had been processed and what Bell thought about the accusations of inept FBI lab procedures.

"O.K. Let's talk evidence," said Bell. "The bomb parts that we

THE INVESTIGATION

recovered from behind RenTech Computers were meticulously logged, collected, brought in here, photographed. And then we had this meeting with the FBI—one of a series. 'We have all the other evidence at our lab in Washington,' they say, 'but it makes sense that the same criminalists look at all the evidence—it's common sense.' You certainly don't want to say, 'No, no, no—we're keeping it.'"

"Because you don't want to give away the investigation," said Penny.

"Right. So we agreed, recognizing that we're going to be able to compare the glues and resins and stuff like that. You really can't do that with a phone call. They have to have that evidence to physically compare and we'd spoken many times with Chris Ronay, who was the lead guy at that time.

"We sent the evidence from the Scrutton case back to the FBI so they could do their analysis, recognizing that if there's an arrest made they're going to be doing the prosecution here in Sacramento. 'So we want the evidence back when you're done with it,' we said. It took us nine months to even get the photographs back. We never did get the physical evidence back. We threatened to go and get it."

"What about the sloppy FBI lab practices we've all been reading about." I said. "The Bromfield Report made the cover of *Time* magazine."

"Of course, we weren't aware of any of that. Initially, we were under the assumption that the FBI was functioning and that they did a good job. I honestly believe they were still doing a good job... doing an excellent job because I had so much respect for Chris Ronay and some of the other criminalists who were looking at the [UNABOM] case. I met and talked with them and discussed the evidence. I have no doubt they were absolutely objective and did everything right.

"We realized we had a problem with the evidence later, but not in this case. We'd shipped some evidence back for DNA work on a couple of murder cases we had here. It was real apparent that their DNA lab was really messed up. In fact we had to dismiss cases on some murder suspects based on inconsistencies in the FBI. They just couldn't agree even amongst themselves. Both the local DA and the judge dismissed all charges. We realized then there were some problems."

PART FOUR

THE NEW YORK TIMES BOMBER
San Francisco / The Nineties

CHAPTER 30
Return in Fire

T*he technophiles are taking us all on an utterly reckless ride into the unknown.*

—UNABOMBER MANIFESTO

FOR SIX YEARS NO ONE HAD HEARD A WORD from the bomber, but it soon became apparent that he'd made the Bay Area his home and center of operations. His new package bombs would all show California return addresses and postmarks, mostly from Oakland and San Francisco. In the meantime he'd almost been forgotten. As for the public, they were unaware there was a *serial* bomber, much less the Unabomber.

The Hermit was restless as June 1993 rolled around. On the fifth he checked into the Park Hotel, paid the three-dollar key deposit, and lodged the night in Room 119. The following afternoon he left, after paying Barbara McCabe thirteen dollars for the stay.

But violence was in the air. "Guns and Waco" was a rallying cry. On June 22, just over two months after the disastrous FBI raid, siege, and burning of the Branch Davidian sect in Waco, Texas, and terrible loss of life on both sides, Charles Joseph

Epstein sat alone in his kitchen. His Noche Vista Lane home sat bayside just north of San Francisco in Tiburon. Dr. Epstein, a painter, physician, and world-class medical geneticist and bio-chemist, was chief of the Division of Medical Genetics, Department of Pediatrics at UC San Francisco, and had recently been featured in a profile in *The New York Times*. Therefore he was not surprised at the volume of mail he'd been getting.

Epstein was best known for locating a gene that might contribute to Down's syndrome and had broken ground with his leading research on that and on Alzheimer's disease. He was a valuable man doing even more valuable research. Much of this research focused on stroke-induced brain damage. His expertise ranged from human embryology to recombinant DNA. Like the Professor, he had studied at Harvard and was a UC professor in 1972.

Epstein, a Guggenheim Fellow in 1973–74, was the author of numerous books. Among them were *The Consequences of Chromosome Imbalance: Principles, Mechanisms and Models, The Neurobiology of Down's Syndrome,* and *Oncology and Immunology of Down's Syndrome.* And he also acted as editor of *Human Genetics.*

The fifty-nine-year-old doctor sat down at 4:30 PM to sort through the mail the postman had brought at 12:30 PM. His daughter, Joanna, one of four children, had brought in the stack, including a parcel she'd retrieved from the mailbox, and put it on the kitchen table.

Epstein first noticed the brown, heavily padded envelope posted with twenty-nine-cent US Flag–Olympic Ring stamps. He might have recognized the name on the return address: Professor James Hill of the Sacramento State Chemistry Department. Hill was an inorganic chemist and head of that university's department. The zip code read "95819," an outdated designation. A year earlier the code had been lengthened to 95819–6057. The postmark showed the letter had been mailed on June 18. The bespectacled geneticist began to open it.

One moment the doctor was in a bright, cozy, immaculate room, the pots and pans hanging perfectly, the cupboards filled with delicate glassware, the curtains billowing gently in the breeze coming in off San Francisco Bay. The next moment it was as if a magician had clapped his hands to perform a monstrous magic trick.

In a flash this scene of domestic tranquility, of home and all that it held for the brilliant scholar, was altered into a howling black hole of fumes and bright lights, of searing heat and burning pain. A whirlwind of rubble seemed to spin round him. A shudder rumbled through the house, and Epstein shook wildly in the grip of a gigantic force. After the final hissing came dead silence.

The padded envelope had erupted in his hands, throwing back his right arm and snapping it in half like a twig, and shrapnel ripped into his abdomen. Hot metal peppered his face and chest. The roaring explosion tore off three of his fingers.

Quickly, help was summoned, and in minutes three medics and a policeman were carrying the geneticist down through the heavily foliaged lane to a waiting ambulance, which rushed him to Marin General. After four-and-one-half hours of surgery, Epstein was listed in fair condition, then upgraded to stable.

What had brought the bomber back on this sunny Tuesday afternoon? Police were not certain he'd actually returned and were naturally cautious at first.

As I said, violence was in the air, mainly bombs. At the time of the blast in Tiburon, prosecutors were preparing for the trial of a group of Muslim fundamentalists in the World Trade Center bombing: Ahmad Jjaj, Mohammad Salmeh, Mahmud Abouhalima, and Nidal Ayyad. The trial was set for September and had occupied the headlines, possibly inciting the jealousy of the long-dormant bomber.

The bomber had used a six-inch length of three-eighths-inch copper tubing sealed on both ends by metal, epoxy, and wood plugs and one-eighth-inch metal pins. A powerful mixture of aluminum powder and potassium chlorate had been tightly packed inside the tubing, and the device was housed inside a handmade redwood box. The mere act of opening the parcel would detonate it. Like many of the bomber's devices, the demolished condition of the exploded bomb made it impossible for anyone to determine what wiring the bomber had installed and how the device had worked. "The exact wiring of this device cannot be determined due to the fragmented condition of the components," the FBI wrote.

"It has been frustrating. You keep chewing on the same thing," said John C. Killorin of the ATF, "hoping to go further, but it's just not there. Ultimately, you reach the point where there is no more work to be done, where you've chased down every conceivable lead, so you just hope that the person has died, or been put in jail or a hospital, or moved away."

About this time, June 1993, students at Sacramento State noticed odd graffiti. Someone had scrawled the symbol "FC" inside a "peace-symbol-like" circle on the walls of several campus buildings and on objects. The word or letters meant nothing then. The word "anarchy" had been painted in black around the circle. After the June 22 attack on Professor Epstein and the mail bomb maiming of Professor Gelernter two days later (see following chapter), the FBI swarmed over the campus like angry bees. As mentioned, the return address on Epstein's lethal parcel had read: "Professor James Hill, Chemistry Department, California State University at Sacramento"—Sacramento State. And so, agents questioned him. "Mr. Hill has been interviewed and has no knowledge of the parcel," they concluded.

"I think every chemistry faculty member of this department had a visit from an agent of the FBI," said Hill, "because the suspicion was strong at that point that the individual had been on campus or was on campus." Professor Hill had noticed the graffiti, which was considered harmless at the time and washed away.

"The FBI certainly did [think a student might be the Unabomber]. They thoroughly studied the records of certain individuals on this campus," continued Hill. "I believe they had to get special warrants to access data on campus. The suspicion is that this person may have used the library facilities. Some of my faculty suggested some students that were strange at times, and potentially might have had interest in explosive-like materials. They may have been identified to the FBI."

Hill could understand the strategy of the bomber in using his name. "If somebody sees my name at that point, it probably wouldn't have been suspicious. They may have wanted to open it because it came from a university.

"Agents were suspicious that he might be an older person who may have been going to school off and on, in different places," Hill concluded.

The Hermit continued his wandering ways. He came and went unseen, unmissed, and lonely. On August 26, he took as his abode Room 105 of the Park Hotel in Helena and left the following day, probably headed back to Lincoln. But who could know? He moved like smoke—insubstantial, leaving no trace, and, once gone, forgotten.

CHAPTER 31
Gelernter

T herefore two tasks confront those who hate the servitude to which the industrial system is reducing the human race. First, we must work to heighten the social stresses within the system so as to increase the likelihood that it will break down or be weakened sufficiently so that a revolution against it becomes possible. Second, it is necessary to develop and propagate an ideology that opposes technology and the industrial system.

—UNABOMBER MANIFESTO

TWO DAYS AFTER THE ATTACK ON CHARLES EPSTEIN, June 24, 1993, a second leader of the computer science community was struck down by the mysterious bomber. On June 23, a padded envelope, similar to Dr. Epstein's, arrived at the New Haven, Connecticut, campus of Yale University, addressed to renowned computer scientist David Gelernter, age thirty-eight. The impish young man who had once studied to be a rabbi was director of undergraduate studies in computer science, an author, and a fine artist. The parcel, mailed June 18, arrived early in the morning, but took several hours to reach its final destination of Gelernter's desk. Chris, an assistant, picked up the package covered with US Flag–Olympic Ring stamps, and saw that it was addressed to his boss, but knew that Gelernter was out of town that day. The return address read: Mary Jane Lee, Chairman Computer Science, Cal-State. Mary Jane Lee had not been chairperson of that Sacramento department for a year. Currently Anne-Louise Radimsky was. Obviously, the sender was working from outdated reference material.

The professor was due to return the next day, a Thursday, so Chris put the package on his boss's desk and left. The following morning, David Gelernter made his way to his fifth floor office. The building, at 8:00 AM, was silent and apparently deserted. Summer classes had yet to start. The building that houses Yale's Computer Science Department echoed with his steps. He sat down at his desk close to 8:15 and saw the package.

Gelernter, a published author, found his fame growing. He made no secret of his displeasure at the way computers were being used in education and had published several articles filled with creative ideas in national forums, including *The New York Times.* He had once worked with the Department of Anesthesiology, Psychiatry and Radiology at Yale Medical School.

Gelernter's accomplishments were as impressive as Epstein's. He had invented a language that allowed desktop computers to achieve the power of supercomputers by linking them in parallel processing. The landmark computer language he had conceived enabled multiple computers to work on a single problem, thus rivaling the expensive supercomputers. He had impishly dubbed it "Linda." David was the name of the Professor's brother, and Linda the name of his brother's wife, a New York professor herself. Gelernter, however, had christened his language after Linda Lovelace, an early adult film star.

The subtitle of Gelernter's *Mirror Worlds,* a book about parallel programming, was *The Day Software Puts the Universe in a Shoebox,* and coincidentally the package before him was the size of a shoebox.

He unfastened the wrapping, tugged the red pull tab, and immediately a mushroom of red flame and smoke lifted him from

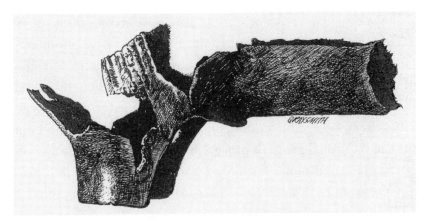

Gelernter pipe bomb fragment.

his seat. Instantly, his right eye stung, shrapnel ripped and bit at his hands and, in microseconds, tore at his chest and abdomen and did more damage to his face. As an artist, his immediate concern was riveted to the state of his eye. If Hauser had been concerned about his fingers and eyes because of his astronaut career, Gelernter's painting career made the same worries foremost in his mind in spite of the pain.

Inside a small homemade redwood box, measuring eight by four by one and a half inches, the Unabomber had hidden a six-inch length of three-eighths-inch copper tubing. He'd sealed the ends with plugs constructed from metal, wood, and glue and held in place with metal pins one-eighth inch in diameter. Packed inside the pipe was a deadly mix of potassium chlorate and aluminum powder. A fusing system was powered by four nine-volt batteries (jackets peeled off like bark from a log) and set in motion by a metal and wood anti-open switch and improvised wooden dowel initiator. Again, the FBI agents were unable to figure out how the wiring inside the pipe functioned because it was fragmented during the blast.

Eugene Sorets, a postdoctoral student in his second-floor room, heard a noise as if "someone had dropped a heavy metal object." He craned his neck upward. The explosion had been near the top of the building, and immediately fire alarms began to sound throughout the cavernous building. Water erupted from the sprinkler system, flowed under doors from various offices, and put out the small fire in Gelernter's office. Meanwhile, the young scientist, intent on saving himself, plunged and weaved blindly headlong down the stairs. He lurched toward the medical center about a half-block away.

He left a trail of blood, bits of bloodied clothing, and his shattered eyeglasses on the stairs. Fourth floor, third, and (finally!), breathing heavily, he reached the second landing and rushed on. He would save himself, he thought. Sorets recalled that "[s]oon I heard groaning and I looked out my window and saw Gelernter running across the street. After the fire alarm went off, I saw blood on the stairs and his bloody shirt lying on the stairway."

Gelernter had rushed out the back door and cut though the parking lot, pushing bystanders who offered help with an agonized shout of "Leave me alone!" Finally, he reached the nearby campus health service.

Later at Yale New Haven Hospital, where he was rushed, the scientist was put under anesthesia and on a respirator. In critical condition, he quickly underwent surgery.

Meanwhile, police dogs, fresh from the recent World Trade Center bombing, sniffed for explosives and weaved warily around the remaining pools of blood on the stairs. But the water had washed away any traces of chemicals, and agents worked over Gelernter's office instead, picking out any possible fragments with tweezers. They collected evidence from the wall, the floor, the furniture, even the ceiling, while one dog howled outside.

As the radio reported the attempt on Gelernter's life, his colleagues were puzzled. "His research is not controversial," said one. "It's aimed at helping humanity."

"He is a very benign, blandish fellow," another said of David. "Everyone is worried and irritated. I know I certainly am not going to open packages in the future without being really cautious."

At midmorning Gelernter's brother, Joel, received an anonymous message at the nearby Veteran's Affairs Medical Center switchboard. Like his sibling, Joel was involved in genetics research as a Yale psychiatrist specializing in that field. He had written highly regarded research on the connection between alcoholism and genetics. The anonymous message was blunt: "You are next."

At Yale New Haven Hospital, doctors were still not certain if David would lose sight in his right eye or what the repercussions of his other wounds might be. Would he be able to paint again? Gelernter's colleague, Bob Dunne, who had known the scientist for many years, said, "I'm shocked to find that the very nice, extremely intelligent guy who was very well respected in the department and community has been the target of such a violent act. I cannot think of anything that could provide a suggestion of why someone would do this."

Two of the staples from Epstein's package and one from Gelernter's parcel evidenced identical tool marks. A "Priority Mail" stamp had been used on both Epstein's and Gelernter's package wrapping, as well as on the previous bomb wrapping of the Fischer and McConnell devices. The same typewriter had been used to write notes to Fischer and to type "Wu—it works! I told you it would.—RV."

Of course, the FBI knew the two bombings had to be connected. Mail bombs to two scientists, both academics, within two days had to be more than coincidence. "It's crazy," said Jim Cavanaugh of ATF. "There are more theories on this guy's motives than there are for JFK's assassination. In fact, we should probably start with Jack Ruby as a suspect. This is an 'Inspector Clouseau' type investigation. We suspect everyone, and we suspect no one."

While Professor Gelernter waited anxiously to find out if his injuries were permanent, he became more and more anxious to get back to his computer and track down the man who'd possibly taken away his painting career. No bomber could touch his fighting spirit.

Much later he spoke to *Time* magazine of the months after his mail bomb maiming. "The public figured that computer technology had been (in some sense) the intended victim," he said in a written piece, "and so I became Mr. Computer Science.... There are computer scientists far more distinguished than I, and to tell the truth, I don't even like computers very much....

"I couldn't care less what the man's views on technology are or what message he intended to deliver; the message I got was that in any society, no matter how rich, just and free, you can rely on there being a certain number of evil cowards. I thank him for passing it along, but I knew that anyway....

"I emerged with great admiration for Senator Dole, whose battlefield injuries were a little like mine; I cribbed my lefty handshake from him, and his example cheered me when things were bad. I'd admired him anyway, but without any sense of personal connection....

"By inclination I'm a writer and a painter.... The explosion smashed my right hand, and for several months I was under the impression I would never paint again; I bitterly regretted the work I had never put down on canvas. But I learned to paint with my left hand and will never again neglect my duties as a painter." Gelernter went on to write a book he'd put off, and published it to much praise. " ...[R]emember and honor the men who were bestially murdered and drink *l'chaim*—to the life of the mind, to the human enterprise that no bomb can touch."

IN THE LATE SEVENTIES the Genentech Corporation programmed a bacterium to produce human insulin by splicing the insulin gene into bacterial DNA, making it possible also to produce human growth hormone in this way. This use of recombinant DNA became known as genetic engineering, techniques that someday may be employed to treat genetic diseases. The design of drugs now includes structure-based drug design in which the three-dimensional structure of the target virus or enzyme is discovered, then a drug is designed that attaches to and changes this structure.

After the attacks on Gelernter and Epstein, Genentech, Inc., south of San Francisco, went on their highest level of security and had all packages and incoming mail into the biotechnology company screened.

Within three-and-a-half months the government would offer more than a $1 million reward for the capture of UNABOM, up from the $60,000 previously pledged for conclusive evidence and the $50,000 before that. The $1 million came from the government, the FBI, the ATF, and the Postal Service, each contributing $150,000 and added to $600,000 donated by the academic and scientific communities—pursuers and victims joined together in a common aim. The FBI's toll-free, twenty-four-hour hotline, (800) 701-BOMB, remained in place, waiting for that vital tip. Hundreds of tips came, but none led them any closer to their quarry.

"I think it's like a hobby with him, when he gets going on it. I think," said Chris Ronay, "he enjoys it almost to the point where he really gets his kicks on this thing. If he's got a job, I think it's something he does when he comes home at night and he plays with it, just like somebody would go to the basement and tie flies.

"He has an uncontrollable urge to fool with this thing as much as possible. And ultimately you have to put it down and have it kill somebody—that's your ultimate gratification. He's leaving a little of himself at each crime scene."

CHAPTER 32

Out with the Old

ON JUNE 24, 1993, FBI DIRECTOR William Steele Sessions still clung to his job as tenaciously as a barnacle on the *Titanic,* steadfastly refusing to give way under mounting pressure. In mid-January of 1993, during the last few days of the Bush administration, the Justice Department ethics office had issued a report charging the white-haired FBI director with a range of ethical violations. These listed infractions included not only the personal use of Bureau aircraft and limousines, but also alleged Sessions had inappropriately used Bureau funds and FBI personnel to construct a $10,000 wooden fence around his Washington, DC, home. Apparently he'd also neglected to pay income taxes on these perks.

Sessions, son of a minister, had been a federal judge in Texas before Ronald Reagan appointed him as FBI head. The Senate confirmed him with nary a conflicting vote, and Sessions was sworn in in September of 1987. Now, halfway through his term,

Sessions had been forced to vigorously defend his ethics simply to stay in office. The inside story in DC was that he had already lost that battle and that just about everybody in DC knew it—except Sessions.

After J. Edgar Hoover's abuses of power during his lifelong term, another omnipotent director was considered unthinkable. Congress had imposed a ten-year limit on the office. Still, no FBI director had ever been fired. Rumor had it that Sessions, by telling President Clinton that, "as a matter of principle," he would never resign in the face of the charges against him, had as good as volunteered to be the first. This very morning Sessions had met privately with Attorney General Janet Reno to discuss his tenure again, vigorously denying any impropriety on his part, but the meeting had not gone well.

Now he attempted to put that meeting out of mind, to focus on the business at hand, a matter too long neglected that had now forced its way back onto the front burner. This was the type of challenge an FBI director ought to be able to sink his teeth into, rather than arguing over expense reports. And the type of challenge that might save an FBI director's career. Sessions was speeding aboard an FBI jet toward a conference in San Francisco to reenergize his Bureau in the pursuit of the most elusive domestic terrorist in US history and to put into effect a drastic change in strategy for those hunting him.

As the embattled FBI chief reached to turn on a light above his seat and opened the blue-covered investigation booklet on his lap, the mocking capital letters UNABOM on the casebook glared up at him. The director had been well briefed and knew that UNABOM had struck at the most famous universities and computer experts since 1978, successfully concealing his identity and

THE INVESTIGATION

motives from three powerful government arms—the Postal Service, the ATF, and the FBI. Insubstantial as a puff of smoke, their quarry seemed even more unknown and uncatchable than ever after fifteen long years.

The contrast with the Bureau's generally outstanding record on domestic terrorism was overwhelming, and discouraging. On one hand Sessions counted off the number of major terrorist bombers the Bureau had pursued. They had gotten all of them, except for this one. The Bureau could point with pride at its triumphs, but this one vexing terrorist had perplexed them for fifteen years.

Bombers, especially when bombing for a cause, as FC was now claiming, usually left behind not only a great deal of useful physical evidence, but a crystal clear motive as well. One of the first big bombing cases the Bureau had helped on, the Mad Bomber case, had been a better-than-textbook-quality example of profiling at its best. But there had been recent equally dramatic victories as well: The VANPAC bombings, just two years ago, had shown the FBI, Sessions's FBI, at its best. Against VANPAC the Bureau played on its own turf: the mass processing of abundant clues through its huge and highly intelligent data-base systems. And just this past February, when the World Trade Center fell victim to the most powerful terrorist bomb ever exploded in the US, Sessions's FBI sent three hundred of its agents into the field within hours and had an arrest in days. Though one terrorism expert later likened the Trade Center bombers to the "Three Stooges," there had been some real detective work to do, and coordinating an investigation that large toward a result that quickly had been a masterwork.

As Sessions gazed out over a sea of white clouds below him he reflected how the Bureau's experience with small radical groups like the Weather Underground in the early seventies and the United Freedom Front, which exploded ten bombs between 1982 and 1984, had given them the insights and experience that had made solving some of these later incidents look almost easy. US domestic incidents of terrorism plummeted from a hundred in the seventies to a mere seven in the nineties. Much of that was due to the calming political climate as the sixties and Vietnam became more distant memories. But good police work played its part. After all, terrorist attacks throughout the globe had increased 11 percent in 1992. That year the US had not had one.

Now, halfway through 1993, already there had been two bombings, both in June, by the man who was many men. The Junkyard Bomber, the University Bomber, the Airline Bomber, *The New York Times* Bomber, or simply UNABOM, who remained the FBI's most wanted domestic terrorist year after year. UNABOM had not only eluded his legions of pursuers, but avoided leaving behind any definite pattern or clear motive for his crimes. Between 1978 and 1987, targeting business leaders and educators, he'd placed twelve bombs in six states, injured twenty-one individuals, and killed one man, Hugh Scrutton. Only through luck had he not claimed more lives. His intention had clearly been lethal.

Then he had gone silent for more than six years. But that was not why he had eluded them. In early 1987, when he was glimpsed in Salt Lake City, they had not even been close. When he had gone silent, they had hoped against hope that he had died, been incapacitated, or even incarcerated for another crime, which unbeknownst to the public, are three of the most common ways serial murders are actually terminated. The Unabomber team had been largely disbanded; several of the important players were now retired. But without fail, since the seventies, the FBI had held an annual conference in an attempt to solve the riddle of the uncatchable man.

Sessions summarized the case in his mind. What had they missed? The truth was there had been little to miss. The evidence by itself said so little. And though the man who was many men clearly had a purpose, up to now that purpose had been clear only to himself.

Up to now.

In the wake of the two June bombings, the first Unabomber activity on Sessions's watch, the Director had begun to pump new life into the investigation. The UNABOM team, largely disbanded, would be regrouped and rededicate themselves to the task. Retired agents from the old team were called back in. Because the bomber appeared to have returned to his old stomping grounds, with his two new bombs stamped with Bay Area postmarks, in a few days Janet Reno would announce that the new UNABOM Task Force, a multi-agency effort to encourage cooperation among the federal agencies, would be headquartered in San Francisco.

True, some in the Bureau reserved some doubt that the two new bombs were the work of a single man. And Sessions, understanding the drama of the moment, took advantage of their skepticism to delay the Bureau's announcement that the old bomber was back at work. He had allowed San Francisco FBI spokesman Rick Smith to tease the press with the possibility that the nineties bomber was the same man as the seventies and eighties bomber. But it would remain a tease until the Director himself convened his news conference and announced the really dramatic news. First, he checked into his hotel, freshened up, called his daughter, who lived in the Bay Area, then thought about what he was going to say.

"Ladies and gentlemen," announced Agent Smith, "FBI Director William S. Sessions."

Sessions strode confidently to the podium. He wore a dark suit, paisley tie, and his trademark round glasses. An American flag and the California state flag flanked him on either side. The FBI seal, imposingly large, dominated the curtain directly behind him. Sessions cleared his throat and began. He spoke in his now-familiar Texas drawl directly into a bank of radio and television microphones marked KGO, KPIX, and KRON and attached to the lectern.

Sessions mentioned the two June bombings and connected them to a past bombing at the University of California at Berkeley computer science building, Cory Hall. "The FBI will go back and look at all similar bombings," he said, "and if there are firm links, that will come from the evidence."

Smith displayed photos of the new bombs, exhibiting a picture of the June 24 Yale explosion first. An associate professor had been seriously injured, Sessions explained, and indicated an enlarged photograph of a black bomb squad truck and Connecticut State police cars crowded in front of a science building.

A second photo depicted a world renowned professor, the target of the June 22 bomb, being rushed on a stretcher to a waiting ambulance. The whole city knew about the bomb that had exploded in Dr. Epstein's hands at his bayside suburban home in Tiburon, California. In the picture, rivet-like marks of the blast were clearly evident on the scholar's face.

So far the story was unchanged. The bombs were made of untraceable materials. The attacks themselves left the motives murky. But then something completely different had happened.

THE INVESTIGATION

The bomber had opened a line of communication.

Mere hours after the explosion at Yale, a *New York Times* staffer named Kris Ensminger opened a letter addressed to her boss, Warren Hoge, an assistant managing editor. She was used to kook mail—"We get a lot of crazy letters." But the cryptic typewritten letter postmarked Monday, June 21, 1993, return address unknown and mailed from Sacramento, seemed not only intelligent to her, but also "something serious."

In the letter, UNABOM predicted the June 22 attack and linked his earlier bombs from the seventies and eighties with a clue. On the letter itself, investigators discovered a faint impression of a second message written previously on the sheet of paper that had been on top of it. "Call Nathan R Wed 7 pm" it read. The actual letter was passed around by the *Times* security staff, and any usable prints were smudged beyond recovery.

"The FBI is seriously studying this letter," said Sessions. An excited Rick Smith identified the one-paragraph communication as "as good a lead as we have." The text ran as follows:

> We are an anarchist group calling ourselves FC. Notice that the postmark on this envelope precedes a newsworthy event that will happen about the time you receive this letter, if nothing goes wrong. This will prove that we knew about the event in advance, so our claim of responsibility is truthful. Ask the FBI about FC. They have heard of us. We will give information about our goals at some future time. Right now we only want to establish our identity and provide an identifying number that will ensure the authenticity of any future communications from us. Keep this number secret so that no one else can pretend to speak in our name.

A nine-digit number followed, 553-25-4394, printed at the bottom and resembling a Social Security number. Future communications through the secret number could be counted on as coming from the same person if the FBI withheld it as suggested, and this was done when the *Times* published the letter on June 25.

The bomber had broken his long silence, decisively and with the promise of future communication. His previous missives to a few victims had been tricks to get them to open packages, part of his disguise. No, it was he himself speaking on his own behalf. Perhaps more revealing than any other line in the letter was "Right now we only want to establish our identity," an ambition his pursuers shared. What had inspired their sudden loquacity? The rash of publicity for other bombers, far less competent then he, when he apparently had always been ignored? Did the crude force of the Trade Center bombing offend his precise sensibilities? In one respect at least he seemed to be showing off in the message. Agents noted that the first three digits of the number were the same as Social Security cards issued to California residents. Task Force members quickly traced it.

The nine numbers were actually valid and were those of a twenty-year-old parolee living in Northern California. Investigators had a hard time accepting that as coincidence, given FC's obsession with wood. Astonishingly, the parolee had a tattoo that said, "Pure Wood." Did UNABOM have an accomplice? The petty criminal apparently had been behind bars at the time some of the bombings occurred, which probably ruled him out. But what a tantalizing clue, or was there another accomplice who had known the convict? Perhaps the bomber himself had once known him?

Now that the bomber had gone public, so did the government.

Immediately after Sessions's press conference the FBI publicly announced that the mysterious bomber had returned and was up to his devilish tricks as he continued to spread random terror.

"The intricacy of the device, the workmanship, the materials, and the manner in which it was constructed all come together to form a signature that has enabled investigators to conclude it is the work of the same person or persons," Milton Ahlerich, FBI special agent in charge in Connecticut, said. "We figured he was dead or in jail or in the appropriate facility, but he's back in a big way, which is all the more maddening."

With the FBI's encouragement the *Times* published the letter, along with a growing number of details released by the Feds. Even the bomber's ID of FC, once the Bureau's precious secret, was now known to the entire nation. Within a few months the FBI would set up a Web site carrying almost all known information, except such details as could inspire copycats, and informing Web browsers of a one-million-dollar reward for information leading to the bomber's capture.

The attack on Professor Gelernter at Yale had excited the interest of East Coast newspapers and television news programs, including several tabloid shows, in the bombings for the first time. The unsolved case now drew hundreds of new tips daily.

As for the sparse writings contributed by the bomber over the long manhunt, the top experts in codes and forensic psychiatry scrutinized them. In desperation, rumor went, the FBI even turned to a psychic.

Chillingly, the letter had promised more attacks on prominent scholars by mail bomb nationwide. Explosions by post were next to impossible to guard against from the post office end—who could screen the 160 billion pieces of mail flowing yearly through

US mailboxes? This prompted Sessions to post a computer message to major universities saying that "professors should be particularly cautious about any packages that contain excessive postage, incorrect names or titles and misspellings of common words on the return address."

The FBI's alert for suspicious parcels was sent over the national computer network used by universities (specifically most university computer science departments), and explained that excessive postage suggested the mailer wanted to avoid going through a post office. Harvard, Yale, and MIT set up training sessions for their respective mail departments. "There has to be a concern for everybody in scientific research," lamented Sessions.

Some colleges, fearing copycats, did not want to be listed publicly as possible targets and warned their faculty on their own. "Watch for telltale signs," they cautioned, "—stains on a package. Explosive chemicals often leave marks; look for erratic writing on the wrapping, and no return address."

"We're telling people to be especially heads-up in light of the Yale and UCSF incidents," said a UC spokesman. Other University of California at Berkeley officials instituted special security measures, and UCSF Police Chief Ron Nelson canceled days off for all twenty-five of his uniformed campus officers and placed them on alert. At all nine UC facilities in San Francisco, patrols were stepped up. Coincidentally, on the day Sessions conducted his briefing, UCSF campus police unearthed a package discarded on college grounds. But it turned out to contain only a manuscript.

The Bureau also began sharing more widely its psychological profile of the bomber, again updated, taking into account the passage of years and any changes in the bomber's pattern. The report

The first sketch of the Unabomber, 3-10-87, by Bob Exter.

San Francisco FBI Chief Jim Freeman standing next to the notorious sketch and telling reporters in June of 1995 that he is "100 percent sure" the Unabomber wrote the jetliner terror letter sent to the San Francisco Chronicle.

AP/MIKE DERER

Grieving Mosser family (left) and emergency scene (below) after ad executive Thomas J. Mosser opened a cassette-sized mail bomb, killing him at his North Caldwell, New Jersey, home on 10-10-94.

WARREN GOLDBERG/SABA

UPI/CORBIS-BETTMANN

Captain John Hauser being rushed away from another Berkeley explosion, 5-15-85, after a bomb, disguised as a loose-leaf binder, blows off most of his right hand, ending his dream of becoming an astronaut.

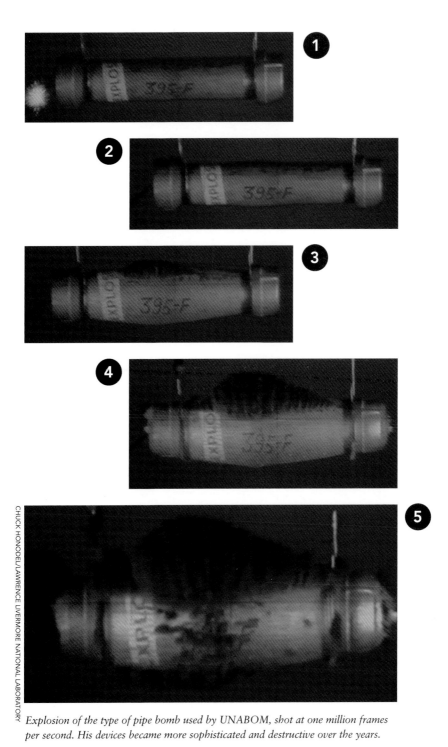

Explosion of the type of pipe bomb used by UNABOM, shot at one million frames per second. His devices became more sophisticated and destructive over the years.

(Above) Investigators prepare to enter Sacramento office ravaged by an explosion that killed timber lobbyist Gil Murray on 4-24-95. (Left) Blood left on pavement outside the door Hugh Scrutton exited, before picking up a bomb disguised as a road hazard.

Bomb fragments from the Unabomber's first lethal device, the bomb that burst Hugh Scrutton's heart in the parking lot behind his Sacramento, California, computer store on 10-11-85.

The Professor's brother David, and Juan Sanchez Arreola, a farmhand. Sanchez assisted David in he the construction of his wilderness cabin on the West Texas plains.

Faithful friend, Sanchez, of Ojinaga, Mexico, holds a Christmas present from his reclusive pen pal of seven years. The Latin phrase reads, "MOUNTAINMEN ARE ALWAYS FREE."

The Professor's brother David, writer and youth counselor in Schenectady, New York, made the most agonizing decision of his life at the beginning of 1996.

The focal point of the Hermit's life, the mailbox was a meeting place for rides and brought news of the outside world and letters from his brother. It was the last point of civilization before the trek to his shack.

Brother David's own remote cabin forty miles north of Mexico. Previously, he'd lived in a hole in the arid land, covered by sheets of corrugated tin and canvas. Photo circa 1980s.

The Hermit's Thoreau-inspired cabin outside Lincoln, Montana, on Humbug Contour Road, near Big River, circa 1996.

The Lincoln Community Library, intellectual home of the Hermit, where the recluse spent countless hours reading and researching his victims in out-of-date journals causing him to incorrectly address packaged bombs.

Author Robert Graysmith at the Unabomber's cabin site after FBI agents uncovered a live bomb and sealed off the area.

(Above) Near the Hermit's feces-fertilized garden is the bucket he used for his shower.

(Right) Plastic containers—possibly used for straining chemicals—hanging around the recluse's shack sway eerily above the root cellar and drying shed.

The gradual twenty-five–year decline of the man the FBI called the most wanted, elusive criminal in history. The Professor, as a shy, innocent-looking high school senior, 1958 (top left); a mathematical genius at Harvard, 1962 (top center); as Campbell Hall professor at the tumultuous University of California at Berkeley, 1968 (top right). The mountainman's Utah driver's license photo, 1958 (bottom left); and the suspect's booking mug shot, 1996 (bottom center). The FBI arrested America's most wanted letter-bomber on 4-3-96, ending an 18-year search. With torn clothes and covered in dirt, the Hermit is taken to Clark County jail in Helena, Montana (center).

Ringed by FBI agents in Helena, Montana, 4-4-96, the Hermit was dressed for court and extradition to Sacramento—the center of attention at last (bottom right).

THE INVESTIGATION

suggested that UNABOM probably labored at menial jobs and spent his formative years in the Chicago area, the site of the first four bombs. Chicago was a good shot as was, to a lesser extent, menial labor. But the profile continued to be misleading in a number of ways, positing that the bomber had resided in Utah, where two bombs were set, and had moved to California. Failed college students, along with disgruntled airline employees and odd ducks reported by coworkers, neighbors, and family continued to be targets of the investigation.

This one dramatic change, toward getting the public involved by communicating as much as possible about the Unabomber, and by implication with him as well, would eventually be the key to solving the case.

In the meantime, however, not much else changed. The tendency toward a self-crippling giantism in the investigation ran on more powerfully than ever, stoked by so many new clues, generating even more new clues. The FBI just naturally has a proclivity for mass high-tech operations, sort of like a Russian infantry campaign commanded by NASA. Their reaction to "Nathan R" for instance was to add every Nathan R in the country to the suspect list and to interview all of them, some ten thousand additional suspects. Similarly, authorities continued to scrutinize the names of more than eighty thousand former residents of Chicago, because Unabomber seemed to have once lived there.

The newly reconstituted Task Force began a series of what they called "Immersion Conferences." One by one they called in everyone connected in any way with the bombings that had occurred so far—all were put up in hotels during the interview sessions in San Francisco where the Task Force was headquartered. They began with the people mentioned on the wrapping of each bomb—sender and addressee, then moved on to secondary subjects.

Some of the names included: Professor Buckley Crist (three long interviews); Professor Ed Smith, graduate student and second victim; John Harris (interviewed a single time); Terry Marker, the security guard who was burned on his left hand (interviewed only once); people on board Flight No. 444; Percy Wood, United Airlines President; Professor John Hauser; members of the Boeing Aircraft Company Fabrication Division in Auburn, Washington; Dr. James V. McConnell (torn away from his worm training experiments); employees of the RenTech Computer Rental Company in Sacramento; and the Salt Lake City witness who briefly glimpsed the Unabomber in the CAAMs parking lot.

James Hill of Sacramento State, whose name was found on the return address of the June 22 bomb posted to Dr. Epstein, was the subject of the most intense and repeated questioning by thirteen agents. Two experts in the field of psychology and computers monitored the conferences.

The UTF continued to work on variants to the profile. While the bombs had grown steadily more sophisticated and effective and the bomber's workmanship was so painstaking in many ways, at the most detailed level the workmanship had always been crude: the overdone soldering, clumsy wire work, the wood carving done with a crude chisel. Some agents floated the idea that UNABOM might have a physical handicap of some sort. Another agent found that personally insulting to the physically challenged.

A Dungeons and Dragons lead had to be checked out; of course it led nowhere. All of this information, even disparaging com-

ments from metalworkers and carpenters about the bomber's cru-
dities were logged in with thousands of new facts from the interviews. The data base swelled until it creaked like an overloaded
wagon. Hitched to this were the investigators, sweating, pulling
like a team of oxen.

THE MORNING AFTER his UNABOM press briefing in San
Francisco, William Sessions flew back to Washington, DC, and
prepared, as *Newsweek* phrased it, to be "dragged kicking and
screaming from his office." Some good news awaited him though.
The FBI had prevented another terrorist bombing while he'd been
out West jump-starting the UNABOM Task Force.

The planned bombing might have been more horrific than the
World Trade Center blast, erupting fire throughout the United
Nations headquarters and funneling smoke and flames into the
Lincoln Tunnel beneath the Hudson River. The terrorists had
scheduled these events to occur symbolically on the Fourth of
July, but a SWAT team of New York City police and FBI agents
had stopped them cold. Just before dawn, authorities burst into a
bomb factory in a Queens garage, surprising five men hunched
over barrels stirring mixtures of fertilizer and diesel fuel to blend
an explosive paste.

"We entered so fast," said James Fox, special FBI agent in
charge, "some of the subjects didn't realize strangers were in the
bomb factory until they had the handcuffs being put on them."

The FBI's watchword for the future became "prevention." The
Bureau had succeeded in quashing the plot early because they'd
infiltrated the gang through an informant. Recently, agents had
also captured eight California white supremacists allegedly
preparing to assassinate Rodney King, who in a sense sparked the

recent LA riots, and then blow up a black church. Over the next years a disturbing number of black churches would be torched by arsonists.

Ironically the FBI had arrested the Lincoln Tunnel plotters the same day that the Yale bomb package detonated. Terrorist groups might in the long run be easier to foil because a weak link always exists in large numbers. But UNABOM worked alone (so far the FBI had no facts to contradict this), which nullified the use of an infiltrator.

As for Director Sessions, sitting gloomily in his capital office, the end was near. Attorney General Reno ordered him to meet with her at the Justice Department on July 17, a Saturday. Bluntly, Reno told Sessions that President Clinton would be forced to fire him if he did not resign by Monday. As the FBI chief departed from his meeting with Reno, he tripped on a curb and fractured his right arm in the fall. That made two times he'd fallen in the same hour, one literally and the other symbolic. Returning from the hospital, Sessions met with reporters in the twilight outside his house and reiterated that he would not, as a matter of principle, resign.

Two days later the protracted standoff ended with a whimper. Clinton was forced to remove Sessions from his post after the attorney general concluded that the Director had shown "serious deficiencies in judgment."

Deputy Attorney General Phillip Heymann met with Sessions in his office and informed him that Clinton was going to call him personally at 3:50 PM. "He will dismiss you," said Heymann. And at exactly that time the president called to do just that, then faxed a letter to the former director formally notifying him of his removal. But at 3:59 PM Sessions still sat stonily in his office.

THE INVESTIGATION

He had not turned in his FBI badge or his credentials. A second phone call came from Clinton, telling Sessions that the firing was to take effect "immediately" and for the Director to begin gathering up his personal effects. At 6:00 PM an agent escorted Sessions to the front door and ended the torture.

Temporarily, the president named Deputy Director Floyd Clark as Sessions's replacement, but the next day forty-three-year-old straight-arrow US District Judge Louis J. Freeh was nominated to succeed Sessions as director. Freeh, a Mafia-busting federal prosecutor, had helped obtain the 1987 convictions of a heroin ring in a case popularly called the "Pizza Connection." He'd spent many years fighting racketeering on New York's waterfront.

The darkly handsome Freeh entered a new FBI, one still reevaluating itself. Sworn in on September 1, he promised the nation and a crowd of 1,500 people gathered in the FBI courtyard that "as we hurtle toward the twenty-first century, we must confront the stark realities of crime and disorder with an unprecedented dedication of purpose. The greatest enemy here is losing faith that we can control and reverse the pandemic of crime."

Back in San Francisco, Agent Rick Smith was thrilled with the choice of Freeh as Sessions's replacement, but he was also worried. Classes were beginning at the UC Medical Center. One of the new seminars offered was how to recognize a mail bomb. Additionally, the *San Francisco Chronicle* ran various articles warning of the danger hovering over the coming fall semester at UC Berkeley. Then, Smith knew, the bomber would have scores of possible targets to choose from. The next device didn't necessarily have to come through the mails. It might come in the guise of an innocuous appearing object lying about a professor's office, possibly in Cory Hall.

But why, after a six-year gap, had the bomber emerged from the safety of his retreat to jeopardize his freedom by presenting the FBI with a host of fascinating new clues to his identity and purpose and whereabouts? Did he just want attention, or was he about to divulge his motive after all these years?

Safe in his lair, UNABOM provided the FBI with three postmarks within the space of a week that placed him in Sacramento, an area he'd killed in eight years previously. Bell and Biondi were still wrestling with that. To the frustrated agents these tidbits were gold. Now if the bomber chose his targets from individuals recently profiled in *The New York Times,* did this mean his elusive motive might be jealousy? Had these leaders excelled in life in ways he never could? Was the powerful emotion of jealousy the key to the bomber's personality? It had seemed suspicious that UNABOM had written a letter to the *Times* to announce his reentrance into the arena of domestic terror on the heels of a quote in the New York paper from the suspected Trade Center bomb ringleader on the enormous damage inflicted. Was the elusive motive as simple as a matter of professional jealousy?

In the turbulent wake of Sessions's departure, Freeh took on the enormous task of tracking down UNABOM—once again, the torch was passed from detective to detective as men dropped out of the hunt and were replaced by other investigators. The bomber outlasted them all. While no one had yet unraveled the reasoning of this clever, possibly insane bomber, not a single agent, retired or active, on the case believed UNABOM would ever stop killing and maiming on his own.

THE INVESTIGATION

EXCERPT FROM FBI UNABOMBER WEB SITE, JANUARY 1994

--- Original message follows ---

Return path:

Received: from local host by cdp.igc.org
(8.6.4/Revision: 1.124)
Tue. 18 Jan 1994 23:39:22 -0800
Date: Tue, 18 Jan 1994 23:39:22 -0880
--- Hit <RETURN> for more---

Mail?

From: Fred Reeves
Message-Id: <199401190739.XAA23164@cdp.igc.org>
Subject: UNABOM - $1,000,000.00 Reward - Series of 14
Unsolved Bombings
Apparently-To:

> UNABOM
> $1,000,000 Reward
> SERIES OF 14 UNSOLVED BOMBINGS

Beginning in May, 1978, a series of 14 bombing incidents have
occurred across the United States for which there is no apparent
explanation or motive. No person or group has been identified as
the perpetrator(s) of these incidents. The explosions have taken
place in seven states from Connecticut to California. As a result
of these bombings, one person has been killed and 23 others
injured, some grievously. There had been no incidents identified
with this series of bombings since 1987. However that changed
in late June, 1993, when a well known geneticist residing in

Tiburon, California, and a renown computer scientist from Yale
University, New Haven, Connecticut, opened packages which had
been mailed to them and both were severely injured when these
packages exploded.

In the past, targets of the bomber have been associated with the
computer industry, the aircraft and airline industry and universities. Seven of these devices have been mailed to specific
individuals and the other seven have been placed in locations
which suggest there was no specific intended victim. All but two
of the explosive devices functioned as designed and exploded. All
14 crimes, dubbed "UNABOM", have had common effects: all
have caused terror, grief, and fear. On September 11, 1985,
Hugh Scrutton, the owner of the RenTech Computer Company, in
Sacramento, California, was killed by one of these diabolic
devices. The two most recent victims narrowly escaped death.

In response to the June, 1993, events, the Attorney General
directed that a Task Force of federal law enforcement agencies be
reestablished to urgently investigate and solve these crimes. The
UNABOM Task Force, consisting of investigators from the FBI,
ATF, and the US Postal Inspection Service, has been operational
in San Francisco and Sacramento, California, since July 12,
1993, and is dedicated exclusively to the investigation of these
crimes.

Among the clues in the case are the following words in what
appears to be a note possibly written by the bomber as a
reminder to make a telephone call: "call Nathan R—Wed 7PM."
The UNABOM Task Force believes that "Nathan R" may be associated, perhaps innocently, with the bomber and that "Nathan

THE INVESTIGATION

R" may have received a telephone call from the bomber on a Wednesday prior to the June, 1993 bombings.

The two most recent tragic bombings illustrate the senseless and tragic consequences of these crimes and demonstrate the urgent necessity of solving this case. This serial bomber will strike again. We do not know who the next victim will be. We do believe that there is someone out there who can provide the identity of the person or persons responsible for these crimes. This person may be a friend, a neighbor, or even a relative of the bomber(s).

UNABOM's chronology is as follows:

1) Northwestern University
Evanston, Illinois
May 25, 1978

A package was found in the Engineering Department parking lot at the Chicago Circle Campus of the University of Illinois. The package was addressed to an Engineering Professor at Rensselaer Polytechnic Institute in Troy, New York. The package had a return address of a Professor at Northwestern's Technological Institute. The package was returned to the addressor who turned it over to the Northwestern University Police Department because he had not sent the package. On May 26, 1978 the parcel was opened by a police officer who suffered minor injuries when the bomb detonated.

2) Northwestern University
Evanston, Illinois
May 9, 1979

A disguised explosive device which had been left in a common area in the University's Technological Institute, slightly injured a graduate student on May 9, 1979, when he attempted to open the box and it exploded.

3) Chicago, Illinois
November 15, 1979

An explosive device disguised as a parcel was mailed from Chicago for delivery to an unknown location. The bomb detonated in the cargo compartment of an airplane, forcing it to make an emergency landing at Dulles Airport. Twelve individuals were treated for smoke inhalation. The explosion destroyed the wrapping to such an extent that the addressee could not be determined.

4) Chicago, Illinois
June 10, 1980

A bomb disguised as a parcel postmarked June 8, 1980 was mailed to an airline executive at his home in Lake Forest, Illinois. The airline executive was injured in the explosion.

5) University of Utah
Salt Lake City, Utah
October 8, 1981

An explosive device was found in the hall of a classroom building and rendered safe by bomb squad personnel.

6) Vanderbilt University
Nashville, Tennessee
May 5, 1982

THE INVESTIGATION

A wooden box containing a pipe bomb detonated on May 5, 1982, when opened by a secretary in the Computer Science Department. The secretary suffered minor injuries. The package was initially mailed from Provo, Utah on April 23, 1982, to Pennsylvania State University and then forwarded to Vanderbilt.

7) University of California
Berkeley, California
July 2, 1982

A small metal pipe bomb was placed in a coffee break room of Cory Hall at the University's Berkeley Campus. A Professor of Electrical Engineering and Computer Science was injured when he picked up the device.

8) Auburn, Washington
May 8, 1985

A parcel bomb was mailed on May 8, 1985, to the Boeing Company, Fabrication Division. On June 13, 1985, the explosive device was discovered when employees opened it. The device was rendered safe by bomb squad personnel without injury.

9) University of California
Berkeley, California
May 15, 1985

A bomb detonated in a computer room at Cory Hall on the Berkeley Campus. A graduate student in Electrical Engineering lost partial vision in his left eye and four fingers from his right hand. The device was believed to have been placed in the room several days prior to detonation.

THE INVESTIGATION

10) Ann Arbor, Michigan
November 15, 1985

A textbook size package was mailed to the home of a University of Michigan Professor in Ann Arbor, Michigan from Salt Lake City. On November 15, 1985, a Research Assistant suffered injuries when he opened the package. The Professor was a few feet away but was not injured.

11) Sacramento, California
December 11, 1985

Mr. Hugh Scrutton was killed outside his computer rental store when he picked up a device disguised as a road hazard left near the rear entrance to the building. Metal shrapnel from the blast ripped through Scrutton's chest and penetrated his heart.

12) Salt Lake City, Utah
February 20, 1987

On February 20, 1987, an explosive device disguised as a road hazard was left at the rear entrance to CAAMs, Inc. (Computer store). The bomb exploded and injured the owner when he attempted to pick up the device.

13) Tiburon, California
June 22, 1993

On June 22, 1993, a well known geneticist received a parcel postmarked June 18, 1993, at his residence. The doctor attempted to open the package at which time it exploded severely injuring him. It has been determined that his parcel was mailed from Sacramento, California.

THE INVESTIGATION

14) Yale University
New Haven, Connecticut
June 24, 1993

On June 24, 1993, a Professor/Computer Scientist at Yale
University attempted to open a parcel which he had received at
this office. This parcel exploded severely injuring him. It has
been determined that this parcel was mailed from Sacramento,
California on June 18, 1993.

At this time, the UNABOM Task Force would appeal to the public
for assistance. For this purpose, a one million dollar reward is
being offered for information which results in the identification,
arrest and conviction of the person(s) responsible. Contact the
UNABOM Task Force at 1-(800) 701-2662.

William L. Tafoya, Ph.D.
Special Agent, FBI
UNABOM Task Force
San Francisco, CA
btafoya@orion.arc.nasa.gov

CHAPTER 33

Death and the River

*A*nd *with wild nature we include human nature,
by which we mean those aspects of the functioning of
the human individual that are not subject to regulation by
organized society but are products of chance, or free will,
or God (depending on your religious or philosophical
opinions)....*

—UNABOMBER MANIFESTO

THE BIG BLACKFOOT WAS DYING. Not the slightest doubt existed in
the Hermit's mind. That magnificent river had once swarmed
with rainbow and brown trout, its cold mountain waters alive
with the zing of fly-fishermen's lines and transparent leaders.
Golden lines, suspended in halos of spray as graceful arcs and fan-
ciful figure-eights, had glittered in twilights that seemingly lingered forever. But somewhere up at the river's head lay trouble—a
long-abandoned mine. The lode festered, pumping out toxins in a
flow as mighty as Big River itself. Arsenic and zinc, by-products
of the past, flowed endlessly, moving among black rocks and
swirling water, killing as they proceeded.

The afternoon wind had fallen, but the trees still murmured
like the dying river. He stood alone on the banks where the Big
River passed Stemple Pass Road and was lost in and reborn in the
spray and the shadow of the day. "It isn't the biggest river we

fished, but it is the most powerful, and per pound, so are its fish," Norman Maclean had written in the thirties. He found them to be the jumpiest, biggest, leanest fish—but not anymore. The bull and cutthroat trout had dwindled drastically. Some twenty years ago a flash rain storm had burst the mine's settling pond, propelling one hundred thousand tons of toxic waste downstream. Soon Big River began to bleed and blacken from these poisons. The steady sedimentation of streams from erosion, combined with settling pond seepage and present toxins, still kill salmon and trout for the entire length of the waterway from its headwaters at Rogers Pass to Bonner, Montana.

This same mine filled a hundred miles of the upper Clark Fork River with mining toxins. The Environmental Protection Agency rated it as the largest site on the Superfund list of highest-priority pollution sites. It would take at least a billion-and-a-half dollars to clean the mine up and return Big River to its former state.

In 1994 all of Lincoln was buzzing with talk of plans by Phelps Dodge Mining Company to establish a gold mine on the Big River. This proposal—to open a huge gold-mining operation in Lewis and Clark country—had alarmed environmental activists in Lincoln such as Becky Garland, Cecil's daughter, one of the few people the Hermit confided in. In addition to running her family's dry-goods store with sister Theresa, she was president of Trout Unlimited, a group fighting against the mine's establishment and legacy of producing acid-laden waste.

"Generally he came into my store in the summertime, and I didn't always work all the time," Becky said later. She did not find him threatening at all. "As far as an actual threat," she recalled, "he was so quiet that that would never have happened. The things you had to [deal with] was that he just didn't smell well. He had a real musky, smokey odor about him and his hair stood straight up...."

"He was almost pathologically shy. He would speak only if spoken to, and if you had some sort of conversation going at all, if he chose to stop it would be immediately. You knew the conversation was over. You knew he was going to leave."

Sometime that summer of 1994 Becky looked up to see the Hermit, neater and cleaner than she'd ever seen him. More talkative than usual, the Hermit spoke of her hard work on behalf of environmental causes. He paused, then said something unusual.

"I'm running out of funds, and I don't know how to go out and get a job. It's been so long since I've done something like that."

The Hermit passed her a handwritten letter, a combination of biography and resumé. Garland was stunned to realize that he was a Harvard grad with a doctorate in mathematics from the University of Michigan, that he'd been a math instructor at Berkeley. The Hermit revealed more to her about himself than anyone in Lincoln would have ever thought possible.

The Hermit traveled that summer and was at the Park Hotel in August. But the Unabomber was silent.

ADVERTISING EXECUTIVE THOMAS J. MOSSER, fifty years old, had been away on business when the package arrived at his house at 15 Aspen Drive in the well-to-do North Caldwell, New Jersey, area. The next morning, December 10, 1994, he sat in the kitchen, pulling his bathrobe tighter around his neck as he waited for his wife, Susan, his two daughters—Kim, thirteen years, and Kelly, fifteen months—and a neighbor child to go shopping for a Christmas tree. Presently, they were in another wing of the home. Mosser passed the time thumbing through the mail, then noticed a package his wife had considered opening several times the previous day, but she had always been called away before she could.

Mosser studied the package, noting it appeared to be about the same size and weight as two video cassettes stacked together. It

looked as if it had at least sixty stamps plastered on it. According
to the typewritten return address on the red, white, and blue
label, one HC Wickel of the Department of Economics at San
Francisco State University, 94132, had sent it and according to
the postmark had done it on Saturday, December 3, from San
Francisco near the university. Wickel, though, had labeled the
parcel to Mosser in care of Burson-Marsteller, a company he'd
left nine months previously. So, whoever Wickel was, he wasn't
too familiar with the firm—he'd misspelled the name as "Burston-
Marsteller." Mosser had joined that company, a public relations
subsidiary of the Manhattan-based Young & Rubicam, one of the
world's largest ad agencies, in 1969. When Mosser left, he joined
the parent company, Young & Rubicam, and only nine days ago
had been promoted to executive vice president and general manager, a promotion featured in both the *Wall Street Journal* and
New York Times the day before the parcel was posted.

During the time Mosser served as Burson-Marsteller's vice
president and chief operating officer, Exxon had been a client of
the firm. In March 1989, the *Exxon Valdez* split open on Bligh
Reef in Prince William Sound and spilled eleven million gallons of
crude oil into the environment. But, contrary to a radical publication, *Earth First!*, printed two months ago, Burson-Marsteller,
and especially Mosser, had no hand in softening the image of the
oil tanker disaster in the nation's press.

The well-connected Mosser shaped public opinion and promoted various technologies but he knew more about the entertainment industry and sports world. "I did not see that he was
tied into the technology industry," said a coworker, although the
previous month Young & Rubicam picked up two computer-
related clients—the Desktop Document Systems division of Xerox
Corp. of Palo Alto, California, and Massachusetts-based Digital
Equipment Corp.

As for his work at Burson-Marsteller, Mosser had helped Johnson & Johnson field inquiries during the Tylenol tampering poisoning cases in 1982, when seven Chicagoans had taken Tylenol capsules someone had laced with cyanide. During his tenure as vice chairman and chief operating officer he handled Coca-Cola's disastrous introduction of new Coke and the successful unveiling of Coca-Cola Classic. In 1984 he organized the cross-country Olympic Torch Run and earlier had served as a member of the New York City Bicentennial Committee.

Mosser decided the man who sent him this package was working from outdated information, and began to open the neatly wrapped white package. The Saturday morning calm was broken by a tremendous explosion, blowing a two-foot-wide hole in the formica counter and decapitating Mosser. Clouds of smoke roiled through the house as Susan rushed from the house crying for help. Their older daughter also ran for help, alerted by her mother's screams. Mosser had been killed instantly by a pipe bomb.

Essex County Sheriff Armando Fontoura called in the ATF who, as they combed through the explosion's debris in the kitchen, identified components unique to past bombs manufactured by the Unabomber. As usual the bomber had fashioned devices from common, easily obtainable nails and other items, fashioning handmade switches and pieces of wood that he'd highly polished. The $9^{1}/_{2}$-by-$7^{1}/_{4}$-by-$2^{1}/_{4}$-inch white cardboard box had been reinforced with more white cardboard on the inside and contained a homemade wooden box. Nestled like a viper within was an aluminum pipe no more than $9^{1}/_{2}$ inches long. Both ends of the pipe had been corked with metal end plugs, and each plug was secured with two metal locking pins.

Inside the pipe he'd packed an explosive mix of sodium chlorate and aluminum, ignited by four nine-volt batteries, an improvised initiator, and an anti-open switch of wood and metal—the

Unabomber's trademark. As if this concoction was not venomous enough, the bombmaker had added fangs to his snake—one-inch-long green paneling nails and double-edged razor blades. The explosion had converted them to slashing and tearing shrapnel. It was a scene right out of Conrad's *Secret Agent*:

> The shattering violence of destruction which had made of that body a heap of nameless fragments affected his feelings with a sense of ruthless cruelty, though his reason told him the effect must have been as swift as a flash of lightning. The man, whoever he was, had died instantaneously; and yet it seemed impossible to believe that a human body could have reached that state of disintegration without passing through the pangs of inconceivable agony....
>
> The inexplicable mysteries of conscious existence beset Chief Inspector Heat till he evolved a horrible notion that ages of atrocious pain and mental torture could be contained between two successive winks of an eye.

DENNIS HAGBERG, CHIEF US POSTAL INSPECTION SERVICE officer in San Francisco, could find no trace of an "HC Wickel" either as a professor or student at SF State. The UNABOM Task Force checked out everyone they could with the last name of Wickel, and asked the public whether that name meant anything to anyone. One caller pointed out that "wickel" means envelope in German.

IN MANHATTAN THREE SUSPICIOUS PACKAGES were called in to the bomb squad, but were discovered to be a calendar, a box of chocolate, and a fruitcake. In Meriden, Connecticut, a package emitting a "funny ticking noise" was revealed to be a phone answering machine.

Back at Young & Rubicam, workers said of Mosser: "Everyone liked him. Why would anyone want to kill him?"

On December 12, Agent Jim Freeman called a press conference, his second in two days, and said: "I want the general public to be particularly alert. [UNABOM] certainly has a familiarity with the Bay Area and San Francisco. Whether or not he is a full-time resident, I don't know.

"He may even appear to be a very nice guy, could easily be the person living next door.... There has been a progression in the sophistication of devices... and the destructiveness of the explosions. He may have no apparent predisposition toward violence. To allay any widespread public concern, it should be noted that all mailed devices thus far have targeted specific individuals."

CHAPTER 34
Targets

AND HOW DOES A MADMAN SELECT HIS TARGETS, for surely the Unabomber was just that. His letters, lifestyle, bizarre behavior, mood swings, obsessive-compulsive behavior, and "shut-downs" had anguished his family. They watched helplessly as he lost touch with reality, eventually suffering delusions. His paranoia was painfully obvious to them as far back as 1971 as well as his growing inflexibility and reliance on associative logic.

As private investigator Susan Swanson, instrumental in the solving of the UNABOM case, told me, "It upsets me when he is called a domestic terrorist. He was mentally ill and this behavior manifested itself in these actions."

FBI Behavior Science Unit profiler John Douglas recognized both the cruelty and cowardice of the bomber, and his ability to elude capture by constantly changing his modus operandi. He altered his M.O. especially in regard to his selection of targets—

universities and airlines in the beginning computer scientists, geneticists, and lobbyists later. Douglas realized the bomber's "signature" was important, writing that this signature was "the unique aspect that was critical not so much to accomplish the crime as to satisfy the perpetrator emotionally."

Thus, the prerequisites for choosing a target focused on satisfying something emotionally lacking in the bomber and selected through associative logic. In the Unabomber's case a large factor was his obsession with wood.

Wood. Wood was everywhere. It haunted his mind, controlled his actions, wood was his goal and mode of attack. He selected as his enemies people who had wood-associated names, addresses, or businesses. Yet the people the Hermit most cared about, even loved, in the little mountain town were named Wood. Danny Wood was the Recluse's friend, Anna Wood sold him supplies at the Grizzly True Value Home Center, and her cousin, Sherri Wood the librarian, found books for him and was his confidant and later protector. "You will not see his reading list," she sternly told the FBI. "That is confidential."

The Hermit lived with wood, in wood (his ten-by-twelve-foot shack enshrouding like a coffin), and around wood (the sighing grove of aspen, the larch, the pine). Wood was his motivation, his totem. And an entire nation would embrace wood and be returned to the wild if the Unabomber had his way.

Probably not enough has been said of the importance of Unabomber's carved little boxes—each fashioned from a variety of woods. The Epstein and Gelernter boxes were mailed the same day in 1993 and proved to be identical. In these cunning boxes I find the most curious qualities of the entire investigation. That a machine of death, an amalgam of wood and metal and electricity, should be so lovingly contained is virtually without precedent. In wild nature the beautiful and brightly colored insects are almost always filled with poison.

I work in an unusual way. I try, like a profiler, to get inside my subject's head. Thus, I wrote this story in a small room, under isolated conditions and on a portable typewriter such as the bomber used. Admittedly this was not a vast departure for me. How, I asked myself after three months of such conditioning, would I have selected my targets if I was the Unabomber? And every time I thought, "Wood." Yet, a second factor must have been less environmental. I saw hurt, jealousy, and revenge. Those who had failed to appreciate his genius, who had rejected him or bypassed the lonely, socially inept professor on the professional track of life, all came under the merciless hand of UNABOM.

But mostly everywhere I looked throughout the tragedy (for it was that on every level, from bomber to the victims), I saw wood. From the glade ringed in wood, the mountain man dispatched his devices into the world. But first he dressed them in handcarved wooden boxes like new clothes. I tried to imagine the genesis of such a strange concept—lovely wooden containers packed with electronic death. Some years ago Truman Capote wrote a nonfiction story about death threats hidden inside hand-carved miniature coffins that were delivered to a killer's selected victims as warnings. Had UNABOM been inspired by that or was it simply a natural outgrowth of a childhood spent carving such boxes?

In madness there is so often a powerful logic. Lewis Carroll, a mathematician like the Professor, showed how close the relationship is between absurdities and logic. His chapters in *Through the Looking Glass* and *Alice in Wonderland* contain chess games and backwards writing, cryptography, and visual puns. The Mad

Queen in Alice's world makes perfect sense in her mind. In the Unabomber's mind there is a similar logic. He chose his targets for reasons that were as blindingly obvious as the sun—to him.

Not all of the Unabomber's victims were specific targets, some were accidental. But the rest were carefully chosen.

"All university people whom we have attacked have been specialists in technical fields," wrote the Unabomber in his manifesto. "(We consider certain areas of applied psychology, such as behavior modification, to be technical fields.)" When UNABOM attacked Professor James McConnell, the psychologist and behavior modificationist, some experts thought the motive of the bombing might have been jealousy over McConnell's successful text, *Understanding Human Behavior*.

McConnell's appearance on the "Steve Allen Show" may have sealed his fate. There he demonstrated how he had programmed flatworms, through light and shock, to follow a maze. When the worms were ground up and fed to new worms, the next generation possessed the learned knowledge of the previous worms. They could successfully work their way out of the maze. Timothy J. Bergendahl, Ph.D., has suggested on the Internet that the Hermit may have chosen McConnell because flatworms inhabited his creek and the behaviorist had attempted to tame a creature of wild nature.

On the other hand a friend of the Professor's family was named O'Connell—even such a minor link as that, and one connected to his brother, might have been enough to target McConnell.

McConnell also taught at Ann Arbor, as in an arbor of trees, at the same time the Professor studied there.

The most obvious victim to be targeted is of course Percy Addison Wood, former president of United Airlines. He not only possessed the middle name of the Professor's former boss at the University of

California, John Addison, but also lived in Lake Forest, Illinois. The explosive book, from Arbor House, delivered to him, carried a leaf logo. The book itself, *Ice Brothers*, may have had meaning to the Professor in his relationship with his own brother.

As noted by John Douglas, Percy Wood had lived in the Bay Area while the Professor taught at Berkeley and served on the Bay Area Air Pollution Board, another position connected with the environment.

Leroy Wood Bearnson of BYU—again the irresistible middle name—was a secondary target of the bomber in May 1982. A package posted from Provo, Utah, with canceled stamps was supposed to be returned to the indicated sender, Bearnson, but was actually delivered to Professor Patrick Fischer at Vanderbilt. Patrick was the last name of his brother's friend, Linda, though she spelled her last name, Patrik.

Hugh Scrutton, though apparently a untargeted victim, had lived in Montana at the same time as the Hermit. He had been at UC Berkeley taking math classes in the late sixties. Had he somehow slighted the Professor, somehow have been singled out some seventeen years later? The device used to claim his life was a block of wood filled with protruding nails.

The accidental maiming of Gary Wright, the CAAMs computer store owner, occurred when he disturbed two two-by-four pieces of wood nailed together.

As for Dr. David Gelernter, the Yale computer scientist, author, and Winslow Homer expert, he shared the Professor's brother's name at a time when the brothers were at odds. At first I had looked to see if Gelernter was associated with anyone named Linda, then learned that was the name of the revolutionary computer language he had developed. David and Linda—always on the Professor's mind.

The identifying number on *The New York Times* FC letter of June 24, 1993, turned out to be a real Social Security number.

Thomas Mosser lived on Aspen Drive, apparently enough to target him as a Unabomber victim. Moss grows on trees. To the bomber it made perfect sense. Mosser lived in North Caldwell, New Jersey, and everyone knows moss grows on the north side of trees.

Mosser had also lived in Oakland as an advertising executive before his move east.

The last victim, chosen from those always-a-year-out-of-date references that the bomber consulted, worked for the Timber Association. It was mailed from OAKland, California.

Jerry Roberts of the *San Francisco Chronicle* received a letter from Isaac Wood. Isaac was the scapegoat brother from the Bible. Return address was "549 Wood Street, Woodlake, California."

The Professor, as I had nearly forgotten, had attended school at a wood-associated place—Evergreen Park High.

The occupations of UNABOM's victims were also a common element. After the 1993 bombings, then, bombs had been dispatched to intellectuals who worked with computers or in high-tech fields. Speculation existed that he might have anti-Semitic tendencies because his 1993 targets were Jewish and some return addresses, some signatures used on letters, had had Jewish-sounding names.

On the other hand, some of the parcel bombs were not addressed to a particular person, but had been abandoned on doorsteps or in parking lots to ensure a nonspecific target. These would attract Good Samaritans. If the intended victim was the person listed on the *return address*, then insufficient postage would send the deadly parcel on to that individual. "I think the victims are symbols, not individuals this person knows and dislikes," said Professor Patrick Fischer, one of the bomber's early, secondarily chosen targets.

Based on the letter to *The New York Times* and the new round of bombings, the FBI suspected UNABOM was periodically choosing his victims from the paper's columns, or one of the six hundred newspapers that subscribed to the *Times,* articles characterizing them as leading figures in their respective fields—two had just announced major breakthroughs in their areas of expertise. However, the bomber was reacting speedily after the articles—possibly too speedily—to dispatch his devices. Was the time between publication and receipt physically possible to have cause and effect? After all, the references in which he looked up the addresses and titles of various people had characteristically been a whole year out of date. For this reason Bill Dennison's successor at the Timber Association, Gil Murray, opened a package addressed to the former chief. The addresses may have been old, but the bomber had been ready to underscore the Oklahoma City tragedy at a moment's notice. Naturally, he had the bombs built and waiting. No one was safe.

With a madman, you could be a target for the slimmest of reasons—but reasons that made absolute sense to him.

CHAPTER 35
Gilbert Murray

But an ideology... must have a positive ideal as well as a
negative one; it must be FOR something as well as
AGAINST something. The positive ideal that we propose is
Nature. That is, WILD nature: those aspects of the functioning
of the earth and its living things that are independent of
human management and free of human interference and
control.

—UNABOMBER MANIFESTO

ON MARCH 13, 1995, the Hermit reached the three mailboxes on
Stemple Pass Road. Across the road stood a square plasterboard
storage shack. Automatically he peered down the mountain thor-
oughfare toward the route Dick Lundberg, mailman of the
Lincoln Stage, used to take. But he'd retired in 1993, and his son
had begun working the family mail line. The Recluse rode his bike
into Lincoln and left it behind George and Carol Blowars' office
before taking the Greyhound which ran twice a day into Helena.
He peered from the window as the bus sped over the winding
mountain pass into the capital. There he checked into Room 120
of the Park Hotel and checked out the following day. Then he
took the Rimrock Trailways line to the Greyhound Bus Lines in
Butte, Montana, to the south.

ON WEDNESDAY MORNING, April 19, 1995, the blast, like the bite of enormous teeth, cut into Oklahoma City's Alfred P. Murrah Federal Building killing 168, the worst single act of domestic terrorism in American history. That same explosion set in motion an inexorable chain of events that resulted in the delivery of UNABOM's most powerful device of all. On the day following this act of domestic terrorism (apparently inspired by the *Turner Diaries,* a racist novel about a militia plot to blow up a federal building in Washington, DC), the Professor posted four letters at an Oakland mailbox.

At four-thirty that evening the FBI offered a $2 million reward for information leading to the arrest and conviction of the Oklahoma City bombers.

This was twice the amount offered for UNABOM's head.

The Professor realized he still had time to post the shoebox-size package in his room, but he decided to place it personally.

On Sunday, April 23, at 10:52 AM, the phone rang at the Association of California Insurance Companies. "Hi," said a rough voice, "I'm the Unabomber, and I just called to say 'Hi.'" No one was there so an answering machine recorded the message. But next morning when the secretary played back the messages that had accumulated over the weekend, she was distracted before she came to that communication. Finally, three hours later, she reported the unsettling information to the police, who passed on the tip to the FBI. Later, officials theorized that the caller might have thought he was phoning the sheriff's office. Their number was only one digit off from the insurance association's.

The next morning, April 24, the Professor's letters began to arrive on the East Coast, breaking his five-month-long silence. Though opened at different times, they all had the same electric effect.

The first letter, single-spaced and crowded onto a little over two pages, was addressed once more to *New York Times* editor Warren Hoge and almost opened by secretary Kris Ensminger, who had opened the 1993 "FC" letter. Recognizing the typeface on the envelope, she left it sealed until the proper authorities could be summoned. Like a river current, rage and an odd ennui ran through the rambling diatribe:

> This is a message from the terrorist group FC. [Here the bomber listed his secret nine-digit identification number, 553-25-4394.]
>
> We blew up Thomas Mosser last December because he was a Burston-Marsteller executive. Among other misdeeds, Burston-Marsteller helped Exxon clean up its public image after the Exxon Valdez incident. But we attacked Burston-Marsteller less for its specific misdeeds than on general principles. Burston-Marsteller is about the biggest organization in the public relations field. This means that its business is the development of techniques for manipulating people's attitudes. It was for this more than for its actions in specific cases that we sent a bomb to an executive of this company.
>
> Some news reports have made the misleading statement that we have been attacking universities or scholars. We have nothing against universities or scholars as such. All the university people whom we have attacked have been specialists in technical fields. (We consider certain areas of applied psychology, such as behavior modification, to be technical fields.) We would not want anyone to think that we have any desire to hurt professors who study archaeology, history, literature or harmless stuff like that. The people we are out to get are the scientists and engineers, especially in critical fields like computers and genetics. As for the bomb planted in the Business School at the U. of Utah, that was a botched operation. We won't say how or why it was botched because we don't want to give the FBI any clues. No one was hurt by that bomb.
>
> In our previous letter to you we called ourselves anarchists. Since "anarchist" is a vague word that has been

applied to a variety of attitudes, further explanation is needed. We call ourselves anarchists because we would like, ideally, to break down all society into very small, completely autonomous units. Regrettably, we don't see any clear road to this goal, so we leave it to the indefinite future. Our more immediate goal, which we think may be attainable at some time during the next several decades, is the destruction of the worldwide industrial system. Through our bombings we hope to promote social instability in industrial society, propagate anti-industrial ideas and give encouragement to those who hate the industrial system.

The FBI has tried to portray these bombings as the work of an isolated nut. We won't waste our time arguing about whether we are nuts, but we certainly are not isolated. For security reasons we won't reveal the number of members of our group, but anyone who will read the anarchist and radical environmentalist journals will see that opposition to the industrial-technological system is widespread and growing.

Why do we announce our goals only now, though we made our first bomb some seventeen years ago? Our early bombs were too ineffectual to attract much public attention or give encouragement to those who hate the system. We found by experience that gunpowder bombs, if small enough to be carried inconspicuously, were too feeble to do much damage, so we took a couple of years off to do some experimenting. We learned how to make pipe bombs that were powerful enough, and we used these in a couple of successful bombings as well as in some unsuccessful ones....

The idea was to kill a lot of business people who we assumed would constitute the majority of the passengers.... But of course some of the passengers likely would have been innocent people—maybe kids, or some working stiff going to see his sick grandmother. We're glad now that that attempt failed....

Since we no longer have to confine the explosive in a pipe, we are now free of limitations on the size and shape of our bombs. We are pretty sure we know how to increase the power of our explosives and reduce the number of batteries needed to set them off. And, as we've just indicated,

> we think we now have more effective fragmentation mater-
> ial. So we expect to be able to pack deadly bombs into ever
> smaller, lighter and more harmless looking packages. On
> the other hand, we believe we will be able to make bombs
> much bigger than any we've made before. With a brief-case-
> full or a suitcase-full of explosives we should be able to
> blow out the walls of substantial buildings.

Obviously, this alluded to the two-and-a-half-ton crude fertilizer and fuel truck bomb used to kill almost 170 people at
Oklahoma City. Again, growing boldness, escalating complacency, pride in his work, and an intense rivalry caused him to
break his silence.

"All the reports of the Oklahoma bombing—all the attention it
received—may have stimulated him to do something he may have
been planning all along, but hadn't picked a date," San Francisco
psychiatrist Fred Rosenthal told the press later. After all, the
Oklahoma terrorists didn't build their devices from handcrafted
components, didn't lovingly sand and polish everything.
UNABOM took pride in his work.

"When there are such big headlines describing the Oklahoma
City explosion as 'the largest bombing of its kind,' it is almost an
invitation to violence," reasoned James Fox, dean of criminology
at Northeastern University in Boston. "It's enough to make
another bomber feel a little envious. It's almost like an addiction,
so that there's greater and greater destruction to achieve the same
satisfaction, so they do it more and more with increasing fre-
quency. After a while, they get so good, they are bolder and no
longer so careful."

One aspect of bombings is emotional detachment, since the
murderer is far away by the time his handiwork detonates. "They
don't do it for the pleasure of seeing the victim take his last breath
of life," said Fox. Michael Rustigan, a San Francisco State crimi-

nologist, agreed. "Quite possibly he was hyped up in terms of Oklahoma City, and saying, 'I can do that, too. And I can get away with it.' This is one type of serial killer that we refer to as a missionary serial killer. There is a cause and a justification. In all these cases there is a monstrous ego that's been wounded. And after a while [striking out] takes on a career of its own, a celebrity thing." The bomber continued:

> Clearly we are in a position to do a great deal of damage. And it doesn't appear that the FBI is going to catch us any time soon. The FBI is a joke.
>
> The people who are pushing all this growth and progress garbage deserve to be severely punished. But our goal is less to punish them than to propagate ideas. Anyhow we are getting tired of making bombs. It's no fun having to spend all your evenings and weekends preparing dangerous mixtures, filing trigger mechanisms out of scraps of metal or searching the sierras for a place isolated enough to test a bomb. So we offer a bargain.

Since UNABOM spoke of "searching the sierras for a place isolated enough to test a bomb," investigators began to question anyone who might have seen the fugitive at work in the California and Nevada Sierra Nevada. Then too, after seventeen years of rage, the bomber had begun to sound exhausted.

> We have a long article, between 29,000 and 37,000 words, that we want to have published. If you can get it published according to our requirements we will permanently desist from terrorist activities. It must be published in *The New York Times*, *Time* or *Newsweek*, or in some other widely read, nationally distributed periodical. Because of its length we suppose it will have to be serialized. Alternatively, it can be published as a small book, but the book must be well publicized and made available at a moderate price in bookstores nationwide and in at least some

places abroad. Whoever agrees to publish the material will have exclusive rights to reproduce it for a period of six months and will be welcome to any profits they may make from it. After six months from the first appearance of the article or book it must become public property, so that anyone can reproduce or publish it. (If material is serialized, first installment becomes public property six months after appearance of first installment, second installment etc.) We must have the right to publish in *The New York Times*, *Time* or *Newsweek*, each year for three years after the appearance of our article or book, three thousand words expanding or clarifying our material or rebutting criticisms of it.

The article will not explicitly advocate violence. There will be an unavoidable implication that we favor violence to the extent that it may be necessary, since we advocate eliminating industrial society and we ourselves have been using violence to that end.

But the article will not advocate violence explicitly, nor will it propose the overthrow of the United States Government, nor will it contain obscenity or anything else that you would be likely to regard as unacceptable for publication.

How do you know that we will keep our promise to desist from terrorism if our conditions are met? It will be to our advantage to keep our promise. We want to win acceptance for certain ideas. If we break our promise people will lose respect for us and so will be less likely to accept the ideas.

Our offer to desist from terrorism is subject to three qualifications. First: Our promise to desist will not take effect until all parts of our article or book have appeared in print. Second: If the authorities should succeed in tracking us down and an attempt is made to arrest any of us, or even to question us in connection with the bombings, we reserve the right to use violence. Third: We distinguish between terrorism and sabotage. By terrorism we mean actions motivated by a desire to influence the development of a society and intended to cause injury or death to human

beings. By sabotage we mean similarly motivated actions
intended to destroy property without injuring human
beings. The promise we offer is to desist from terrorism. We
reserve the right to engage in sabotage.

It may be just as well that failure of our early bombs discouraged us from making any public statements at that
time. We were very young then and our thinking was crude.

Over the years we have given as much attention to the
development of our ideas as to the development of bombs,
and we now have something serious to say. And we feel
that just now the time is ripe for the presentation of anti-
industrial ideas.

Please see to it that the answer to our offer is well publicized in the media so that we won't miss it. Be sure to tell
us where and how our material will be published and how
long it will take to appear in print once we have sent in the
manuscript. If the answer is satisfactory, we will finish typing the manuscript and send it to you. If the answer is
unsatisfactory, we will start building our next bomb.
We encourage you to print this letter.

　　　　　　　　　　　　　　　　　　　　　　　　　FC

[Passage deleted at the request of the FBI]

The second letter arrived at a familiar address, that of David
Gelernter, the Yale University computer scientist and author who
had been seriously wounded in the bomber's June 24, 1993,
attack. The enormous blast had rendered him deaf in one ear, torn
off part of his right hand, and blinded him in one eye. Squinting
at the envelope, Gelernter recognized the return address. It read:
"Ninth Street and Pennsylvania Avenue, Washington, DC,
20535"—FBI Headquarters.

Inside was a mocking, astonishingly cruel, five-paragraph letter
that chastised him for being injured by the device:

Dr. Gelernter:

People with advanced degrees aren't as smart as they think they are. If you'd had any brains you would have realized that there are a lot of people out there who resent bitterly the way techno-nerds like you are changing the world and you wouldn't have been dumb enough to open an unexpected package from an unknown source.

In the epilog of your book, 'Mirror Worlds,' you tried to justify your research by claiming that the developments you describe are inevitable, and that any college person can learn enough about computers to compete in a computer-dominated world. Apparently, people without a college degree don't count. In any case, being informed about computers won't enable anyone to prevent invasion of privacy (through computers), genetic engineering (to which computers make an important contribution), environmental degradation through excessive economic growth (computers make an important contribution to economic growth) and so forth.

As for the inevitability argument, if the developments you describe are inevitable, they are not inevitable in the way that old age and bad weather are inevitable. They are inevitable only because techno-nerds like you make them inevitable. If there were no computer scientists there would be no progress in computer science. If you claim you are justified in pursuing your research because the developments involved are inevitable, then you may as well say that theft is inevitable, therefore we shouldn't blame thieves.

But we do not believe that progress and growth are inevitable. We'll have more to say about that later.

FC

P.S. Warren Hoge of *The New York Times* can confirm that this letter does come from FC.

The bomber specifically challenged Gelernter's 1991 book, *Mirror Worlds or: The Day Software Puts the Universe in a Shoebox... How It Will Happen and What It Will Mean.* In his book, the computer scientist argued that computers that can mimic real life, from sociological events to physical ones, are nearly here. Gelernter believed that such devices would help mankind to explore in depth the underlying factors that affect the "real" world and control such events better.

After the letter to Dr. Gelernter, the last two communications were slightly delayed—threats to two Nobel laureates: Richard J. Roberts, a geneticist at New England Biolabs in Beverly, Massachusetts, near Boston, and Phillip A. Sharp, who had shared the 1993 Nobel prize for medicine with him. Roberts, a Derby, England, native, received his letter first, dated April 20, 1995, and addressed to him at New England Biolabs, Inc. The return address read "Manfred Morari, 2735 Ardmore Road, San Marino, California 91108-1768." He immediately gave it to the FBI. Sharp received his communication, addressed to him as head of the Biology Department, MIT, Cambridge, Massachusetts, and, forewarned by public mention in a UNABOM letter to the *Times*, passed his letter along to the detectives.

Once more experts in the field of genetics had been singled out. Sharp and Roberts had won the Nobel prize for their 1970s research and discovery of the concept of split genes, a discovery fundamental to biotechnology.

The invention of genetic engineering raised many moral questions, among them the troubling dilemma of whether a corporation could own a living thing. When General Electric in Schenectady, New York, developed a genetically engineered bacterium that could devour spills of crude oil like that of the *Exxon Valdez*, they realized that ownership of a life form, in this case an oil-eating bug, was essential to their financial success. Ultimately, in 1980, the Supreme Court ruled 5–4 in *Diamond* v. *Chakrabarty*, that a private company *could* patent a living creature.

UNABOM had identified the "people we are out to get" as scientists and engineers "especially in the critical fields like computers and genetics." The bomber now warned Roberts and Sharp with words, not bombs. "It would be beneficial to your health to stop your research in genetics," he said, implying that if they did not, the two men would face his wrath. Morari, incidentally, was questioned and reportedly had no knowledge of the letter.

THE CALIFORNIA FORESTRY ASSOCIATION (CFA), a single-story, five-thousand-square-foot brick building at 1311 I Street, stood only three to four blocks from the capitol building in Sacramento. Across the street lay the new State Department of Justice building and a block away the Fire Department Headquarters. On Monday, April 24, 1995, at about the same time as the letters back East were opened, a ten-inch by ten-inch by six-inch package—a carved wooden box wrapped in brown paper and nylon filament tape—was left outside the timber headquarters' main entrance.

"It was a typical work day," said Eleanor later. "The receptionist was out that day, so I was filling in for her. I was sitting up at the front desk when the mail arrived, and right on top of the packet of mail was... a package about five inches high—a little shorter than a shoebox, and it was heavy. I would say around eight pounds." Others estimated its weight at somewhere between five and six pounds.

"It had the tape, no strings or anything, around the outer part to hold the thing together."

The typewritten return address read: "Closet Dimensions, Inc.," an Oakland custom furniture store, and was addressed to the forestry group's old name, "Timber Association of California," and to a man who had not been president of the association for a year—William Dennison.

William Dennison had personally chosen Gilbert Murray, forty-seven years old, as his successor precisely because he was such a good man, "a consummate professional" who stood for the best of his profession. The timber industry needed a lobbyist who was untouched by the bad things of the industry. Murray was described variously as "popular," "very honest," "affable," "quiet-spoken, low-key, and solid," "very businesslike, and courteous to the extreme." He was as beloved and bereft of enemies as Thomas Mosser had been.

Murray, an ex-Marine who had survived two tours of duty in Vietnam, had been a forester and studied at UC Berkeley in 1968–69. The Professor was teaching there then. Murray had become president of the state's leading timber lobbying group, having started at the association in 1988 after working with Collins Pine Company near Chester. He'd been applauded for bringing together a group of environmentalists, farmers, timber men, and fishermen who agreed to protect the Coho salmon on the state's North Coast.

The CFA represented the interests of eighty foresters and landowners, and had tried to ease the Endangered Species Act legislation which it felt had hamstrung the logging industry in the state and throughout the Pacific Northwest.

With a $1.5 million operating budget, garnered through assessments on timber company members, the CFA had been successful in supporting a proposal by Senator Slade Gorton to increase salvage logging in the national forests by waiving the Endangered Species Act in such locales as Six Rivers, Tahoe, and Plumas and Eldorado forests. They'd not fared as well on their petitions to have the northern spotted owl declassified as an endangered species and in changing rules in Mendocino County that limited landowners to logging no more than 2 percent of their inventory.

It was hard to imagine a more loving husband and family man

than Gil Murray. He and his wife Connie maintained a close-knit household, and Murray was active with his two sons, Wilson and Gilbert, Jr., eighteen and sixteen years old, respectively—backpacking, snorkeling, and biking at Lake Tahoe or Mount Shasta. The family had even visited the White House and joked in pictures out front. Murray was a known practical joker, and made no apologies for it.

When the well-liked president bestowed the title of communications director on Lisa, one of the six people working at CFA today, he'd made a loyal friend. Lisa, expecting a child, became immensely fond of the balding, likeable executive and lobbyist. Lisa enjoyed sharing every aspect of her pregnancy with him. Gil was in his office when she poked her head in. He was looking forward that night to seeing his oldest son accept an athletic and scholastic achievement award. Wil had already been given a partial scholarship to Cornell. Murray glimpsed the young brunette woman holding something out to him at the door.

"It's my sonogram," she said, "or at least a videotape of it." Lisa, in the fourth month of her pregnancy, knew the baby would be a girl. Murray was enthusiastic and rose to take the cassette. "That's neat," he said, "and you can be sure I'll watch it at lunchtime." He returned to his work.

After lunch, around two that afternoon, Murray left his office to walk to the lobby and sort through the mail. He saw the receptionist was elsewhere, then caught sight of Lisa. "Have you seen Michelle?" he asked.

Lisa shook her head. Meanwhile three staffers approached the desk to see if they had any mail. Almost immediately, they noticed the brown-wrapped package that had arrived on the steps that morning. "Gil came up to the front desk and asked me a question," said Eleanor. "And I showed him the package. 'This came for Bill. Do you want me to forward it on to him?' He picked it up at that point and was looking at it, and there was another gentleman in our office, Bob Taylor, and Jeanette Glenn, who was also there. Murray turned it toward him and saw that it wasn't addressed to him, but to the previous president, Bill Dennison. He thought for a moment, then said: 'Rather than forward it, we might as well look inside and see if it pertains to business.'"

One staffer hefted the parcel and gave it a little shake. He dropped it down on the lobby desk where it lay only inches from Lisa's abdomen. As she reached across to see a letter, her stomach momentarily rested on top of the box. "It's heavy enough to be a bomb," the staffer said. Murray laughed and bent forward to examine the postmark. "At least it's from Oakland, not Oklahoma City," he joked.

They had difficulty in opening the filament-sealed shoe-box sized-package, so Murray said, "Lisa, would you get some scissors to cut it?"

"I never saw the package [close-up] myself," said Lisa, who had not been particularly interested. "I can't speak for the other staff members there, but from what I overhead there was discussion that there could be a bomb. And it was lightly put because you never think it's going to happen to you, that you have any relationship to something so horrible."

As the other employees carried their own piles of mail back to their respective offices, Lisa returned with the shears and began to cut the wrapping. "Here," said Murray, "let me do that for you." He took the scissors from Lisa, and she turned to walk down the hall to her office.

"He'd started to cut through the paper when the phone rang," said Eleanor. "I answered—I was still sitting at the front desk—so I answered the telephone, and it was a woman. To this day, I don't know who she was. And she was asking for a telephone number. I had to put her on hold, get up from the desk, and go back to another part of the office to look through a Rolodex for the number. I don't know how much time elapsed—maybe fifteen, twenty seconds."

"And that's how it ended up in his hands," recalled Lisa. "I had been finishing up a conversation with Gil in the lobby where he was fiddling with the package. It was a brief conversation, and I started walking back to my office which was less than twenty steps away."

In the act of pushing her door closed, Lisa caught a glimpse of Gil Murray bending over the parcel. As with all his actions, there was an intentness as he manipulated the tightly-wrapped tape binding the parcel. An unnatural stillness, an unease, might have filled the dark brick building that afternoon, a suspended beat in that last instant before a flashpoint. It was the tiny nerve that throbs at the core of all tragedies—unseen, unfelt, and unknown to all about it, but later recalled as if experienced and held frozen in time.

"Lisa went back into her office," recalled Eleanor. "Gil was alone in the front part. I was getting ready to answer the phone to give the woman the phone number when the bomb went off. And we were just stunned. At first I didn't realize what it might have been. Then the smoke came billowing through the corridors right outside the door. I lifted the phone at that moment and told the woman—whoever she was—'I'm sorry I can't talk to you—a bomb just went off in our office' and I hung the phone up."

Before Lisa had a chance to sit down, a hollow roar filled the offices and shook the employees like a giant fist. The ensuing blast ripped two doors off their hinges and sent them spinning; chunks of aluminum pipe punched one fist-sized hole after another into the walls and into the recess of the lobby skylight fifteen feet above. Shards of metal, like porcupine quills, quivered in the walls The immense power of the explosion rose as if in a colossal chimney, sucking the air upward and filling the void with howling winds and flames. The smell of chemicals was everywhere, and black smoke choked the lobby, a maelstrom in the inrush of air.

In the outlying offices, nails were pushed outward by the force, flames incinerated the carpet, and the furniture was turned into wood chips. Amidst the reek of chemicals, Gil Murray had ceased to exist.

Like a sonic boom, the shockwave moved outward. Workers below ground felt it, and employees in other offices began to evacuate onto the street. Some likened the detonation to "a Dumpster crashing" or "a car crash or backfire," but all heard something.

"Rat-tat-tat-tat!" Lisa's door shook, and when she flung it open, smoke blinded her. The explosion had taken out the electricity, and the hallway was black. "Gil! Gil!" she cried, shielding her eyes and peering in the direction where she'd last seen him. Her ears were ringing, but she was certain no answer came back. Lisa swung back into her office and felt for the phone. She dialed 911, then raced to the rear of the timber association where the other four workers were exiting to the little alley.

All five watched the exit, expecting their friend to appear at any moment, but Murray never came. Lisa's ears still rang. "I once heard an M-80," she said later, "but this was ten times louder."

"It was a very pristine crime scene we handed over to the UNABOM Task Force," said Sacramento Police spokesman Michael Heenan. "We took in a video camera and extensively chronicled the scene rather than bringing in more and more people. It's an enclosed area, so the collection of evidence was made a lot easier. It's a lot easier to collect trace and chemical evidence indoors." The Scrutton bombing a decade earlier had been entirely different.

Agents with boots pulled up over their street shoes moved gingerly around the crime scene on tiptoe, careful not to miss the slightest clue or pick up anything on their soles. The victim's body, almost completely destroyed, lay where it was until ATF and FBI forensic specialists reached the site.

"His face was ripped off; his arm was ripped off," said the Sacramento Coroner Bill Brown. "There were parts of his body all over the room."

"At first we couldn't figure out if he was trying to kill people or maim them," said the FBI. "Now there's no doubt."

Later reports characterized the corpse as being carried out in eleven bags; one report said paint cans. What sort of bomb contained so much power?

For UNABOM to have assembled such a compact, destructive device he would have needed a considerable amount of time. Clearly, the Oklahoma tragedy was what triggered his use of the bomb, which must have been tested and waiting. To construct his most powerful device yet, UNABOM nested three hand-casted aluminum pipes, each a slightly larger circumference. He'd learned a lot since he used a tin juice can as a containment vessel. Now he knew that the tighter the container, the stronger the seals, the greater the impact. Now, too, he scored the pipes to increase fragmentation. Apparently he had also used relatively difficult-to-buy sodium chlorate.

When Lisa was finally allowed back into the building, she saw for the first time how truly close she had been to being killed. "I was four months pregnant at the time—that could have been me and my baby—she's my miracle baby—especially after what I saw when I went back to my office after things had settled there. Before I went into my office I looked at the doorframe."

The machine-gun-type report she'd heard had been countless pieces of shrapnel slamming into the door. "So I could have still been en route to my office when the bomb exploded," she said later, "but miraculously I was in my office behind my desk." Lisa felt the presence of an angel who had protected her and spared her unborn child.

When the bomb went off, Governor Pete Wilson, a full four blocks away in his office, heard a muffled bang. Later, angered and outraged, he said, "A civilized society cannot tolerate these sorts of heinous actions, and we will bring all forces to bear to see that the perpetrator or perpetrators of this crime are swiftly brought to justice." Janet Reno's office contacted the Sacramento police as agents from the FBI and ATF and Postal Inspection Service reached the scene.

More than three thousand people attended Murray's funeral. Police Chaplain Mindi Russell noted of Connie and the boys, "They're doing horribly. They have lost the most precious person in their life, the dad they loved so dearly, the husband they loved so dearly." Stifling sobs, Wil said, "He taught us about everyday life. I don't know what we'll do without him. He'll always be in our thoughts, our hearts. I miss you, Dad. I love you."

Naturally, California environmental groups feared being tarred with the same brush as the Unabomber. "This is stark-raving mad," said Betty Ball of the Mendocino Environmental Center. "The environmental community is strongly nonviolent and believes in life and would never, ever engage in such acts." Judi Bari of Earth First!, one of the most progressive environmental groups, was equally shocked. "The only time that Earth First! has been associated with a bomb at all is as the victim," she said. "Bombing is outside of the ideology and always has been. It is outside the debate of even the most extreme person in Earth First!"

For the next two months nothing was heard from the bomber.

In the days after the Oklahoma City bombing and the Sacramento explosion that took Gil Murray's life, crank bomb threats flooded northern California. San Francisco P.D. was receiving two to three baleful warnings a day. Meanwhile, a man phoned San Francisco State University. "There are four bombs in four buildings on campus," the anonymous caller claimed. "Guess when they're going to go off." UCSF Medical Center got a threat that specified its ambulatory care center.

In Sacramento, two false threats forced an evacuation, and there were three sightings of suspicious packages in the capitol. One was a harmless briefcase left in a washroom. In the second case a telephone repairman left a box with some wires in the capitol building, and an alert employee reported it. So far Sacramento police had received several hundred requests from state employees on how to protect themselves against the Unabomber. Police mailed out illustrations and pamphlets that told how to spot a letter or package bomb.

Then, in Los Angeles, KCBS-TV reported that they'd learned the name of a major UNABOM suspect—James William Kilgore, forty-seven years old, a San Rafael native who was wanted on bombing charges. Kilgore had been a fugitive since 1975 when he was charged with possession of a pipe bomb in San Francisco. He was also named by federal authorities as a member of the SLA (the Symbionese Liberation Army), the group that had kidnapped Patty Hearst. Police also linked him with the New World Liberation Front and wanted to question him regarding an April 1975 robbery in Carmichael in which a woman customer was shot to death in a Crocker Bank branch. One of Kilgore's bombs allegedly blew up a Marin County deputy sheriff's car.

But Jim Freeman of the Unabomber Task Force said the report was "totally inaccurate." He stated, "To my knowledge there's been no information from anyone in the community that's been brought to the attention of the UNABOM Task Force that he's a potential suspect."

In the *San Francisco Examiner* Tom Bates wrote of the true identity of UNABOM—"He's around in the sixties. He probably doesn't own a car. He is also into physical fitness. He hangs out around universities. And he is willing to do almost anything to get published, including killing by mail and threatening to blow up airliners. But the manifesto is a detailed self-portrait. Could it be telling us exactly who the Unabomber is?"

Bates thought he recognized Leo Frederick Burt, an ex-altar boy and former Marine. Burt had been a fugitive since the August 1970 bombing of the Army Mathematics Research Center at the University of Wisconsin. Burt, forty-seven years old, resembled the Salt Lake City composite sketch and might be living in the Bay Area.

Almost twenty years before, in 1976, the New World Liberation Front planted a Tovak-explosive bomb in a flower planter near some scaffolding on future Senator Dianne Feinstein's house. Tovak would not detonate below freezing, and at 1:30 PM the temperature dropped to freezing and kept the bomb from exploding. The detonator alerted the family when that portion exploded as planned. "We were very lucky," said Feinstein, "very lucky. The scaffolding would have acted as shrapnel."

Now Senator Feinstein thought she was in a position to do something about terror bombings. Available on the Internet were unsigned messages that offered bomb-building information such as how the Oklahoma City bomb might have been made more devastating, bomb construction manuals such as *The Terrorist Handbook* and the *Big Book of Mischief,* and instructions on where to buy ammonium nitrate and fertilizer for bombs. Senator Feinstein wanted to add a provision to the Omnibus Counter-Terrorism Act that would prohibit the dissemination of information pertaining to the manufacture of explosives likely to be used in bombs, and this especially included the Internet, more than

28,000 computer networks working in concert worldwide. She was currently working with constitutional experts to test the proposed language, allowing such exceptions as physics texts.

"Whether you are planning to blow up the World Trade Center or merely to explode devices on the White House lawn, *The Terrorist Handbook* can be an invaluable tool to having a good time," read Senator Feinstein, enumerating the sections of the book that told how to acquire explosives and how to break into college labs for supplies. "It tells what time of day, how to enter a lab, how to jam a lock, how to dress, and where the chemicals are," she said. "It is clearly saying, 'We're going to show you how to do this.' This is not a remote book hidden on the back shelf of a library that some physics student may find. It's going out on the Internet to anybody who might have access to it and might want to engage in a terrorist act. I have a hard time with people using our First Amendment rights to teach others to go out and kill. I must tell you, that's not what this nation is about."

But civil libertarians were equally determined to safeguard individual rights, stating that sharing information is constitutionally protected speech. "The telephone, the fax, the postal system, an overnight express service, a shortwave radio," said University of Wisconsin law professor Frank Tuerkheimer, "are alternate methods of communicating. Trying to stop the flow of information is just not going to work in a free society."

If Senator Feinstein had her way, providing instructions for readers to build a bomb would be a crime (if there is reason to believe they intend to use an explosive device for criminal purposes). Her draft language covered any person who broadcast, distributed, or published information on the manufacture of explosives. "But," said Deputy Assistant Attorney General Robert Litt, "information about bomb-making has been available in bookstores and libraries for years. But the Internet has unquestionably increased the flow of this information. It is now available to millions... criminal laws like the conspiracy statute [already] apply with the same force to the Internet."

A terrorism bill drafted by Senate Majority Leader Bob Dole and Senate Judiciary Committee Chairman Orrin Hatch moved slowly forward as the Senate cut down on amendments to it. Dole's proposals encompassed many of those President Clinton had included in the $1.5 billion antiterrorism package he submitted to Congress a week after Oklahoma City. The president wanted to add a requirement to his plan that compelled manufacturers to add tiny traceable materials, taggants, to any chemicals that could be used to make bombs.

Rob Morse, in an *Examiner* column, had some thoughts on UNABOM's plans to restructure society into smaller units. "The only social instability he has caused is in the families of his victims. He has not disrupted industrial society. Instead he has mangled individual human beings who work in small offices of our society.

"Our industrial society is a web of individuals who are fathers and mothers, sons and daughters. Those who are hurt by bombs and the delusions that propel them... lacking humanity [the Unabomber] is what he hates: a purely industrial being. He manufactures death and fear... his vision is 'to break down society into very small, completely autonomous units.' In fact, all he's done is break apart some widely disparate lives."

In the last two weeks of May, the FBI fanned out over the campuses of Stanford University, San Francisco State, UC at Berkeley, College of Marin's Kentfield and Indian Valley campuses, Sonoma State, and Dominican College. They poked through university art departments where there were foundries to cast bronze and other metals for sculpture. Since UNABOM had been making bombs out of aluminum cylinders, agents were curious about the casting process. They were told that most casting in the university foundries involved bronze. But, one instructor explained, aluminum has a comparatively low melting point, about 1,100 degrees, and the bomber could work his aluminum tubes with a propane torch. When they found a viable suspect, that would be something to look for.

In chemistry labs they looked at former students or employees who may have had access to bomb ingredients. At maintenance shops, at the departments of mechanical engineering and electrical engineering, the search went on.

PERHAPS IT WAS ONLY DAVID'S INNATE GOODNESS, a natural generosity, that kept him sending his brother funds through the mail. Only through the mail did the two seem to touch these days. Possibly, he felt some guilt that he'd not shared his father's estate with his brother, an amount in the neighborhood of $60,000. But with virtually no capital, with virtually no possibility of employment, the Professor kept on through the kindness of his sibling.

The Professor's bank records show that his mother and brother sent him at least $16,800 from 1985 through 1995. As modest as that sum seems for a man with little other income for a decade, it was far more than the $200 or so a year he reportedly lived on. The former math instructor was a lot wealthier than his neighbors suspected.

CHAPTER 36

Suspect List

HE LEFT FEW LEADS, and many of those were deceptive. Yet the federal investigators were overwhelmed by leads. The modern federal approach to investigation can generate leads—mostly false leads—prolifically and with the same almost maniacal focus as the bomber showed in his work.

Major federal investigations, especially those led by the FBI, have a tendency to take on monstrous proportions. The federal agencies can do so much, bring so many resources to bear with their enormous resources and advanced technology. The result is natural: what they can do they do. And the result can be that sound analysis and even common sense can be drowned in a frenzy of activity and a mountain range of data.

Once relatively late in the case, when despite seventeen years of investigation the investigators were no closer to their target than they had been in 1978, an FBI agent, perhaps trying to keep his own spirits up, started reciting for me everything that was being done, the masses of interviews, the growing data base of suspect files cross referenced and multiply linked to other huge FBI data sources. "Look at our data base" he said. "Fifty thousand suspects and growing. We're going to nail this sucker. It's only a matter of time." Of course at the time I was impressed. It is impressive. But later, meditating on the logic, I wondered if they would consider themselves closer to a solution if they had 100,000 suspects in the file, or 200 million. With 200 million suspects they could be sure of having him in there somewhere.

The Hermit never made it onto the list.

The bomber's first two rather ineffectual bombs (if they were his bombs) attracted relatively little federal attention, especially outside the ATF. And even after the initial frenzy caused by the attack on Flight No. 444, the investigation was often a relatively minor affair, especially during the long silence from 1987 to 1993.

Yet even then, the core of the FBI approach was massive in spirit. The soldering techniques and the attack on Flight No. 444 created the largest file to that point. The FBI held great hope that the answer to the Unabomber's identity lay in investigating aircraft machinists. Interviews with airline employees and the men who manufactured the aircraft were added to the now gigantic spider which sported an obscene number of limbs. And of course all incidents were geographically referenced as were all people on the periphery of the attacks. Then technical specialists were called in to analyze every aspect and those results were logged in with every other conceivable connection.

Eventually the data base of combined information from the ATF, postal inspectors, and FBI would be dubbed the "Billion Byte Unabomber Computer." An all-encompassing list of leads—

THE INVESTIGATION

the by-product of a million hours of agents' work—it spread out like the legs of a spider. For instance, one attack on a professor could engender several new legs composed of former students, faculty colleagues, and virtually anyone connected to that campus.

That approach—spread out a big net capturing a huge number of conceivably linkable subjects, and then built more thorough files on those whose connections seemed a bit stronger or whose personas or proclivities or records made them conceivable as serial killers, or bombers, or terrorists—was the foundation for the explosion of data and an unfathomable amount of field work. By various accounts the *priority* suspect list at any given time ranged from fifteen to two hundred names, and the list constantly rotated as nearly all the priority suspects were shed relatively quickly, often because, as additional bombings were linked to the single bomber, one-time suspects would have to have alibis for the later bombings. James Hill of Sacramento State, whose name was found on the return address of the June 22 bomb posted to Dr. Epstein, was the subject of the most intense and repeated questioning by thirteen agents. Two experts in the field of psychology and computers monitored the conferences.

Of course the real glut of information came extremely late in the case, after the 1993 bombings and the letters that followed. Now the constantly changing list of priority suspects kept adding to the enormous morass of facts. There were even a few copycats who believed they were the Unabomber. In the end there was such an abundance of unusable evidence that a special Unabomber Room had to be installed in the FBI Lab.

The New York Times letter received from the Unabomber on June 24, 1993, had contained an unexpected bonus. This was the letter that contained a sentence midway that said, "Ask the FBI about FC." The letter said reassuringly that the FBI had heard of the group FC. Prior to this the FBI had kept the initials FC a secret from the public as they had much of the pertinent information in the investigation. But there turned out to be other initials "secretly" contained within the letter that intrigued the FBI much more.

When the FBI lab got their gloved hands on the letter, they knew immediately that there would be no usable fingerprints on it. As the letter had been passed from curious person to curious person in the *Times* city room on the third floor, an overabundance of fingerprints, all smudged, had attached themselves to the missive.

So at first the technicians had contented themselves with studying the postmark, June 21, 1993. That was important because the letter pointed out that the postmark preceded "a newsworthy event that will happen about the time you receive this letter, if nothing goes wrong. This will prove that we knew about the event in advance, so our claim of responsibility is truthful."

"Well, nothing went wrong," said one technician. "The injuries to Dr. Epstein and Dr. Gelernter prove that." At this point they had yet not received the bomb fragments from Tiburon and New Haven. Thus, they were able to give the envelope their full attention.

When they had exhausted that potential, they focused their attention on the letter itself with even greater fervor. "Let's put it under oblique light," said one. "There seems to be something here."

They crossed the room to a machine that enhanced crushed fibers in paper and made them legible. Sure enough, there was writing there.

"Look, he's written a name on another piece of paper and the impression has carried through." There, standing out boldly was the name, "Nathan R" and the notation to call him on Wednesday at 7:00 PM.

"Who the heck is 'Nathan R'?" they asked.

"Probably a friend of Wu, RV, and FC's." These were names that had turned up in various ways on earlier bombs.

"Is 'R' the last name or a middle initial?"

"Beats me, but let's check out the phone books and then driver's license records across the whole country." This was done and over ten thousand Nathan Rs or combinations thereof turned up in the United States.

"What now?"

"Well, it's obvious. We interview every one of them."

"All ten thousand?"

"All of 'em."

And they did, with absolutely no tangible gain from their almost impossible task. All it did was briefly swell their suspect list by another ten thousand names.

The *Times* letter contained a second valuable clue. A secret identifying number had been provided by the Unabomber.

"It has nine digits," said the agents. "Of course, it's a social security number."

"What are those numbers? Let's see who they belong to."

"553-25-4394."

Quickly, they tracked down their owner. He was a twenty-three-year old man who was apparently in prison. When they interviewed him he had an alibi for many of the bombings, reportedly being incarcerated at the time. However, it was his tattoo that rocked them back on their feet. "PURE WOOD," it read.

THE INVESTIGATION

The investigators were fully aware of the bomber's pathological obsession with wood, both physically and with name-related connections. It was just too much of a coincidence. Though he was ruled to have nothing whatsoever to do with the bombings, the possibility that the real Unabomber had known him somewhere along the line seemed good. They questioned him till they were blue in the face, but like the "Nathan R" and "Wu" leads, this went nowhere, too.

CHAPTER 37
Mail and Packages

T*he revolution must be international and worldwide. It cannot be carried out on a nation-by-nation basis.*

—UNABOMBER MANIFESTO

I HAD WORKED WITH JERRY ROBERTS at the *San Francisco Chronicle* a dozen years before, when I was political cartoonist there, and so it wasn't hard later to envision him opening the letter UNABOM sent him. I imagined his black, neatly trimmed beard was much the same, though surely flecked with some gray by now. Roberts had followed Templeton Peck as editorial page editor.

The letter arrived in a plain white envelope with a return address of Frederick Benjamin Isaac Wood, 549 Wood Street, Woodlake, CA 93286. Woodlake lay in Tulare County about twenty miles northeast of Visalia, home to just over five thousand residents. The postmark showed the letter had been mailed in San Francisco on Saturday, June 24, 1995—three days earlier. Roberts slit the flap and read:

> **WARNING.** The terrorist group FC, called Unabomber by the FBI, is planning to blow up an airliner out of Los Angeles

International Airport sometime during the next six days. To
prove that the writer of this letter knows something about FC,
the first two digits of their identifying number are 55.

"Six days from now?" thought Roberts. When would that be?
The fifty-two-word missive was undated; it might be a hoax. The
short letter made the rounds of the city room, until it landed on
the desk of a reporter who had written many stories on the case.
He recognized it as authentic. Both Roberts and Executive Editor
Matt Wilson were faced with the same dilemma as the eastern
papers—whether or not to publish in the face of a threat.
UNABOM had promised *The New York Times* he'd desist from
terrorism in exchange for publication of his long essay. If faced
with that choice, Wilson later said, "We were willing to take
extraordinary measures to ensure public safety. We'd give serious
consideration to publishing such a document." After notifying the
FBI, Wilson decided to go public with the communication, though
still uncertain of its authenticity. "Given [law enforcement
authorities'] concern and the history of Unabomber violence," he
said, "we feel the public ought to know about this new threat."

The FBI noticed two things about the terse letter—for the first
time the bombmaker had specified a potential target in detail and
in advance. And again UNABOM tweaked their noses in the
return address: "*Frederick Benjamin Isaac*" spelled out the initials
"FBI" and the word "Wood" reminded them of the bomber's
obsession with all things wood.

Early next morning, a Wednesday, the UNABOMB Task Force
apprised the Federal Aviation Administration of the threat to a
jetliner and advised them to take appropriate security precautions. Though not yet certain whether the letter was real or a
hoax, FBI agent Jim Freeman said, "We're erring on the side of
caution, finding it similar enough in its language, characteristics,
and content to earlier letters."

Letter and Package Bomb Indicators

Source: From FBI Files

RECOGNITION POINTS
• Excessive Postage
• Incorrect Titles
• Titles but no Names
• Misspellings of Common Words
• Oily Stains or Discolorations
• No Return Address
• Excessive Weight
• Rigid Envelope
• Lopsided or Uneven Envelope
• Protruding Wires or Tin Foil
• Visual Distractions
• Foreign Mail, Air Mail and Special Delivery
• Restrictive Markings such as Confidential, Personal, etc.
• Handwritten or Poorly Typed Addresses
• Excessive Securing Material such as Masking Tape, String, etc.

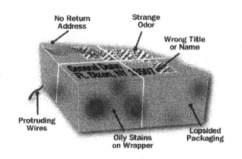

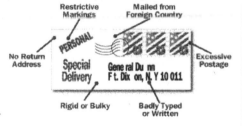

PRECAUTIONS
• Never accept mail, especially packages, at your home in a foreign country.
• Make sure family members and clerical staff know to refuse all unexpected mail at home or office.
• Remember: **It May Be A Bomb.** Treat it as suspect.

Though more than eighty agents from the Postal Service, FBI, and ATF were already working full time on the investigation, Freeman promised their ranks would be "further augmented." Later at an afternoon press conference, Freeman said they were taking the communication "as seriously as you can take it.... Further examination has confirmed that this letter originates from the Unabomber subject. It is a credible threat."

"How sure are you that the letter is from the Unabomber?" asked a reporter.

"Very sure. A hundred percent."

The original of the letter had been flown overnight to the FBI laboratory near Washington, where tests had confirmed its authenticity. Most importantly the letter reaffirmed the bomber's strong connection to the Bay Area, the strongest clue in the case so far. "The most valuable thing is we really believe that the Unabomber lives, works, and operates in the greater Bay Area or around Sacramento," he said. Freeman refused to detail the specific lab tests that had made the connection to the bomber or to emphasize any one theory. "There are a lot of theories out there," he said. "I really don't want to eliminate from the public any kind of suspect."

The FAA sprang quickly into action, warning not only Los Angeles airports but also San Francisco and other airports across the nation to inaugurate special security procedures. FAA spokeswoman Sandra Allen warned airline passengers to be "alert for suspicious bags, parcels, and other items, and to expect delays as a result of the increased security actions. These security measures will be in effect until the situation is resolved."

Federal officials had been criticized for not warning of a possible terrorist bombing of a US airliner just before a Pan American jetliner was blown out of the sky over Lockerbie, Scotland, on December 21, 1988.

Since San Francisco was considered the terrorist's home turf, San Francisco International Airport's (SFO) security was enhanced, even though the facility was not targeted in the letter to the *Chronicle*. Police dogs scrutinized every corner of the airport, and during the first night of the alert officials banned all but ticketed passengers from the boarding area. Policeman Tom Tang, in uniform, guided Pancho, a black-and-tan shepherd, one of eight airport bomb dogs, as he sniffed luggage before it was loaded onto a jetliner. Pancho had an accuracy rate of 95 percent, higher than any bomb-detecting machine.

Airport security measures then considered extreme were put in place, and have largely remained in place since—for instance, requiring picture ID for ticket holders or barring people without tickets from passing the security lines. Unattended baggage was quickly removed. Outside, a special reinforced bomb squad truck sat. A roving SFO Command Post RV crept across the tarmac. Most airlines shut down curbside check-in operations. Many people returned to their double-parked vehicles to discover they'd been towed. Skycaps scrutinized picture IDs. Nearby, patrolmen kept congested traffic moving and kept an eye out for suspicious packages and individuals matching the composite.

At USAir a long line of passengers stretched endlessly into the distance of the cavernous terminal. A red-jacketed, red-haired clerk walked the line repeating, "Have picture ID ready—for the next six days we will be requiring that all your bags be physically searched."

A hundred jets arrived and departed between San Francisco and Los Angeles (LAX) everyday at SFO. And in spite of the heightened security, the checkpoint inspection, the roving cops, and plainclothes surveillance, SFO and LAX remained vulnerable, like all other US airports, to terrorists.

"Airports are Swiss cheese," Marc Cohen, an investigator, told the press. "Most of the security at airports is rent-a-guards, and they are borderline worthless."

Over the past five years the FAA had spent $160 million to protect against airline bombers like UNABOM, but the proper technology remained elusive. How to build a sensitive bomb-detector able to distinguish reliably between a powerful plastic explosive and everyday plastic items? Even the smallest bag might conceal a tiny but powerful explosive. One answer lay in the construction of the plane itself.

Aviation safety experts thought planes might be built well enough to survive a major explosion. If only the FAA could convince airlines to reinforce cargo storage areas. Thus, even if a device made its way into the plane storage area, the detonation would not disable the plane. Because of the added weight and expense, airlines declined such modifications.

After Pan Am flight 103, Congress ordered FAA technicians to develop the technology to screen for bombs. It is still not in place.

Neil Livingstone, a Washington, DC, terrorism expert, presented a chilling thought to the media—"How could anyone be sure the Unabomber was not a member of the airport staff?"

All thirty thousand SFO workers—flight attendants, pilots, bar and restaurant employees, newsstand vendors and booksellers, gift-shop clerks, and janitors were now required to pass their ID cards through special scanning equipment to enter secured boarding areas with passengers who had already been subjected to strict screening. The number of people in secure boarding areas was also dramatically reduced.

People calling SFO asking if it was safe to fly were told not to change their plans, that San Francisco International was a safe airport. Passengers were also advised not to leave their bags unattended or to carry any item aboard given to them by a stranger.

Dave McElhatton announced over Channel 5's "Eyewitness

News" that evening that "within the last half-hour we've learned of a sophisticated device found on a flight from LAX to Sydney, Australia...." Crew members on board the United Airlines jumbo jet carrying 350 passengers discovered a device under a seat some two hours away from Sydney. They herded all the passengers to the front of the aircraft, covered the suspected bomb with heavy rugs, and landed. After everyone was evacuated police found a clock transistor radio wrapped in tape with a line leading to it but it was not a bomb.

A second United Airlines jet, this time on the way to San Francisco, returned to Portland after an anonymous caller said a bomb had been placed aboard.

US Secretary of Transportation Frederico Pena flew into LAX to demonstrate his confidence in its security. He'd already briefed President Clinton and FBI Director Freeh about the unprecedented security measures being undertaken. Pena, dark-haired, wearing rimless glasses, addressed a packed news conference shortly afterward.

"Because of the past history of this individual," he said, "we take this threat very seriously. All of us as Americans are beginning to understand we live in a changed society. We realize that our lives are going to be inconvenienced because of the changing nature of the world. While we have a very large contingent of law enforcement personnel handling security at Los Angeles and other airports, people should exercise common sense and their own individual decisions on whether to fly in and out of LAX."

The afternoon of Wednesday, June 28, 1995, federal authorities shut down California's airmail system, pulling the plug for much of the day. The many million pieces of mail that routinely traveled on passenger planes were diverted to trucks. US airlines earn $1.2 billion annually by carrying airmail, more than any other commodity transported on commercial aircraft. "If you blow out the side of a truck," said Postal Inspector Frank Ducar, "nothing much is going to happen to the truck or the people around it. If it's a plane, it's a different story."

Finally, restrictions on letters began to be lifted. First class and overnight letters *under* twelve ounces moved by air by the end of Wednesday. "Letter-class mail is too small to harbor any type of device that could hurt aircraft," said Fred Ducar.

Over the next fifteen hours, twelve postal inspectors worked to screen tons of packages. They scanned for parcels that matched UNABOM's past mail bombs—excessive postage (not easily traced metered postage), a particular range in weight, and neatly taped seams. They phoned addresses on wrappings to check on the contents of two dozen or so packages. In the end none contained an explosive device. They segregated suspicious packages and had them sniffed by a bomb dog or X rayed.

Though UNABOM had built bombs activated by altitude and trip wires, he'd changed his pattern so completely that some feared he'd constructed a bomb that he could explode at any time by remote control. "The volume of packages is just too tremendous to screen every parcel," said Bill Paul of the Postal Service. "It's almost unreal, the power of one person to affect an entire state."

"None of the nation's airports have the ability to X ray or inspect large volumes of cargo for bombs," said Stephen Alterman, president of Washington, DC–based Air Freight Association. "Businesses have come to depend on overnight shipments. If you slow down the system, you don't just slow down the mail—you slow down the entire business cycle."

UPS ships 11 percent of its twelve million packages a day by air, and during the crisis still guaranteed overnight delivery by 10:30 AM the next day. But they owned their own jets, as did FedEx. Both companies required proof of ID when a customer dropped off a package. "If it's a cash sale," said an employee, "and a package is over a pound, the customer has to let us see inside the package." DHL Worldwide promised next day delivery, but inspected some parcels.

In San Jose a woman passenger asked that her flight be delayed because she was awaiting a relative to deliver her eyeglasses. The stewardess refused, so the passenger said, "There's a bomb in one of my suitcases, and the plane will blow up." They immediately arrested her for making a false bomb threat.

But most people took the mail and plane delays calmly. One passenger discovered the postal slowdown not so inconvenient after all. "I've found that the Internet has really taken care of a lot of my messaging needs," he said. "So I'm kind of beyond US mail in a lot of respects." Hardly the reaction UNABOM expected or wanted.

TO CHRIS RONAY the threat neatly completed the loop back to airliners. "We think he is going to shift from serial bomber to more of a terrorist personality," said Ronay, "which is mass casualties, and that's why we think he's going after airliners."

Now more and more experts noticed the chameleon-like quality of the quarry and how he was becoming increasingly brazen and daring. Dr. Fred Rosenthal, a psychiatrist specializing in the criminal mind, shared some thoughts on the subject.

"Why has he become so bold? He may have some mixed feelings about the things he's been doing. On one hand he's been doing some fairly violent, dangerous acts, and on the other hand he may also be somewhat uneasy about the fact that he's doing these acts, and the letter to *The New York Times* may be an expression of those mixed feelings he now has.

"Oklahoma City made some difference. This individual really wants to be recognized and, I think, wants people to know about him."

Many others thought jealousy over the notoriety of chief suspect Timothy McVeigh in the federal building bombing might be driving UNABOM.

"What you're seeing is an increase in age, and it could well be that this guy is slipping into paranoid thinking. The mid-forties is a ripe old age for a paranoiac personality," said criminologist Robert Ressler, creator of the FBI's Violent Criminal Apprehension Program (VICAP), prototype for criminal profiling methods featured in the film *The Silence of the Lambs.*

"I think he's getting tired," said Ressler, "and that he almost has the capability of resolving all this. If approached properly, I think he's intelligent and creative enough that possibly he could surrender or at least he could agree to cease the bombings."

THURSDAY NIGHT, JUNE 28, 1995 Ted Koppel found the news changing even as he went on the air. "At the top of this program 'Nightline' I told you about a package received by the *Times* today. As I mentioned they did not open it, nor has the FBI told the editors of the paper what was in the package, but those who saw it today told me its size and shape were consistent with the [35,000-word] manuscript the Unabomber wants published.

"Now literally in the last few minutes word has come to us that the FBI has now opened that package, that they have found a letter in it from the man they identify as the Unabomber and that he has said it was never his intention to blow up a plane, but that he simply wanted to cause a stir. When we come back we will be joined once again by Linda Daschle and Richard Roth."

In separate studios Daschle, a young blonde woman in a red dress, and Roth, a serious man in a dark suit, waited through the commercials patiently.

Koppel returned and said, "I'd like to warn all our affiliates that we're going to be going a little bit longer this evening. We had some late information that literally just came in in the last couple of minutes. Rejoining us now is Linda Daschle [deputy administrator of the FAA], and also joining us live here in Washington, Richard Roth, executive director of a company which provides security advice to major airlines and airports. If [the Unabomber] wanted to cause a stir, Ms. Daschle, he sure did that, didn't he? But can you take him at his word either way?"

"Right now, the only information we have from the FBI is that we have a credible threat and therefore as long as we have that information saying that there is a threat to the traveling public, we will keep our security measures in place."

"I'm really not quite sure if I know what that means," said Koppel. "I don't mean to be argumentative with you, but if there's a credible threat as long as the Unabomber is out there—he's been out there for seventeen years—he writes one letter saying he's going to blow up a plane in six days, he writes another letter which the FBI has also identified saying, 'Gee, just funning you, I didn't mean it all along.' Is it a credible threat? How do you decide?"

"FBI makes the decision, Ted," Daschle said, "about whether this threat is credible. In this case, last night they believed it was." But Koppel returned to the point:

"But what we have here," said Koppel, "is quite literally the cost of a stamp and a letter that says 'I'm going to do it,' and if the person has any sort of track record, as the Unabomber does, you can bring a metropolis to a grinding halt...."

THE NEW YORK TIMES RECEIVED A PACKAGE, mailed on June 24, but not opened until June 28 (the day of the jet threat), that had an odd return address. The name of Calgene Inc. of Davis, Yolo County, California, was printed in the upper left-hand corner.

Calgene had created a genetically engineered tomato. In the package was a copy of UNABOM's fifty-six page manifesto and eleven pages of footnotes and corrections. A hand-drawn chart by the bomber had been enclosed as well.

The *Washington Post* received the same material, plus a new letter and copies of UNABOM's letters to the *Times* and *Penthouse*, an adult magazine published by Bob Guccione. The *Post*'s package had been addressed with cutout pieces of paper, but its return address was as bizarre as on the *Times*' package. The name of the apparent sender was Boon Long. A San Jose business executive owned the house on the return address, but rented it out. He told the *San Jose Mercury* he was "devastated.... I never got any publicity," he said. "I'm very low profile and so is the company."

The second letter the *Times* received that June had no mailing date, but was opened on June 29 and read as follows:

> Since the public has a short memory, we decided to play one last prank to remind them who we are. But, no, we haven't tried to plant a bomb on an airline (recently).
>
> In one case we attempted unsuccessfully to blow up an airliner. The idea was to kill a lot of business people who we assumed would constitute the majority of the passengers.
>
> But of course some of the passengers likely would have been innocent people—maybe kids, or some working stiff going to see his sick grandmother. We're glad now that that attempt failed.
>
> We don't think it is necessary for us to do any public soul-searching in this letter.
>
> But we will say that we are not insensitive to the pain caused by our bombings.
>
> A bomb package that we mailed to computer scientist Patrick Fischer injured his secretary when she opened it. We certainly regret that. And when we were young and com-

paratively reckless we were much more careless in selecting
targets than we are now.

"The second letter alone will not dissuade us from taking the
first letter seriously," said a source in the FBI.

FAA spokesman Mitch Barker said, "We will be maintaining
the security measures that went into effect in California as long as
necessary to protect the traveling public."

All day Thursday, June 29, the FAA kept California airports on
"code alert." When Jerry Roberts returned to the *Chronicle*
offices at Fifth and Mission just across from the US Mint, he saw
the police had cordoned off several blocks near the newspaper. At
1:00 PM a suspicious-appearing toolbox had been left at the curb
near the Mission Street entrance by a driver in a blue van. An
hour later the police bomb squad exploded the box, which turned
out to contain only tools.

A similarly provocative briefcase, abandoned at an airline gate
at LAX, caused airport police to rope off the area and summon
the bomb squad, which detonated that suspicious container, too.
Brochures and shattered lighting fixtures showered to the floor.

A young married couple boarding a Marin Airporter shuttle at
SFO noticed a fellow passenger who eerily resembled sketches of
the Unabomber. The husband quickly disembarked and phoned
airport police. Police caught up with the shuttle just north of the
Golden Gate Bridge at 7:30 PM. The suspect, unidentified, was
driven to the Marin County sheriff's office and questioned, but
deputies quickly determined he had no link to the investigation. A
lawyer, who kept dark aviator glasses like the Unabomber's on
throughout a United Airlines jet flight from SFO was also questioned and quickly released.

UNABOM told *Penthouse*, which had offered to print his manuscript, that Guccione might publish the manifesto if the *Times*

and *Post* "relinquished first claim" on the right to publish. If *Penthouse* published the tract, the bomber reserved the right to one more act of violence. In the Guccione letter, four-and-a-half single-spaced, typed pages, only the first two pages asked the *Penthouse* publisher to print his manifesto. The remainder of the letter must not be divulged until the manifesto was published, warned the bomber.

"I sincerely believe if we were to publish the guy, he would stop the killing," said *Penthouse* publisher, Bob Guccione, "because if he didn't, if he enters into an agreement to have his works published, then turns around and kills somebody, then he's denigrating his own work."

Over the Internet, of all things, Guccione offered the bomber a page a month to air his views if he'd stop his murdering and an additional three follow-up messages, one each year thereafter. Guccione, in the space of a month, would take out a full page in the *Times* to appeal to UNABOM. In the meantime, the debate over the ethics of bowing to a terrorist's demands continued.

"The traditional journalist's answer to that is, 'Hell, no! We're not going to print what a terrorist demands we print.'" said Austin Long-Scott, a professor of journalism at San Francisco State. "Nobody gets to tell us what to print. But that's really not a very helpful reaction.

"It's not helpful for several reasons—one is that this person has clearly indicated he can, and will, kill. Number two is that newspapers have been looking for new definitions of news over the last few years. They need to reclaim declining circulations, and they are, in fact, printing more of what people tell them to print. Now it isn't driven by threats, it's driven more by money....

"And while the Unabomber seems to be acting alone from what we know—another question is 'Where do these ideas come from? Is there a thread here? Do his complaints about the industrial society have a solid basis that a lot of people have some concerns about even if they're not organized?'"

RECENTLY WHILE TRAVELING I was reminded of the myriad and permanent changes wrought by UNABOM not only in California, but also throughout the nation. The sign posted on my corner mailbox, in bold red letters on a white background, read, "STOP! Important Customer Information. Because of heightened security, the following types of mail may not be placed in this receptacle: all domestic mail weighing 16 oz. or over, or parcels that bear stamps. Please take this mail, in person, to a retail clerk in a post office." At SFO I was constantly reminded to not leave my bags unattended or take parcels aboard the plane for strangers. I showed picture ID as a matter of course and idled in the long lines for screening and X raying of baggage. Even today, America's greatest home-grown terrorist is still very much with us.

AS FOURTH OF JULY TRAVELERS resigned themselves to delay and fear, letters continued to flow from the now-loquacious bomber. At the beginning of July he sent a letter to *Scientific American* magazine, a mocking diatribe against modern science. "Scientists and engineers constantly gamble with human welfare and we see today the effect of some of their lost gambles—ozone depletion, the greenhouse effect, cancer-causing chemicals... overriding noise and pollution, the massive extinction of species... we strongly deplore this kind of indiscriminate slaughter that occurred in the Oklahoma City event. FC."

UNABOM suggested that his antitechnology views had been first revealed in a letter to the *San Francisco Examiner* back in 1985. I wasn't surprised when the *Examiner* said they had no record of the communication. Carol Fisher, who screened and chose the letters at the *Chronicle* across the alley from the Hearst paper rarely filed original letters longer than six weeks, for legal reasons. But once again this information showed the bomber's close ties to San Francisco.

Just before the Fourth of July, FBI agents fanned out over the Bay Area, spilled into iron and scrap metal yards to question employees about sales of minute amounts of metal and shavings. This time they brought a visual aid with them—a new picture of the man they thought might be the Unabomber.

One of the scrap yards visited was Alco Iron and Metal on Davis Street in San Leandro.

"Have you seen this guy?" one agent asked an employee. "He might have been in the yard trying to buy something."

The investigator passed the clerk a grainy black-and-white, computer-enhanced enlargement of a jittery man captured on video tape. He'd been glimpsed near the site of timber lobbyist Gilbert Murray's killing. He wore aviator-style glasses like those shown on the now famous composite sketch of the bomber. But the man in the photo was heavier, older by some eight to sixteen years, and had a thin mustache. He wore an old-style military jacket.

"I don't know," said the employee. "I can't tell you exactly if it's the same guy. We have a lot of different people come and buy a lot of different stuff."

"What about the purchase of magnesium?" Magnesium burns like a small sun, adding to the intensity of the damage.

"No," said the clerk.

"Keep quiet about the picture I showed you. We don't want word to get out that we have it."

The Sacramento police department said of the video, "We've never made it the centerpiece of our investigation. It's more in the category of something that could prove useful later on. You never know. When you're putting a puzzle together, you never know what piece might fit. So rather than dismissing it out of hand, we thought it was useful to take a more detailed look at it and let the FBI know about it."

In June of 1995, eighty-eight years after Joseph Conrad published *The Secret Agent*, the UNABOM Task Force, having long noted correlations between the novel and their quarry, did something about it. Agents contacted the great scholars of the land to draw possible parallels between Conrad's story of a chemistry professor who resigned from his university and real life.

The most obvious connections were the attempts of Conrad's bomb-constructing Professor to obliterate those "false idols"—technology and science. Conrad had sketched a similar figure (also named the Professor) in his short story, "The Informer." "Explosives were his faith, his hope, his weapon and his shield," the Polish author wrote. The pipe bombs UNABOM placed echoed the Professor's own description of his lethal devices: "'The detonator was connected with the screw top of the can,' the Professor told Ossipon. 'It was ingenious—a combination of time and schock. I explained the system to him. It was a thin tube.... Screwed the top on tight, which would make the connection.'"

Just as the Unabomber kept improving the efficiency and power of his devices, the Professor sought the perfect detonator through his experiments. Other relevant strains ran through Conrad's work that might reflect on the Unabomber. Isolation shot through *The Secret Agent*. "I've got the grit to work alone, quite alone, absolutely alone," says the Professor.

The Professor's thoughts on mankind went as follows: "They swarmed numerous like locusts, industrious like ants, thoughtless like a natural force, pushing on blind and orderly and absorbed, impervious to sentiment, to logic, to terror, too, perhaps.... What if nothing could move them?... A despicable emotional state this, against which solitude fortifies a superior character."

"Next time, or the time after next," Conrad's Professor thinks in Chapter Five of *The Secret Agent*, "a telling stroke would be delivered—something really startling—a blow fit to open the first crack in the imposing front of the great edifice of legal conceptions sheltering the atrocious injustice of society."

Conrad's characters, such as those in *Heart of Darkness*, often abandoned civilization for the wilds. Then there was the odd diet of a character in *The Secret Agent*—he subsisted entirely on raw carrots. Additionally, the fictional anarchist group was called FP, while the Unabomber's "group" was named FC.

Even Conrad's full name might yield a clue to the ivy-bound detectives. Teodore Jozef in English might be Theodore Joseph. Or someone named Conrad or Konrad. Who knew?

CHAPTER 38
Life's Work

*M*any people understand something of what technological progress is doing to us yet take a passive attitude toward it because they think it is inevitable. But we don't think it is inevitable. We think it can be stopped.

—UNABOMBER MANIFESTO

TOM TYLER, AN AUTHORITY IN THE FIELD of psychology of law and an author of a 1990 work, headed up the Social Psychology Department at UC Berkeley. On Friday, June 30, 1995, at 10:44 AM, a package appeared on his desk at Tolman Hall. The nine by twelve-inch thick manila envelope had traveled through the campus mail system before showing up at his office. The serious, dark-haired scholar looked down at the unexpected package, then began to open it though it bore all the telltale signs of suspicious mail.

The package had excessive postage, hand-canceled stamps, and no return address, and bore a typed address on a white-gummed mailing label like all the packages to the *Post* and the *Times*. The FBI had learned long ago that the technophobic bomber never licked these labels, but what about the stamps? They were to be tested for DNA. Campus bomb squad chief Bill Foley had warned the university staff repeatedly, "If you encounter a package, don't open it. We have a bomb squad that's on call twenty-four hours a day. They'll respond and determine if the package is safe or not."

Still, the package bore none of the other common marks of a mail bomb—oily stains or discoloration on the outside of the wrapping, protruding wires or tinfoil, excessive securing material such as tape or string, restrictive marking such as "Confidential" or "Personal," or misspelled words. The Unabomber's mail devices had often given the incorrect or outdated title for the addressee, and Tyler's title was incorrect on the typed label. Yet the incorrect phrase (Social Psychology Group) had been used in a recent May *Chronicle* story on Tyler's take on the Oklahoma City tragedy.

Inside Professor Tyler found a carbon copy of the manuscript sent to *Penthouse*, the *Times*, and the *Post*, sixty-eight pages of typed material—fifty-six of the manifesto, eleven of footnotes, and a one-page personal letter to Tyler, which read:

> Dr. Tyler:
>   This is a message from FC. The FBI calls us "unabom." We read a newspaper article in which you commented on recent bombings, including ours, as an indication of social problems. We are sending you a copy of a manuscript that we hope *The New York Times* will get published for us.
>   The trouble with psychologists is that in commenting on what people say or do they often concentrate exclusively on the non-rational motivations behind the speech or behavior. But human behavior has a rational as well as an irrational component, and psychologists should not neglect the rational component. So if you take the trouble to read our manuscript and do any further thinking about the "unabom" case, we suggest that you should not only consider our actions as a symptom of social or psychological problems; you should also give attention to the substance of the issues that we raise in the manuscript. You might ask yourself, for example, the following questions:

Do you think we are likely to be right, in a general way, about the kind of future that technology is creating for the human race?

If you think we are wrong, then why do you think so? How would you answer our arguments? Can you sketch a PLAUSIBLE scenario for a future technological society that does not have the negative characteristics indicated by our scenario?

If you think we are likely to be right about the future, do you consider that kind of future acceptable? If not, then what, if anything, do you think can be done about it?

Do you think our analysis of PRESENT social problems is approximately correct? If not, why not? How would you answer our arguments?

If you think we have identified some present social problems correctly, do you think anything can be done about them? Will they get better or worse with continued growth and progress?

We apologize for sending you such a poor carbon copy of our manuscript. We can't make copies at a public copy machine because people would get suspicious if they saw us handling our copies with gloves.

FC

Tyler rang the campus police, and Foley and his men rushed to examine the package. They realized instantly who it was from. "Are you afraid?" asked Marie Felde, a UC spokeswoman.

"No," said Tyler, "it's not a threat. I'm intrigued." Later he said to the press, "I'm very pleased. The Unabomber appears interested in providing education about his beliefs. I think discussion about these issues is a far more positive and ultimately more effective way to bring about change than violence. I'll respond to the issues the Unabomber has raised."

Tyler admitted he was taking a risk in contacting the unpredictable bomber, but said, "I'm careful. I look for packages that look a little suspicious but so far I haven't had any problems."

Tyler intended to respond through the media in written form. He suspected that the Unabomber had selected him because of his remarks on the bomber in the *Chronicle* and so chose that local paper as his forum to acknowledge the questions. The FBI gave him their blessing, not editing or censoring Tyler in any way. They hoped the dialogue might provide leads to solve the case.

The campus seemed also to be totally behind him. "I believe in open communication," said one female student. "I think it only promotes the good. It might show the Unabomber that there are other people with different ideas. He seems to me so forcefully suggesting that many people share his view and I don't...." On the Fourth of July Professor Tyler published his open letter to the Unabomber in the *Chronicle*, prefacing his twenty-three-paragraph public response with these remarks to reporter Michael Taylor: "I really appreciated that he tried to educate me, as opposed to just assuming I wouldn't listen and just sending me a bomb. I would rather be having a dialogue with what concerns him and those issues in society."

The following is Professor Tom Tyler's reply to the Unabomber:

> On May 1, the *Chronicle* published an article using both the Oklahoma bombing and the actions of the Unabomber (FC) as examples of general social malaise in America. I was one of several psychologists interviewed for the article.
>
> I have received a letter from FC commenting on that story, along with a copy of his manuscript, "Industrial Society and its Future." I have read the manuscript and am writing this open letter to address the concerns raised by FC, both in his letter to me and in the manuscript itself.
>
> I regret that we cannot communicate more directly. Hopefully, you will read this reply to the questions you have raised. In your letter, you suggest that we look beyond

the questions of whether you have social or psychological problems and consider the substance of the issues you raise in your manuscript. This seems to me a fair request.

There is a widespread feeling of social malaise in our society today and we need to consider why people have those feelings. It is wrong to simply say that people who are dissatisfied are in some way nonrational.

We should also consider whether the structure of society is hurting people and needs to be changed. The manuscript you prepared directly addresses this issue.

I agree that it is important for all Americans to talk about what is wrong with our society and to try to find ways to improve it. By circulating your manuscript you are encouraging us to think about these important issues.

I have tried to read and consider your arguments with an open mind. I think violent actions are wrong, and I am pleased that you have decided to communicate your ideas by sending me (and others) your manuscript.

I cannot completely present or comment on all of the issues you raise in your lengthy manuscript within this letter. But I would like to note what seems to me to be several key arguments. The central point of your manuscript is that the economic and technological changes in our society have had a negative effect on people's lives.

Your concerns about widespread feelings of inferiority and over-socialization into conformity with society's rule are widely shared, as is your suggestion that many people do not find their lives very satisfying. Many people today do feel that they have little control over their lives and few opportunities for autonomy.

As you say, they do not feel that they have power over their lives. I think that your feelings and concerns are widely shared. Many people in America are searching for ways to make their lives more fulfilling. I agree with you that technology is resulting in many social problems and that our society has to address those problems and their solution.

You also argue that industrial-technological society cannot be reformed. Here I am less certain that I agree. There have been increasing signs that people are making choices that create individual freedom and local autonomy for themselves.

People quit jobs in corporations to start their own small businesses, people move from large cities to the country, people voluntarily conserve water, recycle their trash, and lower their use of electricity and natural gas.

People are finding many ways to change their lives in positive ways. It seems to me that the revolution you advocate is already occurring. Instead of being trapped in the system through psychological or biological manipulation, people are finding ways to live better lives. People are developing the type of anti-technology ideology that you advocate in your manuscript.

Of course, many people's lives continue to be difficult, and change takes time.

But, given evidence that people are able to make choices that give them a sense of control, does it not seem possible that society can change?

You suggest two ways of creating social change: Developing an alternative ideology and promoting social stress and instability.

As I have noted, there is already evidence that people themselves are developing an alternative ideology that lessens the importance of technology and increases their control and autonomy over their lives.

But how is it useful to promote social stress and instability, especially through acts of violence?

My impression is that people react to violence by becoming less willing to change. Instead of encouraging social change, threats of violence make people fearful and unwilling to consider new ideas.

How can you encourage people to think about your alternative ideology by creating fear and insecurity?

I think that education is the key to changing people. Would it not be possible to try to develop the core group of intelligent, thoughtful, rational people that you describe in your manuscript?

That core group could articulate and develop a new ideology that allows us to move beyond the problems of technological-industrial society. Many members of our society would welcome new ideas about how to deal with the problems created by technology. That group could change society by showing people a better way to live their lives. Do you have thoughts about how such a group could be formed? Who should be on it? What the most important issues for it to address might be?

Let me close by saying that I especially welcome your suggestion in the manuscript that a "revolution" that changes the economic and technological basis of our society need not be violent or sudden. It can occur peacefully and over a period of decades. In that spirit, I think our society should consider the important issues you raise in your manuscript.

IN PROFESSOR TYLER'S REPLY the distinct impression was of a reasonable man attempting to placate a wild animal, as if Tyler, by speaking softly, might tame the Unabomber. And what could he possibly make of the bomber's query, "If you think we are wrong, then why do you think so?" Second thoughts after having wrought carnage, death, and shattered lives over the past seventeen years?

TIMES **PUBLISHER ARTHUR O. SULZBERGER, JR.,** said on June 4, one month before Professor Tyler responded in print to UNABOM's three questions, that the newspaper would review the bomber's manuscript when it arrived and "make a journalistic decision about whether to publish it."

Twenty-four days later, at night, the voluminous manifesto had finally appeared on the *Times'* steps. Editors were greeted with sixty-two pages of single-spaced text (232 numbered paragraphs and thirty-six footnotes), a page listing grammatical corrections and typographical errors, references to numbered paragraphs, and a hand-drawn chart: "Diagram of Symptoms Resulting from Disruption of the Power Process." The repetitive and difficult, though erudite, text was going to be tough sledding for even the most dedicated reader. The following morning Mike Getler of the *Post* got his copy.

"The manuscript is long, and we're just starting to look at it closely and study our options," said Sulzbeger. "...We will act responsibly and not rashly, knowing that lives could be at stake.... One issue that we find especially troubling is the demand that we not only publish the initial document but then open our pages for annual follow-ups over the next three years. Such a commitment is not easily made."

Over at the *Post,* publisher Donald E. Graham announced, "The *Post* takes this communication very seriously. We are considering how to respond, and we are consulting with law enforcement officials."

Attorney General Reno and FBI Director Freeh met with Sulzberger, *Times* executive editor Joseph Lelyveld, Graham, *Post* president Boisfeuillet Jones, Jr., and editor Leonard Downie, Jr., at the Justice Department in the first of two meetings between the most important people in journalism and law enforcement.

Reno had the editors briefed on the psychological profile of UNABOM. As for a recommendation by the FBI to publish the manifesto, Sulzberger later said, "We wanted the input of people who are considered experts on this. They have been following this guy for seventeen years. Neither Don Graham or I had much experience in dealing with terrorists firsthand."

Behind the scenes the excruciating moral arguments continued: If they published, would they play into UNABOM's hands? If not, would more people die?

PENTHOUSE **PUBLISHER BOB GUCCIONE** had received a call around June 25 from an anonymous person who'd told him to expect "a package" soon from UNABOM. As of June 29, he'd still not received any written communication from the bomber.

Since first rights to publish fell to the *Post* and the *Times,* Guccione took out a full-page advertisement in *The New York Times* on August 3. In his "Open Letter to the Unabomber," Guccione said:

> I am a little miffed and a whole lot disappointed by your recent communication. In your first letter to *The New York Times,* received April 24, 1995, you categorically undertook to "desist from all terrorist activities" if the *Times* or "some other nationally distributed periodical" agreed to publish you manifesto. Well, I agreed! I agreed immediately and without reservation. Within 24 hours of your letter appearing in *The New York Times,* I put out a press release saying that I believed your offer was genuine and that on the basis of that belief, I was prepared (unlike the *Times* and the *Post*) to publish you *fully* and without censorship in the next available issue of *Penthouse.*
>
> Not everyone in the media agrees with that position. Many think that any attempt to strike a deal with you is journalistically unethical and contrary to the proposition that government, big business, and the press do not negotiate with terrorists. I answered those and other accusations in the following manner:
>
> 1) You held no individual newspaper or periodical hostage. You did not insist on publication in any one particular forum failing which you would continue to kill. Had you done so, *The New York Times* would have turned its back and so would I.
>
> 2) I disagreed with the popular belief that you are a serial killer and should be treated like one. I pointed out that serial killers derive the whole of their satisfaction from the act of killing... that killing was an end in itself. In your case, I suggested that killing was merely a *means* to the end. Your objectives are much bolder and infinitely more elaborate.

> You want to change the world! Killing people was your way
> of attracting attention to a personal philosophical doctrine
> with vast socio-political change at its center.
>   3) I further held that anyone who has taken the trouble
> to write a literate 37,000-word, philosophical manifesto
> and who set about killing people to get it published is most
> unlikely to destroy the credibility of his thesis by publicly
> going back on his word. For this reason alone, I do not
> believe that you would kill again.

Guccione boasted next of his magazine's influence, demographics, and awards in an attempt to win over the bomber, but it was obvious that beneath the surface he appeared to be both hurt and angry:

> I am asking you to put an end to all terrorist activities
> now and forever. I'm still the only friend you have in the
> media. Don't let my willingness to publish you make fools
> of us both!

REASONS NOT TO PRINT THE MANIFESTO WERE PLENTIFUL. "Everyone understands that the object of a terrorist is to strike terror," said Terry Francke, director of the California First Amendment Coalition, "and for that you need the maximum publicity—the kind you can get from newspapers."

Publishing UNABOM's views, well-reasoned or not, served the elusive terrorist's aims, provided him comfort, and gave the appearance to the public of "pandering to the whims" of the bomber. To refuse to print the tract would be a dramatic stand against literary extortion. And what about copycats? Would the capitulation of two of the nation's greatest papers deliver the press up to any serial killer as a public forum?

"To print this manuscript, even part of it, is a terrible precedent," said Michael Josephson, a journalistic ethicist. "It's like paying off highjackers. If a person knows they can extort this kind of thing out of the press, where will it stop?" Kenneth Solomon, a terrorism specialist with the Rand Corp. research organization, agreed. "The more you say, the more you propel it and encourage this guy. It's a self-perpetuating fire."

On the positive side of a publishing dialogue was the public's right to know, the lives that might hang in the balance, and the fact that few copycats, in the long run, ever came forward after a forum was offered to a terrorist. In September 1976, a New York–based band of Croatian separatists hijacked a plane and also slew a policeman with a bomb planted in a Grand Central Station locker. They warned that they had a second bomb planted and would explode it if five major US papers didn't publish their 3,500-word manifesto. Among the five papers that ran the propaganda tract were the *Times* and the *Post*. No copycats followed them.

One other point in favor of printing UNABOM's manifesto was that a communication of words, not violent acts, might provide insight into the bomber's mind. His style of writing over a period of time might demonstrate the state of his sanity, declining or healing, and provide leads to track him down. In the sixties and seventies the Environmental Liberation Front, among other left-wing terrorist organizations, set bombs and wrote communiques that they demanded the press print. No paper published them, and the bombings continued.

Most important, publication of the derivative manifesto might make public a peculiar turn of phrase, cadence, phraseology, or expression that might ring a bell with someone. For instance, UNABOM employed the stylistic inconsistency of "consist in," rather than the more common "consist of."

And yet, if published, there was no guarantee UNABOM

wouldn't go ahead and resume his killing spree. He'd lied about the airliner threat. Could he ever be trusted?

On August 2 the *Times* and the *Post* printed three thousand words of quotes from the tract. "The *Post*'s decision to publish excerpts from the manuscript is a journalistic one," said Leonard Downie, Jr., the paper's executive editor. "The decision to publish it in its entirety would be a non-journalistic decision." The excerpts were made available to other newspapers through the Associated Press wires.

In San Francisco, the *Examiner* chose not to print them. "There are too many unanswered questions as to why these particular excerpts were chosen by the two papers for an unprecedented tandem publication at this particular time," said the *Examiner*'s executive editor, Phil Bronstein. "If it is being done in conjunction with an FBI request, the *Times* and *Post* should reveal that. We assist law enforcement and perform what we believe is a public service all the time when we publish photos, drawings, and descriptions of criminal suspects. But we do so understanding full well that we are aiding law enforcement authorities.... If the FBI wants us to publish something as part of an effort to help them catch a suspect, they can ask us, and we'll make a judgment based on their request."

The previous day, August 1, the FBI had acted. They'd sent fifty copies of the treatise to select academics, professors, and scholars throughout the country. "We have to try everything," they said.

George Grotz, an FBI spokesman, thought the fifty professors might be able to assist in the investigation. "Maybe they had him in their class," he said.

"The FBI is taking this investigative step in an effort to determine whether that community might recognize the writer's work or be able to shed light on important or telltale aspects of the manuscript's general topic, the history of science," said FBI

Director Freeh. Freeh thought the manifesto might prompt the recollection of professors who'd seen the bomber's writings at some point over the years.

"It appears the bomber was exposed to the history of science or similar academic disciplines in the late 1970s in the Chicago area, possibly at Northwestern University or the University of Illinois Chicago Circle Campus," said Freeh. "There are indications the bomber continued his education, formally or informally, in the Salt Lake City area in 1980 and 1981.... From there, it appears that the bomber had some sort of contact with the University of California at Berkeley from about 1982 to 1985.

"The UNABOM subject has probably lived in Northern California or traveled frequently through the area since the early 1980s."

Freeh got some help almost immediately. Jack Lesch, an associate professor in history at UC Berkeley, said he thought UNABOM might be well-read, but didn't have formal schooling in the history of science or related disciplines.

"It's clear that the writer has thought about a lot of things and read a lot of things, but I don't see much specifically related to the scholarly discipline of the history of science," said Lesch. "...His vision of things is not scholarly in any sense. It's kind of apocalyptic. He's seeing things rushing toward disaster for the human race..., his kind of radically pessimistic vision of the future is usually not built into an academic discipline."

Publishers, editors, and journalists at large spent almost the entire three-month deadline period debating ethics. The final group meeting between the fourth estate and the FBI occurred just as the Unabomber's deadline was trickling out—September 13, 1995—and it was then that Freeh and Reno urged the two papers to print the text. The *Post* and the *Times* came to the conclusion that printing the thesis *in full* was worth the gamble.

"Jim Freeman had a lot to do with the publishing of that manuscript [the manifesto]," FBI agent Rick Smith told me. "He felt that it was important, and he was able to encourage others to support his position. And he was able then to convince headquarters to do it, convince Department of Justice [and Janet Reno] to do it.

"He was a real key guy and very effective and had more common sense than any other manager I knew in the FBI. If you wrote that Freeman was the architect behind getting the manifesto published you would be right. He was absolutely the architect.

"The case would never have been broken without that. Freeman all along thought public assistance was essential. It didn't matter who it came from."

I had written books dealing with unsolved mysteries set in the Bay area, almost always cases that spanned decades, and did many interviews on such perplexing investigations. When CBS radio interviewed me shortly after we learned that the manifesto was to be reprinted, I said, "No man can write 35,000 words and not tell us something about himself, if not *all* about himself."

In a similar case, I'd spent a decade researching a serial murderer who dressed in a nightmarish black costume, wrote taunting letters to the *Chronicle*, and designed bombs (actually sending diagrams to my newspaper) to blow up school buses. His letters offered many clues to his background and frame of mind.

With the decision to print the manifesto, a net began to close around UNABOM for the first time in seventeen years.

CHAPTER 39
The Manifesto

A *ctually, under certain circumstances, revolution is much
easier than reform.... A revolutionary movement offers to
solve all problems at one stroke.... Revolutionaries work to
gain a powerful reward... and therefore work harder and more
persistently than reformers do.*

—UNABOMBER MANIFESTO

WITH PUBLIC SAFETY AT STAKE, *The New York Times* and the
Washington Post, jointly and with the blessing of Freeh and Reno,
published the full Unabomber treatise. The manifesto filled a special
eight-page insert included in 850,000 copies of the September 19,
1995, issue of the *Post.* Both the ethical responsibility and the nearly
$40,000 printing expense were shared by the two papers.

"It's awfully hard to put too much faith in the words of someone with the record of violence that the Unabomber has," said
Sulzberger of the *Times.* "You print it, and he doesn't kill anyone
else; that's a pretty good deal. You print it, and he continues to kill
people, what have you lost? The cost of newsprint?"

In the Bay area, thousands of readers deluged news vendors
with requests for the *Post* insert. Harold's International
Newsstand usually carried five copies of the Washington paper
daily, but ordered several hundred copies this time out. They were

available just after 7:00 AM at the Geary Street stand on a first come, first served basis.

Meanwhile the text could be found on the World Wide Web at http://pathfinder.com. Time-Warner's Pathfinder service had posted the manifesto on the Internet, giving it the distinction of being the "first epic-length attack on technology to be sent everywhere on a computer network."

The following day the *Oakland Tribune* and *The Alameda Times-Star* also published the complex, densely reasoned tract in full.

"We print the treatise for these reasons," said the *Tribune*:

> 1) Three of the bombings took place in the Bay Area (two in Berkeley, one in Tiburon). Two other bombs were mailed from Oakland, including the most recent one that killed a Sacramento man. The Unabomber may live and work in this area, and much of the investigation is centered in the East Bay. This makes it a local story for the *Tribune*'s unique Oakland-Berkeley readership.
>
> 2) The decision by the *Washington Post* to publish the "manifesto" Tuesday—at the urging of the government—is historic and news all by itself, creating considerable reader demand in the Bay Area.
>
> 3) There is always a chance that publishing the treatise for Bay Area readers could lead to the Unabomber's apprehension....
>
> The *Tribune* condemns terrorism in any form.

UNABOM'S RANSOM NOTE, the most amazing document in the history of serial murder, stated and restated its main premise: "The industrial revolution and its consequences have been a disaster for the human race.... In order to get our message before the public with some chance of making a lasting impression, we had to kill people."

And why was the industrial revolution a disaster? Organized modern society, the Unabomber tells us, "HAS to force people to behave in ways that are increasingly remote from the natural pattern of human behavior."

In his cover letter to the *Post* accompanying his manifesto, UNABOM said, "The industrial-technological system has got to be eliminated, and to us almost any means that may be necessary for that purpose are justified." Besides being a glimpse into a killer's mind, FC's document spoke of science, history, politics, sociology, and "a cataclysmic struggle between freedom and technology." He listed the banes of modern life—accelerating social change, urban overcrowding, man's alienation from nature, and the breakdown of community and family values. "A technological society," argued the self-described anarchist (with his particular brand of anarchism), "must crush those values, and especially human freedom, to sustain itself."

The Unabomber interpreted society as being managed by corporate figures and a shadowy international government elite, all seeking to subvert human freedom. His treatise depicted a future in which humans were at the mercy of intelligent machines invented by computer scientists motivated by money and status, not curiosity.

Technology, he said, had made the situation worse by "permanently reducing human beings and many other living organisms to engineered products and mere cogs in the social machine." Since the Unabomber despaired of ever reforming the system, he advocated a revolution against the industrial system—technical books burned, factories demolished, officials overturned—and a return to nature.

"The positive idea that we propose is nature. That is WILD nature." He believed the purely "natural" world "provided a stable framework, and therefore a sense of security. In the modern world it is human society that dominates nature... thus there is no stable framework."

He devoted long passages to "the psychology of modern leftism," a group he was particularly hard on, though he railed against activists and politicians of the Left and Right. In modern leftism, "feelings of inferiority" were said to account for activism by blacks, feminists, and others, and to "oversocialization" in which lifelong feelings of "powerlessness, defeatism, guilt, etc." are inculcated into children.

UNABOM considered the right of freedom of the press: "Freedom of the press is of very little use to the average citizen as an individual. The mass media are mostly under the control of large organizations that are integrated into the system. Anyone who has a little money can have something printed, or can distribute it on the internet or in some such way, but what he has to say will be swamped by the vast volume of material put out by the media.... Take us, for example. If we had never done anything

DIAGRAM OF SYMPTOMS RESULTING FROM DISRUPTION OF THE POWER PROCESS

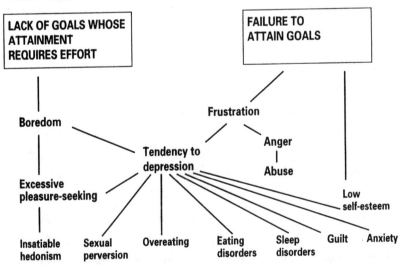

The Unabomber's diagram included in the original manifesto.

violent and had submitted the present writings to a publisher, they probably would not have been accepted.... Even if these writings had had many readers, most of those readers would soon have forgotten what they had read as their minds were flooded by the mass of material to which the media exposed them."

In a category entitled "Human Suffering" he wrote, "The process of de-industrialization probably will be very chaotic and involve much suffering. One has to balance struggle and death against the loss of freedom and dignity.... We all have to die sometime, and it may be better to die fighting for survival, or for a cause, than to live a long but empty and purposeless life."

He concluded with a "Disruption from the Power Process" map, which made the killer's connections between abuse, boredom, frustration, and anger (the overriding emotion in his recent letters and this tract), all paths leading to a central nexus: "Tendency to depression."

THEORIZING THAT THE BOMBER might have attended high school in Chicago or its northern suburbs, FBI agents spread out through the area's schools. The investigators hoped that someone might recognize the language and ideas used in the manifesto as that of a former student.

Terry D. Turchie, the FBI officer overseeing the Unabomber investigation, spoke to the press. "Our efforts right now are concentrated on trying to tie in the Chicago aspects. One of the predominant themes in the manuscript involves this entire idea of the negative impact of technology on society, and he discusses it in the context of the history of science," he said. "He's obviously spent a lot of time thinking it through. Those are probably the most important elements of that manuscript."

Agents requested additional information on nine students at three Niles Township high schools in suburban Skokie and subpoenaed the former pupils' transcripts in September. The FBI had spent the summer winnowing down the list of suspects with the help of Niles teachers. "Do you recall any students who stood out as antisocial or eccentric?" they asked.

At two Chicago universities, current and former professors strained their memories to recollect any lecturers who were anti-science. They couldn't. Students who thought the same way had left no impression in the faculty's minds. A small group of scholars, Science for the People, had been powerfully antitechnology and had occasionally disrupted meetings, once with a thrown tomato. The group, active in the 1970s, had some members at Northwestern, the site of the first bombing, and at the University of Illinois Chicago Circle Campus. Placing the blame for society's ills on technology had its roots in the anti-Vietnam War movement, when the government utilized the universities to construct weapons for scientific warfare.

Late Saturday night, October 7, police in the suburb of Evanston pulled over the driver of a van with expired California license plates. A further check showed the plates didn't match the vehicle's identification number. A search of the thirty-seven-year-old driver's car turned up a .40-caliber semi-automatic pistol, detailed maps of the Northwestern campus, and bomb-making materials.

Police discovered, according to CBS radio news, a typewriter with a font that could match the type used to write the manifesto in the suspect's home. FBI agents questioned the man the next morning. Though initially there was hope that the long-sought Unabomber had been captured, authorities soon realized he was not the terrorist. "Unfortunately, I have to say we do not have the Unabomber," said Police Chief Gerald Cooper.

But the day before the incident, investigators thought they had a little better luck. They spoke with a professor who had once worked at Northwestern's Technological Institute. He'd read the manifesto when the FBI had sent it out to select academicians, and it had reminded him that, back around 1975, a young man had walked into his office and requested that he read an essay the student had written. The paper had railed against a corrupt techno-industrial society. He and the young man had chatted awhile.

"What do you remember about him?" asked an agent.

"His first name was Robert. His last name, I believe, started with the letter 'V.' I'll try and remember the full name. It was a long time ago. I seem to recall he lived in or near Morton Grove. It's eerie how much that paper reminded me of the manifesto."

ON OCTOBER 13, A SMALL Berkeley publisher, Jolly Rodger Press, normally known for printing chess books, brought UNABOM's antitechnology manifesto out in a $9.95 paperback. Publisher Kristan Lawson typed the manuscript into his computer in one sitting while perched on the edge of his bed. Lawson sold three thousand copies of the eleven-thousand–print run.

"To be perfectly honest," he said of his bestseller, "it's boring. It's not even wildly revolutionary. I've read much more inflammatory stuff. I think it's obvious [the Unabomber] was once a member of some left-wing group, and some girl in it spurned him."

The FBI, anxious to keep tabs on a book the bomber himself might want a souvenir copy of, asked Lawson to keep detailed records of all bookstore and individual orders, but the job proved too time-consuming. Thereafter, Lawson made only bulk sales to stores, not single orders. He set aside a portion of the profits for the diatribe's real author, saying, "I will pay him if he contacts me—but I'll have to tell the FBI."

The publication of the manifesto had caused the Bureau to revise its profile of the bomber. The rage inherent in each paragraph, the growing power of his devices, and UNABOM's recent erratic behavior had led them to reclassify him. The investigators now regarded him as less a terrorist than a serial killer, someone who kills to satisfy an inner need, not to advance a political agenda. The tone of his manifesto also led them to speculate that his education was based in the social sciences.

The bomber, experts said, had a need to be right and to make the Bureau look foolish. In his *Scientific American* letter, he laughed at the FBI's theory that he had an obsession with wood. UNABOM wrote that he used wood in his devices only because it was light and strong. In his letter to the *Post* the bomber crowed that he never left prints, even sanding his bombs to erase any subsurface oils that might have gotten into wood and metal.

Newsweek magazine located a copy of the letter the bomber had sent to the *San Francisco Examiner* in 1985. Apparently, the Unabomber had included it in his letter to Guccione as an example of a dry run for his manifesto, with its fastidious grammar. In this tract UNABOM denigrated the "old revolutionary ideologies" and stated that the Freedom Club (FC) "is strictly anticommunist, anti-socialist, anti-leftist" and "this doesn't imply that we are in any sense a right-wing movement. We are apolitical. Politics only distracts attention from the real issue," which is science, technology, the labyrinth of modern society, and the crushing rule of the elite.

The UNABOM manifesto, careful but bland, referred by title to four books—*Violence in America: Historical and Comparative Perspectives* by Roger Lane and edited by Hugh Davies Graham and Ted Robert Gurr; *The Ancient Engineers* by L. Sprague DeCamp; *Chinese Political Thought in the Twentieth Century* by Chester D. Tan; and *The True Believer* by Eric Hoffer. Agents pored over these books, seeking clues.

THE PROFESSOR'S BROTHER CONTINUED his work in Schenectady as assistant director of the nonprofit Equinox Youth shelter, which provided emergency services for troubled teens. David's mother, Wanda, beginning to feel the weight of her years, often visited her son and his wife, Linda. Occasionally she partook of meals with Mary Ann Welch, David and Linda's neighbor. Welch knew of an eccentric elder brother who had never once visited in the five years David and Linda had lived next door. "They're very sweet, extremely polite and truthful people," Welch said later. "They're the kind of neighbors who lend you their car when yours is in the shop, who offer their gardening tools." Everyone said they were neighbors who cared.

News accounts of the Unabomber had said the FBI believed that he'd grown up in Chicago, lived in Berkeley, and occasionally been in Salt Lake City. These locations had nagged at Linda's subconscious in the summer of 1995 because she automatically associated them with David's brother. In August of 1995, Linda, during a vacation in Paris, read in the *Herald Tribune* of a rash of terrorist bombings throughout France. She also heard various news accounts about UNABOM. These stories raised new doubts in her mind concerning the Professor, misgivings she shared with David when he joined her in Paris during the second or third week of August. Although she had never met David's brother, she said, "Hey, you've got this screwy brother. Maybe he's the guy." David laughed, but doubt now took root in his mind.

Back in the States, they attempted to get a copy of the manifesto, but the few copies around had sold out. Time passed and other thoughts occupied their minds because they were shopping for a home and David's mom had been ailing. But Linda's thoughts kept returning to that lingering suspicion. "Come on, Linda," David would say, "you're just being silly." But around the third week in October David read a few pages of the diatribe and saw a few things he couldn't dismiss. Then one day Linda traveled to Union College, where she taught philosophy, and a librarian helped her find the manifesto on the Internet (the *Post* and the *Times* had jointly published the full text on September 19, but the library copy had been stolen). They got the treatise on disk from the reference library, but the computer version had only the introductory portion of the screed. Still, that was enough. For Linda, at least, the pieces came together. She immediately called David, and he came over so they could read the text together.

Linda watched David as he scanned the first six pages of the Unabomber tract and saw his jaw drop. "He couldn't simply dismiss the possibility," lawyer Anthony P. Bisceglie said later, "which surprised him. He had expected to read this and conclude Linda's fears were groundless. But that didn't happen." David spoke later of what he was feeling. "Chills, I think," he recalled. "Felt some anger. I was prepared to read the manifesto and be able to dismiss any possibility that it would be my brother, but it continued to sound enough like him that I was really upset that it could be him."

The pair considered the dates of the two most recent, and lethal, explosions and thought about all the money they'd sent his brother. The two siblings had not actually seen each other since October 1986. In November 1994, the Professor had requested a loan of one thousand dollars, and followed this with a plea for a two-thousand-dollar loan. One month before the mail bomb murder of Thomas Mosser, David sent his brother one thousand dollars in the form of a cashier's check. Then on January 19, 1995, David sent a second check of two thousand dollars, three months before the package to Gilbert Murray was mailed on April 20.

In his December 30 letter, the Professor had explained his request thusly: "I need another $2,000... if and when I get over the present difficulties sufficiently.... There won't be any further requests for loans... if another $2,000 won't do it, then I guess nothing will, so I may as well give up."

"I just felt awful about that," remembered David. "My wife expressed a great deal of anger that money sent, partly hers, might have killed other people."

David, on the counsel of a longtime friend, wrote his brother. "I told him that I regretted very much the strain in our relationship and said I would like to come visit him. I wanted to see him after all these years." The Professor wrote back that the suggestion made him "feel awful and made him feel angry."

In November the Professor fired back with another letter that refused any visit from his brother. He said, "I am not 'suffering, sick or discouraged,' and I don't know what 'indications' you think you have that I am so. But if you want me to get sick, all you have to do is keep trying to communicate with me, because I get just choked with frustration at my inability to get our stinking family off my back once and for all, and 'stinking family' emphatically includes you. So get this straight... I DON'T EVER WANT TO SEE YOU OR HEAR FROM YOU, OR ANY OTHER MEMBER OF OUR FAMILY, AGAIN."

David suffered, unsure of what to do next. "It was horrible, there's no question about that," he reported later. "One concern was if, God forbid, I were in a position to prevent more lives from being lost, I couldn't do otherwise." David's other fear was for his brother's well-being. "It was horrible to me that I was considering my brother to be this person."

Private investigator Susan Swanson had been a childhood friend of Linda's, even predating kindergarten. She and her sister had lived just down the block from Linda in Evergreen Park, Illinois, and they had become inseparable friends right through seventh grade. Naturally, Susan had attended Linda's wedding to David and overheard the good-natured ribbing friends gave the groom, since David had taken twenty-five years to win the hand of his beloved. As the guests mingled prior to the nuptuals, Susan began conversing with a longtime friend of David's. In passing, he told Swanson many details about David's older and troubled brother and some of the odd occurrences in his life. In a short time she had become a minor expert on the Professor's past history.

David's brother seemed unable to stop writing letters, as if this indirect way were his only method of connecting with others. The couple had saved many of the letters, and David scanned through the ones nearest at hand. In them he found nothing definitive, and throughout this excrutiating period he would be pulled hither and thither. "Call Susan," he finally told Linda, "and maybe she can find someone who can do a lingusitic comparison. But don't tell her who the writer is."

Linda and David called Swanson, who worked in the Chicago branch of the Investigative Group Inc., a Washington, DC, firm headed by Raymond Kelly, a former New York Police commissioner. The beleaguered couple asked, "How would you handle a hypothetical case where you knew someone had committed a serious crime?" Without revealing Linda or David's names or where they lived, Susan agreed to undertake the inquiry without a fee and as a friend.

In late November David and Linda discovered more letters. First, he studied the phrases he felt were common to both the bomber and the Professor. Both employed the phrase "eat their cake and have it too," which was a convolution of the usual "have their cake and eat it too." Their mother had often used that phrase. The bomber used "consist in" instead of "consist of."

In one letter, David's brother wrote to relatives that "the average man today is turning into a pawn in a big game played by scientists, businessmen and bureaucrats." In the manifesto, the Unabomber stated "experiments are performed on the public by the scientists and by the corporations and government agencies that pay for their research... the average man gets only the consequences of their social experiments."

At least one elite paragraph his brother had written appeared to be identical to one in the manifesto, even to the point of emphasizing the same word in capital letters: "The radical environmentalists ALREADY hold an ideology that exalts nature and opposes technology." Both the Professor and UNABOM used uncommon spellings for the same words: "wilfully" for "willfully," "analyse" for "analyze," and "intalment" for "installment."

After reviewing the documents, David and Linda decided they had no choice but to get in touch with the FBI. "I guess it's fair to say I felt compelled," he said afterward. "The thought that another person would die and I was in a position to stop that—I couldn't live with that."

But David tossed and turned, torn between duty to society and blood loyalty, obligation to his fellow citizens balanced against the bonds of family. The tragedy was biblical in power, and the brothers of the Old Testament whirled in his mind: Cain and Abel, the firstborn and the younger, the prodigal and the faithful son, Ishmael without his birthright.

Along with the weight of blood and honor on his shoulders, he searched his soul and struggled with his own guilt. What if he had financed a seventeen-year terror? What if he were wrong about his shy, tormented brother—the glare of publicity could destroy him. David had his doubts—the Unabomber had railed against leftists, a subject his brother had not considered important. And what about that first bomb?

The explosive device placed in the University of Illinois Engineering Building parking lot on May 26, 1978, apparently predated his brother's trip to Chicago. He'd arrived on May 30 at the earliest, as far as David could recall. Had his brother actually carried a bomb cross-country by bus, or if he'd built it in Chicago, where had he worked? Could the little shed in the family back-yard have been a bomb factory? Of course, there was the possi-bility that the first two bombs might not have been Unabomber devices at all. The first bomb did not have the excessive soldering, improvised loop switches, initiators (a wooden dowel, a pair of wires, and a bridgewire), or the letters FC, which were on all the other bombs with the exception of the first, second, and third ones. The second bomb, though more powerful and sophisticated than the first, was still far cruder and less powerful than all that followed. True, the first bomb had carried a Eugene O'Neill stamp as had numbers three and six and most of the rest. If some other bomber had placed the first device, perhaps the Unabomber had copied the use of O'Neill stamps. The local press had com-mented on the stamp from the first bomb. Only that would explain the single link.

In the delicate relationship between brothers, could David be certain that this act of both moral principle and social obligation was not some form of unconscious retaliation against a feuding sibling?

Yet even that psychological burden was not the most horrify-ing prospect if he turned in his brother.

What if the government should seek the death penalty, or kill him during a botched arrest like the ones at Waco and Ruby Ridge? He might be saving others' lives at the cost of his brother's.

It hadn't been until the first of October that Linda and David had approached Susan with their problem. And keep in mind that all these delicate, secretive maneuvers, actions that held the poten-tial of life and death for both suspect and possible future victims, in the sheer scope of their importance, were done long-distance. The emotionally charged conversations transpired over a phone hook-up between New York, where the young couple lived, and Chicago, where Susan worked and lived. Eventually Washington, DC, again at a distance and over the phone, would be drawn into the drama. In one of the most important events of her life, Susan would not see the principals face-to-face until the story had played itself out.

"'We suspect a friend of ours of a serious crime,' David told me," Swanson related to me much later. "On December 15, 1995, he told me, 'Let's go ahead [with the investigation]. It has to do with the Unabomber case.' When I realized what he was talking about, I thought, 'Well, maybe it's probably better that he doesn't tell me who the suspect is.' I would rather have not known since up to this point David had not identified who the friend was, but as he talked he described him to such a degree that I recognized him as his brother." David had not known of the long conversation Susan had had with his longtime friend at their wedding, a conversation that had described the Professor.

Throughout late December and into early January, over her weekends and throughout most of her evenings, Susan researched. She held a full-time job as a private investigator during the day, and so the labor took almost all of her waking hours. She researched both the suspect and the Unabomber case, compiling a vast library of articles concerning the perplexing investigation. Though she had a computer at work, Swanson used the database at the Chicago Public Library to discover everything she could that had been printed about the Unabomber.

In between she conducted lengthy interviews with David. As she put through a series of inquiries and calls to the various universities where David's sibling had studied or taught, she certified exact graduation dates and the topics of his various papers, and nailed down the myriad details of the older brother's life that David had been unable to recall.

Indefatigable, Swanson turned her mind to the recepients of bombs from the Unabomber. Swanson then divided them up into two groups—specifically targeted individuals and those who had accidently stumbled across a bomb abandoned in a public area by the Unabomber. First, she researched their pasts, immersing herself in articles, files, and biographical entries that had been written about the various victims prior to their assault. How had the terrorist targeted his victims?

Had he done just what she was doing and pored over biographical information to choose them? Police and FBI agents already knew that in several instances the facts, positions, and addresses of mail bomb victims were approximately a year out of date. If the bomber was researching his victims, he was consulting outdated references, perhaps in some small or remote, underfunded library.

Had the bomber known his selected targets personally? Susan needed to discover if David's troubled brother had ever crossed paths with any of them. When she had learned all that she could learn, Swanson congently summarized her findings and presented a thoughtful analysis of the case, comparing the unidentified suspect's characteristics with the known qualities of the Unabomber.

She was careful and methodical. She handled the probing gingerly, not tipping her hand or alerting the suspect. She especially did not want to do anything that might endanger the elder brother's reputation or reveal Linda and David's interest in the UNABOM case.

Meanwhile, her boss, Raymond Kelly, had suggested Swanson contact Clinton R. Van Zandt, a twenty-five-year veteran of the FBI, once their chief hostage negotiator, now in charge of a security consulting firm in Fredericksburg, Virginia. Swanson contacted him in mid-December and prepared some writing samples. Among the items Swanson sent to Van Zandt weeks later for study were the manifesto and some of David's brother's letters. "I sent a one-page letter, a recent one," she told me later, "and four pages of a letter that he had written ten years earlier. The four-page letter had the most meat to it." David neatly typed the letters and was careful to mask their origin by removing opening greetings, closing signatures, dates, abbreviations, and any biographical information. On page four of the oldest letter he removed an item that might reveal the subject's identity. Close to the bottom of the page, he deleted another fact.

Van Zandt formed two units to compare the letters the Professor had written his brother with the manifesto and designated a second team, academics who specialized in communication analysis, to decide what probability there was that David's brother was the most sought-after criminal in United States history.

But first Van Zandt had some questions for Swanson. "'How old is the subject?' he asked me and I told him. 'And what about his educational background?' he said, and I told him that too," said Swanson. "'And what about his medical background?' and I told him that too."

"I think we confirmed [their] worst fears," said Van Zandt, a behavioral specialist who had retired from the Bureau in 1994. Van Zandt noted that both the Unabomber and the writer of the letters used the phrase "tends to," underlining, expletive marks within the body of the sentences, and quotation marks around selected nouns, a practice used to frighten by giving certain words emphasis. Van Zandt also drew up a personality profile that suggested the bomber was "a male between 45 and 55 with a strong academic background, probably a Ph.D., somebody who had probably taught in a university setting." Sources within the investigation said that analysts studied drawings the suspect had done.

Van Zandt had completed his assignment by New Year's weekend. "The second team," Susan told me afterward, "finished their project sometime in January." A final report I consulted was dated January 29, 1996.

"When I received comparisons, the Friday before New Year's," she told me later, "they included a profile of the subject." Susan spoke with Van Zandt and said of the psychological study, "This is pretty much what I told you." "Yes." "Well, did you share it with the other team in advance of their findings?" "Yes." Later, Swanson told me, "He told me that I gave him pertinent information, but that it didn't influence him." This concerned her, but the comparisons between letters and manifesto were striking, and Van Zandt had produced what was later pronounced a very informative report.

Additionally, the first unit placed the probability that the author of the two letters and the manifesto were the same person at 60 percent. The second unit placed the probability at 80 percent. But he told Swanson the bad news the Friday before New Year's. "Because the analysis contained significant qualifiers, it wasn't something she was ready to take to the bank," lawyer Anthony Bisceglie told me later. "It didn't really reach the level of probable cause."

Meanwhile, David tried to figure out what the findings meant. "Here's a third party who doesn't know my brother," he said, "and saying we can't rule him out." This concerned him, but after all, 60–40 was almost 50–50—still not that strong. He was ambivalent—feeling certain one day, then convinced it could not possibly be true the next. The analysts had learned something of the Professor's background from Swanson, and the peculiar phrasing might be the way all academics talk, strident because they're not getting feedback on their ideas. David now carefully read through the full manifesto and noticed other indications that his brother might be its author. "There was a unique phrase in the UNABOM manifesto which referred to a 'cool-headed logician' which I recognized as my brother's terminology," David later said. It "leapt out" at him because it expressed the Professor's long-held position on the role of art versus science in our society. "These statements marked the UNABOM manuscript as my brother's product because we'd had a running argument for years on these topics."

David recognized, in particular, a paragraph in the first portion of the manuscript, paragraph seventeen:

> Art forms that appeal to modern leftist intellectuals tend to focus on sordidness, defeat and despair, or else they take an orgiastic tone, throwing off rational control as if there were no hope of accomplishing anything through rational calculation and all that was left was to immerse oneself in the sensations of the moment.

David later explained that his brother had long been committed to "rationality" as a guiding principle, and had further remarked that since his ideas were based on a "rational ideal" any action supporting them was justifiable. Once David and Susan got the last results on New Year's Eve, they decided to see about how to go about contacting federal authorities.

After the analysis of Van Zandt and his team, "he was agonizing," Swanson told me afterward. "But once he'd decided to move on," to the next step knowing he'd made the right decision to do what was right, he wanted to do it right away. And this was the moral core of the story—doing the greatest good for the greatest number at the expense of yourself.

David asked Swanson to recommend an attorney to act as a liaison between twixt the FBI and the anguished family.

On a Friday afternoon, January 26, 1996, Swanson called a former classmate from Antioch Law School in Washington, Anthony Bisceglie, a forty-four-year-old white-water canoeing enthusiast and skier with impeccable legal credentials. Later, he would be listed as one of the top fifty lawyers in the District of Columbia by *Washingtonian* magazine, and recognized as a "hero" at the American Bar Association's annual meeting. He had represented many clients in high-profile cases, including Leona Helmsley and Dr. Jeffrey MacDonald, whose federal appeal he was currently handling and whose case was at the center of the FBI lab scandals, and he was extraordinarily skillful in acting as a liaison in sensitive cases. This latter quality, along with Bisceglie's tact, had made Swanson think of him.

When Swanson called Bisceglie, she did not reveal either the Professor's or David's names. Nor did she mention the "UNABOM" case. He appreciated her "great concern about confidentiality." "Someone he knows might have committed a crime," she told him, "a serious crime. Possibly murder. He wants to talk to a lawyer, but at the same time doesn't want a free-wheeling uncontrolled investigation that could result in harm to this person or to others."

"Have him call me," he replied. "Just have him identify himself as a friend of Susan's, and I'll take it from there." David called Bisceglie the following Monday.

Bisceglie was retained for three purposes. First, he was to help determine if David's brother was responsible for the Unabomber crimes. Second, he was to convince the FBI that the suspicions were worthy of investigation and that the inquiry should be executed in such a manner that there would be no harm to the brother's reputation if he could be ruled out. Should the probe be unable to rule him out, Bisceglie wanted to make certain no physical harm came to him. Third, if the worst fears were realized, the lawyer would address the death penalty issue.

None of this cloak-and-dagger intrigue fazed Bisceglie. "I have represented a wide variety of clients," he later told me. "I learned long ago not dismiss people out of hand. At the same time I learned to treat every allegation with a grain of salt. When David first called and started talking about the Unabomber, I sighed and looked up at the ceiling. But after I talked to David, I took it seriously. I realized that this was a very thoughtful and intelligent person who had not come to these suspicions lightly. As we spoke, it became clear I should pay attention.

"I obtained more information from Susan Swanson and pulled public record information from papers on the Unabomber case. I concluded that it did warrant investigation and David authorized me to make contact with the FBI. I contacted an agent in the Bureau I had known for thirteen years as a preliminary step. I called this agent for two reasons—I thought going directly right to the Task Force would be a mistake. They had something like fifty thousand leads. To persuade the Task Force would take some doing. There was no direct evidence that showed he had connections to those crimes, no direct contact to any crime. The chance the client's suspicions would be backburnered was extremely high. My biggest concern was that once the lead was provided they would simply go up and knock on his door one day, and that would be a disaster. I needed to be taken seriously. I needed someone who knew me and would not present the matter in a cavalier fashion. I provided him with only partial information. I wanted caution, not an overreaction. The trick was to get the train out of the station, but not have it run anybody over.

"At this point I still did not know David's name, telephone number, or address. Later that week I provided the FBI with typewritten material and handwriting samples provided by David and Linda for comparison. The FBI didn't have much handprinting, but they had lots of typewriting. Different typewriters, though. We thought this could be a quick way to get some answers. But there was no positive match of the typewriting.

"Later that week, I had a meeting with two agents from the FBI's Washington field office (WFO) here in our conference room [at his Washington, DC, suite of offices]. I provided some additional background and letters."

At that point David was hit by one final blow: "About a week later David called because he had found a typewritten essay his brother had written in the early 1970s. David had been shown this essay by his brother years ago, but he couldn't recall the exact words. He did, however, remember the basic ideas. David recalled that his brother had sent it to different newspapers and columnists. He thought this essay had been destroyed."

CHAPTER 40

A Brother's Anguish

*W*hen a man commits a crime, the earth is made of glass.

—EMERSON

"WHEN DAVID'S MOTHER BECAME ILL, a week after first contacting me, he left for Chicago," Bisceglie continued. "And there in a trunk he discovered the essay."

David had begun sifting through boxes as he helped his mother clean out the house in preparation for a move to Schenectady.

He eventually came upon some letters and a carbon copy of a twenty-three-page essay his brother had written in 1971 (reproduced here for the first time ever in Appendix D).

David called Bisceglie and told him of the essay he'd unearthed in a trunk. "He told me he would send it to me by Federal Express, and I could provide it to the FBI as another typewriting sample.

"I read it, and I reread it. I'd already read the manifesto several times. 'My God,' I thought, 'there are some remarkable similarities in some of the concepts, the style, and the language.'"

Bisceglie was so concerned that he paced round the block, his mind filling with possibilities. Back in the office he rang up the FBI WFO contact and she came right over.

"Did you read it?" she asked. "Yes," he said. "It's making my hair stand on end."

Later he called her and asked, "Have *you* read it?" "Not yet. It's gone to the lab," she said. Bisceglie later told me, "Because of bad matches in the typewriting, they were already beginning to backburner it." He told her to "read it now and make sure the Task Force reads it now." They did and had the same reaction. The next trick was for the agents to get Freeman to read it. Freeman read it and was immediately interested. "Within a couple of days we were told they definitely wanted to meet David, and we negotiated several conditions for this first meeting.

"I spent roughly three months with my office door locked," Bisceglie said. "We did everything we could to keep a lid on this. And the reason for that was to protect, again, [the brother's] reputation and also to protect the integrity of the investigation."

On February 12 Bisceglie wrote his FBI contact that "Our client is fully prepared to cooperate with the Bureau and to comply with its above-described requests conditioned upon receipt of certain written assurances by the Bureau and set forth below.

"First, the Bureau agrees that our client's identity, his cooperation and his role as a source of information shall remain confidential and shall not be revealed to persons other than the authorized Department of Justice employees with a need to know. Our client will be given the status and entitled to Bureau procedures applicable to confidential informants. This confidential treatment by the Bureau shall continue indefinitely, unless and until our client indicates otherwise in writing.

"Second, the Bureau agrees that its investigation of the subject will be conducted in accord with all applicable laws, regulations and guidelines.

"Third, the Bureau agrees that its investigation of the subject, if any, will be conducted in phases beginning with the most discreet and least intrusive measures to minimize any publication of the fact that the Bureau is investigating the subject.

"The first phase could include inquiries with people... but only if a pretext is used. The investigation in this phase should exhaust all investigative steps that do not require authorities to inform anyone that the subject is a Unabomber suspect.

"Once the quiet-phase steps have been exhausted, we would like to be informed of whether the subject has been excluded as a suspect. If he is not excluded at that point, we would like to be notified before the next investigative phase begins.

"If the investigation progresses to the point where the Bureau desires to speak with the subject's mother or the people living in the town where the subject's home resides, we would be notified prior to the start of that phase."

Before the manifesto was received, the FBI didn't know what psychological state the bomber was working from—disgruntled worker, terrorist, or possibly someone suffering from a mental disturbance, Bisceglie explained to me. "Now they knew he had a mental disturbance," he said. Among the worries that consumed both the dedicated lawyer and the anguished brother were the elder brother's fragile psychological state, his heart condition, and the overwhelming stress he endured daily. "Any slips could endanger our client's life," he cautioned them.

"Fourth," Bisceglie's agreement letter read on the last page, "at every stage of the investigation, and during such phases, all efforts to exclude the subject as the Unabomber would be made. The Bureau will keep us informed about the progress and the results of its investigation of the subject on an ongoing basis."

On February 14, Valentine's Day, 1996, after multiple interviews and many discussions, David finally agreed to speak face-to-face with the FBI. Bisceglie would meet with him, and David would turn over his brother's name. David knew this was the turning point. "Either it's an historic occasion," said Bisceglie, "or the beginning of a wild goose chase." One agent said of David, "He was torn, as anyone would be, between doing what is societally right and loyalty to his brother. This was not some guy who walked in with information to collect the $1,000,000 reward."

"That weekend, the seventeenth and eighteenth," Bisceglie told me, "three agents came out from the Task Force. David and Linda came down and stayed at the University Club, since it was discreet, and I could get them a reasonable rate there." Tony was outside counsel for the prestigious University Club only a block away from his firm. This would be the first time Bisceglie would meet David and Linda in person.

"David and Linda were wonderful people," he recalled. "They were bright, articulate, sensitive, concerned, and nervous. They were very worried about Ted's well-being. I was doing everything I could to protect their anonymity.

"We had a fairly open discussion for two days. The agents asked a lot of standard questions. A lot of David's knowledge didn't fit the profile. We still had no evidence of any crime and no evidence that Ted had ever left the state of Montana after 1979. It became as apparent to the agents as it was apparent to me this wasn't going to be an easy investigation. A Recluse who did not have a lot of contact meant that the investigation would eventually require extensive study of business and the way he traveled.

"At the same time we didn't want agents walking into this small community and asking questions about David's brother. If a lot of this investigation would focus on his writings, that meant [initially] getting hold of any letters he'd written.

"David recalled that he'd received many letters when he lived in Texas. The following week he went to his cabin at the FBI's request and retrieved more letters. The FBI kept David busy, which was difficult since he was trying to retain his job and to maintain all outward appearances of normalcy to help his mother. It was now mid-February, and we were concerned that his brother could become more mobile as the snows started melting. The anniversary of the manifesto was coming up, and we had a large concern about government leaks."

As more letters were retrieved by David, Bisceglie and the FBI began doing a parallel analysis of those letters. "There were many statements in the manifesto which could be construed as autobiographical," the lawyer said.

"We maintained a list of every postmark on the letters to compare to the list of dates of [Unabomber] incidents in order to rule him out as a suspect. But we never could do that."

Beginning on February 18, David began to lay out a chronological history of his brother's movements and peculiar behavior over the years from 1967 to the present. He explained how he had contributed $1,050, half the amount needed to purchase 1.4 acres near Lincoln, Montana, where his brother had singlehandedly built a shack along the lines of Thoreau's cabin.

David provided eighty-six letters and the 1971 essay, in which his brother argued the necessity of forming an organization to bring about the cessation of corporate and federal funding of scientific research, to the FBI.

Now the investigators had enough that they felt they would have to speak to David's mother, Wanda. Was this the worst moment of all for him? He had never mentioned his suspicions to her. In the end, it was mere hours before the investigators arrived at Wanda's new home in Schenectady that David told her of his fears and suspicions. Haltingly, he told her of the last few months and of his excruciating decision, the harrowing nights, the haunting dreams.

Wanda said little at first, only, "It can't be. It can't be him." Then she asked, "Where would he get the money to travel? He hates travel. I can't imagine him doing anything violent." She sat back, thoughts racing, and finally said slowly, "You could be right."

"The first concern was for me, I think," said David later. "I believe she knew me well enough. I did not do this lightly."

David was pacing, then crying. "I'm very, very sorry," he sobbed.

Wanda arose from her chair, a frail woman with the world's weight on her shoulders, and hugged him. "I feel awful for what you've gone through," she said.

David experienced an all-consuming "rush of relief," he said later.

But his mother was more worried than she let on. Many long years lay ahead for David to be wracked by recriminations. Her greatest concern was that David might be responsible for his brother's death. "It would be very, very difficult to live with myself knowing that I had delivered my injured, disturbed brother over to be killed," he said later.

The family continued to aid the FBI, on the condition that the Professor never know who'd sent the investigators in his direction. Wanda provided letters her son had written in 1969 and 1970, and an undated letter that said "no one could want better parents."

On March 23, 1996, Wanda read newspaper accounts of the Unabomber, in which he was described as "a loner who is against technology." She agreed that the words fit her son. "People like my son are vulnerable to suspicion. He likes to live alone, likes privacy, is an environmentalist, and he deplores the excesses of technology."

The plain, thoughtful woman still did not truly believe her eldest son could be the long-sought-after domestic terrorist, and felt it was unfair that his lifestyle had led authorities to regard him as a suspect. She paused. Then said, "But if it is him, he must be stopped."

On the same day, David's mother provided the FBI with the carbon copy of the twenty-three-page essay, complete with her lonely son's penciled notations.

CHAPTER 41
Comparisons

*T*hroughout this article we've made imprecise statements
and statements that ought to have had all sorts of
qualifications and reservations attached to them; and some of
our statements may be flatly false. Lack of sufficient
information and the need for brevity made it impossible for us
to formulate our assertions more precisely. All the same, we are
reasonably confident that the general outlines of the picture we
have painted here are roughly correct.

—UNABOMBER MANIFESTO

COMPARISONS OF THE ESSAY (along with handwritten notations the
Professor had made in its margins) and the manifesto fell to FBI
Supervisory Special Agent James Fitzgerald. He painstakingly
directed his experts to conduct a comparative analysis of all of the
Professor's correspondence, documenting the UNABOM letters
and the 34,649-word manifesto with letters the subject had written his brother. In a side-by-side comparison, the experts found
similarities and reproduced some 160 examples.

Of the forty-seven paragraphs in the 6,374-word essay, all but
twelve could be correlated by subject matter with the manifesto.
For instance, David's brother wrote objecting to Perry London's
view in *Behavior Control*—"I simply find the sphere of freedom
that he favors too narrow for me to accept." UNABOM wrote in
his ninety-third manifesto paragraph: "We are going to argue that
industrial-technological society cannot be reformed in such a way

as to prevent it from progressively narrowing the sphere of human freedom," and later the bomber three more times referred to "narrowing our sphere of freedom" and "invades our sphere of freedom...."

In the essay, David's brother wrote of "[d]irect physical control of the emotions via electrodes and 'chemitrodes' inserted in the brain." UNABOM says in paragraph 158, "It presumably would be impractical for all people to have electrodes inserted in their heads."

In the essay the Professor wrote: "...various electronic devices for surveillance. These are being used. For example, according to newspaper reports, the police of New York City have recently instituted a system of 24-hour television surveillance over certain problem areas of the city." In the manifesto, the bomber says, "...there are the techniques of surveillance. Hidden video cameras are now used to collect and process vast amounts of information."

The essay commented on "...all the misery suffered as a result of Victorian repressions, sexual perversions, frigidity, unwanted pregnancies, and venereal disease." The manifesto read: "During the Victorian period many oversocialized people suffered from serious psychological problems as a result of repressing or trying to repress their sexual feelings."

Both the Professor and UNABOM spoke of propaganda and their use in mass culture, such as movies and other entertainment. In both essay and tract, "Big Government" and "Big Business" were mentioned. Then Agent Fitzgerald and his men turned to the letters to compare them with the manifesto.

David's brother, on August 28, 1979, wrote: "... by wilderness I meant a place where our nearest neighbor would be 5 miles away." In the manifesto, UNABOM said, "Many nuclear families lived by choice in such isolation; having no neighbors within several miles." On November 17, 1982, and again on September 21, 1988, the Professor fretted over "...partial destruction of the ozone layer in the atmosphere which is caused by releases of fluorocarbons..." and in a letter almost a full year later wrote: "They predict that in coming years there will be increasing drought... because of the greenhouse effect." UNABOM said in paragraph 169 of his manifesto: "No one knows what will happen as a result of ozone depletion, the greenhouse effect and other environmental problems...."

It appeared an inescapable conclusion that the Unabomber, whoever he was, had read, perhaps even owned a copy of Vice President Al Gore's book, *Earth in the Balance*. Gore had popularized the term "ozone layer" to such an extent that the politician had been dubbed "Mr. Ozone." Fittingly, considering the Vice President's demeanor, often characterized as "wooden," the Unabomber, with his preoccupation with all things wood, was apparently drawn to Gore's ideas. Syndicated columnist Tony Snow later pointed out some of the remarkable similarities between the two texts:

> **WHEREAS THE UNABOMBER WRITES:** "Very widespread in modern society is the search for 'fulfillment.'... (Yet) for the majority of people whose main goal is fulfillment, (technology) does not bring completely satisfactory fulfillment."

> **GORE SAYS:** "Industrial civilization's great engines of distraction still seduce us with a promise of fulfillment. Our new power to work our will upon the world can bring with it a sudden rush of exhilaration.... But that exhilaration is fleeting. It is not true fulfillment."

> **THE DOMESTIC TERRORIST SAYS:** "Technological progress marches in only one direction. It can never be reversed. Once a technological innovation has been intro-

duced, people usually become dependent on it, so that they can never again do without it, unless it is replaced by some still more advanced innovation."

AND GORE WRITES: "Like the Sorcerer's Apprentice, who learned how to command inanimate objects to serve his whims, we too have set in motion forces more powerful than we anticipated and that are harder to stop than start."

UNABOMBER: "Artificial needs have been created.... Advertising and marketing techniques have been developed that make many people feel the need for things that their grandparents never desired or even dreamed of.... It seems for many people, maybe the majority, these artificial forms... are insufficient. A theme that appears repeatedly in the writings of the social critics of the second half of the 20th century is the sense of purposelessness that afflicts many people in modern society."

GORE: "Whenever any technology is used to mediate our experience of the world, we gain power but we also lose something in the process. The increased productivity of assembly lines in factories, for example, requires many employees to repeat the identical task over and over until they lose any feeling of connection to the creative process—and with it their sense of purpose."

Snow even ended his column by switching two passages, labeling a passage by the bomber as Gore's and vice versa, and then asking his readers if they had guessed. It was not easy.

In a September 2, 1986, letter the Professor referred to DeCamp's *Ancient Engineers,* one of the four books mentioned in the UNABOM manifesto. Terry Turchie, assistant special agent in charge, also sought the opinions of scholars and educators and, without revealing the identity of the suspect, provided them with UNABOM writings in order to evaluate their thoughts. One suggested that a book by Jacques Ellul, *The Technological Society,*

ATTACHMENT, 4

A TEXT COMPARISON OF THE 'T'
(TED) DOCUMENTS
AND THE 'U' (UNABOM) DOCUMENTS

'T' DOCUMENTS	'U' DOCUMENTS
T-1. Throughout this letter Ted writes of nature, e.g., "the kinds of woods one finds in Illinois...;" "Mushroom hunter's field guide;" "I found 4 edible plants..." "...parsnip roots..." (edible plants/roots also mentioned in T-9, T-13, T-15, T-16, T-84, T-87, T-169.)	U-14. Paragraph 198 "When primitive man needed food he knew how to find and prepare edible roots,..."
T-1. "...I drove up to Humboldt county for deer hunting." "...we hunted together..." "...details of hunting and fishing laws-..." "...deer hunting is very exciting."	U-14. Paragraph 75 "A young man goes through the power process by becoming a hunter, hunting not for sport or for fulfilment but to get meat that is necessary for food." U-14. Paragraph 198 ...how to track game..."
T-1. "But where to learn all that stuff?" ("stuff" also used in T-9, T-22, T-23, T-27, T-31, T-33, T-34, T-35, T-39, T-49, T-59, T-61, T-66, T-77, T-79, T-81, T-82, T-84, T-85, T-120)	U-7. "We would not want anyone to think that we have any desire to hurt professors who study Archaeology, history, literature or harmless stuff like that..." U-11. "We are very pleased that you've offered to publish our stuff, and we thank you..." "...be to our advantage if we can get our stuff published." "...we'd like to get our stuff published..." "So to increase our chances of getting our stuff published..." U-14. Paragraph 223 "Some readers may say, 'This stuff about leftism is a lot of crap..."
T-1. "More or less ignorant,..." ("more or less" also mentioned in T-2, T-13, T-17, T-22, T-25, T-28, T-52, T-54, T-66, T-73, T-76, T-91, T-92, T-143, T-170.)	U-14. Paragraph 10 "We argue that modern leftists tend to have such feelings (more or less repressed)..." U-14. Paragraph 192 "..the majority of the population, are more or less, susceptible.." ("more or less" used through U-14.)

'T' DOCUMENTS	'U' DOCUMENTS
T-7, Last Paragraph "...hunting and gathering wild fruits...killing an animal for it's meat..."	U14. Paragraph 38 "...time and energy in hunting, though they certaintly didn't need the meat..."
(T-85, Page 2 talks about hunting for meat.)	U14. Paragraph 75 "...hunting not for sport...but to get meat that is necessary for food."
T-7, "...as a cause of, the Industrial Revolution..." "Is it possible...hard work started with the Industrial Revolution?"	Industrial Revolution is mentioned numerous times betwen the U12 and U14 documents. Some examples are:
	U-12. "...who initiated the Industrial Revolution..."
	U-14. Paragraph 160 "The industrial revolution has radically altered man's...way of life."
	U-14. Paragraph 170 "The industrial revolution was supposed to eliminate poverty..." "...the industrial revolution technology has been creating new problems..."
	U-14. Paragraph 184 "Only with the industrial revolution did the effect of human society on nature become really devastating."
T-9. "...partial destruction of the ozone layer in the atmosphere, which is caused by release of fluorocarbons in various technological activities, including but not restricted to use of these gasses in aerosol cans."	U-12. "...the effects of some of their lost gambles: ozone depletion, the greenhouse effect,..."
	U-14. Paragraph 169 "No one knows what will happen as a result of ozone depletion, the greenhouse effect and other environmental problems..."
T-60. Page 1 "They predict that in the coming years there will be increasingly more drought [footnote" because of the 'greenhouse effect.'"	U-14. Paragraph 118 "Thus pesticide or chemical use near a creek may contaminate the water supply hundreds of miles downstream, and the greenhouse effect affects the whole world."

'T' DOCUMENTS	'U' DOCUMENTS
T-28. "...there is no way of travelling side by side. ...that when **travelling**..." ("**travelling**" is also mentioned in T-29, T-43, T-48.)	U-14. **Paragraph 109** "But it was a step along the road that the English-speaking world was already **travelling**..."
T-29. "According to that book on Mexican-American that I sent you, they don't like being considered as **nonwhite**. I don't really think of them as **nonwhite**, myself."	U-14. **Paragraph 40** "In modern industrial society...who work for the rights of **nonwhite** minorities."
T-29. "The ones I've seen look as if they have more Spanish than Indian blood, though it's true that most Mexicans do have a **greater or lesser** amount of Indian blood."	U-14. **Paragraph 42** "...need a **greater or lesser** degree of autonomy..." U-14. **Paragraph 58** "...the power process to a **greater or lesser** extent." U-14. **Paragraph 85** "...the power process to a **greater or lesser** extent."
T-31. "So, you'll understand that with the way things are around here now I often suffer from tension, **anger, frustration**, etc.," "...but under the influence of any sort of worry, **anger, frustration**, etc.," ("**frustration and anger**" also mentioned in T-34, T-92.)	U-9. **Page 7** "You'll ask why we are so angry. You would do better to ask why there is so much **anger and frustration**." U-14. **Paragraph 59** "The more drives there are in the third group, the more there is **frustration, anger**, eventually defeatism, depression, etc." U-14. **Note 6** "**Frustration** leads to **anger**, **anger** to aggression,..." U-14. **Note 7** "DIAGRAM OF SYMPTOMS RESULTING FROM DISRUPTION OF THE POWER PROCESS ... **Frustration Anger** ..."
T-31. "...things would get so built up around here that I would find my cabin and myself **isolated** in the middle of a huge shopping center." ("**isolated**" also mentioned in T-13, T-64, T-84, T-91, T-137.)	U-7. "The FBI has tried to portray these bombings as the work of an **isolated** nut." U-7. "...filing trigger mechanisms out of scraps of metal or searching the sierras for a place **isolated** enough to test a bomb." U-14. **Paragraph 57** "In those days an entire county might have only a couple of hundred inhabitants and was a far more **isolated** and autonomous entity..."

'T' DOCUMENTS	'U' DOCUMENTS
T-128. Page 2 "...it would choose docile people who don't make trouble;"	U-14. Paragraph 65 "...sufficiently docile to go along obediently..." U-14. Paragraph 78 "...Individuals with a weak drive for power...These are docile types..." U-14. Paragraph 163 "...making people sufficiently docile so that their behavior no longer threatens the system." U-14. Paragraph 175 "...will have to be ever more reliable, conforming and docile," "...to engineer people to be docile..."
T-129. Line 3 "...by some form of behavioral engineering"	U-14. Paragraph 58 "...massive behavioral aberration" U-2. Paragraph 1 "...and I am writing my dissertation on the development of the behavioral sciences..." U-2. Paragraph 2 "I have selected the behavioral sciences for study..."
T-129. Line 5 "...if we want to have any individual liberty, we must recognize that we have to pay a certain price for it ..."	U-14. Paragraph 84 "...with negative consequences for individual freedom." U-14. Paragraph 111 "...high cost in individual freedom and local autonomy."
T-129. Line 19 & 20 "...increasingly strict regulations, some of which have already been proposed, regarding the use of automobiles..."	U-14. Paragraph 127 "When automobiles became numerous, it became necessary to regulate their use extensively."
T-129. Line 20 "...any mechanical device with any capacity to do physical harm..."	U-12. Page 3 "...harm caused by technological progress..."
T-130. Line 9 "...make them fit the restricted structure of society..."	U-14. Paragraph 95 "...technological structure of the society..." U-14. Note 33 "...technological structure of a society..."

'T' DOCUMENTS	'U' DOCUMENTS
T-130. Line 15 & 16 "...blame for our environmental problems on excessive individual freedom."	U-14. Paragraph 84 "...negative consequences for individual freedom..."
	U-14. Paragraph 111 "...for technology to strengthen the system at a high cost in individual freedom and local autonomy."
T-131. "It is commonly assumed that scientists are motivated mainly by a desire to benefit humanity."	U-14. Paragraph 87 "Some scientists claim that they are motivated by 'curiosity' or by a desire to 'benefit' humanity."
T-131. Page 1 "...including genetic engineering, electronic surveillance devices, superhuman computers..."	U-4. Page 1 "...genetic engineering (to which computers make an important contribution)..."
	U-12. Page 1 "For the future what will be the consequences of genetic engineering? Of the development of super-intelligent computers...?"
	U-14. Paragraph 130 "(...genetic engineering, invasion of privacy through surveillance devices and computers, etc.)
	(U-14. Genetic engineering used in several other paragraphs - 122, 123, 124, 128, 133, 141, 149, 169, and 177)
T-131. Page 1 "...scientists are motivated mainly by a desire to benefit humanity."	U-14. Paragraph 87 "Some scientists claim that they are motivated by 'curiosity' or by a desire to 'benefit humanity'."
T-131. Page 1 "The supposed benefit to humanity is merely a rationalization that is sometimes used."	U-14. Paragraph 88 "The 'benefit of humanity' explanation doesn't work any better."
	U-14. Paragraph 88 "Did this involvement stem from a desire to benefit humanity?"
	U-14. Paragraph 88 "...not from a desire to 'benefit humanity'..."
T-131.Page 1 "..."scientists love science... because their egos are built around their scientific work."	U-14. Paragraph 40 "Scientific work may be motivated in part by a drive for prestige,..."

had influenced the writing of the manifesto. David said that he believed this book became his brother's "bible," and produced an August 21, 1981, letter in which his brother refers to Ellul and his philosophy.

One scholar said that the Unabomber had paraphrased ideas from two books—*Behavioral Control* by Perry London and William A. Henry III's *In Defense of Elitism*. The Professor had devoted pages of his essay to London in which Professor McConnell, a UNABOM target, is mentioned. Ellul is also mentioned.

David's brother referred to the "edibility of roots" in several notes, such as one dated July 23, 1984. The Unabomber wrote in his manuscript: "When primitive man needed food he knew how to find and prepare edible roots...."

Finally, Fitzgerald and his men completed a fifty-page document demonstrating the similarities they had unearthed.

In Helena, near the subject's home, was a Sylvan Learning Center, one of only three in the entire state. Sylvan placed particular emphasis on mathematical skills. In the entire manifesto, this business was the only one mentioned by name.

And finally the Unabomber had slipped up. When he had posted the letter to Professor Tom Tyler at UC Berkeley, he had evidently *licked the stamp*. The FBI now had his DNA. In a comparison with an envelope flap and stamp licked by David's brother, the subject could not be ruled out as a possible contributor to the DNA detected on the Tyler stamp. Both correspondents had relatively rare DQAI Type 1.1, 2.

"The estimated probability," wrote the FBI, "expressed as a percentage of selecting an unrelated individual at random from the population having DQAI Type 1.1, 2 as detected in these specimens, is approximately 3 percent of Caucasians, 3 percent of blacks, and 5 percent of Southeastern Hispanics and 2 percent of

Southwestern Hispanics." But DNA alone would not be enough in court to convict—3 percent still included an impressive number of people. "David Kaczynski reviewed all the writings attributed to the UNABOM subject," said an FBI report. "He came to the conclusion that based upon content, style, and specific phraseology of the writings that they were written by his brother."

From Valentine's Day on, preparations for the suspect's arrest began to be laid. But first came the tricky part. Agents had to infiltrate a small town where the presence of even a single stranger excited suspicion.

CHAPTER 42
The Arrest of a Mountain Man

The system does not and cannot exist to satisfy human needs. Instead, it is human behavior that has to be modified to fit the needs of the system. This has nothing to do with the political or social ideology.... It is the fault of technology.... No one stops to ask whether it is inhumane to force adolescents to spend the bulk of their time studying subjects that most of them hate.

—UNABOMBER MANIFESTO

LIKE BUGS ON A WINDSHIELD—a few at first speckling the glass, then more and more until they blotted out the Big Sky—strangers blew into Lincoln. Their numbers climbed from a few a day in February to such a multitude in March that the townsfolk, always watchful and mindful of the slightest change, speculated endlessly about the outlanders (when they weren't discussing the constantly changing weather). Such an odd assortment, they wondered— mountain men who were too tidy, postal workers far off their routes, hunters, snowmobile enthusiasts, tourists out of season, lumberjacks, and prospectors—all caught their scrutiny.

One Lincolnite recalled the army of "too shiny" cars he'd seen, all "new rigs." "They were new cars, Fords mostly," he said, "and all were pulling new snowmobiles behind them. And we instantly knew something was up." The newcomers failed to give lifts to people alongside the road, something that was just not done here.

One of the townspeople recognized a man he knew to be an FBI agent, but then realized that the agent often liked to snowmobile over the two hundred miles of trail that radiated from the hub of Lincoln. Routes cut through wildlife winter ranges and along both groomed and ungroomed trails—Keep Cool Creek, Stonewall Mountain (the most difficult), and Cotter Basin (difficult), Upper Copper to Copper Creek and Upper Copper to Snowbank Lane (with steep pitches and possible drifting). But then the true reason for the federal agent's presence and for that matter the presence of so many nonresidents came to him.

Over three hundred miles away on Montana's arid eastern plain at the opposite end of Highway 200, the standoff between Freemen's (Constitutionalists) Movement members and an oddly benign contingent of FBI agents dragged on. The siege began the same day—March 25, 1996—that agents arrested two Freemen leaders, LeRoy Schweitzer and Daniel Petersen, Jr. These antigovernment activists refused to recognize federal authority and held their own Bible-based laws and courts, basing their interpretation on the Constitution and other documents.

Writer Walter Kirin characterized them thus: "Not content to live in the peaceable Montana way, this band of alleged counterfeiters and tax cheats busied itself placing bounties on neighbors. No wonder the locals were set to raid the place before the FBI stepped in. In Montana, screwing the government is your affair, but no one likes a busybody."

Along with neo-Nazis, busily establishing an Aryan homeland in the Pacific Northwest, and white separatists, the modern militia movement was becoming ever-present in Montana.

The Freemen detested government interference and maintained their sovereign individual rights to issue "Dead or Alive" warrants on any elected county official who crossed their paths. As for the twenty-two members holed up at a ranch house on a 960-

acre farm in Jordan, the government wanted them on charges of bank fraud, conspiracy for threatening public officials, and mail fraud.

And that, stated the Lincoln man with certainty, explained why agents were creeping about the town. These men were lying low, waiting to snare any Idaho militia reinforcements passing through Lincoln on the way to Jordan.

But a second resident had a different explanation for the recent infestation of grim-faced young men, each remarkably fit and clean-cut. Recently, gold and platinum deposits had been discovered near the Scapegoat Wilderness to the north. Butch and Wendy Gehring were even now drilling core holes in the clear-cut bluffs above the Hermit's shack south of town. The influx of prospectors, mine experts, and historians researching a book on the long petered-out gold mines that had given the town its birth was now completely understandable.

Sherri Wood, the Lincoln town librarian for the past twelve years, looked up to see a pleasant stranger looking down over her high desk. He introduced himself as "Ralph Grayson, mining enthusiast." Sherri had been one of the editors and writers of the historical society's definitive book on Lincoln's history and mining days. The deluxe, black-bound volume was available down by the beef jerky plant, and it was only logical that she'd be a mining information source. "Grayson," in reality, though, was FBI Agent John Gray working undercover to glean all he could about the Hermit from Wood and her assistant, Mary Spurlin. He knew about the long hours the Recluse had put in at those two long dark tables, and his close friendship with Wood.

In reality, most of the strangers in town—lumberjacks, miners, and hunters alike—were members of the Bureau's top-notch Hostage Rescue Team, trained to survive in the wilds for long stretches of time, enduring the region's frigid temperatures. But these men asked questions about the Hermit on the Hill, quiet and subtle—and in this neck of the woods the only thing folks liked less than questions were the questioners themselves. The agents soon learned the Hermit hadn't been seen for some time.

"What was funny," Chris Waits told me, "is that I was the last one to see him before the arrest. He came downtown and made a right to get some groceries real fast. Rode his bike down. It was cold, and I saw his tracks in the snow. That way I always knew he was out. It was late in the afternoon when I saw his tracks, and I stopped.

"It was real stormy out, and the sun had broken through. This is just a few days before the FBI showed up and started surveillance.

"I pulled up and asked if he wanted a ride. He said, 'No. It would be too much of a problem. I'm getting close, and it would be too much fuss to unload my pack and load up my bike and all that. Pick it up and unload it again.'

"So he declined, and that was the last time I talked to him. The last time anybody saw him. Nobody remembers seeing him since the fall before."

Waits looked back. The circle was complete—their first and last meeting had been identical. A storm came up as the solitary figure pedaled away and was soon lost in the trees.

"We were talked to months before the arrest," one townsperson later told me. "We had no clue what they were questioning us about the Hermit for. We figured he'd sent somebody a letter or something."

"There weren't too many contrary views at the end," FBI Agent Rick Smith told me. "There were a couple [of agents] who thought maybe it wasn't him. Freeman had pretty much convinced everyone that they had the right guy, and he was optimistic. He was on the scene. And Turchie, Noll, Joel Moss. Everybody who was on the Task Force was up there."

Wendy and Butch Gehring lived on a couple of hundred acres about an eighth of a mile from the Recluse's shack, making them just about his nearest neighbors beside Chris Waits and Glenn Williams, who used his shack only on weekends. Carol and George Blowars were a close second in proximity. Then Larry Menards came next. One day Wendy realized that she hadn't caught sight of the Hermit for a considerable time.

"Go on up to the cabin," she urged Butch. "He might be dead."

"I want no part of that," said Butch. In his checkered relationship with the Hermit (their battle over Butch's use of a pesticide that the Hermit thought caused cancer still rankled, and the mill owner harbored suspicions that the Recluse had once sabotaged his sawmill), concern for his neighbor had been dampened. But it was true the Hermit had been looking bad the last time they saw him—red-rimmed eyes, with his "serious-looking" hair more matted than ever.

As for the agents, they were worried. Their plan had been to wait until he went into town with his backpack or caught a lift with the mailman, Lundberg. But certain fears set them to talking among themselves.

"What if he's already mailed the next bomb and we're just sitting here?"

"You've forgotten the manifesto," said one. "He said he'd stop if they printed his message." There was then grumbling among the freezing men about the wisdom of trusting terrorists, domestic or otherwise.

"We'll know once we're inside."

"That is if he doesn't spot us coming, or if it's not booby-trapped."

"What if he blows up the entire cabin while we're at the door?"

"No, we'll just catch him on the way to town on his bike. Then we'll have answers. Well, we *will*, won't we? And we've all the time in the world."

Over the last weeks of March, three FBI sharpshooters kept the shack in sight using their night sniper sights and infrared binoculars. From space, satellites spun by, pinpointing and measuring the property, and capturing it in a series of high-resolution photographs. Objects only a few inches wide showed up clearly. High-flying aircraft also snapped photos of the site and surrounding mountainside. When agents sat down to plan their raid, they could consult any of these pictures to get the lay of the land: "Now over here's the ravine, here's the shack, and over here is Humbug Contour Road." Williams's cabin was photographed from above in reference to the Hermit's cabin. The two huge gardens stood out plainly in the aerial photos, the root cellar, a dark blotch on the hillside, more visible than from the ground.

FBI lookout post.

They hung the forest with microphones until it looked like spider webbing; motion sensors and high-definition television units captured every movement for the waiting men. It showed a brief glimpse of the Recluse as he came out to check his garden, then went back inside. After they had dissected Stemple Pass Road and the road by his house, the agents gradually began to draw the neighbors into their confidence. Butch Gehring would prove to be the most important of these coconspirators.

Agents approached him in a series of visits over a period of weeks, gaining entry through a law enforcement friend. The cop explained to Gehring that he wanted him to meet a man who wanted to build a pole barn. But before the first meeting had concluded, Gehring had figured out that the stranger was an FBI agent more interested in his neighbor's activities than in constructing a barn. "You're right," the agent conceded, drawing the mill owner over to the side. "I'm real interested in your buddy up the gulch." "Why?" The investigator was forced to take Butch into his confidence. Eventually they would have to rent two of his nearby cabins, anyway. These would be blinds from which to watch their quarry.

"Level with me. What's he done?" said Gehring impatiently.

"We suspect him of writing threatening letters to professors back East," said the G-man, only partially revealing the truth. "Are you aware he's well educated?"

"No, I didn't think he was well educated."

"Well, he is. He graduated from Harvard."

Butch later told CBS, "I almost fell over because I had no clue that he had any kind of education."

"Are you aware he taught at Berkeley?" said the investigator.

Within a few minutes the sawmill owner learned more about his shy neighbor than he had in all the seventeen years they'd lived down the road from each other.

Eventually, the agent convinced Butch that an investigation was valid and consulted him on the best way to approach the Hermit.

"Very gently. Very gently," Gehring said. "So it doesn't scare him. The only thing that would really scare Ted would be fourteen people marching up toward his house. My suggestion is that you pose as surveyors. He's really concerned about his property line."

At the beginning of April, Butch and a few of the government men walked up the rocky road to the shack. Soon they came to a steep incline and ascended into the glade. All held maps in hand, and to give the Hermit an opportunity to see the new men so he wouldn't be suspicious of them in the days to come, Butch yelled out, "Hello!" The Hermit stuck his head out, then went back in.

Back at the Gehring's, the truth finally came out. "Frankly," admitted the agent, "I'll just say it—we're looking for the Unabomber."

"And when he said that," Butch recalled later, "I just said, 'No way! He couldn't get out of here. He has no money.'" Gehring thought of what he knew of the Hermit and decided he was harmless.

Wendy was pregnant with twins, and it wasn't until April 2 that Butch let her in on the fact that the FBI had been in town for several weeks. "I didn't want her involved," Gehring said to the *Missoulian*. "She's on an emotional roller coaster [with the pregnancy]. She didn't think Ted could do it. That's when I started telling her about what they'd found in Chicago."

When almost every question from the newcomers focused on the Hermit on the Hill, it wasn't hard to divine their true purpose. Perhaps if the Recluse had been more social, one of those wise to what was going on would have warned him. But the Hermit, working on his book and tending his roots, seemed far removed from any man. In turn the FBI seemed content to let various people in on their plans and equally confident that none would send a warning to their quarry.

On April 3, a Wednesday, Gehring crept through the woods near the cabin and at the base of the hill used his video camera to record the precise bearings of the shack in the clearing. "I was scared. Wouldn't you be?" he said to the *Missoulian*. "It was cold in the morning. It was icy, hard to walk without making a sound."

"Butch told me that he was asked by the FBI to take that video," a townsman later told me. "I know he was the one who walked up there. As he was walking it was a little bit icy and the ground was crunching. Inside the cabin he could hear the Hermit sawing."

Wendy, commenting on the Hermit, said, "He wouldn't talk to you. If you spoke to him he'd answer, but he wouldn't go up and start a conversation with you or anybody else that I saw.... I don't think anything else [other than Butch's plan] would've gotten Ted out of that cabin."

Over at the Seven-Up Ranch Supper Club, Wayne Cashman, the proprietor, had seen agents bustling about for over a month, wearing hiking boots and camouflage pants and packing sidearms on a "training mission." While Butch was filming clandestinely, agents were renting all of Cashman's cabins and motel rooms, and he was packing fifty box lunches for them. The Hermit's neighbors, Carol and George, were indirectly involved in the establishment of the FBI headquarters—she'd arranged the rentals through her realty, and he'd installed the blue roof on the Seven-Up.

As for the federal detectives, they thought they had all the time in the world to play the situation out to a safe conclusion. But they were mistaken.

For more than two days, CBS News had known of the surveillance of the UNABOM suspect in Lincoln and during furious discussions with the FBI had agreed to hold back. Now, however, CNN and ABC were getting ready to scoop them on their own story. CBS knew it had to run the report, if possible without endangering the lives of the agents or the suspect.

Special Agent Donald Sachtleben and a lawyer from the Justice Department raced fifty-five miles to Helena, secured a written request for a search warrant from a federal judge, and, after getting the judge's signature, raced back to Lincoln. There were times when having to speed paid off. CBS intended to run their story at noon, and the agents rushed to bring about the arrest by eleven o'clock.

Three men approached the shack, maps in hand. They could hear the rush of Poorman's Creek and the wind rustling the leaves on the trees. This was the closest look they'd had at the root cellar carved into the mountainside. The gardens had been recently watered and a long black hose stretched toward the stream. The

Attachment #A

The premises to be searched is described as a faded reddish in color wood cabin structure approximately 10' x 12' in size, no eaves, with a single door on the up canyon end of the cabin, a single window on the trailside of the cabin located where the roof and the wall join, and a single chimney at the peak of the roof on the up canyon end of the cabin. This cabin is located on 1.4 acres of land approximately 1/4 miles up Canyon Creek from the Gehring Lumber Company in Lewis and Clark County, State of Montana. The cabin has an access road from the cabin of Glen Williams which comes off of a logging skid road. The cabin is the last cabin up Canyon Creek. This cabin and surrounding area is further depicted in three sketches attached to the search warrant and incorporated as Exhibits A through C. These sketches were drawn by United States Forest Service Officer Jerry Burns who has specific familiarity with the area at and around the cabin. Attached to the search warrant and incorporated as Exhibit D is a photograph of the cabin from the Lewis and Clark County Assessor's office. Exhibit E, attached to the search warrant and incorporated is an aerial photograph depicting the cabin and its orientation to the Williams Cabin. A legal description is attached as Exhibit F.

This search warrant requests authorizatiokn to search the premises described above and all surrounding areas within the approximate 1.4 acres that comprise the property of Theodore John Kaczynski. The areas to be searched include any area above and below ground that could be used to store, secrete or conceal any items of property as described in the search warrant. In order to carry out the search of the areas below ground, electronic detection equipment may be necessary to examine areas that may conceal or contain objects. Trenching and or digging equipment may be necessary for the same purpose.

Attachment A of Turchie warrant request.

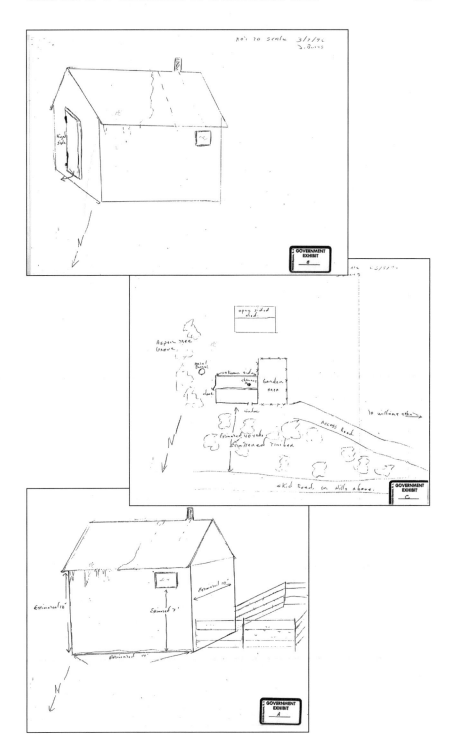

plastic containers of lamp oil suspended from tree limbs swung noiselessly to and fro. They stopped near the Hermit's trash pit, which was filled with cans he'd discarded. Many canisters of Hershey's Cocoa were scattered by the trees, and the cannibalized red bike that he'd used to construct his wide-tired bicycle stood upright in ice-brittle weeds. A pile of wood he'd chopped was heaped on the densely packed forest floor of rotting snowbanks and decayed leaves. The canopy of trees above reduced the light to dappled shadows that moved like fish in a stream.

"Hey, Ted. Hey, Ted!" the agent posing as a Park Service employee called out. His two assistants, also disguised as Park Service men, trailed, although the Hermit was aware of only two of the men. The door finally opened and the Recluse stuck his head out. "Hey, Ted, can you help me find on this map where a line is?"

The Hermit remained where he was. They'd given up on catching the suspect in town because the CBS reports were due to be aired any moment. The agent knew that he had guns in the cabin; neighbors had told him that much. Again, the fear of the shack's being booby-trapped and exploding, killing them all, flashed across his mind.

Conrad's Professor, fueled by rage alone, habitually carried with him the means of his own destruction. In *The Secret Agent* he says of the police:

> I don't think there's one of them anxious to make the arrest. I don't think they could get one of them to apply for a warrant. I mean one of the best. Not one." "Why?" "Because they know very well I take care never to part with the last handful of my wares. I've it always by me." He touches the breast of his coast lightly. "In a thick glass flask.... I shall never be arrested. The game isn't good enough for any policeman of them all. To deal with a man like me you require sheer, naked inglorious heroism.

"Ted, we need to talk," said the agent. "I'm trying to find this line right here." He walked down there and let the Hermit come to him. As soon as he was close, the "ranger" said, "I'm looking for this line right here."

The Hermit leaned forward to look. He was fit from all his work, but seemed frail and sick, as if he'd been under the shack and not above it. At that moment the agent grabbed his right arm and pulled him out and away from the cabin door. Instantly, the other agent grabbed his other arm and slapped cuffs on him. He struggled, but only a little bit, trying to shake them off and slide back into his shack. Through the open door they saw thick soot covering the walls and smelled wood smoke.

A concerned Butch Gehring asked later, "Any throwing him down or anything like that?" "No," said the agent, "absolutely not."

Then they took him to one of the nearby buildings they had rented, the chalet visible on their walk to the gully, and began an interrogation. The first thing the Hermit said was, "Don't talk to me about the UNABOM case." For the next five hours he talked about little things, fishing, and his beloved garden.

Meanwhile CBS had reached a senior FBI official in Washington, DC, at noon EST, just fifteen minutes before CBS newsman Jim Stewart was to go on the air and announce the raid presumably in progress. No objections were raised, and the network decided to go ahead. After all, they'd held up the story for two days at the request of the Bureau.

The CBS report on the arrest of "the best suspect" in the UNABOM investigation aired just after noon, one hour after the actual arrest in Lincoln. CBS broke into regular programming after learning that CNN and ABC were preparing to announce the raid. CBS news anchor Dan Rather said, "Like every other American journalist worthy of the name, we try to strike an ethical balance between the duties of citizenship and the duties of journalistic integrity. The record on this clearly shows we did."

"There was a great deal of consternation about CBS breaking that story," said one FBI source. "This was a case of the news driving the investigations rather than the investigation driving the news." Some felt that the CBS report forced the Bureau to act prematurely. But CBS vice president Lane Venardos said, "We're satisfied we held off as long as we possibly could hold off and as long as the FBI expected us to hold off." He believes that the investigation was not hampered at all.

"Because of the CBS News decisions, the FBI was able to carry out the arrest with complete surprise, and neither the defendant nor the FBI agents were injured," the Bureau stated. "CBS News acted in a memorably responsible manner, placing the well-being of the public ahead of its own interests. The FBI is grateful, and we are certain that the public is grateful to CBS News as well."

Janet Reno held a press conference at 1:58 PM EST on April 4 and explained the charges made against Kaczynski in Helena: "He has been presented today in federal district court in Montana, charged as a result of the search with one count of Title 26, United States Code, Section 5861, which is possessing—illegally possessing a destructive device. Nothing further can be said at this time."

"Ms. Reno," asked one reporter, "are you finished? Let me ask a negative. Has the Department or the FBI ruled out any accomplices to this suspect or alleged accomplices to the suspect?"

"As you know," she replied, "I really cannot comment on a pending matter."

"Ms. Reno, is he the Unabomber?"

"As you know, I really cannot comment on a pending matter."

"Ms. Reno, this subject has lived in this remote cabin for about twenty years. He had no car, no electricity, yet somehow he's supposed to allegedly get around the country mailing explosives and other missives to some very particular targets. Given those facts, can the Department or the FBI even at any point rule out any accomplices—that this is one person?"

Carol and George Blowars, the Hermit's friends and neighbors, had known little of what was going on until that afternoon when a friend called for George with hot news.

"Well," he says, "they caught the Unabomber up at Stemple Pass."

"The Unabomber didn't mean a thing to me. We were so far removed from it up here I had no idea what he was talking about. He said, 'Well, they're supposed to have picked him up by your house.' From that point on everything just went crazy.

"As I was coming home that day I saw the same herd of elk— there are usually about five hundred of them—that we fed all winter. There were a couple of hundred down on the Gehring ranch as you're coming up the flats across the open spot there. The sky was so blue, and the elk were all grazing peacefully on those rolling hills. Then I came around the corner before you turn in here to the house. There were like fifteen to twenty press cars parked on our driveway all the way through the curve. There were cameras in the middle of the road so you couldn't get by. And that was the thing that stuck in my mind—'Nothing will ever be the same here because of this thing.'"

THE EXPLOSIVE ORDINANCE DISPOSAL (EOD) squad immediately secured the ground around the shack and made the initial entry, where they saw a dark, soot-encrusted room still smoky from a recent fire. Their job was to ensure the safety of the follow-up search by the Evidence Response Team (ERT). EOD discovered a few suspicious packages and began to take X rays of each before they were removed or touched in any way. FBI Agent Donald

Sachtleben observed jars and later wrote in his affidavit:

> I observed chemicals and other materials that, in my opinion, are designed and intended for use in manufacturing a destructive device, namely a pipe bomb, and from which a destructive device could be readily assembled, including what appears to be a partially completed pipe bomb.

> Containers containing powders labeled as "KCL03" (potassium chlorate), "NaCL03" (Sodium chlorate), "Sugar," "Zinc," "Aluminum," "Lead," and "Silver Oxide." Necessary ingredients in the preparation of explosives include an oxidizer and a fuel. Sugar, zinc, aluminum, lead and silver oxide all can serve as fuels, and potassium chlorate can be combined with either aluminum or sugar to create an explosive material. Similarly, sodium chlorate can be combined with aluminum to create an explosive.

> Solid case ingots, one of which is labeled aluminum. I observed on the floor shiny metal filings consistent with aluminum. Aluminum can be used as an additional fuel and a catalyst in an explosive mixture.

Within three hours of beginning the search, investigators found a three-ring notebook. Sachtleben wrote, "I also observed notebooks that contain what I recognize to be diagrams and notes that are consistent with the manufacture of destructive devices such as pipe bombs.... Ten three-ring binders," he continued:

> These binders contain page after page of meticulous writings and sketches which I recognize to be diagrams of explosive devices. These diagrams depict cross-sections of pipes and electrical circuitry commonly used with boxes which could be used to contain, conceal and transport explosive devices. The notebooks also contain hand-written notes in Spanish and English which describe, in part, chemi-

cal compounds which can be used in various combinations
to create explosive charges for use in explosive devices.
After consultation with an FBI chemist, it appears that the
notes reflect the proper proportions for such mixtures.

The interrogation of the suspect dragged on so long that light
was failing by the time Special Agent Thomas Mohnal and his
demolition team entered the possibly booby-trapped cabin. That
the cabin had no electricity delayed them even further, but they
saw great potential in the stacked boxes, jars of chemicals, and
scattered tools.

Mohnal, a Supervisory Special Agent (SSA) Examiner in the
Explosives Unit, had graduated from Lycoming College,
Williamsport, Pennsylvania, with a Criminal Justice degree. In
1982 he worked as a Physical Science Technician in the FBI lab,
and after graduation from the Basic Demolition and Improvised
Explosive Device Technology Center at Indian Head, he was
appointed a Special Agent of the FBI. In 1990 Mohnal graduated
from the US Army's Hazardous Devices School in Huntsville, a
center for training "render safe" techniques to law enforcement
civilians. He's also conducted literally thousands of examinations
of bombing evidence in the past seven years.

That evening they told the converging press from all over the
world that the search was "going very slowly because we're not
sure if it's booby-trapped. We have an explosives team X raying
everything before we touch it.... We don't have make-or-break
evidence yet. We have some writings that match up, but we don't
have his tools yet. We want the irrefutable mother lode of evidence."

Though the agents had repeatedly brought up the Unabomber,
the Hermit had kept the conversation neutral. "I would like to
talk about anything else but that," he said. Finally, the agents just
told him, "You're under arrest."

As agents scanned, the X rays revealed and confirmed their worst fears—a live bomb! In seconds they had evacuated the remote little shack. As they stood, at just after 4:00 PM, in the gold-tinged glade amid the white swinging buckets and smoldering fire pit, more than one must have thought, "It's not over yet."

CHAPTER 43
An Improvised Explosive Device

T he United States is the world's most technologically advanced country. As for economic or other disruption that might be caused by the elimination of scientific progress—this disruption is likely to be much less than that which would be caused by the extremely rapid changes brought on by science itself.

—UNABOMBER MANIFESTO

AS POLICE WALKED THE HERMIT THROUGH THE STREETS of Helena in handcuffs, he was dressed in the colors of the forest—greens and tans, his matted hair wild as the leaves on the forest floor, his beard streaked and mottled with gray. As the nation watched him on television, you almost expected to see twigs entangled in that beard. But it was the eyes that held the attention—tired, red-rimmed, alternately lethargic and penetrating. His hands were reddened and filthy as if he'd been rolling in the dirt.

The Recluse was portrayed in the press in the next few days as smelling bad and being filthy, but later interviews showed that this was untrue. Perhaps he'd been beaten by the police. But that had been denied. Perhaps his health explained his wasted look, but it apparently was something more. Had he been underground somewhere?

Though his hair still had the wild look of the forest, some of the arrogance of his old profession seeped through. He had the confident, almost sly, certainly unruffled appearance of a mathematics professor. Attired now in a brilliant orange prison jumpsuit, a beige tweed jacket over it, and wearing a pair of open-toed leather sandals, he shuffled along in wrist and ankle shackles. He'd been bathed and photographed and now possessed a calm he'd lacked earlier.

As the Hermit walked the gauntlet of the press, did Conrad's last lines for the *Secret Agent* run through his mind?

> And the incorruptible Professor walked too, averting his eyes from the odious multitude of mankind. He had no future. He disdained it. He was a force. His thoughts caressed the images of ruin and destruction. He walked frail, insignificant, shabby, miserable—and terrible in the simplicity of his idea calling madness and despair to the regeneration of the world. Nobody looked at him. He passed on unsuspected and deadly, like a pest in the street full of men.

In the presence of his public defender, Michael Donahoe, the Hermit—now identified publicly as Theodore John Kaczynski—

stood before Judge Charles C. Lovell at 11:24 AM in Courtroom
No. 551 in the United States Courthouse. More properly, the proceedings against the Recluse were not an arraignment, the initial
step in the criminal process wherein the defendant is formally
charged with an offense, but a presentment. If the appearance
comes shortly after the arrest, it is properly a presentment, since
no plea is taken, at least not if it's a felony charge.

The proceedings began with the usual formalities, ascertaining
first that the Hermit's full name was Theodore John Kaczynski,
and then the court read the only charge against him at that time:
"that you knowingly possessed components from which a
destructive device such as a bomb can be readily assembled....
This carries a penalty for violation of that law of a term of imprisonment of not more than ten years, a fine of not more than
$10,000 or both...."

At 11:43 AM, Judge Lovell returned the defendant to the care
of US marshals. As he passed the phalanxes of press the Professor
did not bow his head, but smiled slightly.

The Professor was locked into his seven-by-ten-foot cell, not
much different from his tiny cabin, placed behind bulletproof
glass, and kept under a twenty-four-hour suicide watch. During
the mornings the deputies let him jog in an outside exercise area
and watched him peruse thick books on medieval and ancient
history.

The young, stern-faced agents and the more seasoned senior
agents of the FBI—some dressed convincingly as fishermen—
rarely dropped their poker faces. But once the cameras were put
away and the crowds had drifted off, they lit up with unrestrained
joy and enjoyed a feast of hand-cut salmon steaks and beer at the
lodge/command post.

"After eighteen years of beating our heads against the wall and
being taunted by this guy, you can't believe how good it feels to

have the son of a bitch," said one agent. Some detectives wore T-shirts with Jeanne Boylan's composite sketch of UNABOM on the front and the words, "FBI HQ for Unabomber Bust 4/3/96" on the back.

They loved the Wild West atmosphere of the area. A sign at one cafe read, "Please Check Your Guns and Cellular Phone at the Counter."

Bright and early on Thursday, the day after the arrest, federal agents began to probe again. Inside the cabin they ferreted out a partially completed pipe bomb and four pieces of copper pipe—galvanized metal, copper, and plastic—with copper plates sealing one end. All had been hidden in the rafters.

The inventory noted an "improvised explosive device contained in a cardboard box, wrapped in plastic bags with various tape and rubber bands." An improvised detonator and a plastic jar contained triggering devices.

Three rolled-up pieces of paper seemed to contain "logs of experiments to determine the optimum pipe dimension and combination of explosive materials in various weather conditions." Additional handwritten notes featured chemical compounds that could be used to create explosives.

Altogether there were 232 books, including volumes on chemistry, electrical circuitry, and bomb-making, sixteen notebooks or binders, and a white piece of paper with some kind of mathematical equations on it. There were seven rolled-up maps, a "Samsonite briefcase containing a University of Michigan degree," and "yearbooks in a green plastic bag." Among the notebooks, papers, and letters sat a box containing various papers, news clippings, bus schedules, addresses of corporate officials, and San Francisco maps.

There was explosive black powder and smokeless powder and the electrical components that detonated explosives—batteries, soldering wire, and electric wires—and aluminum ingot, which could be employed as a fuel and a catalyst in an explosive mix.

Inside the cabin agents discovered a hooded jacket, a blue-zippered hooded sweatshirt, and two pairs of plastic sunglasses. They appeared similar to the eyewitness description of the Unabomber planting a bomb at a computer store in Salt Lake City. Various firearms were also recovered—a bolt-action .22-caliber rifle, a .25-caliber gun, a Remington model .30-06, a .22-caliber black-handled revolver, and a handmade gun.

At 4:00 PM the detailed search of Ted's cabin was halted when EOD X rayed a package prepared for mailing and saw the outline of a destructive device inside, fully assembled and probably live. Quickly, the cabin was evacuated according to a plan worked out prior to the search. Agents contacted a bomb expert at Sandia National Laboratory in Albuquerque, New Mexico, and the technician set out immediately for Montana in order to deactivate the improvised explosive device.

Upon the demolition expert's arrival, he began the excruciatingly slow deactivation of the bomb. While this went on, the detectives realized that the bumpy road leading to the Hermit's cabin would be unsafe to travel with any sort of destructive device. Construction workers graded the dirt road so that the newly discovered bomb could be taken from the cabin safely and transported to a neutral site. The bomb was not removed until late in the day on Friday, April 5.

That day, police found two typewriters, and later a third. The typewriter that produced the manifesto had a spacing of twelve characters to the inch (elite), the numeral three was filled with ink from extensive use, and the lowercase letters "r" and "m" leaned to the right. Agents believed that one of the other two found on Thursday was used to type the tract. Both machines were flown to the FBI forensics lab where experts would attempt to link the documents to the typewriter by microscopic analysis of minute variations in the shapes and positioning of the letters, which change as typewriters wear.

The *San Francisco Chronicle* had a typed UNABOM letter and asked two expert typewriter repairmen to estimate what machine produced it. Willi Kitz, one of the experts, said the jetliner bomb threat letter was typed on a Royal manual of 1940s vintage. He pointed out a capital "A" with a faint top and an unaligned lower case "t." "It's always possible that another typewriter in the world is worn in exactly the same way as this one, but it would be unlikely. Maybe I wouldn't convict him just on the typewriter alone. But I'd be fairly sure." Mike Jaeger of the Typewritorium also noted the misaligned "t," the lowercase "r," and the right-leaning "m." Jaeger could tell the Unabomber's machine had been repaired and said that repairs leave markings that give a typewriter a unique look, like fingerprints.

Tools also leave their fingerprints on metal or a screw. Electron microscopes might reveal minute scratches on the drills, drill bits, hacksaw blades, and wire cutters in the cabin. Similar scratch-marks on bomb debris might link the tools to the Unabomber.

Investigators found the sheer bulk of written material in the shack astounding. They ferreted out ten three-ring binders with page after page of meticulous writings and sketches, which they recognized as diagrams of explosive devices. The sketches included cross sections of pipes and electrical circuitry of bomb devices.

What if the Professor had been digging under his rustic shack? That would explain the red-eyed, grubby look agents saw when they arrested him. Beneath the shack was a root cellar the Recluse had dug, and Butch Gehring had apparently seen it. "The hole to the cellar," he was quoted in the press, "was three feet deep and tight for a person to go down into. But once inside, the cellar was six-feet by twelve-feet [long], and four-and-a-half-feet high."

The FBI requested permission to carry out a search below ground. "Electronic detection equipment may be necessary to examine areas that may conceal or contain objects" read Attachment A of the warrant request (page 406). "Trenching or digging equipment may be necessary for the same purpose."

"In addition to the above-described premises, agents have located a root cellar," wrote Agent Terry Turchie. "Because of the poor physical condition of this underground room, experts are being consulted to determine what if any precautions should be taken before any subsequent entry is made."

A volunteer with the Lincoln fire department helped agents explore the tunnel system near the Professor's mountain cabin two days after G-men arrested him. This was according to a published report in the *Helena Independent Record*. Federal authorities refused to describe the extent of the complex tunnels, where they were located in relation to the shack, or whether anything was recovered from them. When the cabin was removed for evidence and the area surrounded by a chain-link fence, the root cellar remained as I saw it when I visited the scene later. In the photos my associate Penny took it is obvious that the area had not yet been explored, but fissures showed the existence of a world below. Speculation was that this is where a secret bomb lab existed. What was the truth?

Are there tunnels beneath the Hermit's land or not? Waits would not elaborate, but only said, "It boils down to an age-old knowledge that when it's thirty below zero above ground—it's forty *above* underground."

On Friday at 3:40 PM, two days after the Hermit's arrest, patches of snow stood stark against the ground. A thin line of smoke marked Humbug Contour Road as a lone truck made the curve past the sawmill and started up to the cabin. Soon it returned carrying a suspected bomb.

At 4:05 PM, in the clearing by Butch's colorful collection of antique cars, an ATF agent arrived in a full, white bomb protection outfit and dark helmet, looking like a deep-sea diver. Other agents talked, waiting to see what would come next. A sawdust pile had been converted into a table where they could study the item. Nearby, the big white control van bristled with tall antennae and a TV dish hummed with energy.

Saturday, a methodical search began again, but the searchers were wary of other concealed devices or booby traps. Turchie told ERT members that they were to search only during the daylight hours, but in Montana this meant an evening that stretched until 10:00 PM and a dawn that was bright at 6:00 AM.

"It's at least similar," said one agent, discussing the paper-wrapped cylindrical parcel publicly. "There are general similarities [to bombs built by the Unabomber], but we have to subject them to detailed analysis." Another official said, "It was as if once he found the right design, he stuck with it." The FBI lab thought the bomb matched the 1995 bomb that killed Sacramento timber lobbyist Gilbert Murray. "It's bizarre. I saw the thing—the similarities are remarkable," said one lawman. "It's very similar in shape and size and the materials used to construct it—including wood."

The triggering switch, like a metal and wood sandwich, had colored wires springing out like the Hermit's hair.

The package was ready for mailing, secured with tape, and had a phony return address. The FBI began warning potential targets in the Northwest, mainly timber industry executives, that there was a chance a bomb had gotten past them and was in the mail. Meanwhile, the live bomb was detonated.

"They brought the device out in front of Butch's CAT, or rubber-tired "skidder," then they had Snoopy the Robot—we did watch that from the gate here—they had the robot walk down to where the CAT was," said Carol. "The guy got off the CAT, parked it, and then the robot took the device out of the front end loader.

"They had a hole dug out in the sawdust and they had a makeshift table constructed out of some stumps and boards. That's where they did whatever they did. He walked with it and put it over on the table and then they had a couple of the people in flack suits come in and work on it. They allowed us to stand way out in the field and watch from a distance."

Agents exploded the device at a distance where they could see it from their fence but were not damaged by the blast. Other neighbors heard the explosion and reported it to the local authorities, including the FBI, who declined to elaborate.

Butch and Wendy Gehring watched, too, and later told CBS-TV, "We saw what appeared to be a bomb squad pull up in a U-Haul trailer with some very sophisticated, safe-looking equipment... a robot."

"It looked like a tin box," said Wendy.

"And what did you think when you saw the bomb squad going up and that item coming down?"

"I was mad! Yeah, sure. Disappointed and mad. Sick. Still sick."

"How you could do that to other people is unbelievable," said Wendy.

"Why do you feel sick?" asked reporter Randall Pinkston.

"You just do," said Butch. "It makes you sick to think somebody could do that to somebody and to think for that many years he's been living right there that close to you and your family."

On April 9, a Tuesday, the same day the main floor of the cabin was finally cleared, Judge Lovell rejected a motion by various media organizations to unseal search warrant information and agreed to a federal request to extend the warrant through

Monday, April 15. "There were explosive devices and components which have necessitated very thorough examinations by X ray equipment.... The presence of these devices caused some delay in the execution of the warrant and the completion of the search."

Restrictions on the air space over the shack had been lifted Sunday, briefly allowing news helicopters to photograph the cabin on video from the air. Judge Lovell ordered the cabin sealed for an additional thirty days past the warrant expiration date of April 8 and further forbade journalists access to the property actually to see the cabin. FBI agents guarded the entrance to Humbug Contour Road and began working on a chain-link fence around the cabin to seal it from the public.

Special Agent Terry Turchie of the Unabomber Task Force explained the endless comings and goings from the cabin. "Short of destroying the entire premises during an initial search, there are few options other than multiple searches to ensure that every relevant wire and nail will be retrieved," he said.

On April 10 snow began to fall again and the agents erected two tan-colored tents to stay dry as the work of loading the trucks proceeded. One geodesic dome had hot air ducts that kept the big tent inflated. Evidence went into the huge white motor home, was catalogued, then stored in a U-Haul truck. They'd even erected a flag pole with the Stars and Stripes. At 11:12 AM the FBI prepared to fence in the cabin behind chain link and barbed wire. At 1:06 PM Butch Gehring in white overalls drove his orange skidder up the hill past scattered drifts of snow.

"Agents walked up and down that road for days packing, making marks on it, and giving it identifying numbers," recalled Carol.

News of a possible list of Unabomber victims surfaced as early as April 9, but official sources quickly discounted it. "There's no list of victims per se. At least I don't think so," remarked a federal source.

"There are a lot of lists, a lot of writings, but no target list I know of," said another. "There is a general consistency in the written plans and the physical evidence found at the cabin scene with the Unabomber's work. But there's no list of names found in the shack, only publications that have the names of some of his targets."

Leaks to the press continued to vex the investigation, and Janet Reno drafted a strong memo to all UNABOM investigators and prosecutors. She titled the memorandum "Unauthorized Disclosure of Investigative Information." This Friday, she wrote:

> Media reports concerning the UNABOM matter purport to disclose very detailed information relating to the investigation. Some of these reports assert that the information emanates from sources involved in the investigation.
>
> These kinds of unauthorized disclosures are damaging to the investigation, and inconsistent with the manner in which professional criminal investigation is undertaken. The government, when it speaks about a case, should do so in the courts. The disclosures, whether true or not, are completely inappropriate.
>
> While the public interest in this investigation is understandable, it is imperative that all federal law enforcement personnel adhere strictly to established policies for dealing with the media.

An equally outraged Director Freeh issued a similar memo five days later. He wrote:

> I ordered an investigation early this month of whether any FBI employees have leaked investigative information from the UNABOM case. The investigation is being conducted by the FBI's Office of Professional Responsibility and will seek to uncover all information pertaining to any improper actions by FBI employees. Unauthorized disclosure of investigative information or other confidential mate-

rial will lead to immediate firing from the FBI and possible prosecution.

Supposedly a handwritten list of more than seventy names of corporations had been discovered in the shack. According to sources, Charles Hurwitz, president and CEO of Maxxam Inc., the parent company of Pacific Lumber; Jim Geisinger, president of the Northwest Forestry Association in Portland, Oregon; David Ford, president of the independent Forest Products Association in Portland, and Fibreboard Corporation of Walnut Creek, California; and James Eisses, former executive vice president at Portland's Louisiana-Pacific Corporation, were mentioned.

Word came that several handwritten lists included the name and address of the University of California at Berkeley's bioengineering program, several members of Berkeley's math department, a current graduate student, and two professors in the bioengineering section—a hundred faculty members and fifty-five grad students there were researching such things as finding a use for genetic tissue to fight disease.

Robert Vaught, a UC Berkeley math professor, and math Professor Emeritus John Addison were found on a list in the cabin. "Seriously, we have no idea why we were on this list, but I am not worried because the man is now in custody," said Addison. "We hope this was just a list of his favorite professors."

Other math professors reportedly mentioned were Professors Shoshichi Kobayashi, Tosio Kato, David Gale, Heinz Cordes, Morris Hirsch, Leon Henkin, and Lester Dubins.

One handwritten list contained the words "Airline Executive," and "Computer Industry," partially gleaned from an "Eco-F—'s Hit List" of 110 "anti-environmentalists." The tract was printed by the anarchist group Live Wild or Die.

And Friday, April 12, the search moved even more slowly back into the attic of the shack. Investigators ascertained that this space was congested with boxes and possible booby traps. The Feds now maintained that they'd been premature in saying that one of the two typewriters recovered was used to type the UNABOM letters.

During the same week, however, federal agents became certain they'd found the original typed antitechnology manifesto. "It would be another nail in his coffin," said Laurie Levenson, a law professor at Loyola University. "I have never seen one little shack with so much evidence. It's the ultimate FBI scavenger hunt. This is his life, his entire existence—it's his life's work."

In San Francisco, former US Attorney Joseph Russoniello said if it was the original draft, it would greatly strengthen the prosecution's circumstantial case. "The prosecution had to connect the occupant of the cabin with the author of the manifesto, and they had to connect the occupant of the cabin with the physical evidence found at the bomb site," he said.

At 12:59 PM on April 14, a press helicopter dropped, darting like a wasp over the Hermit's cabin. One agent leaped into a four-wheeler and roared toward the gate to raise hell about the closeness of the camera-mounted copter. Before the newscopter flitted away into the Big Sky, it made one final pass over the army of men carrying evidence downhill, the thirty four-wheel-drive units (everyone the Feds could get from Boise to Billings), and even the battalion of camping reporters at the gate leading toward Florence Gulch. "There was never another soul up there but the FBI from the moment they came," Carol said.

Agents had completely secured the area through checkpoints that kept out visitors and press alike. They routinely seized cameras and film from the neighbors to keep all activities within the perimeter secret. In this book you learn for the first of the frenzied activity that went on within for a month and a half.

George and Carol could have gotten into their property by taking Stemple Pass gravel road about nineteen miles through, come
out on Fletcher Pass, and driven where Humbug Contour Road
toes across Mount Baldy. But this time of year it was gated to protect the elk.

On Tuesday, April 16, the inventory overview was unsealed by
Judge Lovell. The harvest of a twelve-day-long search was carefully
catalogued in a 34-page, 720-item list of evidence—including the
chemical compounds, five rifles and handguns, books, diagrams,
tools, and material used to construct bombs—forty boxes of evidence were carted up that steep hill to where Butch Gehring's
sawmill stood. Nine days earlier, the snails' pace of the search had
been about two-thirds completed as trucks carried the evidence to
the Seven-Up, FBI headquarters in Lincoln.

ABC News reported that agents had found intricately carved
wooden boxes the size of videocassettes, some made from four
different types of wood, inside the shack. On May 14, the FBI
announced that they had discovered the Unabomber's secret nine-
digit identifying number during the previous month's search of
the shack. DNA analysis of saliva on stamps the bomber licked
seemed to fit the suspect's DNA profile. Forensic experts also
announced that they'd matched a typed UNABOM package label
with one of the three typewriters retrieved.

"It was sort of interesting that it was Ted," said Carol. "He
was different, but never was I afraid of him. When the prosecut-
ing attorney was here, he really was interested in that. I'm sure
they're going to go for the fact he's not mentally capable of making correct decisions.

"One FBI guy made an interesting statement to me. He asked
me two or three days after they'd arrested him... 'Well, what do
you think of your friend, Ted, now?' he said.

"'Well, I guess friend Ted's got his butt in a jam.'

"'Friend Ted's going to get a lethal injection,' he said.

"That turned me against them so bad because I thought that was completely the wrong thing for agents to be saying to me."

"I wrote him a little note," said Carol Blowars, "shortly after he was arrested.... I just wrote this little note and put it away in my desk drawer. I didn't do anything with it 'cause I don't know what I'm getting myself into. I don't want to be involved in something I really shouldn't be—this kind of high-profile deal.

"And so I never did mail that letter. His attorney, the FBI's people, and his public defender have been here twice to visit us. I'm not sure why, because we really don't have that much to offer. This one girl said, 'You really should send your card because he's very depressed.' No one has corresponded with him apparently—at least nobody that lives up here. So I added a little bit more to the note and then I sent both cards to him and never have heard back from him."

However, mailman Dick Lundberg's wife, Eileen, told me that Ted has been writing back to her. She attributes this to the fact that she and Dick have refused to talk to the press, which Kaczynski appreciates. Like several of the Lincoln folk who knew Ted, she does not believe he should receive the death penalty.

"I was one of those people who used to get up on the soapbox and say, 'I believe in the death penalty,'" she said. "I believe if you do something wrong, you should pay for what you do. But I've always noticed the victim. It's a whole different outlook on it now. I have seven children, all grown, but you know when you've been raising them you try and teach them if you do something wrong, you have to pay for it. And so it's taken us a year—it was kind of like having a death in the family, it really was. We went through a mourning period." The death penalty is the reason they won't speak to the press, fearing any interview might be held against them if they are called as character witnesses during the "penalty phase" of the trial. "If saying something now would jeopardize anything we could say at that time—we wouldn't want to do anything."

"We had no idea how intelligent he was," she told me, "'cause he never talked down to you. We just had no idea. We have known him for over twenty years. From the time we first came to Lincoln we have known him.

"We all mind our own business here in Lincoln. Everyone would say to us. 'Good heavens! Didn't you have a clue?' No, we had no clue. You didn't ask people, you just accepted people at face value. He didn't do anything to us."

After the arrest and the media invasion, young readers of the *Blackfoot Valley Dispatch* spoke their minds. Mostly they were fifth and sixth graders.

Liz Garland wrote: "My mom [Becky] says that Ted would never harm us. When I heard all this I was scared. I didn't want to go home. I now let my mom handle the mail. Mom said Ted Kaczynski hated technology. Maybe that's why he bombed people. This is very scary, but I'll survive. I hope."

"Personally, I think that the attention Lincoln is getting is bad," said Sarah. "Now many people will think Lincoln is not safe or has a lot of bad people. If only people could hear all the good things about our town. Lincoln is a friendly place and the good people outnumber the bad people by far. I also think the media exaggerates the truth. Everytime I turn the channel on television I hear a different story. Sometimes it make me wonder if the media doesn't make up half of the story they tell. I think the media wants too much out of the people of Lincoln. They seem very pressuring, although we don't know much about Mr. Kaczynski because he was a very reclusive person."

And finally, Jami wrote, "I think the Unabomber is guilty. The

'96 APR 11 ʰᵐ

LOU ALEKSICH, CLERK

DEPUTY CLERK

IN THE UNITED STATES DISTRICT COURT

FOR THE DISTRICT OF MONTANA

HELENA DIVISION

* * * * * * *

IN THE MATTER OF THE SEARCH
OF THE RESIDENCE OF THEODORE
JOHN KACZYNSKI AND
SURROUNDING 1.4 ACRES

MCR 96-6-H-CCL

ORDER

* * * * * * *

This matter comes before the court on application of Sherry
S. Matteucci, United States Attorney for the District of Montana,
by Assistant United States Attorney Bernard F. Hubley for an
Order to Secure Premises pursuant to 28 U.S.C. § 1651.

It appears that the application is made in good faith, and
that based on the affidavit of ASAC Terry Turchie, there is
reasonable belief that the premises belonging to Theodore John
Kaczynski, located in Lewis and Clark County, being 1.4 acres of
land containing thereon a one-room cabin, approximately 10 feet
by 12 feet with a loft, should be secured pending the completion
of the execution of the search warrant for those premises that
was issued by this court on April 3, 1996, and pending the
completion of any further searches and investigations that may be
necessary at the described premises after the results of the
initial search have been obtained and analyzed. It also appears
to the court that it is possible there may still be explosive
devices on the premises and the general public should be
protected by preventing its access thereto.

Accordingly,

IT IS HEREBY ORDERED, pursuant to 28 U.S.C. § 1651, that the
Federal Bureau of Investigation maintain custody and control of
the above-described premises and that all persons are prohibited
from entering thereon without the express approval and under the
supervision of the Federal Bureau of Investigation for a period
of 30 days from the date of this order or until further order of
this court.

IT IS FURTHER ORDERED that copies of this order be posted on
said property and its perimeter in conspicuous places clearly
visible to all persons.

The Clerk is directed forthwith to notify the parties of
entry of this order.

Done and dated this 11ᵗʰ day of April, 1996.

CHARLES C. LOVELL
United States District Judge

Copy of actual warrant request nailed to trees surrounding Kaczynski's property.

FBI has found a lot of things to prove he's guilty. If he is guilty, they should put him in jail. The people should not want to kill him. If he's innocent, he could still be put in jail for the making of bombs."

On April 29, at 8:06 AM, agents strung yellow police "Do Not Cross" tape across all the trees surrounding the Hermit's shack. A fence had been completed to seal off the cabin and three strands of barbed wire ran all along the top. A tent fluttered nearby, reinforced with two-by-fours. At 7:28 AM on May 2, they brought up a generator to Poorman's Creek, and the men at the sawmill could hear it start up.

Five days later, at 7:00 AM, a truck went up and word came that the Recluse's cabin was to be moved up the incline and then down to the mill. The shack looked odd on the cleared plain, as odd as Butch's collection of brightly colored cars. On the same day, residents glimpsed one of the FBI's rented four-wheel vehicles towed into a town garage, front blackened and windshield smashed. One of the Feds had rolled it by driving the way he customarily did at home. He'd been unused to the mountainous terrain. Drawled a local, "Our tax dollars at work." That afternoon, the Hermit's former neighbors, Larry Menard and Butch, traveled up the road to assist the investigators.

On May 9, agents began to wrap the green-roofed, red-sided cabin in preparation for an airlift by Huey. It had been in the paper, and all of the neighbors cautioned against such a move.

"To me the smartest thing to do," said Carol Blowars, "and this is my idea—Our neighbor back there is a logger. He's got a big flatbed truck that he packs a CAT around on. Ted's house is like a storage shed like they sell at building supply stores except that the peak of it is very high.

"And so why don't they just call Larry. The press can't see 'cause we're all up here. Lay the house down on Larry's truck and then go out in the middle of the night when the press goes home. They always start leaving about dark.

"And by golly, the next day that's what they did. Agents stopped and visited with us and I told them my idea. 'But,' he said, 'it's too high to go on a truck.' 'Well, lay it on its side,' said George. 'The eaves are real short and it wouldn't hurt. If anybody can run with an oversize load in the nighttime and convince the DOT that it's all right to do it, it surely should be the FBI.'"

Neighbors visualized the lawsuit the Hermit would have if the house fell during a helicopter airlift and killed someone. Meanwhile, agents lifted the Recluse's homemade bike into the back of a white truck, a sign the end was near. But that afternoon, at 1:35 PM, sirens split the mountain stillness. The Lincoln School was evacuated because of a bomb threat. Fire engines and trucks filled the highway and officials anxiously scoured Highway 200 awaiting the arrival of the Helena Bomb Squad. The scare turned out to be a cruel hoax.

On May 14 at 7:14 AM, a witness made his way past guards to the former site of the cabin. The tent still stood and old bike parts were scattered about the ground. Inside the chain-link fence a fissure in the earth showed among the piles of wood and debris. Rain began to fall and the intruder noted the Recluse's hatchet sunk deeply into a reddish stump. Raindrops pattered against a blue canvas.

By 7:27 AM the men below had the cabin up on four beams and an agent began to cover over the shack's chimney for transport. Inside the back of a red truck the worker easily reached the roof of the cabin. With a graceful movement he rolled a turquoise tarp over the roof. Behind him, Butch's skidder stood ready to lift. By 6:06 PM they'd moved the cabin onto its side. Soon the rolled green tar-paper roof was covered over and they'd flipped the folded tarp open and down over both sides of the roof to cover the cabin proper. "And that's the last we'll see of his cabin," said a local. The little shack looked like a wrapped present. A strong wind ruffled the plain, and they repositioned the cabin on Larry's red flatbed truck and reinforced it.

The job seemed done at 7:44 PM. Black dogs had broken through the perimeter, outfoxing the guards, and moved like blurred streaks across the pale field. When they reached the house that appeared to be striding all about Mount Baldy, they sniffed as if smelling for fear. Enough Big Sky light lingered to illuminate the area clearly and at 8:03 PM it was easy to photograph the five Feds in dark-blue jackets and white-coveralled workmen. Methodically, the men cinched up the cables securing the shack to the truck. At first the peak of the roof jutted toward the truck's cab, but they kept adjusting it as if the cabin were restless.

At 8:17 PM they affixed a yellow banner with black lettering that read WIDE LOAD to the truck. A minute later, Butch's yellow skidder—its shape as crouched as a bird of prey—moved over the house and repositioned it so that the roof faced down, peak toward the truck's rear, and the cabin's foundations tilted forward and braced.

A gentle rain set in making the blue landscape glisten and the men made the final adjustments of the shack. Brilliant red running lights on the cab glowed in the wet. At 9:19 PM the truck, lights flashing, began to crawl so slowly it was almost imperceptible. The area was now dark and deserted. Larry drove down behind some pines, made ready to back up and out to take the road back toward the sawmill. He slid expertly into the tight turn, warning lights flashing madly behind his head. Three minutes later he moved down the road, then parked to wait until no press could possibly be about. He was successful. The photos and videotape I have are the only ones ever taken of the moving of the old shack with all its mystery.

"Larry went home," recalled Carol, "and then everybody left. All the FBI guys except for their skeleton crew which they kept up here to guard it. We didn't hear Larry go, but at one in the morning he set out on his trip. Nobody even knew he went out of here till they got into Malmstrom Air Force Base at Great Falls."

Finally, at midnight the wrapped cabin slid out on Stemple Pass Road, a house gone walking. Mist beat against it, a vaporous haze that shimmered and reflected upon itself in images that were lost and alternately reborn like the wreaths of spray in the froth of Big River. The red truck sped on into the Big Sky until the shack was lost from sight to the kind folks of Lincoln—forever.

Exclusive photos taken inside the restricted area of the FBI wrapping the Hermit's cabin and moving it down the mountain.

CHAPTER 44
Going to Trial

T*he system HAS TO force people to behave in ways that are increasingly remote from the natural pattern of human behavior.... It isn't natural for an adolescent human being to spend the bulk of his time sitting at a desk absorbed in study. A normal adolescent wants to spend his time in active contact with the real world.*

—UNABOMBER MANIFESTO

THE SUN BEHIND THE PRIVATE FBI JET lay low on the distant horizon.

Sunday, a day early, at 11:30 AM June 23, 1996, a sleek US Marshal jet swept into Mather Air Force Base carrying the suspected Unabomber. An armored, black suburban truck with dark-tinted windows backed up, and Ted Kaczynski, hands and feet shackled and weighed down by a white bulletproof vest (the same he had worn under his tweed jacket in the Helena courtroom), shuffled inside. Within a moment a long line of motorcycles, police cars, and a helicopter sped him fifteen miles to Sacramento.

Streets swept clean of bystanders, police sharpshooters huddled on buildings, casting a watchful eye on their surroundings, awaiting their arrival. Even as the caravan crawled downtown toward the Sacramento county jail, rumor circulated about the Hermit's cabin. A full-sized replica of the shack might be an exhibit in the "highest profile trial" ever to be held in the capital.

As they brought Ted in, a one-and-one-half-hour lockdown was instituted at the new jail. They ushered him into the eighth floor of an isolated section of the west tower, a section reserved for inmates who required maximum security. He would have no contact with them, and little interaction with the other jail personnel. His meals were slid into the cell he would occupy for all but one hour a day. During that single hour, Kaczynski could exercise or shower.

Much had preceded this point in his life: On Monday, April 15, 1996, Kaczynski's lawyer, Michael Donahoe, had asked Judge Lovell to dismiss the federal charge of explosives possession against his client. He argued that government media leaks had led to "a lethal media blitz" and "poisoned" the pool of prospective jurors.

Assisted by co-counsel Tony Gallagher, the chief federal defender in Montana, Donahoe requested all evidence seized during the cabin search be returned, because government agents had "deliberately and systematically leaked information to the media" and tainted their client's constitutional rights.

On Wednesday, a federal grand jury heard testimony and looked over evidence related to a single count of possessing bomb-making materials. Lovell chastised the government for hundreds of news leaks, saying, "The defendant is not entitled to perfect treatment, and this is not a perfect world. But he is entitled to fair treatment, and if he is indicted, he is entitled to a fair trial."

Assistant US Attorney Bernard Hubley admitted federal agents had talked to the press, but that none of those disclosures had infringed on the suspect's rights.

Ted Kaczynski appeared amazingly altered—attired in a pale green long-sleeved shirt, khaki pants, and black Gore-Tex hiking boots, with his beard trimmed and his wild hair cut. He smiled for the first time as the twenty-five-minute court session concluded.

On June 19, two and a half months after Kaczynski's arrest, a ten-count grand jury indictment was handed up on what would have been the forty-eighth birthday of UNABOM victim Gil Murray. The defendant faced three counts in the death of Murray: transporting an explosive device with intent to kill or injure, mailing an explosive device with intent to kill or injure, and using an explosive device in a crime of violence.

In the death of Hugh Scrutton on December 11, 1985, the defendant was charged with one count of transporting an explosive device with intent to kill or injure. The counts carried a maximum sentence of death or a mandatory sentence of thirty years in prison.

They also charged Kaczynski with mailing two devices from Sacramento on June 18, 1993—the Epstein and Gelernter attacks. For each of the two bombs, the government charged three counts: transporting the device with intent to kill or injure, mailing an explosive device with intent to kill or injure, and using an explosive device in a crime of violence. This last count carried a mandatory thirty-year sentence.

California Governor Wilson called upon the Justice Department to bring the trial to Sacramento, where he believed the strongest case could be made against Kaczynski. "Californians would hope and expect that the federal government would seek the most severe penalty against him: the death penalty," said Wilson. Although a federal prisoner had not been executed since 1963, a federal crime law enacted in 1994 hugely increased the number of crimes subject to the death penalty. As for the Unabomber's crimes stretching from May 1978 to February 1987, federal law prohibits prosecution of most felonies more than five years old.

The case was assigned through random draw to US District Judge Garland E. Burrell, Jr., in Sacramento. Nominated to the federal bench by President Bush, Burrell was confirmed by the Senate in 1992, after years working in the city attorney's office, district attorney's office, and US attorney's office.

Burrell, the first African American federal judge in Sacramento, was cautious, compassionate, and methodical. Because he had devoted his career to civil litigation, Burrell had little criminal trial exposure. Known for painstaking, "slowly-delivered opinions," Burrell expected everything in the lengthy, complex trial to be "airtight."

"Judge Burrell is not Judge Ito," said US Attorney Donald Heller, referring to the OJ Simpson trial judge. "He will be in tight control of his courtroom. You will not have lawyers spouting off and carrying on. You'll see the case move much more quickly and efficiently."

Quin Denvir, fifty-six, former state public defender under Governor Jerry Brown, headed the defense team. He was an esteemed appellate and trial lawyer and came with a first-class academic list of credentials. A Chicago native, son of a trial lawyer and brother to a law professor, Denvir was known as the "complete lawyer." He graduated from Notre Dame and received his law degree from the University of Chicago School of Law before working with one of Washington, DC's big law firms, Covington and Burlin. Along with his brother, he moved to California in 1971 to work for California Rural Legal Assistance.

The current federal defender in Spokane, Judy Clarke, would assist him. As head of the federal defense office in San Diego, Clarke was called "the patron saint of defense lawyers."

Robert Cleary, 40, a smart, unflappable career prosecutor, would head a six-person prosecution team. Cleary could boil complex matters down into simple concepts. A graduate of William and Mary, and Fordham Law School, he began his career in 1985 as a prosecutor in the Justice Department's tax fraud office. Two years later he became an assistant US attorney in the southern district of New York. Since November 1994, he's served as first assistant attorney in the north district of New Jersey, responsible for handling the office's most sensitive, high-profile cases.

Six to eight crates of photographs and documents that the Feds turned over to Denvir as part of routine discovery of prosecution evidence weighed in at 1,400 pounds. The time it would take the defense attorney to comb through the evidence would delay the trial. Because of the unusual, complex case, federal laws requiring a speedy trial were waived.

Judge Burrell allowed the defense almost a full year to prepare for the trial, setting the day for November 12, 1997. He also set a number of other dates for the following spring and summer to deal with defense motions to throw out any evidence seized at the defendant's home. During a seventy-minute November 22 court session, as prosecution and defense lawyers argued when to hear motions, Kaczynski joked with Dennis Waks and Judy Clarke, defense lawyers seated on either side of him.

Denvir likened the case to a "huge antitrust case… just a monster case." The prosecution predicted their portion of the case would take approximately four months, and Denvir said the defense probably not as long.

Kaczynski would also be charged with the murder of Thomas Mosser. But Mosser had been killed in New Jersey. Denvir wanted the Mosser case transferred to Sacramento and a single trial held there on all Unabomber charges. On December 10, 1996, US District Judge Dickinson Debevoise spoke with Kaczynski in a video teleconference between the prisoner as he sat at a conference table in the public defender's library in Sacramento and the judge's New Jersey courtroom.

"Is the video quality adequate?" asked Debevoise.

"Yes, Your Honor, I can hear," said Kaczynski, dressed in a

brown tweed sport coat and open collar shirt, his beard neatly trimmed. In Newark, the prisoner's image appeared on four television monitors in the courtroom. "Do you waive your right to be present in person in New Jersey?" asked the judge.

"Yes, I did sign the waiver."

Ultimately the judge sided with the defendant's legal team. "Why try this case twice?" he asked. A trial in New Jersey would unduly burden the defense, he said, while they sought to prepare for a California trial.

Federal Magistrate Gregory Hollows ordered Kaczynski to provide samples of his handwriting by printing phrases and words entered in the journals unearthed in his shack. The more than twenty thousand pages of journals, maintained the government, contained handwritten confessions to all sixteen Unabomber attacks. Hollows called them "perhaps *the* critical evidence in this case." Denvir argued that the prosecution already had more than eight hundred pages of letters that his client had mailed his mother and brother, enough for analysis. However, prosecutors needed specific words and phrases from the diaries, and the magistrate agreed, ordering the defendant to provide samples within thirty days.

On Tuesday, April 1, 1997, Hollows ordered the prosecution to allow him to examine law enforcement files in private to determine the truth of the defense's charge that federal law enforcement officials exaggerated important information when they persuaded a federal judge to issue a warrant for a search of the defendant's cabin. Both said that the affidavit in support of the warrant entailed deliberate "falsehoods and omissions" tying Kaczynski to the Unabomber crimes. Denvir also complained that the prosecution had not given the defense the investigatory files that mentioned other suspects considered during the long manhunt.

On Friday, May 23, Quin Denvir accused the FBI of using a misleading, incomplete affidavit to persuade a federal judge to grant them a search warrant for the defendant's shack. "It's hard to believe the judge wasn't put under pressure," he said. "The government was saying, 'The media's going to break this story and we won't have a chance to get in there.'"

To obtain the warrant, FBI Special Agent Terry D. Turchie had written a 104-page brief, detailing the bombs and noting similarities between the manifesto and letters Kaczynski had written his brother, David. Turchie delivered his affidavit, along with six exhibits, to Judge Lovell at 8:00 AM on April 3, 1996, the morning of the raid on the suspect's cabin. Thirty minutes later, Lovell received thirty-nine more pages, then an additional eleven pages shortly after.

"I don't believe he could have read all that in that time," Denvir said.

"I have problems with the [idea] that the judge may not have read it all," said Burrell. "A judge makes sure he or she has read everything."

On June 9, 1997, prosecutors asked Judge Burrell for permission to link Kaczynski with *all* the UNABOM explosions, presenting quotes from his personal journal that included descriptions of placing some bombs.

"The bombs charged in the indictment are not isolated incidents. Rather they are part of a series of steps that the defendant took in his eighteen-year bombing spree," wrote prosecutors. "It is the entire string of UNABOM activities, viewed as a whole, that most persuasively links Kaczynski to the charged crimes." The government also said it had found over a thousand pages of "lab notes" Kaczynski had written in a scientific log, detailing his attempts to increase the effectiveness of his lethal machines.

Federal prosecutors unsealed excerpts from the suspect's diary in a forty-three-page motion and claimed that Kaczynski had admitted to all the bombings in thousands of pages of handwritten journal dating back to 1969. Final entry, claimed the prosecution, was February 1996. Agents said they were able to crack the numeric code used in the journal through a "key" they found in the shack.

"Kaczynski's writings confirm that he sought to identify the reasons that his early bombs failed to inflict greater damage and to improve upon those bombs as his scheme progressed. It stands to reason," read the report, "that one does not become a master bomb builder overnight or through happenstance. Rather, as in this case, that expertise can only be developed through trial and error and through repeated experimentation."

Most of the 22,000 pages discovered in the cramped shack told of Kaczynski's everyday life—"a day-to-day journal of his activities like 'my day in the woods' or 'what I ate today.'" The journal, declared the prosecutor, includes "Mr. Kaczynski's admissions, detailed admissions to each of the sixteen UNABOM devices."

Back in 1996, the state claimed to have discovered a copy of the Unabomber manifesto that constituted "the backbone of the government's case." What had been discovered was a copy of Kaczynski's 1971 essay [see Appendix A], probably left by accident in the cabin by an investigator.

The core of the prosecution's case was circumstantial, but as Chris Ronay said, "Circumstantial evidence adds up. This kind of evidence isn't voodoo or magic. You have to conduct what we call intercomparison examinations. Comparison exams can be visual, chemical. There's handwriting analysis, fingerprint analysis, DNA analysis, tool marks exams that can be done. If two pieces of metal, plastic, wood or tape are broken from each other, they can be microscopically matched back together to say they were one piece.

"The Unabomber's devices aren't that sophisticated. They are... so unusual that any lay juror would have no problem [seeing their similarities] and the evolution from simple to more complex. It would be very hard to take the first and last alone and say these are the same. I couldn't do it. But when you see the steps in between, you can see that progression, and it's quite evident when it's pointed out to you."

"Just because there's an arrest of a reclusive bright guy with an interest in bombs doesn't mean they've caught the Unabomber," said Marcus Topel, a defense attorney. "There's a lot of technical evidence and it's years after the fact. You've got hurdles—Is there enough evidence to show he mailed those bombs? Can you tie the death bombs to him? Can the government prove he wrote that tract published in *The New York Times*? It might be a good case to defend.

"By no means should the government feel a surplus of confidence. You go right at the FBI profile, show how many other people it fits, and immediately show that Kaczynski is not necessarily the guy." Topel also believed there was an "underlying sympathy for Kaczynski's politics in a large segment of the population." He remarked that "in a circumstantial evidence case, it's important to tap into that sympathy and allow him to get the benefit of the doubt. He looks good, he's smart—he's just a white, middle-class guy."

Gerald Uelmen, one of the OJ Simpson "Dream Team" defense attorneys, believed "Kaczynski's case could be the spectacular trial of the century." He favored the defense moving quickly and early to suppress evidence, to question the validity of the search warrant. "It requires prosecutors to justify each seized item," said the Santa Clara University School of Law professor.

Uelmen further suggested that the defense might raise reasonable doubt about the state's forensic work and show that

Kaczynski was mentally disturbed and incapable of understanding that "what he did was wrong."

But the insanity defense rarely works, and many lawyers believed that to play that card at all would be disastrous—the bomber's conduct was "far too elaborate and meticulous for a crazy man."

On June 27, Judge Burrell finally denied a defense motion to suppress all the evidence seized from the cabin. "A nontechnical common-sense and realistic [reading of the affidavit showed it offered] a substantial basis for concluding a fair probability that... evidence of a crime would be found in defendant's home."

"We must continue on," said Denvir. "We've come to kind of always hope for the best and expect the worst. That's criminal defense."

AMIDST THE GRIM COURT PROCEEDINGS some levity surfaced, Jay Leno and David Letterman told countless jokes about the case that so fascinated the nation. Letterman suggested the top ten signs showing that your brother was the Unabomber, among them: "Whenever they show a sketch of Unabomber on TV, he says, 'What a good-looking guy!' 'Subscribes to *Dangerously Quiet Loner* magazine,' 'Even in baby pictures, he's wearing a hood and sunglasses,' and 'Favorite cable channel? TNT.'" Top ten things found in the Unabomber's cabin—"A fridge full of 'Hungry Psycho' frozen entrees" and "Jimmy, the 'Unapoodle.'"

In the days following the arrest of Kaczynski, bumper stickers appeared on the World Wide Web on a site promoting the Unabomber as a presidential candidate. "Write-in for President—Unabomber. If elected he will not serve."

These few moments of light, however, came in a tale that now darkens.

THE UNABOMBER'S SAGA ENCOMPASSED enough compelling stories for a dozen books—a young, pathologically shy Harvard grad and mathematics professor enamored of Conrad's *Secret Agent* who might have taken on the role of that novel's bomb-planting professor; the story of a Hermit in the wild who raged against runaway technology; the chronicle of a master criminal who inexplicably sprang from a loving home and good education to outwit the authorities; the narrative of a taciturn Recluse, tender with children, a good neighbor who kept a warm friendship with a Mexican farm laborer for eight years—all are his legend. A lonely man who yearned for a wife and child, but was crushed by past rejection. He employed despicable methods to drive home a message that nonetheless resonated in the hearts of many gentle people. His concern for the wilderness, his disdain of modern computers, appealed to those who felt powerless in the face of the advancing technologies that destroyed individuality and tore the family unit apart.

He had terrified a nation, halted the mails, disrupted air traffic, and made a free nation far more security conscious than it ever wanted to be. Constantly metamorphosing, the bomber altered his targets, his pattern, his types of devices, method of delivery, the geography of his crimes, and personality. These ever-changing guises made it impossible for him to be caught by police methods, as he outmatched supercomputers and brought tragedy and lifelong pain to the families of victims; he cut short promising careers and took life. Did he struggle with that decision? I would like to think that it was hard for the bomber, and that he finally committed the unspeakable acts because of a greater good in his eyes, after an anguishing searching of his soul.

An environmental savior, a political activist, or Luddite saboteur? How real were the bomber's stated goals as an agent of social change? Even Jack the Ripper has been presented as a well-meaning social activist who perpetrated horrors calculated to draw attention to Whitechapel's grinding poverty. But the bomber did seem to believe.

Computers threatened his no-longer-fashionable mathematical studies. "Some mathematicians kid themselves too...," Kaczynski had written. "Some claim to have proved that human mathematical researchers can never be replaced by computers. What they have actually proved is that there is no finite algorithm enabling a computer to solve every mathematical problem. But... there is no finite algorithm enabling a human to solve every mathematical problem either...."

"A computer will never be successful at introducing new axioms because it has no 'mathematical intuition.' But mathematical intuition is arrived at through experience... computers of the future will be able to develop mathematical intuition...."

"There is every reason to assume that computers will eventually possess creative capacities surpassing those of the greatest human geniuses."

The existence of his 1971 essay leads me to believe his sympathies did lie in pro-environmentalism areas. Ultimately, this man, who exchanged the physical world for an abstract landscape of intellectual sterility, and conducted a long-distance reign of terror, was not any freer than those he criticized as being chained to their computer terminals. But despite his great intellect, he had a sense of absolute right that enabled him to act in a very single-minded way.

The story of an isolated genius striking out against society's perceived ills pales before the high moral struggle of brother turned against brother. In this struggle lies the moral core of the tale—the battle between blood and society. From Abel and Cain to the Civil War and to the present, brothers in conflict have provided chronicles of emotional impact. One gentle brother, agonized, torn between questions of right and wrong, of loyalty to family and duty to his country. Anxious to make certain no other lives were lost, David accomplished what the most advanced technology, a million dollar reward, a toll-free, twenty-four-hour hotline, the Internet, and three powerful government agencies could not—he made a crucial connection between his brother's writing style, a delicately carved cylindrical box made for their mother, and UNABOM.

David might have saved at least one more life—a live bomb ready to mail was found in the shack.

AFTER KACZYNSKI'S ARREST AN interesting theory arose—San Francisco detectives alerted by a local amateur sleuth, Michael Rusconi, began to investigate the possibility that Ted was also the infamous, uncaught Zodiac, a hooded bomb-making Bay Area serial killer. Among the possible links were that Kaczynski lived there from 1967 until 1969, the period that Zodiac's confirmed murders took place; that Ted once signed a high school yearbook with a crossed-circle symbol like Zodiac's; that Zodiac had mentioned Deer Lodge, Montana, near Lincoln in a letter; and that both wrote bragging letters to the *Chronicle*. Both men had knowledge of bomb-making and complex number systems, enjoyed taunting the police, and demanded that newspapers publish their writings or expect more killings. Zodiac and UNABOM both threatened to blow up a highly visible mode of transportation (school bus and jetliner), then revealed that it was a bluff. Zodiac, because of a Taurus astrological symbol used in his letter, was thought to have been born under that sign. Kaczynski was a Taurus.

I thought the similarities fascinating but purely coincidental. Descriptions of the stocky, lumbering, powerfully built Zodiac did not jibe with the slender mathematics professor. The tone of both men did not match in any way. Zodiac spoke with a flamboyant, romantic, pop culture-driven vernacular. The Unabomber wrote in dry, academic, terse prose.

SHORTLY AFTER HIS BROTHER'S ARREST, David Kaczynski was sickened to discover that the public had learned that he was the one who had turned over letters and documents that resulted in Ted's arrest. "He's mad. We no longer have a relationship," said one FBI agent. The Kaczynski neighbor, Bob Welch, watching the media swarming around their house, said, "They don't deserve this terrible mess. They're solid gold." He knew the pain that had wracked David in reaching his decision to turn his brother over to the authorities. "A lot of soul-searching went into this," Welch told the press.

Finally, in a series of interviews with the *Washington Post, The New York Times,* and on the television show, "60 Minutes," David revealed his story to the nation.

"Through the years," he told the *Post,* speaking of his brother's communications with the family, "the letters have shown sudden and unpredictable mood swings, a preoccupation with disease, extreme phobias, compulsive thinking, and an inability to let go of minutiae. One senses a psyche that feels itself terribly isolated and threatened in the world, tormented by its own complexities, unable to hold things in their proper perspective or to find comfort, security or rest for itself.

"Our interest from the beginning was to protect life, and if this government were to process this like a cold and calculative machine, I would have to conclude my faith in the system was misplaced. What would a future family member in a similar situation think if I were repaid with my brother's death? It would be the ultimate disincentive for anyone else to cooperate with our justice system."

On May 25, 1996, David, accompanied by his lawyer, Anthony P. Bisceglie, gave *The New York Times* a six-hour interview in which he revealed more of how he gradually came to the "horrible" realization that his own brother might be the Unabomber. "It was really chilling," he said.

"Clearly part of my whole involvement in coming forward in this whole thing was a respect for life, that human life is really valuable, that certainly Ted did not in my mind have adequate justification," he said. "If he did attack people and kill people, that was wrong. But by the same token, I feel it would be very wrong if he were killed in the name of some notion or principle of justice. I think it's important that people see him as a human being.

"I think the interests of justice are best served in this case by the truth, and I think that truth from my point of view is that Ted has been a disturbed person for a long time and he's gotten more disturbed. It serves no one's interest to put him to death, and certainly, it would be an incredible anguish for our family if that were to happen." Bisceglie had petitioned Attorney General Reno to spare Kaczynski's life on the grounds that being mentally ill is a "mitigating factor" under the law. These circumstances can include severe mental disturbance and an inability to appreciate the wrongfulness of one's actions.

"I think," said David, "he's a person who wanted to love something and... it gets so complex. He failed to love it in the right way because in some deep way, he felt a lack of love and respect himself.

"What amazes me the most about it is that somehow—if he in fact did kill and maim people—he had put a wall around that part of himself.... I think his ability to have a conscience, to have sympathy for people, created for him a people problem he could not solve except by walling those feelings."

In early 1997 the family and Bisceglie argued their objections to the death penalty before a closed door Justice Department review board. Such a review committee sits in all potential death penalty cases. "If there is a death sentence in this case, then families down the road might not turn in their relatives," said Bisceglie.

Department officials argued that turning in a bomber was the right thing to do regardless of the penalty and that no criminal could hope to escape the death penalty by turning himself in. Further, relatives of future criminals would still have a motive for cooperating with the police—arranging a peaceful arrest that avoided shooting during capture. Finally, said the department officials, diaries seized from the cabin show that Ted Kaczynski planned the bombings carefully, constructed his bombs with maximum harm to people in mind, and criticized his own creations when they malfunctioned or left only minor injuries. He vowed to build bigger, more dangerous bombs for later attacks.

"Lock him up or put him in solitary, anything," argued Bisceglie, "just not the death penalty." The family had particularly wanted David's role kept confidential. Mary Ann Welch, their neighbor, had seen David and Linda days before the arrest and they had looked drained. "This man had the courage to turn his brother in," she said later. "This mother had the courage to turn her own son in. They both put the safety of society before their family, for the good of those they didn't know."

Although Janet Reno opposed the death penalty on a personal level, her boss, President Clinton, supported it and she had pledged to enforce it, having already authorized the death penalty fifty-eight times. On Thursday, May 15, 1997, just as my photographer and closest friend, Penny Wallace, and I were returning from Ted's cabin site in Montana, Reno demanded the death penalty for the suspected Unabomber.

"Imagine what his brother must feel like," Penny said. "He

turned in his brother to save lives and it may cost his brother his own."

"I can't imagine a tougher decision," I said.

After receiving Reno's approval, prosecutors filed a four-page memo in Sacramento federal court announcing that "a sentence of death is justified, and the United States will seek the death penalty," and calling Kaczynski a "continuing danger to the lives and safety of other persons." The state contended that he "lacks any remorse for any of the murders" and has a "low potential for rehabilitation." A debate among legal circles erupted about the propriety of getting the capital penalty for someone whose family turned him in asking for leniency in exchange for their cooperation.

After Bisceglie had been notified of Reno's decision, he told David and Wanda that their pleas for mercy had been ignored. "The family is devastated by this development, and they are in seclusion at this time," said Bisceglie to the press. "We believe that the attorney general's decision is a terrible mistake, but we remain hopeful that justice will ultimately prevail in this tragic case."

During this century the federal government has executed thirty-four people, two of them women, on charges ranging from murder to conspiracy to commit espionage. But the federal government has not executed a prisoner for over thirty years, the last being the 1963 hanging of Victor Feguer (for kidnapping) at the Iowa State Penitentiary. Since 1973, sixty-nine death row inmates have been freed by court order before they could be executed. With the conviction of Timothy McVeigh for the Oklahoma City bombing, the number of prisoners sent to death row since 1976 reached thirteen.

During the "60 Minutes" interview with Mike Wallace in 1996, David, Wanda Kaczynski, and David's wife, Linda, had spoken of the devastation Ted had experienced when he learned of his brother's marriage plans. "It was as if I had somehow betrayed him," David said. "It was so totally unexpected. He'd never met Linda… pages and pages of criticism of me."

In other circumstances, Ted had written his mother, "So generally if I… showed any weakness I found I couldn't come to you because you're simply using me as a defenseless butt…. I'm supposed to be your precious little genius."

Commenting on the letter on the show, David said, "This is not the same mother that I grew up with. This is a fiction or a fantasy." Ted had also written, "The rejection I experienced even affected me physically. Of course you wonder why David is two inches taller than I. I have read two different studies that purport to show rejection during adolescence tends to stunt growth."

Wallace then read a letter Ted had written David: "There is nothing that would ever be important enough so that you'd have to get in touch with me. Even if Ma dies I don't want to hear about it." At this Wanda began to cry. When Ted had stopped writing his mother, Wanda wrote one more time to ask to visit him. In reply he wrote David: "Every time I get a letter from a family member, my heart pounds and I'm going to die." When Wanda sent postcards instead, saying only "Hope things are better," Ted wrote David—"The whole world, the Post Office and everything, knows what's on those cards. Please, I'm getting desperate, what do you want to do? Kill me? Don't send me any mail."

"His feelings about our family bear no relationship to the reality of family life that we experienced. These were loving supportive parents," said David. Linda and David became so concerned over Ted's deterioration that they forwarded two of his letters to a psychiatrist in 1991. "He saw the possibility of violence," said Linda.

"We were advised that it was extremely difficult to have someone committed," she said, and David added, "We were told that he had to be a danger, a demonstrable danger to himself or others."

"The next best thing," said Linda, "we got in contact with one of his doctors up in Montana and David called the doctor and asked the doctor to please refer him to therapy."

"The only way he spoke his mind," said David of his brother, "or related to people was through letters.... A part of me very strongly believes if Ted harmed and maimed people, he could not have done it face to face because he, in some way, distanced himself from the consequences of what he was doing." Elsewhere David said, "I work with people all the time. His dynamics I never followed. I love him. And I can't help but love him. But I can't condone what he did.... It would be very, very difficult to live with myself knowing that I had delivered my injured, disturbed brother over to be killed."

Ted's friend, Juan, put it simplest—"At the thought, my head is full of thorn."

Librarian Sherri Wood corresponds with Ted in Sacramento. If he is convicted and given the death penalty, she told the *Wall Street Journal,* "I will support it. For a long time I tried to hate him, I really did, but I just couldn't. Now I write letters to somebody I knew until April 3, 1996.... The man I knew was my friend."

I COULD NOT GET THE Kaczynskis out of my mind. Watching the "60 Minutes" interview over and over, I was touched by their evident sincerity and overwhelming pain. David had waited twenty-five years for the woman he loved, and watching Linda's bright intelligence I understood why. In my mind's eye I could see them now.

Wanda and David did the only thing they could—they waited. A jetliner droned above and leaves dropped from the trees. The sidewalk grew empty except for two black dogs. Ted would not write, but they waited. Ted would not write, yet they listened to each tick of the clock and scanned the sun-drenched street. In the golden light a figure appeared at the crest of the block, walking fast, long strides like the opening and closing of scissors, eyes down, fixed on the pavement, back bent beneath a pack.

FASTER, LEGS STRIKING OUT, HEAD DOWN, he came on. The good people who had made the right decision, the good people who had prayed and waited, also watched. The solitary figure, head bent under the weight of his pack, was closer now. On Wanda's table sat the homemade wooden box her troubled son had sent her, a perfect cylinder, carved from a Lincoln forest tree limb. The light colored the wood amber. Ted had topped it with a black, carved raven and characteristically criticized his work—"The claws are too long and the box is not quite right, but I had promised it to you and so the contract is fulfilled."

A long shadow from the approaching man stretched across the pavement. The sun was behind the figure, shifting and reforming it like the spray off Big River. Then he was recognizable—only a man—only the mail. He walked and nobody else looked at him. He passed on like a shadow and soon vanished up a street devoid of life.

CHAPTER 45

Unanswered Questions

HAD THE HERMIT BEEN DIGGING under his rustic shack? What else would explain the grubby appearance the nation saw in those first pictures as agents escorted him through the streets of Helena on the way to Clark County Jail, his hair so covered with dirt that it looked red-brown rather than his normal salt and pepper. According to some neighbors, the Recluse had carved out a root cellar beneath the shack *in addition* to the one next to his shack. After all, he'd had a good twenty-five years and the seclusion to do pretty much whatever he wanted to do on his acre and a quarter.

Why does it matter?

Until we know where he made the bombs, this case cannot be closed, nor the possibility of an accomplice ruled out.

On May 8, 1996, the *San Francisco Examiner* reprinted a story from the Helena *Independent Record* that seemed to authenticate the many rumors I'd heard about a possible underground lab:

FBI SEARCHED TUNNELS BY KACZYNSKI'S SHACK, read the headline. "The FBI searched an underground tunnel system near Theodore Kaczynski's mountain shack shortly after the Unabomber suspect's arrest last month according to a published report.

"The *Independent Record* of Helena reported Wednesday that a volunteer with the fire department in nearby Lincoln helped federal agents explore the tunnels two days after Kaczynski was taken into custody.

"The newspaper report didn't describe the extent of the tunnel complex or say where it is located in relation to the 10-by-14-foot plywood and tar-paper cabin. It also didn't say whether anything was recovered from the tunnels."

According to another published report, Butch Gehring had apparently seen something. "The hole to the cellar," he was quoted as saying, "was three feet deep and tight for a person to go down into. But once inside, the cellar was six-feet-by-twelve-feet, and four-and-a-half-feet high." The same article reported, "Meticulous about what he ate, Kaczynski dug a root cellar underneath the cabin where he apparently stored vegetables and allegedly worked on bombing projects...."

Did Gehring or the writer mean the root cellar which was visible in the mountainside across from the two huge gardens and little shack? Carol Blowars had described *that* root cellar for me: "There's two doors that go into the mountain—like two garage doors, you know how garage doors open out." When I saw these doors they did not seem a tight squeeze, so I had to think that the remarks referred to another cellar.

Then there was the FBI's request as described on Attachment A of Agent Terry Turchie's remarkable affidavit. That last paragraph ran as follows:

> **This search warrant requests authorization to search the premises described above and all surrounding area within**

the approximate 1.4 acres that comprise the property of
Theodore John Kaczynski. The areas to be searched include
any area above and below the ground that could be used to
store, secrete or conceal any items of property as described
in the search warrant.

In order to carry out the search of the areas below
ground, electronic detection equipment may be necessary to
examine areas that may conceal or contain objects.
Trenching or digging equipment may be necessary for the
same purpose.

"In addition to the above-described premises, agents have
located a root cellar," wrote Agent Turchie. "Because of the poor
physical condition of this underground room, experts are being
consulted to determine what if any precautions should be taken
before any subsequent entry is made."

Why should I not just go up and look? Well, when the cabin
was removed for evidence, beginning its bizarre walk down
Mount Baldy before being trucked out by neighbor Larry Menard
at midnight on May 14, 1996, bound for Malmstrom Air Force
Base, the area was sealed off. Agents surrounded the site with a
chain-link fence. The root cellar or tunnel system remained undis-
turbed behind that fence, with its very convincing federal "Keep
Out" signs. Nevertheless, I determined to see for myself.

The Hermit's neighbors, George and Carol Blowars, allowed
me and my photographer, Penny Wallace, onto their private property. In the golden glow of those long evenings peculiar to the
Scapegoat Wilderness and the Continental Divide, they led us up
by the back way and down a glorified dirt path, Humbug
Contour Road near Poorman's Creek. The shack stood one-quarter mile up Canyon Creek from Butch's lumber company. We
passed the alpine house that jutted over the trail and that the FBI
had used to observe their suspect.

We followed an incline down to the Recluse's glen. As the day faded, our shadows grew impossibly long and we dropped, step-by-step, down to the cabin. I was struck by the strange white hanging buckets that swayed noiselessly from the trees. Too many to be showers. Were they for separating chemicals as shown in the famous "Black Book" beloved by anarchists and militia types? A red bike, cannibalized for parts, jutted from the grass. Outside, where the front door to the cabin had been, the plastic and glass bottles he'd stacked there remained. Environmentalist or not, he was just as messy now as he was when his Harvard room was covered with a thick layer of odorous mess.

The wind whispered through the lodgepoles, aspen, and ponderosa pine surrounding us. Nearby, Poorman's Creek ran and, alongside, Ted's spring-fed hand pump still lay in the grass. His tumble-down root cellar, the one we already knew existed was cut into the mountain. In this cellar, the Hermit kept the parsnips and carrots he lived on. In the distance the Big River, the Blackfoot, a victim of pollution, rushed like the wind in the trees and ran "straight and hard."

The Hermit had built his shack as an exact replica of Thoreau's cabin at Walden, and I imagined his root cellar had been fashioned in a similar manner.

"I dug my cellar in the side of a hill sloping to the south," Thoreau wrote, "where a woodchuck had formally dug his burrow, down through sumac and blackberry roots and the lowest stain of vegetation, six feet square by seven deep, to a fine sand where potatoes would not freeze in any winter...."

Penny leapt the creek at its narrowest, two feet, and we worked our way past the still-flourishing gardens. Both measured larger than the cabin had been—the largest, measuring nine hundred square feet, was fifty feet away from the fenced cabin, and had its own ten-foot-high barbed-wire fence around it. I looked down into a fissure on the cabin site. Darkness showed below, but heads of lettuce showed no digging had been done. Contrary to the *Independent Record* story, no network of tunnels had been explored. At least not yet. Could it still be there?

The suggestion of a world underground thrilled me. But I had already learned that a rumored delivery of a load of cement to the Hermit, which could have been used in tunnel construction, had never occurred. The driver for Lincoln's only cement company told me the cement was never delivered. But one of the early paperbacks published on the Unabomber had claimed the delivery was authenticated with a receipt discovered by the FBI.

I certainly would like this one to be true because it suggests the reinforcement of underground tunnels. But the fantastic and fugitive manner in which the Hermit supposedly unloaded the mixing truck, hefting one wheelbarrow full after another up the hill and out of sight, seemed a bit too good to be true. Just as likely, the rumor started with a delivery to one of Ted's neighbor, which can be documented. And yet, even without cement, a tunnel network built over twenty-five years is more than a romantic possibility. As Chris Waits, reportedly the Hermit's oldest Montana friend, and now a prosecution witness, points out, "It boils down to an age-old knowledge that when it's thirty below zero aboveground—it's forty *above* underground."

Perhaps the FBI has dug it up by now, and we will find out about it at trial. For quite aside from the Hermit's need for shelter, the still-unanswered question is: Where were the bombs made? That was why I had entertained the idea of an underground lab in the first place.

Despite some cosmetic shortcomings, metal pipes and fittings tooled by the Unabomber were executed well enough technically that investigators in the Bay Area and Sacramento had scoured metal shops, college art departments, and chemistry classrooms to find where he made them. Metal shavings used as shrapnel, complicated fittings, and holes drilled through double layers of concave metal at least suggest professional metalworking tools, electric drills and metal-cutting bits, and welding equipment, and maybe even the works for casting aluminum. The FBI even suspected the bomber was casting some of his own pipes, especially the ones made of metals with low melting points, such as aluminum. Police investigators had certainly told me that the reason they searched machine shops and student foundries was that they believed the bombs had been made with electric tools and welding torches. I did ask a welding designer if it was possible to do serious metal-work, including welding in a shack with no electricity and even no has torches. His answer: It is just barely possible, using a very hot fire pit, and assuming that the bomb maker had a vice to hold the pipes while they were being hand-drilled. But he was speaking of bare possibilty. Even considering the Professor's patience and perseverance it seems far fetched for the shack to have been a bomb factory. Certainly the prosecution should be searching for a lab. Perhaps they have found one.

But when the Hermit's cabin was searched, investigators found only a welding-type mask, some melted fragments of metal, seven large drill bits, one drilling base, and a manual (i.e. not power) drill with a blue and red wooden handle. In a shack with no electricity or running water, how had he run, in effect, a machine shop? The mask indicated he welded at some point, but where? How had he drilled through two layers of metal with no electric drill or metal-cutting bits?

Where is the lab? Will we find out at the trial? Will it be in the interest of either the defense or the prosecution to follow up this point?

One inconsistency in the case against Kaczynski leads to another possibility: A bank deposit slip dated December 11,

1985, reportedly places the former mathematics professor elsewhere in Montana while a Unabomber attack was going on in Sacramento. Kaczynski was apparently depositing money in one of the three checking accounts he had while in the Helena area on the same day a bomb was physically placed by the Unabomber in the windswept lot behind Hugh Scrutton's RenTech computer store. It would have taken Kaczynski twenty-five hours by bus from Helena to reach the site of the store in Sacramento, California. Turchie wrote in his detailed affidavit that "UTF has been unable to determine as yet, whether this posting date accurately indicates that Theodore Kaczynski personally made a deposit on that day." Moreover, of the registration slips that I recovered from the Park Hotel in Helena, thirty in all, none matched well the date of the Scrutton murder. Over the years Ted had used the hotel as a sort of halfway house before setting off for parts unknown. He apparently stayed there before leaving on a trip and upon returning. For almost all the murders we can identify a hotel stay within a few months on either side of the murder date. Not so for Scrutton. Kaczynski's last stay in 1985 was in the summer and then not again until March of 1986.

The bomb that killed Scrutton included an FC signature and is no doubt a Unabomber device. But could Kaczynski have been there himself to place it?

Is there an unwilling, willing, or unknowing confederate somewhere who helps the Unabomber? Two Unabombers? A knowing accomplice, admittedly, does not seem to fit in with the most solitary of men. But even if the bombs were manufactured in that primitive little house by Poorman's Creek, where were they tested?

The Hermit had befriended Chris Waits, a Lincoln pianist, construction worker, and welder. Was the accused more devious than the townsfolk suspected? Had he befriended Waits to gain access to his friend's equipment, to root through his scrap heap (scrap heaps were common at many other places in the mountain town, though) for the material that first caused him to be named the Junkyard Bomber. Waits owned a desolate gulch miles from any habitation. Did Kaczynski use Waits to gain access to that remote area so he could test his bombs? No one ever heard explosions near the cabin, so any test detonations must have been a considerable distance into the wilderness. The Unabomber said in one communication that he did test his devices in the mountains. "It's no fun having to spend all your evenings and weekends preparing dangerous mixtures, filing trigger mechanisms out of scraps of metal," he wrote *The New York Times* in his FC letter of April 20, 1995, to Warren Hoge, "or searching the sierras for a place isolated enough to test the bomb." Since Waits, who purports to have been a friend of Ted's for almost the Hermit's entire stay in Lincoln, will be a prosecution witness as of this writing, time may tell.

Speculation about just where these bombs were constructed leads to another possibility—that the first two bombs may not have been the suspect's. They were conspicuous in their technical crudeness. The first did not even have an electrical switch, being triggered instead by a nail sprung by a rubberband to strike match heads, thus igniting smokeless powder. They were not contained in wooden boxes or signed FC. True, the third bomb (the airliner bomb) also lacked an indestructible signature, and yet the bomber later claimed responsibility for that bomb in a letter to Hoge. "The idea was to kill a lot of business people who we assumed would constitute the majority of the passengers."

So since we know of at least one early bomb (the airliner bomb) that definitely was Kaczynski's and yet was not signed FC, maybe the absence of the signature on the first two bombs is less significant. On the other hand, the physical similarities between the first two bombs and the airline bomb may have been exaggerated. The smokeless powder in the Flight No. 444 bomb was supposed to be one of the powerful links. But as later exposés of the FBI crime lab showed, the assertion that there was smokeless powder in the airline bomb may not be justified. Further weakening the link is that the debris of the first bomb was discarded, making later comparisons impossible, and the second bomb, also discarded, was never even examined by the FBI (the ATF lab did, however, study both devices at some point), who were responsible for the analysis linking the first bombs and the airline bomb.

In that dimness that comes so close to the end of our story, when the landscape should have been illuminated with brilliant truth, I thought of another question: "Where did he build his first two bombs, the Illinois bombs, if they were indeed his?" The suspect was staying with his parents and brother at the family home. He apparently arrived in Illinois so close (possibly after) to the placement of the first device in the Engineering Building parking lot at the University of Illinois on May 26, 1978, that you have to ask "where did he build it and when?" Ted Kaczynski began his job at FC, Foam Cutting Engineers, on June 26, 1978. Says the FBI, "According to David [Kaczynski], his brother returned to Chicago from Montana a few days, to no more than 30 days before starting this job." And did the accused carry a live bomb on his lap on a jouncing Greyhound bus all the way from Montana to the main terminal in Chicago?

Did he reach the university, bound across the parking lot, and place this device in time to meet his brother?

The second device, in a "Phillies" brand cigar box, was placed in Room 2424 of the Technical Building of Northwestern University. Where, in the time the accused was living with his parents, did he find the time or a place to construct a second bomb?

The one link that runs through most of the bombs is the use of one-dollar "Eugene O'Neill" postage stamps. At first this seems like overwhelming evidence of a single bomber. Unfortunately, this is not the case; the first bomb received newspaper coverage in the Chicago and Evanston areas and the O'Neill stamps were mentioned. Ted Kaczynski, who was in the area, could have read the local papers and could have copied that motif. In all likelihood the first bombs were the product of UNABOM, but those questions trouble me now as they did in that darkening garden by Big River.

On the other hand, the accused may have been responsible for bombs not associated with the Unabomber. In 1969, while Kaczynski taught at the University of California at Berkeley, at the height of radical campus politics, a gasoline bomb was placed in Wheeler Hall on campus. Not one group, left or right, ever claimed responsibility for this device. In fact all vehemently denied any connection. An early effort and an unanswered question that almost certainly will never be answered.

Then there is the question of insanity, Ted's responsibility, and the death penalty.

Mental illness is apparent in Ted's letters as far back as the seventies.

Here again an unanswered question. To what extent was Ted's behavior the product of the mind-bending antidepressant medication trazodone, with its side effects—gross hyperactivity, threats of violence, loss of impulse control, flights of fancy, paranoia, aggressive behavior, and hallucinations? Trazodone, doctors caution, should not be prescribed to anyone with mental difficulties, suicidal tendencies, or heart problems. Ted suffered from them all, yet reportedly took the medicine daily. How much of the Unabomber sprang from "trazodone-induced mania," as reported in the medical literature?

WITH THE GLUT OF INFORMATION leaked to the media just after the arrest (and just who high up in the Bureau or Task Force was doing that? Another question that should be answered), the FBI's earliest fear began to come true. Some of the accounts, sightings of the Hermit supposedly going about his grim business over the years, seemed almost too good to be true. A few, at least from my vantage point, started to appear doubtful.

Some of these accounts, contrary to published stories, apparently do not stand much scrutiny:

For instance, in Sacramento, the Royal Hotel's night clerk's recollection, quoted in papers, ran as follows:

"He was familiar. The only thing that really, really made me remember his using hindsight, was his demeanor, how he spoke. He was quiet... if it wasn't for all this, I'd be expecting to see him about now."

The clerk said Ted stayed almost annually during the last five years and at $27.50 a night. Federal agents reportedly were unable to find proof of these visits in the form of registration cards, neither under Kaczynski nor his alleged alias "Konrad," or "Conrad."

Then, at a local book store also in Sacramento but some thirty blocks from any bus station, staffers recollected a familiar character, "Einstein," "a wild-appearing, unwashed man who spent spring days in the Tower bookstore browsing in the science section." With Kaczynski's arrest, clerks identified him as "Einstein" and pointed out margin notes in a copy of Eric Hoffer's *True Believer* as the arrested man's work. Possible, but doubtful.

Ted's reaction to the emergency code (red line beneath the stamp) used to notify him of his father's death has been published and mentioned in the affidavit and had come from many sources. Supposedly it demonstrates the defendant's coldness. Published reports had him replying, "This was an inappropriate use" or "appropriate use" of the code informing him of an emergency. But this may be a fabrication. According to another source close to the investigation, Kaczynski phoned his mother in tears, and commiserated with her, when he learned of his father's death. Quite a different spin. I was even told there was no red-line code.

In the twilight, I asked myself if Kaczynski had broken his own nose, in an attempt at disguise, after being sighted at CAAMs computer store on February 20, 1987. After seeing the accused on television, forensic artist Jeanne Boylan theorized, based on her extensive knowledge of physiognomy, that his nose had been broken five to six times and possibly in reaction to the composite sketches circulated of the Unabomber. Others speculated that, if Ted were indeed the bomber, he had injured his nose testing explosive devices in the wilds of Montana or the Sierras.

FINALLY, WHERE HAD THE FBI gone wrong? Their reliance on a profile that was diametrically opposed to the accused Unabomber— "neat, keeps a well-running car... thirties or forties in age," and resistance to Agent Bill Tafoya's profile, which made the Unabomber a man in his fifties and living in a remote area, were certainly a mistake. Only Tafoya's profile suggested the true depth of the bomber's silence, the vastness of his isolation. And since it was that silence and that isolation that did so much to render the Bureau's usual investigative techniques useless, this was a crucial mistake.

A man in a remote area with but a handful of friends and acquaintances, by definition frustrated the FBI's favorite technique: linkage—between suspects, victims, possible suppliers, co-workers, friends—the search for the one witness who does not know he is a witness until he is asked the right question. Linkage is what the "billion byte" Unabomber computer was built for. Linkage is the reason fifty thousand suspects seemed to the investigation to be a resource, not an abyss. The right profile might have suggested that linkage would not work and that other techniques should be tried.

The principal alternate approach was the one Jim Freeman, Bob Bell, and others had espoused—the public should have been informed earlier of the existence of a serial bomber and of enough relevant details to help with *both* discovery *and* prevention. Through such a simple act as informing college professors to be wary of any unsolicited parcels bearing "Eugene O'Neill" stamps, much pain could have been avoided, careers preserved, and lives saved. When Freeman convinced Janet Reno to push for publication of the manifesto, the Unabomber's days were numbered. The solution, this last Task Force chief knew, would come from the public. It was ironic that the Unabomber insisted on publication of the very thing that would lead to his identity.

How could a poverty-stricken man, riding a bike, living in a shack with no electricity or running water, spread fear from coast to coast, and elude the police for almost eighteen years? As Ted's friend, Chris Waits, said, "It's a scenario no one would ever believe."

Darkness claimed the wild dell as Penny and the two neighbors trudged up the steep road toward civilization. I ran to join them and never looked back, knowing the remaining questions would answer themselves in time. Ahead, Big River roared on as it had and would, for thousands of years.

APPENDIX A

A Chronological List of Unabomber Package Bombs Placed in the US During a Seventeen-Year Reign of Terror

1. May 25, 1978: A device, addressed to Professor E.J. Smith at Rensselaer Polytechnic Intitute and apparently from Professor Buckley Crist, discovered in a parking lot at Northwestern University, Evanston, Illinois, injures a security guard, Terry Marker.

2. May 9, 1979: A bomb, contained in "Phillies" brand cigar box abandoned in a common area, injures a civil engineering student, John Harris, in Northwestern's Technological Institute.

3. November 15, 1979: Twelve to fourteen people suffer from smoke inhalation when a package bomb rigged to a barometer to explode at 34,500 feet detonates imperfectly in the forward mail compartment of American Airlines Flight No. 444. The 727 was flying from Chicago to National, but made an emergency landing at Dulles International Airport.

4. June 10, 1980: United Airlines President Percy Addison Wood is injured by a book bomb sent from "Enoch Fischer" to his Lake Forest, Illinois, home. The booby-trapped book is Sloan Wilson's *Ice Brothers,* an Arbor House book.

5. October 8, 1981: A bomb placed in the third floor hallway of Bennion Hall Business Building at the University of Utah in Salt Lake City is discovered by a maintenance worker. The EOD team X rayed, then defused the device. No one was injured.

6. May 5, 1982: Janet Smith, a secretary to Professor Patrick C. Fischer at Pennsylvania State University, is injured at Vanderbilt University in Nashville when she opens a package with canceled stamps that had trailed her boss across

many states. Fischer was on sabbatical in Havana when the wooden box inside that contained a pipe bomb exploded. The return address reads Dr. Leroy Wood Bearnson, the probable target.

7. July 2, 1982: Diogenes Angelakos, a professor of electrical engineering and computer science, is injured in Room 411, the faculty lounge at the Cory Hall Mathematics Building at the University of California at Berkeley. He had picked up a cylinder thinking it was a student project. Angelakos suffers serious injuries to his right hand, arm, and face. But the worst result of the cowardly attack is that the professor can no longer care for his ailing wife, who passes away a month later. However, UNABOM is seen for the first time, by janitor Ricky Timms.

8. May 15, 1985: Aspiring astronaut John Hauser is injured by a device disguised as a three-ring binder attached to a plastic file box. It had been left for days in a computer room, Room 264, Cory Hall Computer Science Building on UC Berkeley campus. Hauser suffered serious injuries to his right hand, including permanent nerve damage and the loss of four fingers.

9. June 13, 1985: King County Sheriff's Bomb Squad safely disarms a bomb mailed to the fabrication division of the Boeing Company in Auburn, Washington. It had been delivered on May 8. Return address was Weiburg Tool & Supply in Oakland, California.

10. November 15, 1985: James V. McConnell, a professor of psychology at the University of Michigan at Ann Arbor, is deafened and a research assistant, Nick Suino, is injured by a booby-trapped package mailed to him from "Ralph C. Kloppenberg," Department of History at the University of Utah.

11. December 11, 1985: Hugh Campbell Scutton is killed by a bomb found behind his RenTech Computer Rental Store in Sacramento, California. Left by a dumpster, the device had the appearance of a block of wood with nails protruding. Its intention was to attract a good Samaritan.

12. February 20, 1987: Gary Wright is injured by a device disguised as a block of wood with four nails protruding behind his CAAMs computer store in Salt Lake City. The Unabomber is glimpsed for a matter of seconds and the first composite sketch is made within twenty-four hours. Freelance artist Bob Exter draws a new sketch by March 19, 1987. Seven years later, Jeanne Boylan draws the now-famous composite of the Unabomber, which reaches iconic stature.

13. June 22, 1993: Dr. Charles Epstein, a world famous geneticist, is maimed at his Tiburon, California, home by a mail bomb enclosed in a padded envelope. Epstein was a professor at the University of California at San Francisco Medical School.

14. June 24, 1993: Dr. David Gelernter, inventor of the computer system "Linda," is badly injured in his Yale University office in New Haven, Connecticut. The package was mailed from Sacramento with a return address listed as Mary Jane Lee, Computer Science, California State University. Gelernter, an artist, author, and computer expert, arrived at his office early in the morning and opened a package identical to Epstein's. The mail bomb inflicted serious injuries to his ear, eye, and hand.

15. December 10, 1994: Thomas Mosser, a New Jersey advertising executive, is killed by a powerful bomb mailed to his North Caldwell, New Jersey home on Aspen Drive. The return address read HC Wickel, Department of Economics, San Francisco State University. No such person existed.

16. April 25, 1995: Timber industry lobbyist Gil Murray is killed by the Unabomber's most powerful bomb yet in the lobby of the California Forestry Association in Sacramento. The return address was Closet Dimensions, Oakland, and was addressed to Murray's predecessor, William Dennison.

Selected Inventory of Items Recovered from
Humbug Contour Road 30, Box 27, Lincoln, Montana,
the Shack of Theodore Kaczynski

Green canvas US Army backpack.

Wood-handled hammer.

One package of saw blades.

One long-handled black knife.

Saw (handsaw).

One box of Mead envelopes, one package of self-adhesive labels, and one package of hole reinforcers.

One plastic bread bag, secured with a shoelace, containing five small containers: 1) an orange plastic bottle with white plastic lid, with masking tape around it, with handwritten note "Thermite laced with chlorate mixture"; 2) an orange plastic container, with white plastic cap, with masking tape on it, with handwritten notation "exp. 118"; 3) an orange plastic bottle with white plastic lid, with masking tape around it, with handwritten notation "$KCLO_3$+ S + charcoal + mucilage"; 4) an orange plastic container with white plastic cap, with masking tape around it, with handwritten notation "Al + S"; 5) a small metal container, silver color, with masking tape around it, with handwritten notation "Smokeless powder from Remington 30.06 bronze points."

Metal can with handwritten notation "12:00 AM," containing two metal castings.

Round metal Calumet Baking Powder can with white paper label secured with masking tape, with handwritten notation "Na_2CO_3—impure. Probably contaminated with [$NaHCO_3$], NaCl, and $NaCLO_3$. This is the first lot of crystals removed March 23. And second lot."

Two small white cardboard boxes, labeled "Potassium chromate K. CrO, for lab use only, Hagenow Labs, Inc., Manitowoc, Wis.," in a white plastic shopping bag.

One small clear glass jar with white metal cap, with handwritten notation "washed charcoal very finely ground"; contains black powdery substance.

One clear glass jar with white metal cap, with picture of a lion on the cap and the name Wagner, with masking tape around jar, with handwritten notations "curic hydroxide?" (crossed out) and "probably basic carbonate $Cu_2(OH)_2CO_3$"; contains blue powdery substance.

Six books: Eastern mysticism, Basimov's *Guide to the Bible, Holy Bible-Dictionary Concordance, Come the Comrade, Les Misérables.*

Partial section of wooden box.

Piece of label from the wooden box.

Jar of white crystalline substance and note "ammonium nitrate."

Two bottles labeled "aluminum" and box lid with experiment info.

Various containers marked "aluminum materials."

Misc. pipes and cordage.

Misc. cans, string, plastic, and metal.

Metal parts and pieces.

Welding-type mask.

Chains, locks, and possible traps.

L-shaped pipe.

Section of pipe.

Bomb components.

Two rolls of brown paper marked "3qq," can containing wire marked "qq" and documents.

Box marked "1 or 10 q or qq" (handwritten), metal tubes, wiring, springs, ball trigger in tinfoil, stapler, 9V battery, and small copper-colored tubing.

Copper-colored tubing removed from Item L-32.

Five bottles labeled "saltpeter."

Plastic bag marked "3q."

Glass container with off-white drills.

Container of white powder labeled "$KCLO_3$ [unreadable] potassium 99.95%

pure."

Six sealed bottles labeled "sulfur."

Plastic bag and container of yellow powder labeled "sulfur."

Large plastic container labeled "$NaCl_3 + NaCl$."

Can with matches and wood fragments.

Small ratchet, tweezers, and a pocket knife.

Four measuring spoons.

Tools in a can.

1-Gal. jug labeled "abietic acid," and sample taken from the jug (two plastic bags).

Bottle labeled "ammonium nitrate NH_4NO_3."

Gray case containing typewriter.

Typewriter parts.

Section of pipe.

Bottle of white powder labeled "NaCl."

Folded papers with chemical residue.

Four copper tubes.

Plastic jar containing triggering devices, each numbered with masking-tape tag.

Three pairs of scissors.

Wood-handle file.

Seven large drill bits.

Great Neck #50 hacksaw.

One drilling base.

One handsaw.

One tube of Duro Super Glue.

One T-shaped metal pipe or bracket with serial number GH-4.

One Hanson, Model 1509 scale, wrapped in brown paper with masking tape.

One metal can labeled "Del Monte Whole Leaf Spinach," containing melted metal fragments.

One brown plastic oblong Hershey canister with lid.

One coil of wire and metal parts.

Once package of Mead brand typing paper, with bottom half in paper and strapping tape.

One Calumet Baking Powder canister containing one red Le Watch brand watch, watch parts, and misc. metal parts.

One brown plastic oblong container, containing one mousetrap.

One piece of inner-tube valve, and one orange plastic bag containing wire.

One small brown plastic bottle labeled "Nature Made Therapeutic M [unreadable]," with paper label attached with masking tape, with handwritten notation "aluminum filings from our big block of cast aluminum 5.1 oz."

One cut portion of a battery, "Radiosonde, NSM-6135-01-054-2098, VIZ Mfg. Co., 335 E. Pierce St., Philadelphia, PA, 19144, USA, Patent No. 3205.096," wrapped in a piece of newspaper dated Nov. 22, 1995, page 4 of the *Consumer Press*.

Small plastic container with strip of black tape around it and torn white handwritten label, "Lima Duras De Hierro Parcialmente Limpias," containing brownish-black powder believed to be aluminum.

Three yellow rubber gloves: one labeled "Ansell" brand; another labeled "Large, Playtex, Dover, Del."; all three with wrists cut off.

Group of metal fasteners, bundled together with blue rubber band.

Two white homemade envelopes, one with handwritten notation "wire," the other "dump."

Hand drill with blue and red wooden handle.

Six cast metallic objects.

Cone-shaped metallic casting.

One cast metallic object.

One cylindrical Quaker Yellow Corn Meal cardboard canister containing two spools of solder.

One cylindrical Quaker Oats cardboard canister containing wires, a switch, and an alligator clip.

Bottom half of cardboard instant-milk box of screwdrivers with masking-tape label "254," a wire brush, a level, three paintbrushes, a paper bag containing small square magnets and misc. metal parts.

One Calumet Baking Powder canister containing machined metal parts.

One small Shopper's Value tomato paste can containing resisters and a tan plastic shopping bag containing resisters.

Seven rolled-up maps.

Quaker Yellow Corn Meal container with handwritten notation "transformer" on top, containing electrical wire and misc. electrical parts.

One metal Hershey's Cocoa can containing misc. metal parts.

Misc. pieces of metal, including tin-can lid, ball of aluminum foil, two pieces of splintered hardwood, wrapped in a sheet of newspaper, front page of *Missoulian*, dated Friday, Sept. 16, 1988.

One metal can containing misc. [grinding] wheels and pieces of metal.

Small orange plastic bottle with white plastic cap, with piece of masking tape around it, with handwritten notation "AgCl, slightly photo-decomposed."

One whitish plastic bottle with black cap, label "manganese dioxide (technical) contact with other material may cause fire. Do not grind. Do not breathe dust. 8J28D, 1/4 lbs. Analytical & Research Chemicals, Inc."

Small glass jar with red and white checkered metal cap containing white flaky substance, with masking tape around it, with handwritten notation "NH_4Cl [ammonium] chloride Exp. 136."

Small brown plastic bottle with white plastic cap, with notebook paper label taped on with masking tape with handwritten notation "Na_2CO_3 from Red Devil lye. Should be reasonably pure, if Red Devil lye is. (No, not very pure)."

One pair of pliers.

One white porcelain mortar and pestle, wrapped in *Consumer Press* newspaper dated April 5, 1995, page 26, and secured with a yellow rubber band.

Rod-shaped pieces of dark-colored/blackish powder, wrapped in a handwritten note inside a red and white checkered bread bag.

Three bundles of clear glass tubing; one wrapped in a page of *Consumer Press* newspaper dated June 21, 1995, and secured with yellow and white rubber bands; another is wrapped in large-pocket bubble wrap, with handwritten notation "5 mm pyrex tubing"; another is wrapped in large-pocket bubble wrap with handwritten notation "10 mm pyrex tubing;" all wrapped together in a *Missoulian* newspaper dated Jan. 16, 1991.

Whitish plastic bottle with white cap labeled "orange." The bottle had a white paper label secured with masking tape. The label contained the following handwritten notation: "$Fe(OH)_2$ partially (or wholly?) oxidized to $Fe(OH)_3$ Exp. 51, lot E."

Small brown plastic bottle labeled "therapeutic M" with masking tape around it, with handwritten notation "lead acetate, lead hydroxide, lead carbonate, unknown proportions, not very pure."

White plastic bottle with white metal cap. Bottle contained a label, "McKesson boric acid crystals NF," and had a small white price tag "112-1755, K3MME, Bergums 1.93."

Small tan cardboard box labeled "Fuel compressed, trioxane, ration heating, F.S.N. 9110-263-9865, 3 bars, specification: MIL-F-10805C, Can-Tite Rubber Corporation, Inwood, L.I., New York, 11696."

One whitish plastic Raspberry Super Sip bottle with white plastic cap with masking tape across cap and around cap and masking tape around bottle with handwritten notation "AgCl."

Clear glass jar, with whitish plastic stopper type cap, with white paper label secured with handwritten notation "amorphous carbon (made by heating sucrose)," containing a black powdery substance.

Oblong whitish plastic container with black cap, with black tape and masking tape around the cap label "Aldrich Scientific, P3191, 500g. Potassium Carbonate, Anhydrous Granular Technical, K, Co, FW 138.21, Aldrich Scientific, 5415 Jackwood Dr., San Antonio, TX 78238-1897, Lot 9C06G."

Round cardboard canister, label "Old-Fashioned Quaker Oats," with handwritten notation on the top "rubber tubings, funnels, bulbs, etc." The canister contains assorted pieces of rubber tubing, a small piece of glass tubing, a black rubber stopper, two metal clips, and one smaller round cardboard canister. The smaller canister is a Quaker Yellow Corn Meal container with handwritten notation on the top "plastic and glass tubing, short pieces." This smaller container contains assorted pieces of plastic and rubber tubing, several black rubber stoppers, and two metal clips.

One round cardboard Old Fashioned Quaker Oats canister containing an electronics tester, serial number 800341385, with handwritten note on masking tape on front "note: when on 'high' the ammeter gives incorrect reading. See Exp. 242."; and a second handwritten note on top of canister, "ammeter," between two intersecting pieces of masking tape.

One yellow and black plastic True Value flashlight with light bulb in it but no batteries.

Cardboard box with US Post Office metered mail "Kansas City, MO, Oct. 27, '76," containing various spools of twine, bundles of string, and numerous strips of leather.

ITEM	DESCRIPTION
MF 30	BROWN PLASTIC RAIN COAT
MF 31	KNIFE
MF 32	MAPS OF LOCAL AREA (2 MAPS)
MF 33	CANVAS GREEN/BROWN FACE MASK AND BLACK CANVAS FACE MASK
MF 34	RADIO AND MAP OF LINCOLN, MT., AREA
MF 35	WHITE RAGS TIED TOGETHER
MF 36	PLASTIC BAG WITH TWO FISH HOOKS, STRING, AND TWO BOXES OF MATCHES.
MF 37	POCKET KNIFE
MF 38	PIECES OF WOOD IN PLASTIC
MF 39	PLASTIC GARBAGE BAG/BAG CONTAINING CLOTHING STRIPS
MF 40	IODIZED SALT IN BOTTLE
MF 41	AMMO PACK AND WATER PROOF MATCHES
MF 42	PIPE APPROXIMATELY 6 1/2 FOOT LONG
MF 43	HAND-MADE GUN WITH SPENT CARTRIDGE
MF 44	WOOD BOARDS IN FOIL
MF 45	DEBRIS
MF 46	MISC. WOOD WITH SCREWS AND NAILS TO INCLUDE PIECES FROM THE WOOD BIN ITSELF, BED, AND BED FRAME
MF 47	ONE LARGE PIECE OF WOOD BIN
MF 48	ONE BOTTLE OF TRAZADONE/ANTI-DEPRESSANT

Reproduction of actual FBI page of listed items seized from Ted Kaczynski's cabin in April 1996. Evidence seized from the cabin filled forty-one boxes.

APPENDIX C

(A) Ted Kaczynski's registration card from the Helena, Montana Park Hotel, he used the "halfway house" as a launching point for his mysterious trips.

(B) Kaczynski's name, in a rare script signature. The FBI later uncovered twenty-two Park Hotel registration cards as evidence.

(C) The defendant's last Park Hotel visit in 1985. No documents show he stayed there before or after the Hugh Scrutton Christmastime murder later that year.

APPENDIX D

INDUSTRIAL SOCIETY AND ITS FUTURE

by FC

The actual manifesto title page and first two pages copied from original as typed by the Unabomber, never reproduced in type or photocopy before. The first page is corrections provided by the bomber and mailed to *The New York Times* and *Washington Post* on June 22 and 24, 1995. The *Times* and *Post* made these corrections before running the eight full page manifesto supplement on September 19, 1995.

Regarding Note 16 of the following manuscript:

If copyright problems make it impossible for this long quotation to be printed, then please change Note 16 to read as follows:

16. (Paragraph 95) When the American colonies were under British rule there were fewer and less effective legal guarantees of freedom than there were after the American Constitution went into effect, yet there was more personal freedom in pre-industrial America, both before and after the War of Independence, than there was after the industrial revolution took hold in this country. In <u>Violence</u> <u>in</u> <u>America</u>: <u>Historical</u> <u>and</u> <u>Comparative</u> <u>Perspectives,</u> edited by Hugh Davis Graham and Ted Robert Gurr, Chapter 12 by Roger Lane, it is explained how in pre-industrial America the average person had greater independence and autonomy than he does today, and how the process of industrialization necessarily led to the restriction of personal freedom.

CORRECTIONS

Please insert the following corrections in the manuscript before it is printed.

Location	Now is	Should be changed to ·
Paragraph 10 Line 5	have such feelings	have some such feelings
Paragraph 30 Line 6	"liberation"	"liberation"
Paragraph 30 Line 8	them,	them.
Paragraph 63 Line 6	paragraphs 78-80	paragraphs 80-82
Paragraph 64 Eighth line from bottom	life. 12	life[12].
Paragraph 72 Line 6	"safe sex).	"safe sex").
Paragraph 75 Fifth line from bottom	dterioration	deterioration

Paragraph 84 Third line from bottom	poit	point
Paragraph 90 Line 5	No doubt to majority	No doubt the majority
Paragraph 95 Line 6	government.16	government[16].
Paragraph 97 Line 4	only certain	only a certain
Paragraph 120 Line 2	thana	than a
Paragraph 121 Line 4	the good parts	the "good" parts
Paragraph 124 Last line	system.20	system[20].
Paragraph 128 Eighth line from bottom	influence.21	influence[21].
Paragraph 141 Line 6	xxxxx sovle	solve
Paragraph 151 Last line	system.27	system[27].
Paragraph 152 Line 3	freedom.28	freedom[28].
Paragraph 156 Last line	presseure	pressure
Paragraph 163 Fourth line from bottom	typed-over correction of word "be" is unclear	be
Paragraph 183 Line 4	colon after "nature" is unclear	nature:
Paragraph 193 Last line	politics.32	politics[32].
Paragraph 219 Line 15	goal.35	goal[35].
Paragraph 220	inposing	imposing

In these pages it is argued that continued scientific and technical progress will inevitably result in the extinction of individual liberty. I use the word "inevitably" in the following sense: One might--possibly--imagine certain conditions of society in which freedom could coexist with advanced technology, but these conditions do not actually exist, and we know of no way to bring them about, so that, in practice, scientific progress will result in the extinction of individual liberty. Toward the end of this essay we propose what appears to be the only thing that bears any resemblance to a practical remedy for this situation.

I hope that the reader will bear with me when I recite arguments and facts with which he may already be familiar. I make no claim to originality. I simply think that the case for the thesis stated above is convincing, and I am attempting to set forth the arguments, new and old, in as clear a manner as possible, in the hope that the reader will be persuaded to support the solution here suggested--which certainly is a very obvious solution, but rather hard for many people to swallow.

The power of society to control the individual person has recently been expanding very rapidly, and is expected to expand even more rapidly in the near future. Let us list a few of the more ominous developments as a reminder.

(1) Propaganda and image-making techniques. In this context we must not neglect the role of movies, television, and literature, which commonly are regarded either as art or as entertainment, but which

Actual 23 page 1971 essay written and typed by Ted Kaczynski. Ted made penciled notations in the margins. SSA FBI Agent Fitzgerald and his team made correlations between the essay, Ted's correspondence, and the manifesto.

2.

often consciously adopt certain points of view and thus serve as propaganda. Even when they do not consciously adopt an explicit point of view they still serve to indoctrinate the viewer or reader with certain values. We venerate the great writers of the past, but one who considers the matter objectively must admit that modern artistic techniques have developed to the point where the more skillfully constructed movies, novels, etc. of today are far more psychologically potent than, say, Shakespeare ever was. The best of them are capable of gripping and involving the reader very powerfully and thus are presumably quite effective in influencing his values. Also note the increasing extent to which the average person today is "living in the movies" as the saying is. People spend a large and increasing amount of time submitting to canned entertainment rather than participating in spontaneous activities. As overcrowding and rules and regulations curtail opportunities for spontaneous activity, and as the developing techniques of entertainment make the canned product ever more attractive, we can assume that people will live more and more in the world of mass entertainment.

(2) A growing emphasis among educators on "guiding" the child's emotional development, coupled with an increasingly scientific attitude toward education. Of course, educators have always in some degree attempted to mold the attitudes of their pupils, but formerly they achieved only a limited degree of success, simply because their methods were unscientific. Educational psychology is changing this.

(3) Operant conditioning, after the manner of B. F. Skinner and friends. (Of course, this cannot be entirely separated from

3.

item (2).)

(4) Direct physical control of the emotions via electrodes and "chemitrodes" inserted in the brain. (See Jose M. R. Delgado's book "Physical Control of the Mind".)

(5) Biofeedback training, after the manner of Joseph Kamiya and others.

(6) Predicted "memory pills" or other drugs designed to improve memory or increase intelligence.

(The reader possibly assumes that items (5) and (6) present no danger to freedom because their use is supposed to be voluntary, but I will argue that point later. See page 15 .)

(7) Predicted genetic engineering, eugenics, related techniques.

(8) Marvin Minsky of MIT (one of the foremost computer experts in the country) and other computer scientists predict that within fifteen years or possibly much less there will be superhuman computers with intellectual capacities far beyond anything of which humans are capable. It is to be emphasized that these computers will not merely perform so-called "mechanical" operations; they will be capable of creative thought. Many people are incredulous at the idea of a creative computer, but let it be remembered that (unless one resorts to supernatural explanations of human thought) the human brain itself is an electro-chemical computer, operating according to the laws of physics and chemistry. Furthermore, the men who have predicted these computers are not crackpots but first-class scientists.

4.

It is difficult to say in advance just how much power these computers will put into the hands of what is vulgarly termed the establishment, but this power will probably be very great. Bear in mind that these computers will be wholly under the control of the scientific, bureaucratic, and business elite. The average person will have no access to them. Unlike the human brain, computers are more or less unrestricted as to size (and, more important, there is no restriction on the number of computers that can be linked together over long distances to form a single brain), so that there is no restriction on their memories or on the amount of information they can assimilate and correlate. Computers are not subject to fatigue, daydreaming, or emotional problems. They work at fantastic speed. Given that a computer can duplicate the functions of the human brain, it seems clear in view of the advantages listed above that no human brain could possibly compete with such a computer in any field of endeavor.

(9) Various electronic devices for surveillance. These are being used. For example, according to newspaper reports, the police of New York City have recently instituted a system of 24-hour television surveillance over certain problem areas of the city.

These are some of the more strikingly ominous facets of scientific progress, but it is perhaps more important to look at the effect of technology as a whole on our society. Technological progress is the basic cause of the continual increase in the number of rules and regulations. This is because many of our technological devices are more powerful and

5.

therefore more potentially destructive than the more primitive
devices they replace (e.g., compare autos and horses) and also
because the increasing complexity of the system makes
necessary a more delicate coordination of its parts. Moreover,
many devices of fundamental importance (e.g., electronic computers,
television broadcasting equipment, jet planes) cannot be owned
by the average person because of their size and costliness. These
devices are controlled by large organizations such as corporations
and governments and are used to further the purposes of the
establishment. A larger and larger proportion of the individual's
environment--not only his physical environment, but such factors
as the kind of work he does, the nature of his entertainment, etc.--
comes to be created and controlled by large organizations rather
than by the individual himself. And this is a necessary consequence
of technological progress, because to allow technology to be
exploited in an unregulated, unorganized way would result in
disaster.

Note that the problem here is not simply to make sure that
technology is used only for good purposes. In fact, we can be
reasonably certain that the powers which technology is putting
into the hands of the establishment will be used to promote good
and eliminate evil. These powers will be so great that within a
few decades virtually all evil will have been eliminated. But, of
course, "good" and "evil" here mean good and evil as interpreted
by the social mainstream. In other words, technology will enable
the social mainstream to impose its values universally. This
will not come about through the machinations of power-hungry
scoundrels, but through the efforts of socially responsible

8.

in children, who can deny it to them? But it will be equally
impossible to argue against any of the other steps that will
eventually lead to the complete engineering of the human
personality. Each step will be equally humanitarian in its goals.

There is no distinct line between "guidance" or "influence"
and manipulation. When a technique of influence becomes so
effective that it achieves its desired effect in nearly every
case, then it is no longer influence but compulsion. Thus influence
evolves into compulsion as science improves techniques.

Research has shown that exposure to television violence
makes the viewer more prone to violence himself. The very existence
of this knowledge makes it a foregone conclusion that restrictions
will eventually be placed on televised violence, either by the
government or by the TV industry itself, in order to make children
less prone to develop violent personalities. This is an element
of manipulation. It may be that you feel an end to television
violence is desirable and that the degree of manipulation involved
is insignificant. But science will reveal, one at a time, a
hundred other factors in entertainment that have a "desirable"
or "undesirable" effect on the personality. In the case of each
one of these factors, knowledge will make manipulation inevitable.
When the whole array of factors has become known, we will have
drifted into large-scale manipulation. In this way, research
leads automatically to calculated indoctrination.

By way of a further example, let us consider genetic
engineering. This will not come into use as a result of a
conscious decision by the majority of people to introduce genetic
engineering. It will begin with certain "progressive" parents
who will voluntarily avail themselves of genetic engineering

9.

opportunities in order to eliminate the risk of certain gross
physical defects in their offspring. Later, this engineering
will be extended to include elimination of mental defects and
treatment which will predispose the child to somewhat higher
intelligence. (Note that the question of what constitutes a
mental "defect" is a value-judgement. Is homosexuality, for
example, a defect? Some homosexuals would say no. But there is
no objectively true or false answer to such a question.) As
methods are improved to the point where the minority of parents
who use genetic engineering are producing noticeably healthier,
smarter offspring, more and more parents will want genetic
engineering. When the majority of children are genetically
engineered, even those parents who might otherwise be antagonistic
toward genetic engineering will feel obliged to use it so that their
children will be able to compete in a world of superior people
--superior, that is, relative to the social milieu in which
they live. In the end, genetic engineering will be made compulsory,
because it will be regarded as cruel and irresponsible for a
few eccentric parents to produce inferior offspring by refusing
to use it. Bear in mind that this engineering will involve
mental as well as physical characteristics; indeed, as scientists
explain mental traits on the basis of physiology, neurology, and
biochemistry, it will become more and more difficult to distinguish
between "mental" and "physical" traits.

Observe that once a society based on psychological, genetic,
and other forms of human engineering has come into being, it
will presumably last forever, because people will all be
engineered to favor human engineering and the totally collective
society, so that they will never become dissatisfied with this

10.

kind of society. Furthermore, once human engineering, the linking of human minds with computers, and other things of that nature have come into extensive use, people will probably be altered so much that it will no longer be possible for them to exist as independent beings, either physically or psychologically. Indeed, technology has already made it impossible for us to live as physically independent beings, for the skills which enabled primitive man to live off the country have been lost. We can survive only by acting as components of a huge machine which provides for our physical needs; and as technology invades the domain of the mind, it is safe to assume that human beings will become as dependent psychologically on technology as they now are physically. We can see the beginning of this already in the inability of some people to avoid boredom without television and in the need of others to use tranquilizers in order to cope with the tensions of modern society.

The foregoing predictions are supported by the opinions of at least some responsible writers. See especially Jacques Ellul's "The Technological Society" and the section titled "Social Controls" in Kahn and Wiener's "The Year 2,000".

Now we come to the question: What can be done to prevent all this? Let us first consider the solution sketched by Perry London in his book "Behavior Control". This solution makes a convenient example because its defects are typical of other proposed solutions. London's idea is, briefly, this: Let us not attempt to interfere with the development of behavioral technology, but let us all try to be as aware of and as knowledgeable about this technology as we can; let us not keep this technology in the hands of a scientific elite, but disseminate it among the population at large;people can then use this technology to manipulate themselves and protect ~~themselves against manipulation~~ by others. However, on the grounds that "there must be some limits" London advocates that behavior control should be imposed by society in certain areas. For example, he suggests that people should be made to abhor violence and that psychological means should be used to make businessmen stop destroying our forests. (NOTE: I do not currently have access to a copy of London's book, and so I have had to rely on memory in describing his views. My memory is probably correct here, but in order to be honest I should admit the possibility of error.)

My first objection to London's scheme is a personal one. I simply find the sphere of freedom that he favors too narrow for me to accept. But his solution suffers from other flaws.

He proposes to use psychological controls where they are not necessary, and more for the purpose of gratifying the liberal intellectual's esthetic sensibilities than because of a practical need. It is true that "there must be some limits"-- on violence, for example--but the threat of imprisonment seems to be an adequate limitation. To read about violence is frightening, but violent crime is not a significant cause of mortality in comparison to other causes. Far more people are killed in automobile accidents than through violent crime. Would London also advocate psychological elimination of those personalities that are inclined to careless driving? The fact that liberal intellectuals and many others get far more excited

12.

over violence than they do over careless driving would seem to indicate that their antagonism toward violence arises not primarily from a concern for human life but from a strong emotional antipathy toward violence itself. Thus it appears that London's proposal to eliminate violence through psychological control results not from practical necessity but from a desire on London's part to engineer some of his own values into the public at large.

This becomes even clearer when we consider London's willingness to use psychological engineering to stop businessmen from destroying our forests. Obviously, psychological engineering cannot accomplish this until the establishment can be persuaded to carry out the appropriate program of engineering. But if the establishment can be persuaded to do this, then they can equally well be persuaded to pass conservation laws strict enough to accomplish the same purpose. And if such laws are passed, the psychological engineering is superfluous. It seems clear that here, again, London is attracted to psychological engineering simply because he would like to see the general public share certain of his values.

When London proposes to use systematic psychological controls over certain aspects of the personality, with the intention that these controls shall not be extended to other areas, he is assuming that the generation following his own will agree with his judgement as to how far the psychological controls should reach. This assumption is almost certainly false. The introduction of psychological controls in some areas (which London approves) will set the stage for the later introduction of controls in other areas (which London would not approve), because it will

13.

change the culture in such a way as to make people more receptive
to the concept of psychological controls. As long as any
behavior is permitted which is not in the best interests of the
collective social organization, there will always be the
temptation to eliminate the worst of this behavior through
human engineering. People will introduce new controls to eliminate
only the worst of this behavior, without intending that any
further extension of the controls should take place afterward;
but in fact they will be indirectly causing further extensions
of the controls, because whenever new controls are introduced,
the public, as it becomes used to the new controls, will change
its conception of what constitutes an appropriate degree of
control. In other words, whatever the amount of control to which
people have become accustomed, they will regard that amount as
right and good, and they will regard a little further extension
of control as a negligible price to pay for the elimination of
some form of behavior that they find shocking.

London regards the wide dissemination of behavioral
technology among the public as a means by which people can protect
themselves against psychological manipulation by the established
powers. But if it is really true that people can use this
knowledge to avoid manipulation in most areas, why won't they
also be able to use it to avoid being made to abhor violence,
or to avoid control in other areas where London thinks they
should be controlled? London seems to assume that people will be
unable to avoid control in just those areas where he thinks
they should be controlled, but that they will be able to avoid
control in just those areas where he thinks they should not be
controlled.

14.

London refers to "awareness" (of processes relating to the
mind) as the individual's "sword and buckler" against
manipulation by the establishment. In Roman times a man might
have a real sword and buckler just as good as those of the
emperor's legionaries, but that did not enable him to escape
oppression. Similarly, if a man of the future has a complete
knowledge of behavioral technology it will not enable him to
escape psychological control any more than the possession of a
machine-gun or a tank would enable him to escape physical control.
The resources of an organized society are just too great for
any individual to resist no matter how much he knows.

With the vast expansion of knowledge in the behavioral
sciences, biochemistry, cybernetics, physiology, genetics, and
other disciplines which have the potential to affect human behavior,
it is probably already impossible (and, if not, it will soon
become impossible) for any individual to keep abreast of it all.
In any case, we would all have to become, to some degree, specialists
in behavior control in order to maintain London's "awareness".
What about those people who just don't happen to be attracted to
that kind of science, or to any science? It would be agony
for them to have to spend long hours studying behavioral
technology in order to maintain their freedom.

Even if London's scheme of freedom through "awareness"
were feasible, it could, or at least would, be carried out
only by an elite of intellectuals, businessmen, etc. Can you
imagine the members of uneducated minority groups, or, for
that matter, the average middle-class person, having the will
and the ability to learn enough to compete in a world of

psychological manipulation? It will be a case of the smart
and the powerful getting smarter and more powerful while the
stupid and the weak get (relatively) stupider and weaker; for
it is the smart and the powerful who will have the readiest
access to behavioral technology and the greatest ability to
use it effectively.

This is one reason why devices for improving one's
mental or psychological capabilities (e.g. biofeedback training,
memory pills, linking of human minds with computers) are
dangerous to freedom even though their use is voluntary. For
example, it will not be physically possible for everyone to
have his own full-scale computer in his basement to which he
can link his brain. The best computer facilities will be
reserved for those whom society judges most worthy: government
officials, scientists, etc. Thus the already powerful will be
made more powerful.

Also, the use of such mind-augmentation devices will
not remain voluntary. All our modern conveniences were originally
introduced as optional benefits which one could take or leave
as one chose. However, as a result of the introduction of these
benefits, society changed its structure in such a way that the
use of modern conveniences is now compulsory; for it would be
physically impossible to live in modern society without
extensively using devices provided by technology. Similarly,
the use of mind-augmenting devices, though nominally voluntary,
will become in practice compulsory. When these devices have
reached a high development and have come into wide use, a person
refusing to use them would be putting himself in the position

16.

of a dumb animal in a world of supermen. He would simply be
unable to function in a society structured around the assumption
that most people have vastly augmented mental abilities.

By virtue of their very power, the devices for augmenting
or modifying the human mind and personality will have to be
governed by extensive rules and regulations. As the human mind
comes to be more and more an artifact created by means of
such devices, these rules and regulations will come to be rules
and regulations governing the structure of the human mind.

An important point: London does not even consider the
question of human engineering in infancy (let alone genetic
engineering before conception). A two-year-old obviously would
not be able to apply London's philosophy of "awareness"; yet
it will be possible in the future to engineer a young child
so that he will grow up to have the type of personality that is
desired by whoever has charge of him. What is the meaning of
freedom for a person whose entire personality has been planned
and created by someone else?

London's solution suffers from another flaw that is of
particular importance because it is shared by all libertarian
solutions to the technology problem that have ever come to my
attention. The problem is supposed to be solved by propounding
and popularizing a certain libertarian philosophy. This
approach is unlikely to achieve anything. Our liberty is not
deteriorating as a result of any antilibertarian philosophy.
Most people in this country profess to believe in freedom. Our
liberty is deteriorating as a result of the way people do their
jobs and behave on a day-to-day basis in relation to technology.

17.

The system has come to be set up in such a way that it is usually comfortable to do that which strengthens the organization. When a person in a position of responsibility acts to eliminate that which is contrary to established values, he is rewarded with the esteem of his fellows and in other ways. Police officials who introduce new surveillance devices, educators who introduce more advanced techniques for molding children, do not do so through disrespect for freedom; they do so because they are rewarded with the approval of other police officials or educators and also because they get an inward satisfaction from having accomplished their assigned tasks not only competently, but creatively. A hands-off approach toward the child's personality would be best from the point of view of freedom, but this approach will not be taken because the most intelligent and capable educators crave the satisfaction of doing their work creatively. They want to do more with the child, not less. The greatest reward that a person gets from furthering the ends of the organization may well be simply the opportunity for purposeful, challenging, important activity--an opportunity that is otherwise hard to come by in this society. For example, Marvin Minsky does not work on computers because he is antagonistic to freedom, but because he loves the intellectual challenge. Probably he believes in freedom, but since he is a computer specialist he manages to persuade himself that computers will tend to liberate man.

The main point here is that the danger to freedom is caused by the way people work and behave on a day-to-day basis in relation to technology; and the way people behave in relation to technology is determined by powerful social and psychological

18.

forces. To oppose to these forces a comparatively weak force like a body of philosophy is simply hopeless. You may persuade the public to accept your philosophy, but most people will not significantly change ̶t̶h̶e̶i̶r̶ ̶b̶e̶h̶a̶v̶i̶o̶r̶ ̶a̶s̶ ̶a̶ ̶r̶e̶s̶u̶l̶t̶. They will invent rationalizations to reconcile their behavior with the philosophy, or they will say that what they do as individuals is too insignificant to change the course of events, or they will simply confess themselves too weak to live up to the philosophy. Conceivably a school of philosophy might change a culture over a long period of time if the social forces tending in the opposite direction were weak. But the social forces guiding the present development of our society are obviously strong, and we have very little time left--another three decades likely will take us past the point of no return.

Thus a philosophy will be ineffective unless that philosophy is accompanied by a program of concrete action of a type which does not ask people to voluntarily change the way they live and work--a program which demands little effort or willpower on the part of most people. Such a program would probably have to be a political or legislative one. A philosophy is not likely to make people change their daily behavior, but it might (with luck) induce them to vote for politicians who support a certain program. Casting a vote requires only a casual commitment, not a strenuous application of willpower. So we are left with the question: What kind of legislative program would have a chance of saving freedom?

I can think of only two possibilities that are halfway plausible. The discussion of one of these I will leave until

later. The other, and the one that I advocate, is this: In simple
terms, stop scientific progress by withdrawing all major sources
of research funds. In more detail, begin by withdrawing all or
most federal aid to research. If an abrupt withdrawal would
cause economic problems, then phase it out as rapidly as is
practical. Next, pass legislation to limit or phase out research
support by educational institutions which accept public funds.
Finally, one would hope to pass legislation prohibiting all large
corporations and other large organizations from supporting
scientific research. Of course, it would be necessary to eventually
bring about similar changes throughout the world, but, being
Americans, we must start with the United States; which is just as
well, since the United States is the world's most technologically
advanced country. As for economic or other disruption that might
be caused by the elimination of scientific progress—this
disruption is likely to be much less than that which would be
caused by the extremely rapid changes brought on by science
itself.

I admit that, in view of the firmly entrenched position of
Big Science, it is unlikely that such a legislative program
could be enacted. However, I think there is at least some chance
that such a program could be put through, in stages over a
period of years, if one or more active organizations were formed
to make the public aware of the probable consequences of continued
scientific progress and to push for the appropriate legislation.
Even if there is only a small chance of success, I think that that
chance is worth working for, since the alternative appears to be
the loss of all human freedom.

This solution is bound to be attacked as "simplistic", but

20.

this ignores the fundamental question, namely: Is there any
better solution or indeed any other solution at all? My personal
opinion is that there is no other solution. However, let us not
be dogmatic. Maybe there is a better solution. But the point is
this: If there is such a solution, no one at present seems to
know just what it is. Matters have progressed to the point where
we can no longer afford to sit around just waiting for
something to turn up. By stopping scientific progress now, or
at any rate slowing it drastically, we would at least give
ourselves a breathing space during which we could attempt to
work out another solution, if one is possible.

There is one putative solution the discussion of which I
have reserved until now. One might consider enacting some kind
of bill of rights designed to protect freedom from technological
encroachment. For the following reasons I do not believe that
such a solution would be effective.

In the first place, a document which attempted to define
our sphere of freedom in a few simple principles would either
be too weak to afford real protection, or too strong to be
compatible with the functioning of the present society. Thus, a
suitable bill of rights would have to be excessively complex,
and full of exceptions, qualifications, etc. and delicate compromises.
Such a bill would be subject to repeated amendments for the
sake of social expedience; and where formal amendment is
inconvenient, the document would simply be reinterpreted. Recent
decisions of the Supreme Court, whether one approves of them
or not, show how much the import of a document can be altered
through reinterpretation. Our present Bill of Rights would
have been ineffective if there had been in America strong

21.

social forces acting against freedom of speech, freedom of
worship, etc. Compare what is happening to the right to bear
arms, which currently runs counter to basic social trends.
Whether you approve or disapprove of that "right" is beside
the point--the point is that the constitutional guarantee
cannot stand indefinitely against powerful social forces.

If you are an advocate of the bill-of-rights approach to
the technology problem, test yourself by attempting to write a
sample section on, say, genetic engineering. Just how will
you define the term "genetic engineering" and how will you
draw the line, in words, between that engineering which is to
be permitted and that which is to be prohibited? Your law will
either have to be too strong to pass; or so vague that it can
be readily reinterpreted as social standards evolve; or
excessively complex and detailed. In this last base, the law
will not pass as a constitutional amendment, because for
practical reasons a law that attempts to deal with such a
problem in great detail will have to be relatively easy to
change as needs and circumstances change. But then, of course,
the law will be changed continually for the sake of social
expedience and so will not serve as a barrier to the erosion of
freedom.

And who would actually work out the details of such a
bill of rights? Undoubtedly, a committee of congressmen, or a
commission appointed by the president, or some other group of
organization men. They would give us some fine libertarian
rhetoric, but they would be unwilling to pay the price of real,
substantial freedom--they would not write a bill that would
sacrifice any significant amount of the organization's power.

22.

I have said that a bill of rights would not be able
to stand for long against the pressure for science, progress,
and improvement. But laws that bring a halt to scientific
research would be quite different in this respect. The prestige
of science would be broken. With the financial basis gone, few
young people would find it practical to enter scientific
careers. After, say, three decades or so, our society would
have ceased to be progress-oriented and the most dangerous of
the pressures that currently threaten our freedom would have
relaxed. A bill of rights would not bring about this relaxation.

This, by the way, is one reason why the elimination of
research merely in a few sensitive areas would be inadequate.
As long as science is a large and going concern, there will
be the persistent temptation to apply it in new areas; but this
pressure would be broken if science were reduced to a minor
role.

Let us try to summarize the role of technology in
relation to freedom. The principal effect of technology is to
increase the power of society collectively. Now, there is a more
or less unlimited number of value-judgements that lie before
us; for example: whether an individual should or should not
have puritanical attitudes toward sex; whether it is better to
have rain fall at night or during the day. When society acquires
power over such a situation, generally a preponderance of the
social forces look upon one or the other of the alternatives
as Right. These social forces are then able to use the
machinery of society to impose their choice universally; for
example, they may mold children so successfully that none ever
grows up to have puritanical attitudes toward sex, or they may

23.

use weather engineering to guarantee that rain falls only at
night. In this way there is a continual narrowing of the
possibilities that exist in the world. The eventual result will
be a world in which there is only one system of values. The
only way out seems to be to halt the ceaseless extension of
society's power.

I propose that you join me and a few other people to
whom I am writing in an attempt to found an organization
dedicated to stopping federal aid to scientific research. I
realize that you will probably reject this suggestion, but I
hope that you will not reject it on the basis of some vague
dogma such as "know██████ is good██████████ the hope of
████ Okay, knowledge is good, but how high a price, in terms
of freedom, are ███ going to pay for knowledge? You may be
understandably reluctant to join an organization about which
you know nothing, but you know as much about it as I do. It
hasn't been started yet. You would be one of the founding
members. I claim to have no particular qualifications for
trying to start such an organization, and I have no idea how to
go about it. I am only making the attempt because no better-
qualified person has yet done so. I am simply trying to bring
together a few highly intelligent and thoughtful people who
would be willing to take over the task. I would prefer to
drop out of it personally because I am unsuited to that kind
of work; in fact I dislike it intensely.

TOTAL P.31

APPENDIX E

UNITED STATES DISTRICT COURT

HELENA DIVISION, DISTRICT OF MONTANA

FILED
'96 APR 3 AM 9 ...

In the Matter of the Search of

the residence of Theodore
John Kaczynski and surrounding
1.4 acres more particularly
described in Attachment #A and
exhibits A through F all of which
are attached hereto and incorporated
herein by reference

SEARCH WARRANT

CASE NUMBER:

30

'96 APR 15 A ...
FILED

TO: Terry D Turchie, Special Agent, Federal Bureau of Investigation, and any Authorized Officer of the United States

Affidavit having been made before me by Terry D. Turchie, Special Agent, Federal Bureau of Investigation, who has reason to believe that ()on the person of or (x) on the premises known as:

the residence of Theodore John Kaczynski and surrounding 1.4 acres more particularly described in Attachment #A and exhibits A through F all of which are attached hereto and incorporated herein by reference

in the State and District of Montana there is now concealed property, namely:

those items particularly described in the affidavit of Terry D. Turchie which is incorporated herein by reference (those pages describing the items to be seized are set forth as Attachment #B)

I am satisfied that the affidavit and any recorded testimony establish probable cause to believe that the person or property so described is now concealed on the person or premises above-described and establish grounds for the issuance of this warrant.

YOU ARE HEREBY COMMANDED to search on or before April 12, 1996 (not to exceed 10 days) the person or place named above for the person or property specified, serving this warrant in the daytime and making the search (in the daytime -- 6:00 A.M. to 10:00 P.M.) and continuing the search until complete (at any time in the day or night as I find reasonable cause has been established) and if the person or property be found there to seize same, leaving a copy of this warrant and receipt for the person or property taken, and prepare a written inventory of the person or property seized and promptly return this warrant to the United States District Court as required by law.

April 3, 1996   0910   at   Helena, mt.
Date and Time Issued   City and State

U.S. District Judge   Charles _____
Name and Title of Judicial Officer Signature of Judicial Officer

First page of Turchie affidavit, filed early on April 3, 1996. Note altered date as agents raced the clock.

IX

ITEMS TO BE SEIZED

213. Based on all of the information contained in this affidavit, which establishes a continual and consistent pattern' of conduct between 1978 and the present date, and based on the expert opinion of Supervisory Special Agent of the FBI's Explosive Unit, who has stated that probable cause exists that all of the below-listed items would be utilized in the manufacture, construction, assembly, packaging, and mailing of the explosive devices, your Affiant believes that probable cause exists that the following items, which are evidence of said violations, and are the fruits and instrumentalities of the foregoing crimes, are currently being stored at the premises of Theodore John Kaczynski, located in Lewis and Clark County, in

98

Reproduction of actual Attachment "B" of the Turchie affidavit. List of items prepared by FBI agent Terry Turchie and presented to Judge Lovell on April 3, 1996. Attacked later by the Kaczynski defense team, Quin Denvir and Judy Clarke, as being "overly broad."

the State of Montana, more particularly described in the
Application and Affidavit for Search Warrant and Attachment A,
previously incorporated by reference.

214. Tools and other instruments or items which have
been used, can be used, or are intended to be used in the
manufacture and/or construction of improvised explosive devices
or the components thereof. These items include, but are not
limited to, saws, files, metal punches, drill bits, sanding
devices, hammers, chisels, drills, vice or similar jawed tools,
abrading equipment, soldering and brazing equipment, wire
strippers, screwdrivers, staplers, safety wire and other pliers,
various hand tools for cutting steel bar stock, grinders,
sandpaper, leather working tools, pots or other containers used
to melt lead and aluminum, tools and associated materials used in
the casting of lead and aluminum, machines and tools which cut
metal pipe, tools used for cross-referencing circumference to
diameter, rulers and other various measuring devices, abrasive
cloths, steel wool or iron wire.

215. The following explosives, chemicals or other
substances which have been used, can be used or are intended to
be used in the manufacture or construction of improvised
explosive devices, or the components thereof: These items
include but are not limited to, firearms ammunition, smokeless
powder, black powder, aluminum and aluminum powder, gasoline
containers, barium nitrate, magnesium, potassium chlorate,

99

potassium perchlorate, sulfur, potassium sulfate, ammonium
nitrate, sodium chlorate, matches, or other pyrotechnic mixtures
and constituents.

216.   The following items, which have been used, can be
used or are intended to be used to house or contain improvised
explosive devices and the components thereof: These items
include, but are not limited to, cigar boxes, wood, wooden boxes,
wooden blocks, scrap wood and wood sources such as boxes,
pallets, cabinets and crates, hollowed-out books, the book
entitled the "Ice Brothers" by author Sloan Wilson, or portions
thereof, notebooks, loose leaf binders, or other plastic
containers.

217.   The following items and materials which have been
used, can be used or are intended to be used as component parts
of improvised explosive devices: These items include, but are
not limited to, metal tubes/pipes, cans, switches, barometers,
springs, batteries, dowels, plugs, screws, pins, nuts and bolts,
nails, staples, fishing line, straps, washers and brackets,
rubber bands, cord, wire, flashlight bulbs, alligator clips, and
lead split shot, tire weights or similar item, any form of
aluminum metal or scraps, sheet metal scraps and shims.

218.   The following items which have been used, can be
used or are intended to be used in the construction or assembly

100

of improvised destructive devices: These items include, but are
not limited to, solder, epoxy, glues and other adhesives or
caulking materials, varnish, lacquer, paint, wax and wax paper,
lead, solid silver bar, metal debris, explosive residue and
debris, gloves, plumbing sink traps, tape, gasket material and
twine.

219. The following items which have been used, can be
used or are intended to be used as exterior packaging materials:
These items include, but are not limited to, boxes, envelopes,
mailing labels, rubber stamps, rubber stamp kits, postage stamps,
wrapping paper, padded envelopes, stenciling sets, ink pens, ink
pads, and scales.

220. Typewriters.

221. Any and all documents, photographs, papers,
written materials, books, diagrams, schematic drawings, video
tapes, computer generated or stored information or other
materials which relate to the manufacture, construction and/or
assembly of improvised explosive devices or any of the components
thereof.

222. Any and all receipts, invoices, purchase orders,
sales slips or other documents and materials relating to the

101

purchase or procurement of any and all materials and tools which
have been used, can be used, or intended to be used in the
design, manufacture and construction of improvised explosive
devices; said documents would include, but are not be limited to,
those which denote the purchase or obtainment of any or all items
previously listed in paragraphs A through H.

223. Any and all documents, photographs, papers,
written or printed materials, books, video tapes, computer
generated or stored information or other materials and indicia
which relate to the names of, "Wu", the initials "R.V." and "FC",
"The Ice Brothers" a book written by Sloan Wilson, "The History
of Violence in America," a book written by Hugh Graham and Ted
Gurr, "Chinese Political Thought in The 20th Century", a book by
Chester C. Tan, "The Ancient Engineers", a book by L. Sprague de
Camp, "The True Believer" by Eric Hoffer, Ralph C. Kloppenburg,
Enoch W. Fischer, or any of the previously identified persons,
names, mailing addresses, or bombing incidents which appear in
this affidavit. These items will also include any lists of
previous or future targeted individuals or victims.

224. Any and all documents or computer generated and
stored information, including but not limited to, appointment
books, diaries, journals, calendars, telephone toll records,
receipts, bank statements, credit card statements, motel
receipts, canceled checks, travel itineraries, canceled airline

102

tickets, car rental contracts or other receipts which denote
Theodore Kaczynski's travel and whereabouts between 1978 and the
present date.

225. Any and all documents, materials, and
correspondence relating to Theodore Kaczynski's affiliation or
association with educational institutions and universities,
airlines, airline fabrication plants, scientific and professional
groups or organizations, and computer companies.

226. Any and all literature, documents, materials,
books, correspondence, membership lists, written materials, or
computer generated and stored lists which relate to the identity
of any co-conspirators who may be involved in any of the
aforementioned bombing incidents.

227. Any and all literature, documents, materials,
books, correspondence, or computer generated and stored
information relating to or showing an interest in or affiliation
with any movement or group advocating violence, revolution or
anarchy.

228. Any and all documents and other indicia of any
kind showing ownership or control of the premises described in
Attachment A or under the control of Theodore Kaczynski,

103

including but not limited to, rental agreements, contracts of sale, deeds, leases, utility and telephone bills, keys.

229. Any and all documents and other indicia of any kind showing ownership or control of storage facilities, safe deposit boxes, other commercial or rental properties, rented or owned by Theodore Kaczynski, which could be used for the storage of the above-mentioned items, including but limited to rental agreements, leases, contracts, deeds, keys and access devices.

230. Based upon the facts presented herewith, your affiant has reason to believe that there is probable cause to search the premises belonging to, owned by, and/or under the control of, Theodore John Kaczynski, and therefore request that a warrant be issued authorizing a search for the aforementioned items of evidence related to the violations mentioned herein.

/s/
_____
Terry D. Turchie
Assistant Special Agent in Charge
Federal Bureau of Investigation

SWORN AND SUBSCRIBED TO BEFORE ME
THIS 3RD DAY OF APRIL, 1996

/s/
_____
United States District Judge

UNITED STATES DISTRICT COURT FILED

HELENA DIVISION, DISTRICT OF MONTANA 96 APR 4 AM 10 58

LOU ALEKSICH, JR. CLERK

BY

DEPUTY CLERK

UNITED STATES OF AMERICA   CRIMINAL COMPLAINT

V.

THEODORE JOHN KACZYNSKI   CASE NUMBER:

I, Donald J. Sachtleben, Special Agent, Federal Bureau of Investigation, the undersigned complainant being duly sworn state the following is true and correct to the best of my knowledge and belief.

On or about April 3, 1996, and before, in Lewis and Clark county, in the State and District of Montana defendant did, knowingly possess a firearm -specifically, components from which a destructive device such as a bomb can be readily assembled - which is not registered to him in the National Firearms Registration and Transfer Record

in violation of Title 26 United States Code, Section 5861(d) . I further state that this complaint is based on the following facts:

See attached affidavit incorporated herein by reference

(X) Continued on the attached sheet and made a part hereof

_____
Signature of Complainant

4/4/96   at   Helena, Montana
_____   _____
Date   City and State

CHARLES C. LOVELL
U.S. District Judge   _____
Name and Title of Judicial Officer   Signature of Judicial Officer   april 4, 1996

The minor charge which allowed the feds to hold the suspect while they gathered evidence for more serious crimes and FBI agent Donald Sachtleben's observations of what lay inside the shack on Humbug Contour Road. Thursday, April 4, 1996.

1   an arrest warrant. The items described herein are based only on a preliminary search and there

2   remains a considerable amount of items to be located and reviewed.

3   4.   I personally participated in the search. As set forth in more detail below,

4   during the search I observed chemicals and other materials that, in my opinion, are designed and

5   intended for use in manufacturing a destructive device, namely a pipe bomb, and from which

6   a destructive device could be readily assembled, including what appears to be a partially

7   completed pipe bomb. I also observed notebooks that contain what I recognize to be diagrams

8   and notes that are consistent with the manufacture of destructive devices such as pipe bombs.

9   5.   In order to construct a pipe bomb, one needs either a commercially

10   manufactured explosive or an improvised explosive, a casing, a device to detonate the explosive,

11   and a power source for the detonating device. During the search I observed materials from

12   which all of these could be made. In particular, during the search I observed the following:

13   1.   Ten three-ring binders, which have been partially reviewed. These binders contain page after page of meticulous writings and sketches which I

14   recognize to be diagrams of explosive devices. These diagrams depict cross-sections of pipes and electrical circuitry commonly used in the construction of

15   such devices. In addition, they contain sketches of boxes which could be used to contain, conceal and transport explosive devices. The notebooks also contain

16   hand-written notes in Spanish and English which describe, in part, chemical compounds which can be used in various combinations to create explosive charges

17   for use in explosive devices. After consultation with an FBI chemist, it appears that the notes reflect the proper proportions for such mixtures. From

18   investigation from other FBI agents I am aware that Theodore John Kaczynski is able to write Spanish.

19

       2.   Pipes that appear to be galvanized metal, copper and plastic. Four of the

20   copper pipes had plates affixed to one end, which is one of the first steps in the construction of a pipe bomb. I did not observe any indoor plumbing or any other

21   apparent structural need for such piping on the premises.

22   3.   Containers containing powders labeled as "KClO3" (potassium chlorate), "NaClO3" (sodium chlorate), "Sugar", "Zinc", "Aluminum", "Lead" and "Silver

2

Oxide". Necessary ingredients in the preparation of explosives include an oxidizer and a fuel. Sugar, zinc, aluminum, lead and silver oxide all can serve as fuels, and potassium chlorate or sodium chlorate can be oxidizers. For example, potassium chlorate can be combined with either aluminum or sugar to create an explosive material. Similarly, sodium chlorate can be combined with aluminum to create an explosive.

4.   Solid cast ingots, one of which is labelled aluminum. I observed on the floor shiny metal filings consistent with aluminum. Aluminum can be used as an additional fuel and a catalyst in an explosive mixture.

5.   C cell batteries and electrical wire. From my experience I am aware that these materials can be used to provide the power for a device used to detonate explosive material such as the mixtures described above.

6.   Three rolled-up pieces of paper attached to one another, containing what appear to be logs of experiments to determine the optimum pipe dimension and combination of explosive materials in various weather conditions.

7.   During a preliminary search of the loft, a package was located. Visual examination determined that it was a cylindrical package wrapped in paper and secured with tape. An X-ray of the package revealed what appears to me to be a partially completed pipe bomb, including threaded pipe, wire and other electrical components.

8.   Several books including ones on the construction of electrical circuitry and chemistry.

9.   Numerous tools, including mechanical drills, drill bits, hack saw blades, wire cutters, and a roll of solder, all of which would be necessary to convert the materials I have described above into a pipe bomb.

6.   Based upon my experience in the investigation of the use of destructive devices, my examination of the above-described materials, and my review of the writings and sketches in the binders, it is my opinion that these components were designed to be, could be, and were intended to be readily assembled into a destructive device such as a pipe bomb. In my opinion, the premises contained all of the necessary ingredients and materials to manufacture such a destructive device.

3

7.   A search was conducted by ATF on April 4, 1996 of the National Firearms Registration and Transfer Record. That search failed to locate any record of Theodore John Kaczynski having authorization for the possession or manufacture of a destructive device.

_____

S/A Donald J. Sachtleben

Subscribed and sworn to before me this 4th day of April, 1996.

Charles J. Lovell

United States District Judge

4

BIBLIOGRAPHY

Over a four-year period, commencing February 1993, the author drew the material in this book from taped interviews with friends and neighbors of the suspect, and from investigators and police. The author consulted federal court documents, deeds, hotel registration records, FBI reports, personal notes, private bank records, personal letters, newspaper files, and television programs. The author also visited sites involved in the story, including San Francisco, California; Salt Lake City, Utah; Chicago, Illinois; Washington, DC; Lincoln, Montana; the Hermit's shack in Lincoln; and the Park Hotel in Helena. He rode the same bus lines that the Hermit did and typed on a typewriter similar to the Hermit's. Of special value was the in-depth affidavit filed by FBI Special Agent Terry D. Turchie and the almost nine hundred pages of original documents subsequently filed in the Helena, Montana, courthouse. Two valuable books on the case were published soon after the Hermit's April 3, 1996, arrest. The author consulted both, as he did the Unabomber Website, where some of the nation's best minds provided constructive information and theories.

BOOKS

David Bower and Steve Chapple. *Let the Mountains Talk, Let the Rivers Run.* New York: Harper Collins West, 1995.

Joseph Conrad. *The Secret Agent.* London: Penguin Books, 1963. The model for the Unabomber's life.

Delta Group. *Improvised Munitions, Black Book, Volume 1.* El Dorado Arizona: Desert Publications, 1972.

William Dietrich. *The Final Forest.* New York: Simon & Schuster, 1992.

Roger DiSilvestro. *Reclaiming the Last Wild Places.* New York: John Wiley & Sons, 1993.

Fyodor Dostoyevsky. *Notes From the Underground.* Vermont: Charles E. Tuttle, 1994. A psychological study that parallels the Hermit's life.

Nancy Gibbs, Richard Lacayo, Lance Morrow, Jill Smolowe, David Van Biema, and the Editorial Staff of *Time* Magazine. *Mad Genius—The Odyssey, Pursuit and Capture of the Unabomber Suspect.* New York: Warner Books, 1996.

Peter C. List. *Radical Environmentalism.* Belmont, California:

Wadsworth Publishing Company, 1993.

Norman Maclean. *A River Runs Through It.* New York: Pocket Books, 1976, 1992. The best book about the Montana Blackfoot River region.

W.C. McRae and Judy Jewell. *Montana Handbook.* Chico, California: Moon Publications, 1996.

Leonard Michaels, David Reid and Raquel Sheer, edit. *West of the West, Imagining California.* San Francisco: North Point Press, 1989.

Marc Mowrey and Tim Redmond. *Not In Our Backyard.* New York: William Morrow & Co., 1993. Valuable for its chapter on early Lincoln environmentalist Cecil Garland, protector of Big River.

Mark Olshake and John Douglas. *Unabomber—On the Trail of America's Most-Wanted Serial Killer.* New York: Pocket Books, 1996. The creator of profiling takes an astute look at the Unabomber.

Ed Phillips. *Crisis in the Atmosphere.* Phoenix: D.B. Clark & Co. Pub., 1990.

Don Pitcher. *Berkeley Inside/Out.* Berkeley: Heyday Books, 1989.

Rolling Stone Environmental Reader. Washington, D.C.: Island Press, 1992.

W.J. Rorabaugh. *Berkeley at War, The 1960's.* Oxford: Oxford University Press, 1989. An important source for those who want to know more of the period.

Kurt Saxon. *The Original Poor Man's James Bond.* El Dorado, Arizona: Desert Publications, 1991.

Henry David Thoreau. *Walden & Other Writings.* New York: The Modern Library, 1965. The mountain man's Bible, which the Unabomber gave a perverse twist.

Root Wells. *The Anarchist Handbook, Volumes 1 and 3.* Miami, Florida: J. Flores Publications, 1992.

Jay Robert Nash. *Bloodletters and Badmen.* New York: Warner Paperback Library, 1975.

NEWSPAPERS

Exclusive news articles consulted;

Serge F. Kovaleski. "Kaczynski Letters Reveal Tormented Mind." *Washington Post,* January 20, 1997.

"Conrad Novel May Have Inspired Unabomb Suspect." *Washington Post,* July 9, 1996: A01.

Lorraine Adams. "A Stranger in the Family Picture." *Washington Post,* July 16, 1996. These were fabulous, valuable interviews.

Mike Taylor and Susan Sward. "The Unabomber is Here." *San Francisco Chronicle,* Thursday, April 18, 1996, and follow-up story to their exclusive on April 19, 1996, on the possibility of a passport worker having turned Kaczynski in as the Unabomber to her superior. The federal workers's claim seems, to the author, to be valid, Taylor and Sward were consistently the best two Bay Area reporters on the Unabomber story.

"November 28, 1995, Letter to Juan

Sanchez Arreola from Theodore J. Kaczynski." In Spanish. Published and translated by the *New York Times*. February 17, 1994 and May 17, 1994; and February letters to Sanchez from Kaczynski included on the Internet on *The Truth is Redacted* Website, and in the Turchie affidavit. Letter to Joe, October 1, 1974, as appeared in the *San Francisco Chronicle* and government file.

Washington Post. Exclusive on Ellen Tarmichael. April 1996.

David Johnston and Jimmy Scott. "Exclusive on Unabomber." *New York Times*, May 26, 1996.

Other articles consulted or cited in the following newspapers: Washington Post, New York Times, San Francisco Chronicle, San Francisco Examiner, San Jose Mercury, Chicago Tribune, Boston Globe, The Missoulian, Blackfoot News, AP, USA Today, Los Angeles Times, and Sacramento Bee.

New York Times. "Unabomber." October 7, 1993.

Washington Post. "Unabomber." November 27, 1993.

Robert D. McFadden. "Mail Bomber Links an End to Killings to his Manifesto." *New York Times*, June 30, 1995.

Quentin Hardy. "Ted Kaczynski Sat Here, in the Library Sherri Wood Runs," *Wall Street Journal*, August 12, 1997.

San Francisco Chronicle: Reportage by Michael Taylor, Susan Sward, Kevin Fagan, Benjamin Pimentel, Kenneth Howe, Suzanne Espinosa Solis, Jamie Beckett, Tori Minton, Peter Sinton, Gavin Power, Pamela Burdman, David Dietz, and others.

Herscher in Oakland, Bill Wallace from Montana for the *Chronicle*, Edward W. Lempinen, Marc Sandalow, and Mike Sullivan.

San Francisco Examiner: Reportage by Tom Abate, Seth Rosenfeld, Sally Lehrman, Louis Trager, April Allison, Monica Valencia, Stephen A. Capps, and others.

UNABOM. "The Manifesto." Mailed from San Francisco on June 24, 1995, and received by the *Washington Post* and *New York Times* on June 27 and June 28, 1996, respectively. Published as *Post* eight-page supplement on Tuesday, September 19, 1995.

Mick Holien. "Interview with the Gehrings." *Montana Missoulian*, April 3, 1997.

Blackfoot Village Dispatch. "Town Comment on the Case." May 2, 1996, Vol. 9, #12.

Tony Snow. "U 'Gores' Technology," *Detroit News*, September 21, 1995.

MAGAZINES

Lance Morrow. "The Power of Paranoia." *Time*, April 15, 1996.

Time. David Gelernter piece on his reaction to the arrest of a suspect and his feelings about his future and art. April 15, 1996. "A Victim Replies." Written by the computer scientist and author especially for *Time*.

Nancy Gibbs. "Under the Microscope." *Time*, April 28, 1997.

Time. "FBI Labs." April 28, 1997.

Newsweek. "Who Is He?" May 8, 1995.

Newsweek. "Chasing the Unabomber." July 10, 1995. 40–46.

Newsweek. "The Mind of the Unabomber." April 15, 1996.

Newsweek. "Bomb Free Airports." July 29, 1996. 35.

US News. "Twisted Genius." April 15, 1996.

People. The Lone Stranger." April 15, 1996.

Sharon E. Epperson and Elaine Shannon. "The Squeaky-Clean G-Man.: *Time* August 2, 1993.

George J.Church, Richard Behar, Elaine Shannon, and Scott Gregory. "The Terror Within." *Time*, July 5, 1993.

Bill Turque and Susan Miller. "Cleaning Up a Messy Bureau." *Newsweek*, July 26, 1993.

Robert Wright. "The Evolution of Despair." *Time*, August 28, 1995.

Robert Bly. "On the Mind of the Unabomber Suspect." *Time*, April 22, 1996.

TELEVISION SHOWS

News Programs and Television Shows featuring the UNABOM case, many with exclusive interviews. Videotapes of evening news programs span February 15, 1993, to the present. Broadcasting stations are NBC, CBS, ABC, CNN, PBS, KTVU, Court TV, USA Network, KPIX, and KGO.

60 Minutes. Wanda, Linda, and David Kaczynski interviews by Mike Wallace on CBS, Sunday, September 15, 1996. A most extraordinary interview of an exemplary family.

Nova. "The Bombing of America." PBS, April 16, 1996. The best filmed program on UNABOM, including a demonstration of an exploding pipe bomb and an end plug marked FC.

Unsolved Mysteries premiere program of new season: Robert Stack, speculation on Zodiac and the Unabomber. Robert Graysmith, as consultant, was guest interviewed on show, and provided drawings and handwriting samples for both. September 20, 1996.

Maury Povitch and *Leeza* shows. Interviews with composite sketch artist, Jeanne Boylan, 1994 and 1996. Also, author appeared with her on *Rolanda*, June 9, 1994.

Leeza. Ted's Friends and UNABOM victims. April 1996.

ABC-TV, exclusive story on Professor Saari and the possibility that the defendant had submitted a manuscript to him shortly before the first device attributed to the Unabomber was detonated at Northwestern University. April 30, 1996.

NBC-TV, with Tom Brokaw. Lengthy discussion of the Unabomber case.

Nightline. ABC-TV. Thursday, June 29, 1995. Packages arrive during show and are commented on as story is breaking. Extensive quotes.

Eye to Eye. Connie Chung, December 16, 1993.

America's Most Wanted. Fox Network, November 23, 1993.

UNABOMBER: The True Story, (Docudrama) with Dean Stockwell, Robert Hays as David Kaczynski. September 11, 1996, made-for-cable move, USA Network.

USA Network. Live, one-hour discussion with principals in the Unabomber case, 11:00 PM following movie, September 11, 1996, hosted by Charlie Rose.

LETTERS, ARTICLES AND ESSAYS BY THEODORE KACZYNSKI

Ted Kaczynski. A 1971, twenty-three–page essay. Filed in support of the search of the Hermit's cabin, and provided to the FBI by Wanda and David Kaczynski.

Letter to Editor, *Saturday Review,* February 28, 1970.

Various dated and undated letters contained within the *Turchie* affidavit. Attachment four of the affidavit.

"Boundary Functions." Defendant's mathematics thesis. Eighty pages.

FBI DOCUMENTS, UNITED STATES DISTRICT COURT WARRANTS, AFFIDAVITS, ETC.

FBI Special Agent Terry D. Turchie. *The Affidavit in Support of an Application for a Warrant to Search Kaczynski's Lincoln Cabin.* On April 3, 1996, Turchie submitted his affidavit for permission to search the residence, adjoining buildings, and surrounding land. Search continued through April 14. On April 15, the government filed a 34-page search warrant *Return.* 104 pages. Original affidavit submitted and accepted, sworn and subscribed to by Judge Charles Lovell on April 3, 1996.

The author consulted and worked from the entire typewritten affidavit, in essence the government's case against Kaczynski. Pages five to seven comprise an introduction, but it is the "Chronology of events," running from pages seven to forty-nine, that provide the most valuable information to anyone interested in the UNABOM case. Turchie, in clean, detailed prose, and utilizing what he'd learned since 1994 when he was designated the Assistant Special Agent in Charge (ASAC) of San Francisco's National Foreign Intelligence Program (to include continued management oversight of the UNABOM investigation as the SSA for UTF), described each device and the events surrounding their detonation. He identified bombs as Explosive Devices #1 through #16. Turchie lists each of the bomber's communications and discusses similarities between the bombs—fusing systems, construction, wooden box construction, typewriter impressions, the letters "FC," tool marks, return addresses, and types of stamps used.

Turchie's statement of Probable Cause commences on page fifty-nine and contains DNA results from the testing of a postage stamp sent by the defendant (to his brother on a letter), to the postage stamp licked by the Unabomber (on his letter to Dr. Tom Tyler). Letters and testimony from David Kaczynski, comparisons to Ted's essay, etc., run to page ninety-five. A valuable chronology of Ted Kaczynski's movements over twenty-five years is detailed by David. The letter, "As you know I have no respect for law of morality…" is included here, as are many others and articles the suspect had written. On pages ninety-six and ninety-seven Turchie makes a plea for search authorization and prolonged execution of same. On the last pages he lists items to be seized, and it is the generality of these instructions that Kaczynski's lawyers base their pleas that the warrant was inadequately framed and is overly general. Were they to prevail, all evidence seized in the cabin would not be admissible.

UNABOM. "Industrial Society and Its Future" (by FC). Author worked from photocopy of the actual manifesto, including typographical errors and corrections, sent to the *Post* and *Times*. Includes three pages of corrections never printed. Two hundred twenty-seven paragraphs and eight pages of notes.

ATTACHMENT #4: A text comparison of the "T" (Ted) Documents and the "U" (UNABOM) Documents. Document intended for internal FBI use only. Pages one through fifty, and quotes letters, essays, articles, and manifesto in comparison.

Inventory of Items Seized at the Residence of Theodore Kaczynski, HCR #30, Box 27, Lincoln, Montana.

Thirty-four–page detailed listing. Author worked from xerox copy of actual document.

The author has copies of all warrants and motions filed in the United States District Court for the District of Montana, Helena Division. These, along with civil/criminal minutes of court proceedings, were consulted in the writing of this book.

Jerry Burns. U.S. Forest Service Officer. Diagrams and schematics of the Kaczynski tract and surroundings: Exhibits A,B,C. The author consulted these diagrams in the completion of his map and in chapter construction.

FBI Photographs of the bombs, recovered components, and reconstructions.

The photographic case file of the Unabomber's first lethal bomb (the Scrutton attack), showing all components of the bomb and the crime scene.

The author made extensive use of photographs and a secretly made video of the FBI at work within the area, which was sealed for miles around Ted's cabin. These pictures were taken with a telephoto lens by camouflaged sources and have never been reproduced until now. The photos span from the arrest to approximately mid-May 1996. Author's collection.

INFORMATION ON THE INTERNET; INTERESTING ARTICLES AND THEORIES ABOUT THE UNABOMBER

Unabomber Investigation facts and analysis by *Timothy J. Bergendahl* (at AOL)

Includes the following:

The Oklahoma City manifesto

The Trazodone Factor *(another person writes about Trazodone)*

Ignotum Per Ignotius: Did Unabomber Punish James Vernon McConnell Because The Professor Trained a Worm Taken from Wild Nature?

The Ancient Engineers and Unabomber (at Redacted)

UNABOMB Facts, Writing, and Analysis by Ross Getman

The Unabomber as a frustrated writer P.S. May 16, 1997.

News, Updates and Commentary August 1996.

Evidence, Leads, Clues, and Unanswered Questions June 26, 1996.

Review of 2 Books

Reviews of UNABOM TV programs

Sloan Wilson's books

Ross pointed out several glaring inaccuracies in media coverage of the case to me during an hour-long interview. His input helped me doubt in the right areas.

Among the Papers in Kaczynski's Cabin (linked 9/7/96) by Anne Eisenberg, *Scientific American*, June 1996. "One FBI agent told me that Kaczynski packed his handwritten notes into boxes and then stored these in a wooden loft he built.... Over the years, I had occasionally wondered if my writing would draw the Unabomber's gaze, but the knowledge that it may actually have done so was unsettling," commented Eisenberg on the net.

Murder by Numbers by Mark Seltzer, Feed (linked 9/4/96). Explores our cultural obsession with serial killers.

Murder by Numbers by The Police.

Retired UNABOM claims at Idea Futures (linked 8/29/96)

The Hostage Brain (linked 8/18/96) "...science has no solid explanation of why they act the way they do, how they can be identified in time to prevent tragedy, and what, if anything at all, could be done to prevent the mental disorders that have engulfed them and crippled or killed their innocent victims."

Unabomber's Aims Analyzed from Stamps (linked 8/8/96)

Associated Press, Sunday, August 4, 1996 (Washington Post, page 23) "The Unabomber apparently chose his postage carefully, using Frederick Douglass stamps when he wanted to injure his targets, and stamps of Eugene O'Neill when he intended to kill, according to an analysis by a former federal agent."

Opinions Vary On Whether Unabomb Suspect Will Damage Science's Image

by Thomas W. Durso, *The Scientist*, June 10, 1996 (linked 8/2/96)

UNABOMBER FALLOUT: Stories about the eccentricities of Unabomber suspect Theodore

Kaczynski have topped the news since his April arrest, leaving observers to ponder if such reports will reinforce "mad-scientist" stereotypes in the public's mind. [The author noted tremendous outrage among mathematicians and true anarchists over their roles as perceived by the general public and continued stereotyping as "weird."]

The Unabomber, Terrorism, and Performance (linked 7/17/96). A Short Essay on the Transmission of Ideas, by Phillip Robertson. "There are crimes of passion and crimes of logic. The boundary between them is not clearly defined. We are living in an era of premeditation and the perfect crime. Our criminals are no longer helpless children who could plead love as their excuse. On the contrary, they are adults and they have a perfect alibi: philosophy." Albert Camus, "The Rebel". 1954

1907 Conrad Novel May Have Inspired UNABOM Suspect, by Serge F. Kovaleski, Washington Post, July 9, 1996, page A01 (linked 7/10/96)

John Douglas, FBI Profiler, (Ret.). Investigative Support and Behavior All Science Units, Quantico. Interview by author.

INDEX

Note: In subheadings, T. Kaczynski refers to Theodore, while D. Kaczynski refers to David.